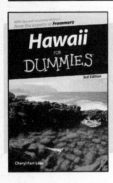
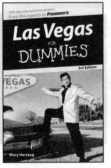

Maui
FOR
DUMMIES®
2ND EDITION

by Cheryl Farr Leas

WILEY

Wiley Publishing, Inc.

Maui For Dummies®, 2nd Edition

Published by
Wiley Publishing, Inc.
111 River St.
Hoboken, NJ 07030-5774
www.wiley.com

Copyright © 2005 by Wiley Publishing, Inc., Indianapolis, Indiana

Published simultaneously in Canada

For general information on our other products and services, please contact our Customer Care Department within the U.S. at 800-762-2974, outside the U.S. at 317-572-3993, or fax 317-572-4002.

For technical support, please visit www.wiley.com/techsupport.

Wiley also publishes its books in a variety of electronic formats. Some content that appears in print may not be available in electronic books.

Library of Congress Control Number: 2004118373

ISBN: 0-7645-7403-5

Manufactured in the United States of America

10 9 8 7 6 5 4 3 2 1

2B/QT/QS/QV/IN

WILEY

About the Author

Cheryl Farr Leas may live on the mainland, but she's a Hawaii girl at heart. She fell in love with Diamond Head, aloha wear, and mai tais in 1994 and has had trouble staying away ever since. Whenever she's not on the islands, she and her husband, Rob, call Phoenix, Arizona, home.

Before embarking on a writing career, Cheryl served as senior editor at Macmillan Travel (now Wiley) where she edited the *Frommer's Hawaii* travel guides for the better part of the 1990s. Now happy to be a globetrotting writer and consultant, Cheryl also writes *Hawaii For Dummies*.

Dedication

This book is for Rob, for loving Maui as much as I do.

Publisher's Acknowledgments

We're proud of this book; please send us your comments through our Dummies online registration form located at www.dummies.com/register/.

Some of the people who helped bring this book to market include the following:

Editorial

Editors: Kelly Ewing, Project Editor; Marc Nadeau, Development Editor

Cartographer: Roberta Stockwell

Consumer Editorial Supervisor and Reprint Manager: Carmen Krikorian

Editorial Assistant: Melissa S. Bennett

Senior Photo Editor: Richard Fox
Cover Photos: Front Credit: © Omni Photo/Index Stock Imagery. Description: Wai'anapanapa State Park, Woman hiking; Back Credit: © Darrell Wong/Getty Images. Description: Windsurfing in front of huge wave.

Cartoons: Rich Tennant, www.the5thwave.com

Composition

Project Coordinator: Michael Kruzil

Layout and Graphics: Lauren Goddard, Barry Offringa, Melanee Prendergast, Heather Ryan

Proofreaders: David Faust, Carl William Pierce, TECHBOOKS Production Services

Indexer: TECHBOOKS Production Services

Publishing and Editorial for Consumer Dummies

Diane Graves Steele, Vice President and Publisher, Consumer Dummies

Joyce Pepple, Acquisitions Director, Consumer Dummies

Kristin A. Cocks, Product Development Director, Consumer Dummies

Michael Spring, Vice President and Publisher, Travel

Brice Gosnell, Associate Publisher, Travel

Kelly Regan, Editorial Director, Travel

Publishing for Technology Dummies

Andy Cummings, Vice President and Publisher, Dummies Technology/General User

Composition Services

Gerry Fahey, Vice President of Production Services

Debbie Stailey, Director of Composition Services

Contents at a Glance

Maps at a Glance

Table of Contents

Introduction

● ●

Maui really lives up to its heady promise of a carefree beach vacation. It can fulfill everyone's unique island dream — whether you're
6 or 60, single or the head of a growing family, the *Survivor* type or a newly
minted millionaire. You just need to know what you want from your Maui
vacation and how to make it happen.

Planning a trip to Maui is easy — too easy, in fact. Far too many people
head off blindly, without exerting the little bit of effort it takes to tailor a
vacation to their own needs, tastes, and desires. So just knowing that
you want to look before you leap puts you well ahead of the pack.

And picking up this guidebook shows that you have the right instincts
about your vacation planning.

About This Book

Maui For Dummies, 2nd Edition, separates the wheat from the chaff — or
the husk from the pineapple, as it were. An island vacation, after all, is
supposed to be easy and fun, and your trip planning should be easy and
fun, too.

I've done the legwork for you, and your vacation will benefit accordingly.
I'm not afraid to take a stand to help you decide what to include in your
island vacation — and, even more important, what *not* to include. I understand that you work hard to set aside a few precious weeks of vacation
time, and that, no matter how much money you have, you don't want to
waste it. The time to figure out your strategy is now, in the planning stage,
not after you get to Maui.

Everyone's tastes and special needs are different, of course — that's why
you're reading this book. In the following pages, I give you the tools that
you need — *just* what you need, not too much — so that you can make
smart decisions about what works for you and what doesn't. I try to give
you the clearest picture of your choices and options so that you can make
informed decisions easily and efficiently.

Because this book is a reference guide, you don't need to read it from
cover to cover — unless you want to. Instead, you can start reading at
any point and flip to the parts that specifically address how you want to
spend your vacation time. That way, you can concentrate on finding out
exactly what you want to know at any given time.

Think of building your Maui vacation as assembling a jigsaw puzzle. This book helps you find the correct puzzle pieces so that they interlock smoothly. The finished product should reflect the vacation *you* want, not somebody else's image of what your island paradise should be.

Conventions Used in This Book

The structure of this book is nonlinear: You can dig in anywhere to get information on a specific issue without any hassles. To that end, I list hotels and restaurants alphabetically with actual prices and frank evaluations to make your search even easier.

I also include exact prices for everything, although you should keep in mind that those prices are subject to change. However, even if prices rise slightly during the lifetime of this edition, the information you have on hand gives you a good idea of what to expect.

In order to make it even easier to find accommodations, restaurants, and activities within your budget, I use a system of dollar signs that you can quickly scan. These symbols show a general range of costs for one night in a hotel or one meal at a restaurant (including appetizer, entree, dessert, one drink, taxes, and tip). Use the following table as your guide to deciphering the dollar signs:

Cost	Hotel	Restaurant
$	Less than $100	Less than $15
$$	$100–$175	$15–$25
$$$	$175–$250	$25–$40
$$$$	$250–$375	$40–$70
$$$$$	More than $375	More than $70

In addition, I use these abbreviations for credit cards:

AE: American Express

DC: Diners Club

DISC: Discover

MC: MasterCard

V: Visa

To make pertinent information stand out, attractions and main telephone numbers (usually toll-free) are in **bold** typeface. The telephone numbers have little telephone icons next to them, too.

Foolish Assumptions

As I wrote this book, I made some assumptions about you and your needs as a traveler:

- ✔ You may be an inexperienced traveler looking for guidance when determining whether to take a trip to Maui and how to plan for it.

- ✔ You may be an experienced traveler who hasn't had much time to explore Maui or its beaches, and wants expert advice when you finally do get a chance to enjoy them.

- ✔ You're not looking for a book that provides all the information available about Maui or a comprehensive list of every hotel, restaurant, and attraction on the island. Instead, you're looking for a book that focuses on the very best places and the most unique experiences.

How This Book Is Organized

Maui For Dummies, 2nd Edition, is divided into six parts. You can read each chapter or part without reading the preceding chapter, but as you read, I may refer you to other chapters for more information on certain subjects.

Part 1: Introducing Maui

This first part gives you an overview of what Maui is like, so you can start getting excited about all the fun that lies ahead. It includes

- ✔ An easy-to-scan list of the very best of the best — my personal picks of Maui's top hotels, restaurants, beaches, golf courses, and more

- ✔ A quick overview of Hawaiian history and culture

- ✔ An introduction to Hawaiian foods and traditions (How else do you know whether you want the _saimin,_ the _poke,_ or the _opakapaka_ — and whether or not you want to save room for a little _haupia_ for dessert?)

- ✔ Time-tested advice on how to divide your time so that you see the best of Maui without sacrificing that all-important beach and relaxation time

- ✔ The details on when to go: A complete calendar of events, tips on avoiding the crowds, and the lowdown on Maui's weather patterns

Part II: Planning Your Trip to Maui

In this part, I get down to the serious trip preparation, including

- ✔ How much you can expect your trip to cost and how to save if money is a concern
- ✔ The pros and cons of planning your trip on your own, using a travel agent, and buying an all-inclusive package deal
- ✔ The ins and outs of flying to Maui
- ✔ Special considerations for families, seniors, travelers with disabilities, and gay and lesbian travelers
- ✔ A how-to guide for couples who want to tie the knot in the Aloha State
- ✔ Getting ready to go, from the pluses and minuses of buying travel insurance to renting cars to making advance luau reservations to *akamai* (smart) packing tips

Part III: Settling into Maui

This part covers everything you need to know when your plane touches down, including

- ✔ Navigating Maui's airport
- ✔ Driving around Maui and figuring out the island's geographical layout
- ✔ The very best places to stay: hotels, resorts, B&Bs, and condos in all price ranges
- ✔ No-holds-barred reviews of Maui's best restaurants, whether you want a gorgeous oceanfront setting or a funky local joint, Maui's best burger or sophisticated Hawaiian Regional Cuisine

Part IV: Exploring Maui

You came to Maui for this part, didn't you? I show you the most beautiful places on Maui and tell you all about the island's best adventures and activities, including

- ✔ An array of beautiful beaches
- ✔ Watersports galore, including fabulous snorkel cruises
- ✔ Amazing whale-watching
- ✔ The otherworldly sunrise at Haleakala National Park
- ✔ A scenic drive along the Heavenly Road to Hana
- ✔ A complete shopper's guide
- ✔ The lowdown on where to party when the sun goes down

In addition, Maui has an incredible array of attractions, but some curious travelers may want to venture off the beaten path to explore two destinations that are among Hawaii's best-kept secrets:

- ✔ Molokai, where your own trusty mule can carry you on an unforgettable journey down lush sea cliffs to discover a hidden leper colony
- ✔ Lanai, where two world-class luxury hotels offer you the chance to truly get away from it all

Part V: The Part of Tens

Every *For Dummies* book has a Part of Tens. If Parts I through IV are the meat of a travel sandwich, think of these fun top-ten-list chapters as dessert.

Chapter 18 gives you the lowdown on Maui's fabulous dining scene. You find a menu guide to Hawaii's incredible seafood, tips on what to expect at a luau, and hints on how to enjoy authentic local foods and traditions.

Chapter 19 tells you how to ditch the tourist look and act like a local, with tips on everything from how to pronounce those tongue-twisting place names to getting to know a few points of island-style etiquette.

Chapter 20 focuses on everybody's favorite topic — romance! I provide some tips to make your romantic getaway unforgettable.

Quick Concierge

The Quick Concierge puts facts about Maui at your fingertips, from the lowdown on taxes to Web sites where you can find accurate online weather forecasts and everything in between. You also get toll-free numbers and Web addresses for all the major airlines, car-rental agencies, and hotel chains for easy reference. And, in case you want more information, I give you the contact numbers for all the local visitor bureaus you may want to consult.

Icons Used in This Book

Think of the following icons as signposts. I use them to highlight especially helpful advice, to draw your attention to features you don't want to miss, and to introduce a variety of topics.

This icon points out useful advice on things to do and ways to schedule your time.

Watch for the Heads Up icons to identify annoying or potentially dangerous situations, such as tourist traps, rip-offs, time-wasters, and other things to avoid.

This icon highlights attractions, hotels, restaurants, or activities that are particularly hospitable to children or people traveling with kids.

 This icon highlights money-saving tips or particularly great values.

 Money is no object with this icon, which indicates the absolute finest places and experiences that Hawaii has to offer.

 This icon highlights any plans that you should make before you leave home.

Where to Go from Here

As you read through this book and start to formulate your vacation, remember this: The planning really *is* half the fun. Don't think of choosing your accommodations and solidifying the details as a chore. Make the homebound part of the process a voyage of discovery, and you'll end up with an experience that's rewarding, enriching, and relaxing — *really*. Have a blast with it. Happy planning!

Part I
Introducing Maui

"We're going to Maui this year during the cliff diving, flame dancing, knife throwing festival just to, you know — relax."

In this part . . .

This part of the book introduces you to the wonders of Maui. You discover why so many people are drawn to the magical Valley Isle, and you begin to shape the basic outlines of your trip. I help you figure out when to go, with information on Maui's climate, its least crowded (and expensive) seasons, and a full calendar of special events.

Chapter 1

Discovering the Best of Maui

*I*n Maui, every day can be a slice of paradise. It's a breathtakingly beautiful place that exudes a generous spirit of genuine aloha. And it doesn't take a lot of cash or over-elaborate planning to get to the heart of Maui. This lovely island has a way of making travelers kick back and savor life's simple pleasures in their purest form. Here, everybody can feel like royalty: A simple beach apartment can be your castle, a fresh papaya and a cup of robust Kona joe your princely breakfast, a joyous aloha shirt your royal robe.

But if you're looking for more worldly luxuries, that's great, too — because vacation is about having what you want. Maui certainly doesn't lack for places to pamper yourself.

This chapter gives you a sneak preview of the absolute best that Maui has to offer — the cream of the crop. Each of these places and experiences is discussed in detail later in this book; for now, you can skim them all at a glance and whet your appetite. As you read through the book, keep your eyes out for the "Best of the Best" icons.

The Best Luxury Resorts

If money is no object, Maui has no shortage of places to park yourself in style. There's a string of terrific upscale resorts along the shores of West Maui (particularly in Kaanapali) and South Maui (in Wailea).

As an extra-added bonus, most of Maui's resorts have recently added brand-new spas that raise the art of relaxation and pampering to a new level. What could be better than a massage on the beach? (Maybe a massage on the beach *with* a mai tai, too?) The following are a few of my favorite luxury resorts:

- **Grand Wailea Resort & Spa:** Many tout the reserved understatement of the neighboring Four Seasons, but I'm underwhelmed. Instead, I prefer this grand beach palace, with its exclusive tropical theme park vibe, big and beautiful guest rooms, and over-the-top treats at every turn. Hawaii's best pool complex awaits your (very lucky) kids, and you can indulge in the islands' finest spa. The luxurious Napua Tower offers such extra amenities as personalized concierge service. See Chapter 10.

- **Hotel Hana-Maui:** Rejoice — for the Hotel Hana-Maui is glorious once again. After years in the doldrums, this breathtaking resort at the end of the "heavenly" Hana Highway has been reborn as a luxurious haven of genuine Hawaiiana thanks to the folks behind Big Sur's Post Ranch Inn. This elegant hideaway is reason enough to cruise to the remotest end of the island. See Chapter 10.

- **Four Seasons Resort Maui:** This resort isn't my favorite on Maui — the Grand Wailea is grander and the Fairmont Kea Lani is a better value in the luxury category — but there's no arguing with the star power of this ultradeluxe hotel. The guestrooms are oversized, service is exceptional, and don't be surprised if you recognize a famous face or two lounging by the pool. However, beware of those "oceanview" rooms that overlook the driveway, as they can put the kibosh on your island-perfect mood. See Chapter 10.

- **Kaanapali Alii:** Luxury condo living hardly gets better than this high-rise beachfront condo complex — and with square footages between 1,500 and 1,900 square feet, the whole family can make themselves at home. Prices are high — but so is quality, and you'll get far more luxury for your money than you will if you and the kids are shoehorned into a pricey hotel room or two. See Chapter 10.

The Best Good-Value Accommodations

Maui is full of wonderful, although expensive hotels, but you can also find plenty of good-value accommodations on the island:

- **Fairmont Kea Lani Maui:** Sure, this fanciful Moorish palace on the sand is pricey, but it gives you so much more for your money than Maui's other luxury resorts. For the same price as a standard hotel room at other places — and sometimes less — you enjoy a large one-bedroom suite with a complete entertainment system (including stereo and DVD) and a huge marble bathroom. See Chapter 10.

✔ **Kaanapali Beach Hotel:** This charming, older beachfront hotel is the last hotel left in Hawaii that gives you a real resort experience at a moderate price. The resort brims with genuine aloha spirit and good value — and the on-the-beach location can't be beat. See Chapter 10.

✔ **The Whaler on Kaanapali Beach:** This well-maintained 1970s luxury condo complex sits front and center on golden Kaanapali Beach, making it the ideal island home for travelers who want homestyle comforts. The individually owned and decorated condos aren't quite as large and luxurious as those at Kaanapali Alii, but they are comfortable, quiet, and wonderfully located, and a much better value than your average oceanfront hotel room. See Chapter 10.

✔ **Noelani Condominium Resort:** This top-notch oceanfront condo complex is both an excellent value and a really enjoyable place to stay. Every unit — from the value-minded studios for two to the family-friendly two- and three-bedroom apartments — boasts an ocean view and all the comforts of home. See Chapter 10.

✔ **Best Western Maui Oceanfront Inn:** Want to stay on the beach without paying usually exorbitant oceanfront-hotel prices? This freshly renovated small hotel is an excellent option. It's located at the quietest south end of Kihei, just north of ritzy Wailea, on golden sands offering excellent snorkeling and swimming. It's a great choice for couples; families who need space to spread out should book at the neighboring **Mana Kai Maui** instead. See Chapter 10.

The Best Restaurants

The increasingly sophisticated Valley Isle rivals Oahu as the fine dining island of choice for vacationing gourmands. Whether you want a casual burger or a lavish meal with fine wine, Maui's got just the ticket.

The island's waters are so pristine that the wealth of fabulous seafood on Maui's menus should come as no surprise. What you may not have expected is the degree to which Maui's chefs celebrate the bounty of this fertile island, showcasing its fresh produce and tropical fruits.

Maui's location at the crossroads of the Pacific also guarantees that you can enjoy an incredible culinary adventure, sampling an authentic taste of Japan, China, Vietnam, Thailand, and Malaysia.

And did I mention that you get to enjoy most of your meals in beautifully situated oceanfront restaurants to boot?

✔ **Mama's Fish House:** My absolute favorite choice on Maui is this delightful seafood house, which offers a magical combination of food, ambiance, and service. Sure, prices are high — but the tiki-room setting is an archetype of timeless Hawaii cool, and fresh island fish simply doesn't get any better than this. See Chapter 11.

✔ **Nick's Fishmarket:** This Mediterranean-accented seafooder at the Fairmont Kea Lani gets everything just right: food, wine list, setting, and service. The ambience is romantic to the max, too, making this an ideal South Maui choice for a special occasion meal for two. See Chapter 11.

✔ **Roy's Kahana Bar & Grill/Roy's Nicolina Restaurant/Roy's Kihei:** Nobody should miss the opportunity to eat at one of the restaurants of Roy Yamaguchi, king of Hawaii Regional Cuisine. This liege is still at the top of the heap in the Pacific culinary world, and his food still shines. No matter which dining room you choose, you'll find a casual ambiance, friendly service, and an oversized menu of dim sum, appetizers, imu-baked pizzas, and creative main courses that allow you to eat as special-occasion or affordably as you wish. See Chapter 11.

✔ **Sansei Seafood Restaurant & Sushi Bar:** D.K. Kodama's two island sushi palaces offer some of the best dining on the island. The innovative menu — composed primarily of pan-Asian seafood dishes with multicultural touches — has won justifiable raves from fans around the globe. Japanese accents set the tone, and the ambiance is festive and casually sophisticated. It's one of the most satisfying dining experiences in the islands; don't miss it. See Chapter 11.

The Best Beaches

Maui boasts an array of wide, breathtaking beaches — more than 80 in all. Luxurious golden sands stretch beside calm turquoise waters, while palm trees sway in the wind. These settings are what make great vacations. Even in the most crowded months, you can easily stake out your own little slice of paradise.

And not that you need any more incentive, but Maui's best resort coasts face west, so you can mosey over to a beachfront bar right on the sands and conclude your day by toasting a Technicolor sunset.

✔ **Kaanapali Beach:** This fabulous, crescent-shaped beach is reminiscent of the Waikiki of yesteryear, before the entire world made it their destination of choice. There's something for everyone here: crystal-clear snorkeling, thrilling wave jumping, golden sands inviting hours of sunbathing, even beachfront bars for that perfect middle-of-the-day mai tai. See Chapter 12.

✔ **Hookipa Beach Park:** Come to watch the world's best windsurfers pirouette over white-capped waves at this glorious North Shore beach. Surfers have eminent domain in the mornings, while the colorful windsurfers take over in the afternoons. The action is equally breathtaking at any time of day, especially when the winter waves are in top form. See Chapter 12.

✔ **Baldwin Beach Park:** If you're looking for an off-the-beaten-path place to spend the day away from the crowds that populate so many of Maui's beaches, but you don't want to sacrifice golden sands or glorious turquoise surf to do it, this Paia-area beach is the one for you. Pick up a picnic lunch, bring a blanket, and stretch out on the sand — you've found the perfect place to bask in the Maui sun. Heed the lifeguard warnings, though — the surf can get rough here, especially in winter. See Chapter 12.

✔ **Hamoa Beach:** This remote, half-moon-shaped beach near the end of the Hana Road is one of the most breathtakingly lovely in all of Hawaii. Expect surf that's the perfect color of turquoise, golden-gray sand, and luxuriant green hills serving as the postcard-perfect backdrop. The beach is generally good for swimming and waveriding in the gentle seasons, but stick close to the shore because you're in open, unprotected ocean. Stay out of the water entirely in winter. See Chapter 12.

The Best Activities & Attractions

The sheer variety of watersports available — diving, surfing, boogie boarding, kayaking — is astounding. What are you waiting for? Go on, get out and explore the great blue ocean.

✔ **Snorkeling:** Even if you're not usually the sporting type, you don't want to miss the chance to try snorkeling on Maui. The waters offshore are so clear that snorkelers are guaranteed to see clouds of tropical fish in every color of the rainbow, and possibly even a green turtle or two. You can see a stunningly beautiful underwater world. See Chapter 12.

✔ **Whale-watching with the Pacific Whale Foundation:** Whale-watching is a premier activity in the islands from mid-December until mid-March; in some lucky years, the great humpbacks remain in Hawaii's warm waters into April. Boats are available to take you whale-watching, but I love the Pacific Whale Foundation for its excellent naturalist guides and its commitment to protecting these gentle giants. If you don't want to splurge on an expensive cruise, you don't need to — the foundation also operates a **Whale Information Station** on the road to Lahaina, where you can spot humpbacks from shore with an expert for absolutely free. The Pacific Whale Foundation can also take you out on terrific snorkel cruises year-round, even when the whales aren't in town. See Chapter 12.

✔ **Diving Molokini:** This sunken volcanic crater is one of Hawaii's top dive spots thanks to calm, clear, protected waters; an abundance of marine life — reef dwellers to manta rays; and exciting viewing opportunities for every level of diver — even first-timers. You don't dive, and you're not ready to learn? No worries — Molokini offers excellent viewing for snorkelers, too. Molokini is only reachable by boat, so see Chapter 12 for recommended outfitters.

✔ **Visiting Haleakala National Park:** The massive, 10,023-foot-high dormant volcano that sits at the heart of the Valley Isle is Maui's biggest natural attraction. It's crater looks like a barren moonscape; no wonder that NASA's astronauts have used it for space exploration training. Haleakala is best known for its mystical sunrise vistas, as crowds of visitors arrive in the dark at predawn hours to watch the spectacle of dawn breaking over the crater. But take heed, early morning phobes: You can enjoy this wonderous park at anytime of day. See Chapter 13 for details.

✔ **Driving the "Heavenly" Road to Hana:** Hawaii's most spectacular drive is well worth a day of your vacation. For 52 winding miles, this blissful highway takes you past flowering gardens, spectacular waterfalls, and magnificent ocean vistas. Start early and keep in mind that it's all about the drive, not about getting to the end of the road. Rent a convertible for maximum effect. See Chapter 13.

✔ **Learning to surf:** Believe it or not, surfing is easier than it looks — and there's hardly a feeling finer than conquering a wave. A number of good surfing schools guarantee that you'll be hanging ten in a single two-hour lesson. My Maui favorite is the **Nancy C. Emerson School of Surfing.** See Chapter 12.

✔ **Hitting the links:** If you love golf, don't miss the opportunity to play at least one of Maui's premier courses. Glorious Kapalua is the best, but you have a bounty of quality courses to choose from, duffers. See Chapter 13.

✔ **Getting a bird's-eye view:** Touring Maui by helicopter gives you a whole new perspective as you swoop over the island's otherwise inaccessible heartland, where nature has been unspoiled by modern man. You'll scale the desolate peak of Haleakala National Park and enjoy a breathtaking view of the road to Hana that takes an hour instead of a day. It's expensive, but worth it. See Chapter 13.

✔ **Shopping the Valley Isle:** Maui has become a premier shopping destination, especially for those who eschew traditional chains for boutiques that are artful, offbeat, or unique. The charming, funky surf town of Paia and sophisticated, cowboy-infused Makawao are best for creative spirits, while Kaanapali's Whaler's Village and the Shops at Wailea offer creative choices and art-filled galleries in elegant, open-air environments. See Chapter 14.

The Best Luaus

The best luaus are in high demand, so book your spots before you leave home to ensure access.

✔ **Old Lahaina Luau:** Hawaii's most authentic and acclaimed luau is justifiably celebrated, and a real treat to experience. Come early to watch craftspeople at work in the lovely oceanfront setting; you can also watch as the luau pig is unearthed from its underground oven, where it's been slow-cooking all day. The live hula show is dazzling. You simply can't do better than this. See Chapter 11.

✔ **The Feast at Lele:** The folks behind the Old Lahaina Luau (see preceding entry) also operate this interesting twist on a traditional luau. The Feast at Lele is an excellent alternative for romance-seeking couples, or anyone who would prefer a luau with a more upscale demeanor, a more intimate setting, and/or a fine-dining twist. The multicourse meal and thrilling performance troupe reach beyond the Hawaii tradition to celebrate the food and culture of the South Seas as well, and the beachfront setting can't be beat. See Chapter 11.

Chapter 2

Digging Deeper into Maui

In This Chapter

▶ Discovering the fascinating story of Hawaii's past

▶ Experiencing the joys of island-style dining

▶ Mastering a few key Hawaiian words and phrases

*Y*ou've had a stressful day at the office. The kids have been driving you crazy, and you realize that everybody in the family needs a break. Or maybe you've just had it with gray skies and gloomy weather.

Then the idea comes, and it's a gem: *Maui*. Ah, Maui.

Just thinking about a Maui vacation warms the soul, doesn't it? Turquoise ocean, white sand, toasty sun. Surfers riding crested waves as emerald-green cliffs rise up to meet a sweet blue sky. Palm trees swaying in the breeze as the strum of a slack-key guitar carries you into tropical reverie. . . .

Vacation is the ultimate antidote to the stresses and strains of daily life — and no destination is more relaxing and restorative than Maui. On this exquisite island, days of soaking up the island sun are interwoven with adventure and plenty of friendly aloha.

Introducing the Valley Isle

The Hawaiian Islands are just a hair's breadth larger, in total landmass, than the state of Connecticut — but oh, what glorious square miles they are. The islands are actually the summits of underwater volcanoes that have grown tall enough, in geologic time, to peek above the waves. (All the volcanoes are dormant except for two on the Big Island.) A volcanic core gives each island a breathtakingly rugged mountainous heart.

Most of the island development is at sea level, along the sunny coastal fringe of each island. Thanks to Hawaii's proximity to the equator, those coastal areas experience near-perfect weather year-round: temperatures in the high 70s or low 80s, clear skies, and gentle trade winds.

The eight main islands are Oahu (oh-*wa*-hoo), the hub of the Hawaii island chain, and the "neighbor" islands: Maui (*mow*-ee); Hawaii, or the Big Island, as it's commonly called; Kauai (ka-*wah*-ee); Molokai (mo-lok-*eye*); Lanai (la-*nah*-ee); Niihau (nee-*ee*-how); and Kahoolawe (ka-hoo-o-*la*-wa).

Oahu is the most populous of the islands, but Maui is the most popular, hands down. When people think Hawaiian paradise, they usually think Maui. Almost everyone who comes to Maui falls in love with the island, and for good reason: The second-largest island offers the ideal mix of unspoiled natural beauty and tropical sophistication, with action-packed fun and laid-back island style.

Here are just a few breathtaking facts about this wondrous isle: Maui has 81 accessible beaches — with more miles of swimmable beaches than any other Hawaiian island. At the island's heart sits a national park — featuring Haleakala, the world's largest dormant volcano. About 3,000 humpback whales visit Maui every winter — out of the 8,000 that populate the entire planet. It's no wonder that the readers of *Condé Nast Traveler* regularly vote Maui "Best Island in the World" and even "World's Best Travel Destination" year after year after year.

Maui does have a few caveats, however. The Valley Isle is more like the mainland than any other place in Hawaii (yes, even Honolulu, Hawaii's capital and biggest city). There's even some L.A.–style traffic. (Maui generally has only one main road going in each direction.) The highways and minimalls look comfortingly familiar, or annoyingly so — it all depends on your perspective.

Although hotels have a bit more breathing room on Maui than they do in Waikiki, the shoulder-to-shoulder resort development is far more urban than what you find on the Big Island or Kauai. Maui also has the highest-profile population of relocated mainlanders. A quicker pace of living prevails, which can make Maui feel more like Southern California than Hawaii, especially in the resort areas. A dash of touristy cheesiness has invaded the old whaling town of Lahaina, and Kihei's dominant architectural style is high strip mall.

But the mainland-style development doesn't detract from the island's natural beauty. Maui really is a tropical paradise, with golden beaches, misty tropical cliffs, and countless waterfalls along the Heavenly Road to Hana, one of America's most spectacular drives. Offshore are two of Hawaii's finest snorkel and dive spots. Onshore, at the summit of one of the island's two great mountains (between which lies the valley for which the island is nicknamed) is Haleakala National Park, a wild, otherworldly place that's hugely popular with hikers, bicyclers, and sunrise-watchers. Sixteen golf courses enthrall duffers, while a bounty of *Food & Wine*–worthy dining keeps sybarites satisfied. Hawaii's finest luau, some excellent theatrical entertainment, and an energetic party vibe in Lahaina make Maui the best choice for travelers who enjoy after-dark activities. With so much to do, you can easily fill a week or ten days — and you'll be ready to come back for more.

Maui

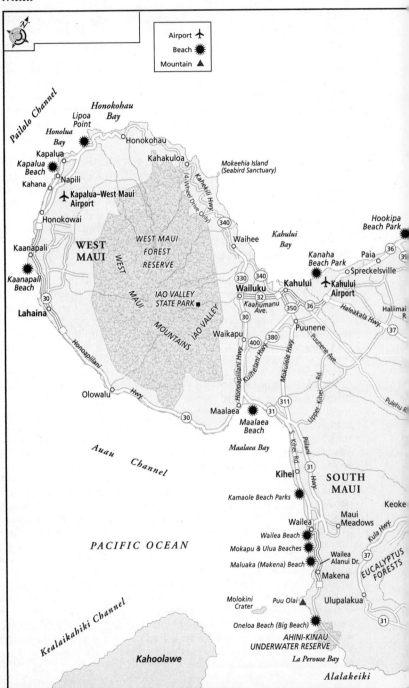

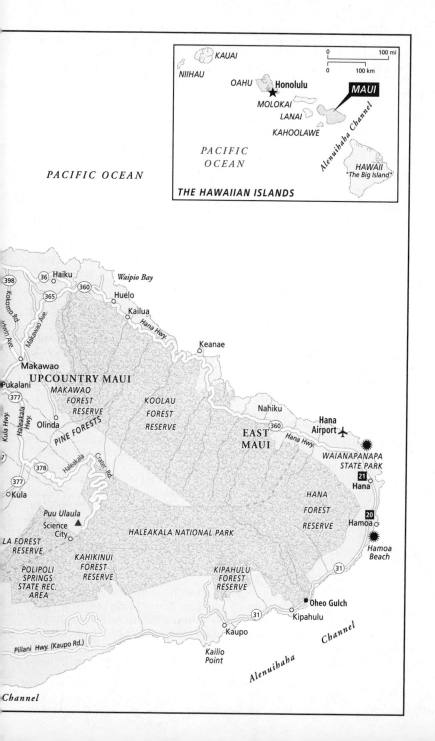

Everybody loves Maui, so expect a few crowds and some high price tags. I've heard an increasing number of complaints about overdevelopment in the last couple of years. Maui's resorts tend to be more expensive than resorts on the other islands, and the high cost of all those available activities doesn't help matters. You can drop a bundle if you choose to splurge.

But you can find good values, too — you just have to know where to look. And that's where this book comes in. It's your key to discovering Maui's best: the island's best values, its loveliest beaches, its most unforgettable experiences, and its authentic spirit of aloha. In the pages that follow, I steer you away from the overpriced and overcrowded and help you design the island getaway that's right for you.

Maui Nui: Molokai and Lanai

Geologists believe that, sometime around one million B.C., the summit of Haleakala volcano broke the surface of the ocean. Flows from this volcano and adjoining ones joined to form a large prehistoric "underwater land mass called *Maui Nui,* or "Big Maui." Encompassing Maui Nui was not only the island of Maui, but the neighboring islands of Molokai and Lanai, plus the unpopulated island of Kahoolawe.

Today, Maui County comprises Maui and its two sister islands, Molokai and Lanai. In prehistoric tradition, the tripartite island group is often called Maui Nui. Both Molokai and Lanai are covered in distinct chapters near the end of this book and can be visited on day trips from the Valley Isle or on extended stays. I recommend visiting one or both of these islands only if you have significant vacation time or a particular yen to explore off the beaten path.

The most Hawaiian isle: Molokai

Sleepy Molokai is a rural island that's largely untouched by modern development (although, as residents like to boast, they do have KFC now). This lean, funky, scruffy little place is often called the most Hawaiian island because it's the birthplace of the hula, and it has a larger native Hawaiian population than any other in the chain. Although it offers some lovely, secluded beaches and a few other adventure-style activities, the island's most famous site is Kalaupapa National Historical Park, a world-famous 19th-century leper colony that can only be reached by mule, prop plane, or helicopter. See Chapter 16 for complete coverage.

The private island: Lanai

Staying on Lanai (pop. 3,500) is less a Hawaiian experience and more a generic park-yourself-at-a-resort vacation. There's little or nothing to do here, which is the entire idea of this getaway island. Just about everything that *is* here is completely handled through the two megaexpensive resorts that have taken over this humble little place: the English manor house-style lodge at Koele, which sits on the cool, misty peak of the island, while the Manele Bay Hotel sits on the beach, Hawaii style. Both hotels are slated to become members of the ultraposh Four Seasons chain — arguably the finest hotel and resort brand in the world — sometime in 2005, which will certainly enhance the Lanai experience for those looking for a leave-it-all-behind luxury escape. Lanai's fans love the total pampering and utter solitude. (Bill Gates booked up the entire island so that he could get married here beyond the prying eyes of the media and public a few years back.) See Chapter 17 for complete coverage.

History 101: The Main Events

Hawaii's historic tapestry is far richer than the story that can be shared in these few pages. If you'd like to immerse yourself in the whole story, pick up *Shoal of Time: A History of the Hawaiian Islands* (University of Hawaii Press) by Gavan Daws. Both definitive and delightful to read, *Shoal of Time* is the ideal one-volume history of Hawaii. From the geological formation of the islands through statehood, the Hawaii story is so well told that it reads like a novel. It's so rich with detail that the characters who shaped Hawaiian history come alive in its pages.

A.D. 700: The first Hawaiians arrive

The first Hawaiians arrived by canoe from Tahiti and the Marquesas Islands, some 2,500 miles to the south, as part of a greater Polynesian migration. They likely came ashore first at the southernmost Big Island, where they found a pristine and blessedly empty island, roiling with fire from the volcanoes at its heart.

An entire Hawaiian culture grew from these first settlers. As islanders migrated throughout the chain, each island became its own distinct kingdom. The inhabitants built temples, fish ponds, and aqueducts to irrigate taro plantations. Sailors became farmers and fishermen. The *alii* (high-ranking chiefs) created a caste system and established taboos. Ritual human sacrifices were common. Life was both vicious and blissful — just like the islands' breathtaking landscapes. Piilani was crowned as Maui's first king in the late 1300s.

1778: The "modern" world arrives

For more than a thousand years, no Hawaiian ever imagined that an outsider would ever appear in these remote "floating islands." But in 1778, Captain James Cook sailed into Waimea Bay on Kauai on his ship the *Resolution* — where he was welcomed as the Hawaiian god Lono.

Cook stumbled upon the Hawaiian Islands quite by chance. He named them the Sandwich Islands, for the Earl of Sandwich, a great friend and first lord of the British admiralty, who had bankrolled the expedition. The Big Island would ultimately be the death of the world-famous explorer — but not before stone-age Hawaii entered the age of iron, and the West forged a permanent foothold in these virgin islands. Gifts were presented and objects traded: nails for fresh water, pigs, and the affections of Hawaiian women. The sailors brought syphilis, measles, and other diseases to which the Hawaiians had no natural immunity.

Cook never made it to Maui before his unfortunate demise. Captain Jean François de Galaup de La Perouse docked at Makena in 1787, becoming the first foreigner to set foot on Maui soil.

La Perouse ignored the King of France's orders to claim Maui for France, but Maui's days as an independent island were numbered, anyway. In 1790, King Kamehameha I defeated the forces of Maui's last king, Kahekili, using guns seized from a British ship to establish his iron-fisted rule. By 1810, all of the Hawaiian Islands were united as one kingdom — and the new Hawaiian monarchy welcomed the west with open arms. In 1819, the first whaler arrived from Massachusetts, establishing Lahaina's reputation as the whaling capital of the Pacific. The first New England missionaries were not far behind: They arrived on Maui in 1823. Victorian mores overtook island style, and eventually subsumed it; hula was abolished in favor of reading and writing, and neck-to-toe dress became the norm. The first sugar mill began operations in 1828, bringing industry to Maui. The same year, the first high school west of the Rocky Mountains, Maui's Lahainaluna High, opened, firmly establishing western-style education in the islands.

At the same time, missionaries also played a key role in preserving island culture. They created the 13-character Hawaiian alphabet and began recording the islands' history. Until this time, history was only passed down from generation to generation orally, in memorized chants.

The children of the missionaries became the islands' business and political leaders. They married Hawaiians and stayed on the islands, causing one astute observer to remark that the missionaries "came to do good and stayed to do well." More than 80 percent of all private land was owned by non-natives within two generations. Sugar cane became big business, and planters imported immigrants by the thousands to work the fields as contract laborers. The first Chinese came in 1852, followed by Portuguese in 1878, and Japanese beginning in 1885. These immigrants would have a lasting and influential impact on island culture that persists to the present day.

King David Kalakaua — known as the "Merrie Monarch" for the elaborate parties he threw — ascended to the throne in 1874, marking the beginning of the end of the short-lived Hawaiian monarchy. He performed a couple of acts of note, however: He built Iolani Palace in 1882; lifted the prohibitions on the hula and other native arts; and gave Pearl Harbor to the United States. In 1891, King Kalakaua visited chilly San Francisco, where he caught a cold and died. His sister, Queen Liliuokalani, assumed the throne.

1893: Paving the way for tourism and statehood

On January 17, 1893, a group of American sugar planters and mission-ary descendants, with the support of U.S. Marines, imprisoned Queen Liliuokalani in her Honolulu palace, where she penned "Aloha Oe," the famous song of farewell. The monarchy was dead. Hawaii was now an American territory ruled by the powerful sugar cane planter Sanford Dole. He and his cohorts — known as the Big Five — controlled the entire economic, social, and political life of the islands, including Maui. Sugar was king, and the native Hawaiians became a landless minority.

The first tourists to the islands were hardcore adventure travelers — among them Mark Twain — who came to the Big Island in the late 1800s to see the roiling Kilauea volcano. But the new industry didn't stick until transportation improved and the sugar industry became too expensive to support.

In 1901, W. C. Peacock built the elegant Moana Hotel (now the Sheraton Moana Surfrider) on Waikiki Beach. After a concentrated marketing effort in San Francisco, 2,000 tourists came to Waikiki in its first big tourism year, 1903. Tourists came by steamship; the sailing took four and a half days. By 1936, visitors could fly to Honolulu from San Francisco on the *Hawaii Clipper,* a seven-passenger Pan American plane; the flight took 21 hours, 33 minutes. Modern tourism was born and was doing brisk business — until the Japanese arrived, that is.

On December 7, 1941, a Japanese air raid wreaked havoc on the American warships parked at Pearl Harbor, drawing the heretofore reticent United States into World War II. Martial law was declared throughout Hawaii for the duration of the war.

1959: Setting the stage for today's Hawaii

The harsh realities of war gave way to the lighthearted culture of *Blue Hawaii,* Trader Vic's, and Arthur Godfrey. Hotels sprouted along the cur-vaceous beach at the foot of Diamond Head known as Waikiki. Resorts finally arrived on Maui in 1946, when the Hotel Hana-Maui (now gloriously restored) opened its doors.

In 1959, this blossoming paradise became the 50th state of the United States. That year also saw the arrival of the first jet airliners. Postwar Americans had disposable cash, and now Hawaii was an easy flight away. Visitors began to arrive in droves — and tourism as we know it was off the ground, surpassing sugar as the premier industry of the islands. Kaanapali — Hawaii's first master-planned resort — debuted on Maui's curvaceous northwest shore in 1961.

Tired of the plastic aloha that had supplanted genuine island culture, Hawaiian elders started making a concerted effort to integrate traditional hula, chant, visual arts, and values into the experience of visitors. In 1976, the Hokulea, a replica of an ancient Polynesian voyaging canoe, set sail from Maui for Tahiti, reversing the ancestral journey and reestablishing ties to the ancient past. Tourism and hospitality employees are now educated in Hawaiian history, culture, and genuine aloha spirit. The culture that was once clipped at the root has now come back in full bloom — and, thankfully, it's stronger than ever.

Building Blocks: Local Architecture and Design

Thanks to blessedly mild weather that includes cooling year-round trade winds and temperatures that don't vary by more than 15 degrees Fahrenheit from January to July, Maui thrives on open-air living. A seamless blend of indoors and out is the prevailing architectural style. Why put up a wall when there's no reason to keep the weather out — or the dazzling view?

The local architectural style is called *kama'aina,* or native born. Kama'aina is a style rich in beautiful simplicity and island tradition. True kama'aina architecture is generally open plan, in keeping with the importance of multigenerational family living and the strength of the community spirit — and to capitalize on those gentle ocean breezes. Decoration is simple but beautiful, generally focused on the shapes, materials, and hues of nature.

The finest homes are fitted with natural woods, such as *ohia* floors and gleaming *koa* furnishings. Koa is a gorgeous slow-growth hardwood that has been a favorite of local artisans for centuries thanks to its deep palette and rich grain. Crafts and furnishings made from the wood are increasingly expensive, simply because koa is a slow-growth wood that takes decades to replenish. If you can afford a piece to take home — perhaps a jewelry box or a hand-turned calabash — you'll likely treasure it as a family keepsake for generations to come, as island families do.

Not all native materials must necessarily be expensive, however. Some of the most beautiful and tropically evocative home furnishings are crafted of simple, light materials like bamboo and rattan. Most floor coverings are woven mats, soft and cool on bare feet. The finest are tightly woven *Lauhala,* crafted from pandanus leaves by talented artisans.

The beautiful shapes and hues of Hawaii's bold fauna have woven their way into the island's favorite fabrics, too. Boldly hued tropical barkcloths — nubby cotton fabrics that wear well and say "Old Hawaii" with their large-leafed tropical and storytelling patterns — are famously suited to the islands.

Despite its glitz and glamour as a tourist destination, Hawaii is fundamentally a farming and fishing community — and the story is abundant in its streetscapes. Simple plantation cottages were built to house the workers brought in from all over the world to farm the islands' abundant sugar, pineapple, and taro fields; now, plantation style is the most pervasive architectural style in the islands, especially on the still-rural neighbor islands. With their single-story style, bright facades, and sloping roofs (many still crafted of corrugated aluminum), plantation cottages embody the simple beauty of island life. A more elaborate, multistoried style originated as the plantation manager's home. Lahaina's Best Western Pioneer Inn (see Chapter 10) offers a charming example of this design style, albeit with a seafaring bent. Ranch life predominates in the cool upcountry of Maui, where plantation life gives way to *paniolo* (cowboy) style. Paniolo-style is built for somewhat cooler weather; as a result, you're likely to find it to be a bit more familiar. Expect ranch-style homes with island touches such as brightly painted exteriors and broad porches, best evidenced in the Haleakala foothills in and around the town of Kula. Grander buildings take on Victorian details and the aura of the Old West. The storefronts of Makawao, in upcountry Maui, have a distinct cowboy feel, as do the western-style storefronts of old Wailuku town and Paia, the funky cowboy-turned-surf town on the road to Hana.

The whaling town of Lahaina was a missionary bulkhead, as the town's architecture evidences. Wailuku's Baldwin Home Museum (see Chapter 13), built in 1831 and Maui's oldest surviving house, is the best example of imported Victorianism on the islands.

Maui is roughly halfway between Asia and the mainland United States, so the Asian influence is pervasive in island architecture and design. Pagoda-style influences are evident in residential and commercial architecture throughout the islands, especially in areas that absorbed the wealth of Chinese and Japanese immigrants who came to work in the fields generations ago, and stayed.

A Taste of Maui: Local Cuisine

About a dozen or so years ago, Hawaii Regional Cuisine was born. Local chefs were tired of turning out a stodgy menu of continental fare that was unsuited to Hawaii living. So they began to celebrate the bounty of the islands, emphasizing the use of fresh locally grown (often organic) produce, tropical fruits, the freshest seafood, and island-raised beef. Their light, creative combinations often feature Asian accents as a nod to Hawaii's multicultural heritage.

This type of cuisine is often disguised under other names — Euro-Asian, Pacific Rim, Indo-Pacific, Pacific Edge, Euro-Pacific, Island Fusion, and so on — but it all falls under the jurisdiction of Hawaii Regional Cuisine. Although there are variations, you can expect the following keynotes: lots of fresh island fish; Asian flavorings (ginger, soy, wasabi, seaweed, and so on) and cooking styles (searing, grilling, panko crust, wok preparations) galore; and fresh tropical fruit sauces (mango, papaya, and the like).

Maui has lured some of the world's finest chefs to its kitchens. Thanks to its proximity to the Pacific Rim and its large Asian population, the island boasts a wealth of Chinese, Thai, Vietnamese, and Japanese restaurants. And if Asian fare isn't your thing, you'll find plenty of other options, from the French classics to good ol' ranch-raised, fire-grilled steaks. Maui's cooks have even managed to put their own spin on some of the world's most revered foods — pizzas, burgers, and burritos — with rousing success.

Seafood lovers, rejoice: Maui offers you an astounding array of fresh-caught fish. In fact, you may find yourself puzzling over lists of unfamiliar fish on island menus. See Chapter 18 for a handy list of definitions that help you decide what to try.

Lest all this unfamiliar food talk makes you think otherwise, remember that the majority of Hawaii islanders are red-blooded, flag-waving Americans — and they love a good burger just as much as your average mainlander.

Real local food is generally starchy and high in calories, so the Atkins crowd will want to skip the traditional plate lunch, which usually consists of a main dish (anything from fried fish to teriyaki beef), "two scoops rice," an ice-cream-scoop serving of macaroni salad, and brown gravy, all served on a paper plate. Plate lunches are cheap and available at casual restaurants and beachside stands throughout the islands.

Chapter 18 takes a more in-depth look at the diversity of wonderful taste sensations just waiting to be discovered on Maui.

A Word to the Wise: The Local Lingo

Everyone on Maui speaks English, of course. But a number of Hawaiian words and phrases regularly pop up in everyday conversation.

You probably already know the Hawaiian word *aloha* (a-*lo*-ha), which serves as an all-purpose greeting — hello, welcome, or goodbye. It's a warm and wonderful word that expresses the sense of peace and hospitality that epitomizes the islands.

You'll definitely need to learn the word *mahalo* (ma-*ha*-low), which means "thank you" and is used extensively throughout Hawaii.

Here's a handy list of other words you may encounter:

- **Hale** (*ha*-lay): House
- **Haole** (*how*-lee): Foreigner or Caucasian (literally "out of breath" — pale, or paleface); a common reference, not an insult (usually)
- **Hula** (*hoo*-lah): Native dance
- **Kamaaina** (ka-ma-*eye*-nah): Local person

- ✔ **Kapu** (*ka*-poo): Anything that's taboo, forbidden
- ✔ **Keiki** (*keh*-kee): Child
- ✔ **Lanai** (*lah*-nigh): Porch or veranda
- ✔ **Lei** (lay): Garland (usually of flowers, leaves, or shells)
- ✔ **Luau** (*loo*-ow): A celebratory feast
- ✔ **Mana** (*ma*-na): Spirit, or power
- ✔ **Muumuu** (moo-oo-*moo*-oo): A loose-fitting dress, usually in a tropical print
- ✔ **Ono** (*oh*-no): Delicious
- ✔ **Pau** (pow): Finished or done
- ✔ **Pupu** (*poo*-poo): Starter dish, appetizer

Say what? How to pronounce Hawaiian words

The Hawaiian language has only 12 characters to work with — the five vowels (*a, e, i, o,* and *u*) plus seven consonants (*h, k, l, m, n, p,* and *w*). Consequently, Hawaiian words and names tend to be long and difficult, with lots of repetitive syllables.

The vowels are pronounced like this:

a	*ah* (as in father) or *uh* (as in above)
e	*eh* (as in bed) or *ay* (as in they)
i	*ee* (as in police)
o	*oh* (as in vote)
u	*oo* (as in too)

Almost all vowels are sounded separately, although some are pronounced together, as in the name of Maui's county seat, Wailuku, which is pronounced "Why-*loo*-koo."

 The simplest way to pronounce a Hawaiian word or name is to approach long words or names as a collection of short syllables. Accents almost always fall on the second-to-last syllable. All syllables end with vowels, so a consonant will always indicate the start of a new syllable.

The Hawaiian language actually has a 13th character: the glottal stop, which looks exactly like a single opening quotation mark (') and is meant to indicate a pause. I've chosen not to use the glottal stop throughout this book; it's often left out in printed Hawaiian and on things like store and street signs. Although serious Hawaiian-language students insist on using the glottal stop, you don't need to worry about it as a visitor; just ignore it when you see it.

Background Check: Recommended Books and Movies

Studying up on Hawaii can be one of the most fun bits of "research" you'll ever do. If you'd like to learn a bit more about the islands before you go — which I encourage — these books and movies are an enjoyable way to do it.

Books

In addition to *Shoal of Time* (see the section "History 101: The Main Events," earlier in this chapter), one of my all-time favorites is *Hawaii* (Random House) by James Michener, the epic, Pulitzer Prize–winning novelist who loved the island's heart and soul. Michener's novel charts a similar course as Daws's book, but this fictionalized account has the style — and the can't-put-it-down appeal — of a beach read. This is a great way to get a real feel for the past without delving into serious non-fiction. The missionary chapters are focused on Lahaina, so *Hawaii* is especially suited to a Maui visit.

Another intriguing work of fiction that tells the story of Hawaii, albeit on a smaller scale, is Kiana Davenport's *Shark Dialogues* (Plume).

Want to learn the stories of Pele, Maui, and the other gods and supernatural creatures, both fiery and benevolent, that comprise Hawaii's mystical backstory? Check out *Hawaiian Mythology* (University of Hawaii Press) by Martha Warren Beckwith and Katharine Luomala. Steven Goldberry's *Maui Demigod* is a well-regarded historic novel focused on the multifaceted character who slowed the sun in order to dry his mother's tapa cloth, as legend has it.

Hundreds of books tell the personal stories of the great figures of Hawaiian history. One of my favorites chronicles the life — and bloody Big Island death — of the great, devastating seafarer who introduced Hawaii to the western world: *Farther Than Any Man: The Rise and Fall of Captain James Cook* (Simon & Schuster) by Martin Dugard. Only a sliver of the book is about Hawaii, but it articulates the British colonial mindset beautifully.

University of Hawaii Press's richly illustrated *Atlas of Hawaii* is a fascinating source for everything you ever wanted to know about Hawaii's physical geography, weather patterns, population, and the like. An ideal gift for natural science buffs who want to delve deeper.

Albert J. Schutz's *All About Hawaiian* (University of Hawaii Press) is a great pocket-sized reference for those who would like to know just a bit more about the Hawaiian alphabet and language, including how to pronounce all those funky place names.

Want to bask in the glory of Hawaii as innocent vacationland, in the days of Matson Cruise Lines, Duke Kahanamoku, and Don Ho crooning "Tiny Bubbles," when Waikiki really was paradise? *Leis, Luaus and Alohas: The Lure of Hawaii in the Fifties* (Island Heritage) by Fred E. Basten and Charles Phoenix, is the book for you. This vibrant coffee-table book will really put you in the mood for a mai tai.

Some beautifully illustrated books tell the story of the aloha shirt in all of its silky, full-color glory. Best of the bunch is *The Aloha Shirt: Spirit of the Islands* (Beyond Words Publishing) by Dale Hope and Gregory Tozian. Broader in its reach — but no less beautiful — is Linda B. Arthur's *Aloha Attire: Hawaiian Dress in the 20th Century* (Schiffer Publishing).

Both craft and horticulture fans will find Ronn Ronck's *A Pocket Guide to the Hawaiian Lei: A Tradition of Aloha* (Mutual Publishing) to be an easy-to-carry reference to Hawaii's most visible and popular creative ritual: lei making and wearing.

If you can manage to find it, no book exudes the genuine spirit of living in Hawaii like Jocelyn Fujii's *Under the Hula Moon* (Crown Publishing Group) a gorgeous blend of photos and text with an introduction by Paul Theroux.

Hawaii culture is predicated on the wisdom of its elders, passed down through the generations. *Voices of Wisdom: Hawaiian Elders Speak* (Booklines Hawaii Ltd.) by M.J. Harden, features interviews with 24 respected island elders, gorgeously illustrated with black-and-white portraits by photographer Steve Brinkman. This beautiful and easy-to-read book is a perfect primer for anyone who wants to embrace Hawaii's rich heritage and the cultural renaissance the islands have experienced over the last two decades.

Chicken Soup from the Soul of Hawaii (HCI) by Jack Canfield, Mark Victor Hansen, Sharon Linnea, and Robin Stephens Rohr, really captures the magic of the island in one slim volume featuring some of the islands' most beloved stories. This book is a delightful introduction to the spirit and substance of Hawaii life and culture for those who want to set the tone but don't care to dig too deep.

Rita Ariyoshi's *Maui on My Mind* (Mutual Publishing) is a gorgeously written and illustrated coffee-table book focused on the beauty and magic of the Valley Isle. If you have a reluctant traveler in your group, this enticing collection of text and photos will change their tune.

If you have a hard time finding any of these books — or if you want additional suggestions from Hawaii's rich library — two Big Island bookstores serve as particularly good resources: **Basically Books (☎ 800-903-MAPS** or 808-961-0144; www.basicallybooks.com) and the **Kohala Book Shop** (☎ **808-889-6400;** www.kohalabooks.com). Both offer online catalog browsing and ordering services.

Movies

Gorgeous Hawaii has served as a backdrop for countless TV shows and movies, from *Hawaii Five-O* ("book 'em, Dano") to *Pearl Harbor*. Here are just a few of my favorites, all available on DVD.

The epic Academy Award winner *From Here to Eternity* (1953), starring Montgomery Clift, Frank Sinatra, Burt Lancaster, and a bevy of other Hollywood big names, tells the story of the attack on Pearl Harbor with gravity and intimacy. The location shots are gorgeous, even in black-and-white.

Blue Crush (2002) is a silly surf movie that nevertheless captures the genuine heart of Oahu's North Shore surf culture. The stunning photography alone is worth putting up with the plot — you'll feel like you're riding the waves yourself. (***Note:*** Although the movie was filmed on Oahu, its original working title was *Surf Girls of Maui.*)

Breathtaking Kauai hosts the dinosaur-dotted jungle of *Jurassic Park* (1993). Of course, Spielberg didn't exactly discover Kauai; Hollywood had discovered the Garden Isle's silver screen magic decades before. For the best retro views, check out Elvis in *Blue Hawaii* (1961) and *South Pacific* (1958), filmed on the north shore of Kauai, whose stunning Bali Hai mountains shape the film's incrediblebackdrop. And even flying Elvises can't upstage the gorgeous scenery when *Honeymoon in Vegas* (1992), starring Nicolas Cage and Sarah Jessica Parker, moves to Kauai.

One of my absolute favorite movies about Hawaii is the little-seen *Picture Bride* (1994), which tells the story of a young Japanese girl who sails to Hawaii in 1918 to marry a man — a laborer in the sugar cane fields — whom she has never met. This stirring and beautiful movie is well worth seeking out.

You and the kids may want to check out *George of the Jungle* (1997), starring Brendan Fraser, which was partially filmed on Maui. Maui is also featured in *Die Another Day* (2002), starring Pierce Brosnan as James Bond. Garry Marshall's movie version of the Anne Rice novel *Exit to Eden* (1994), starring Rosie O'Donnell and Dana Delaney, was filmed largely on Maui and Lanai, but I'm not sure that's a worthwhile reason to rent this unfortunate film.

Chapter 3

Deciding When to Go

. . . .

In This Chapter
▶ Decoding the secrets of the travel seasons
▶ Figuring out Maui's climate
▶ Avoiding the crowds
▶ Zeroing in on special events

. . . .

Situated in the north Pacific just 1,470 miles above the equator, Maui enjoys fabulous weather year-round. Winter is virtually nonexistent. Severe storms are a rarity. Even those times considered the "off-season" — spring and fall — are gorgeous, which means that those of you on a budget can save a bundle if you choose the right dates.

Still, some times are better than others — especially for those travelers who prefer to avoid crowds. This chapter reveals when everybody else comes to Maui so that you can either join the party or avoid it like the plague.

Revealing the Secret of the Seasons

Maui's high season is during the winter months, from the second half of December through mid-April, when people flee the cold, snow, and gray skies of home for the warm sun and bathing-suit temperatures of Hawaii. During this winter high season, prices go up, and resorts can be booked to capacity, particularly during the holiday season. Book far in advance for a trip during this period and expect to pay the highest prices. While not nearly as bad as Christmastime, Easter week can also be crowded because West Coast families flock to the islands for a few days of sunshine over spring break.

Summer (mid-June through August) is a secondary high season in Maui. Because so many families travel over the summer break, you won't find the bargains of spring and fall, but you may still do better on accommodations, airfare, and packages than in the winter months.

Maui's off-seasons have traditionally been spring (from mid-April to mid-June) and fall (from Labor Day to mid-December) — which, paradoxically, also happen to be the best seasons in Maui in terms of reliably great weather. Herein lies the secret of the seasons: In spring and fall, hotel rates traditionally drop, package deals abound, airfares are often at their lowest rates of the year (sometimes as cheap as $400 round-trip from the West Coast, or less), and you can expect consistently clear skies and 80°F days after you arrive.

Because the weather is relatively constant year-round, the decision on when to visit Maui is ultimately up to you. You can bet that no matter what time of year you arrive, you can enjoy prime island conditions. Your decision really boils down to how much you want to spend, how important it is for you to escape a harsh winter back home, how willing you are to deal with crowds, and what's available.

Understanding Maui's climate

Maui lies at the edge of the tropics, so it really has only two seasons: warm (winter) and warmer (summer). Temperatures generally don't vary much more than 15°F or so from season to season, depending on where you are. The average daytime summer temperature at sea level is 85°F, while the average daytime winter temperature is 78°F.

Temperatures stay even steadier when you consider the coastal areas alone: The average summer high is 87°F, while the average winter high is 82°F — not much difference. Nighttime temps drop about 10 to 15 degrees — less in summer, a little more in winter. August is usually the warmest month of the year; February and March are the coolest months. Almost-constant trade winds bring a cooling breeze even in the hottest weather.

The island's *leeward* side (the west and south shores) tends to be hot and dry; the *windward* side (the east and north shores) is generally cooler and wetter. For sun-baked, desertlike weather, visit South Maui or West Maui. When you want lush, junglelike weather, go windward toward Hana on the northeastern shore.

Locals say that if you don't like the weather, just get in the car and drive — you're bound to find something different. That's because the island also has many microclimates, which are highly localized weather patterns based on a region's unique position and topography.

The mountains of Upcountry Maui are much cooler than the coastal areas, and the higher you go in elevation, the cooler it gets. Thus, if you travel inland and upward, the weather can change from summer to winter in a matter of hours. If you visit Haleakala National Park, for example, you climb from sea level to 10,000 feet in just 37 miles. Don't be surprised if the temperature is 30 to 35 degrees cooler at the summit than at the beach.

In general, November to March marks Hawaii's rainy season, while summer is considered the dry season. The weather can get gray during the rainy season — but, fortunately, it seldom rains for more than three days in a row. Winter isn't a bad time to go to Maui; the sun's just a little less reliable, that's all.

The good news about Maui's rainy season is that it's almost never raining *everywhere,* even in winter. So if it's raining on your parade, just get in the car and drive — you'll likely reach a sunny spot in no time. (The south and west coasts are usually your best bet.)

Charting sea changes

Maui's ocean waters stay warm year-round. The average water temperature is a warm 74°F, and reaches a jump-right-in 80°F or so in summer.

Wave action, though, varies greatly between winter and summer, and from coast to coast. Maui's beaches tend to be as placid as lakes in the summer and autumn months. In winter, swells hit the north-facing beaches and the surf goes wild (attracting daredevil surfers, who are fun to watch, even if you're not brave enough to face monster curls yourself). South-facing beaches generally remain calm and friendly to swimmers and snorkelers of all ages and abilities throughout winter, although spring and early summer bring south swells right about the time north-shore waves flatten out.

If the waves are too powerful for you, seek calmer conditions by taking a short drive to another beach that's more sheltered. In Chapter 12, I recommend the best local beaches, including the safest for inexperienced swimmers. When in doubt on where to go, ask your hotel staff or call the local tourist office for recommendations — and watch for warning flags and posted conditions at the beach.

A few important words about ocean safety: Never turn your back on the ocean when you're at the beach. A big wave can come out of nowhere before you can say aloha. Always watch the surf, even if you're just taking a casual stroll along the shoreline. Also, ocean conditions can change dramatically in a matter of hours; surf that was safe for swimming one day can develop a dangerous undertow the next. Get out of the water when the big swells come.

And lastly, don't be shy about wearing floaties or a life jacket if it makes you feel more comfortable in the water.

Avoiding the crowds

Yes, coming to Maui during certain times is a bad idea if you're allergic to crowds. At the very least, you should know what you're getting into.

The entire nation of Japan basically shuts down over Golden Week, which falls annually in late April or early May and encompasses three Japanese holidays. Japanese tourism to Hawaii is down across the board due to Japan's faltering economy, but you won't notice the falloff during Golden Week. (Oahu is more crowded, but Maui fills up, too.) Be sure to book hotels, interisland air reservations, and car rentals well in advance.

Halloween in Lahaina is a major event; up to 20,000 people come for the festivities. Booking your Lahaina hotel room a year or more in advance isn't too early. You shouldn't have a problem elsewhere on the island, though.

And keep in mind that the islands are at maximum capacity during the Christmas holidays; spring break and Easter week can also be crowded. Stay at home during these seasons if you don't want to fight crowds or pay top dollar.

Perusing Maui's Calendar of Events

Check out the following rundown of the top events that take place annually. This brief list is merely a sample, of course. For a complete rundown, as well as the latest events information, go to www.visitmaui.com; also check out www.calendarmaui.com. For events on the island of Molokai, visit www.molokaievents.com; a current events calendar for the island of Lanai is posted at www.visitlanai.net/lanaievents.html.

Don't assume that the other events don't need any planning. Call ahead before any event because you may need tickets, details may have changed, and so on.

In addition to the following listings, I encourage you to check the active events calendar at the **Maui Arts & Cultural Center** in Kahului, where events run the gamut from art exhibits, local entertainers, and film screenings to international entertainers like David Sedaris and the Who. Go online at www.mauiarts.org, where you can also buy tickets, or call the box office at ☎ **808-242-7469.**

> ✔ **January and February:** 'Tis the season for world-championship golf in paradise. The season kicks off with the first PGA event of the year, the **Mercedes Championships** at Kapalua Resort (☎ **808-669-2440;** www.kapaluamaui.com), starring the the previous year's tournament

champs. Next up is the **Wendy's Champions Skins Game** at Wailea, Maui (☎ **808-875-7450**). Expect top-ranked talent at both events. Check www.pgatour.com for complete details on each event, including how to purchase tickets.

✔ **January through April:** These months are Maui's prime **whale-watching season,** when humpback whales — the world's largest mammals — make their way from frigid Alaska to the balmy waters of Hawaii. Because whales prefer water depths of less than 600 feet, these endangered gentle giants come in relatively close to shore. You can see them regularly from the beach in prime season, spouting and *spyhopping* (peeking above the waterline to "spy" on what's going on). They often prefer the west, or leeward, sides of the islands.

Maui is the best spot in Hawaii for whale-watching because the giants love to frolic in the channel separating the Valley Isle from Molokai and Lanai. The best onshore vantage is West Maui's MacGregor Point, a large pullout on the ocean side of Highway 30, halfway between Maalaea and Lanai. The nonprofit Pacific Whale Foundation operates a **Whale Information Station** there that's staffed by friendly naturalists daily from 8:30 a.m. to 3:30 p.m. from December through April. Just stop by — they even have high-powered binoculars you can use — or call ☎ **800-WHALE-1-1** (800-942-5311) or 808-249-8811 for more details.

If you happen to be in the islands during whale season, you don't want to miss seeing these remarkable behemoths. You can often spot them from land, but I also recommend the best whale-watching cruises in Chapter 12.

✔ **Mid-January or early February:** The annual **Hula Bowl Maui All-Star Football Classic** features the United States' top college players competing at Maui's War Memorial Stadium. The all-star event is preceded by **HulaFest Week,** a week full of football-oriented fun, including a team luau, a surf classic, autograph sessions for the public, and more. Ticket orders start being processed on April 1 for next January's game, so be sure to call ☎ **808-874-9500** well in advance of kick-off time (or visit www.hulabowlmaui.com, where you can find out more and order tickets online). If you can't be present, the game is usually broadcast live on ESPN.

✔ **Mid-January:** The **Molokai Makahiki Festival** brings the most Hawaiian Isle to full life with this annual celebration of traditional hula and games, Hawaiian arts and crafts, and food. Call ☎ **808-553-3673** or visit www.molokai-hawaii.com for this year's schedule.

✔ **Late January through early February:** Help ring in the **Chinese New Year** in Lahaina. Events include a traditional lion dance in front of the historic Wo Hing Temple, plus food, music, fireworks, Chinese crafts, and much more in a full-blown technicolored street festival. Call ☎ **888-310-1117** or 808-667-9175, or visit www.visitlahaina.com. February 9, 2005, ushers in the year of the rooster.

✔ **Mid-February:** The Pacific Whale Foundation honors the majestic humpback whale with the **Great Maui Whale Festival,** a full winter-long calendar of events that culminates in mid-February with **Whale Week,** featuring a parade, a regatta, special whale-watching events, and much more. Call the foundation at ☎ **800-942-5311** or 808-249-8811 or go online to www.greatmauiwhalefestival.org or www.pacificwhale.org for all the details. Check with the foundation for the date of the Great Whale Count, when you can help count the number of humpbacks visiting Maui's waters; it usually falls at the end of the month.

✔ **Mid-March:** The second humpback-themed celebration of the season rules Maui during the **Ocean Arts Festival,** Lahaina's own two-day series of special events honoring the island's most high-profile visitors, including whale-watching, an outdoor arts festival, games, and a touch-pool exhibit for kids. Call ☎ **888-310-1117** or 808-667-9193 or go online to www.visitlahaina.com, for this year's schedule.

✔ **Easter Weekend:** Maui's annual **Ritz-Carlton Kapalua Celebration of the Arts** is the premier interactive Hawaii arts and culture festival. Well-known artists give free hands-on lessons in hula, chant, Niihau shell lei making, tapa cloth making, primitive clay firing, and more. Events include a traditional luau, kids' activities, and live entertainment of the highest order. Call ☎ **800-262-8440** or 808-669-6200 or visit www.celebrationofthearts.org for this year's schedule and reservations.

✔ **March or April:** Want to understand the appeal of that mysterious local food staple, the taro root? Attend the **East Maui Taro Festival,** at the Hana Ball Park in Hana, a two-day celebration that includes exhibits, lectures, food booths, live entertainment, and traditional arts and crafts. This is a homegrown local event rather than a touristy one. For this year's schedule, call ☎ **808-264-3236** or visit www.tarofestival.org.

✔ **Early or Mid-April:** Rubber duckie, you're the one! The Sheraton Maui in Kaanapali adds a competitive bent to bathtub fun with their **Annual Charity Rubber Duckie Race,** during which some 500 rubber fowl race across the resort's lagoon pool, with prizes awarded to top finishers. Call ☎ **808-662-8025** for this year's date and details.

✔ **Late April:** Celebrating the bounteous glory of Hawaii agriculture is **The Ulupalakua Thing,** an annual festival sponsored by the Maui Agricultural Foundation, drawing chefs, farmers, and foodies from around the islands to celebrate what's fresh in Hawaii-grown and -made foodstuffs. There are plenty of demonstrations, entertainment, and sampling to be had, and the setting — at Tedeschi Vineyards at Ulupalakua Ranch, on the golden southwest slope of Haleakala — is as bucolic as they come. Call ☎ **888-808-1036** or **808-878-2839** for this year's schedule and advance tickets or visit www.ulupalakua thing.com.

✔ **May 1:** May Day is **Lei Day** in Hawaii — and cause for big-time rejoicing. Although the most extensive celebrations are held on Oahu, expect a festive atmosphere on Maui as well; a number of island resorts, including the Wailea Marriott and the Fairmont Kea Lani, host their own Lei Day celebrations. Contact the Maui Visitors Bureau for a list of events — or merely don a fragrant garland, smile, and greet everyone you see with a warm, festive "aloha!"

✔ **Early May:** All-star golf returns to Kapalua for the **Verizon Hawaii Hall of Fame Pro-Am and Championship.** Call ☎ **808-669-8870** or visit www.kapaluamaui.com.

✔ **Mid-May:** The Most Hawaiian Isle celebrates the birth of hula annually with **Molokai Ka Hula Piko Hula Festival,** a music- and dance-filled one-day event held at Molokai's Papohaku Beach Park. Call ☎ **808-658-0662** or visit www.molokaievents.com for this year's schedule and details.

✔ **Mid- to late May:** A major Maui cultural event, **In Celebration of Canoes,** honors the voyaging canoe that united Polynesia for two weeks in May. Cultural delegations from Pacific island nations come together with master carvers to create Polynesian canoes from wood logs throughout the event. Hosts from Hawaii welcome each nation in a traditional 'awa ceremony at the beach. Lahaina hosts cultural arts demonstrations and performances, a parade, ancient warrior demonstrations, Polynesian crafts, and food. On the final day, a ceremony launches the carved canoes at sunset, with entertainment. Free admission to most events. Call ☎ **888-310-1117** or go to www.mauicanoefest.com or www.visitlahaina.com.

✔ **Mid-June:** The **Maui Film Festival at Wailea** is Hawaii's very own version of Sundance, with five days and nights of premiere screenings, parties, and celebrity appearances, plus Hawaiian cultural events for island flavor. Call ☎ **808-579-9244** or 808-572-FILM or visit www.mauifilmfestival.com for complete program information.

✔ **June 11 (or nearest weekend):** In honor of the great chief who united the Hawaiian Islands, **King Kamehameha Day** — Hawaii's longest-running holiday, since 1871 — is celebrated as a statewide holiday, with massive floral parades, slack key guitar concerts, Hawaiian crafts shows, and plenty of partying. Probably the best event is the celebratory floral parade through Maui's old Lahaina town, which concludes with a food and craft fair, demonstrations of ancient warrior skills, and other entertainment; call ☎ **808-667-9193** or 888-310-1117 or visit www.state.hi.us/dags/kkcc or www.visitlahaina.com for details.

✔ **Late June:** Hawaii's finest musicians — and those who appreciate them — gather annually at the Maui Arts & Cultural Center for the **Ki Hoalu Slack Key Guitar Festival,** an all-day outdoor event for the entire family. Bring a picnic and settle in for a day of soothing sounds from an all-star lineup. Call ☎ **808-242-7469** or visit www.mauiarts.org.

✔ **July 4:** Maui celebrates **Independence Day** with appropriate panache all over the island. Kaanapali celebrates with free activities focused on families from noon to 5 p.m. at Whalers Village. Or celebrate upcountry style at the Makawao Parade and Rodeo, with a street parade, a genuine rodeo, and other cowboy fun. Lahaina offers old-fashioned 4th of July fun, including a free fireworks show at 8 p.m. (Front Street is closed to traffic from sunset to 9 p.m.) Call ☎ 800-245-9229 for the schedule of events in Kaanapali, ☎ 808-572-2076 for Makawao events, or ☎ 888-310-1117 for Lahaina schedules (or visit www.visitlahaina.com).

✔ **Early July:** Lanai celebrates the precious pineapple with the daylong **Annual Pineapple Festival,** which takes place at Lanai's Dole Park on the Saturday closest to July 4th. Themed events celebrating Lanai's plantation and paniolo (cowboy) history include pineapple eating contests and live local entertainment, culminating in fireworks. It's a spirited, local-style celebration. Call ☎ 800-947-4774 or 808-565-7600 or go online to www.visit lanai.net.

✔ **Early July:** World-famous winemakers and chefs gather, along with appreciative gourmands, on Maui annually for the highly acclaimed — and appropriately grand — **Kapalua Wine & Food Festival,** a bounteous weeklong series of wine tastings, cooking demonstrations, and gourmet meals prepared by celebrity chefs. It's well worth attending if you fancy yourself a foodie. Make your arrangements well in advance because this event is hugely popular. Call ☎ 800-KAPALUA (800-527-2582), or visit www.kapaluamaui. com and click Events for details.

✔ **Early August:** The annual **Hawaii International Jazz Festival** presents a weekend of first-class jazz at the Hawaii Theater Center in Honolulu in late July, followed the next weekend by an equally stellar lineup at the Maui Arts & Cultural Center. The festival features evening concerts and daily jam sessions by jazz and blues artists of local, national, and international renown — an absolutely wonderful event! Call ☎ 808-242-7469 to buy tickets to Maui performances, or ☎ 808-528-0506 to purchase tickets in Honolulu. The complete schedule is available at www.hawaiijazz.com.

✔ **Early August:** The **Maui Onion Festival,** held in Whalers Village, Kaanapali, showcases the sweetest onions in the world through food vendors, entertainment, tastings, a farmers market, and a Maui Onion Cook-Off. Call ☎ 808-661-4567 or go to www.whalers village.com.

✔ **Third Friday in August:** Hawaii became the 50th state on August 21, 1959, which is now celebrated as **Admissions Day** on the third Friday in August; all state-related facilities are closed.

✔ **Mid-September:** Running exactly 26.2 miles from Kahului to Kaanapali, the **Maui Marathon** is regularly named one of the ten most scenic marathons in North America. It's no wonder that runners converge on the Valley Isle from around the world to burn rubber here. Call ☎ **808-871-6441** or visit www.mauimarathon.com for this year's date and entry information.

✔ **Mid-September through October:** 'Tis the season in Hawaii for statewide **Aloha Festivals.** Each week from mid-September through October is Aloha Week on a different island, with events running the gamut from parades and royal balls to ethnic days and street festivals. This week is serious celebration time. Go online to www.alohafestivals.com for a complete schedule of events.

✔ **Mid-September: Taste of Lahaina and the Best of Island Music** is Maui's biggest foodie event. Some 30,000 people flock to the Lahaina Special Events Arena to sample the signature dishes of Maui's top cooks throughout this weekend festival, which also includes cooking demonstrations, wine tastings, and nonstop live entertainment. The weekend before the main event features Maui Chefs Present, an elegant $100-a-plate dinner and cocktail party featuring about a dozen of the island's best chefs. Call ☎ **888-310-1117** or visit www.visitlahaina.com for details.

✔ **Early October:** The **Maui County Fair** is Hawaii's oldest and largest county fair. Expect a parade, rides, games, exhibits, live entertainment — all with an island twist, of course. Held at the Wailuku War Memorial Complex. Call ☎ **800-525-MAUI** or 808-242-2721, or visit www.calendarmaui.com, for this year's details.

✔ **Late October through early November:** The **Aloha Classic World Windsurfing Championships,** the final event in the Pro Boardsailing World Tour, is held at Maui's Hookipa Beach, universally considered to be the best windsurfing beach on the planet. These daredevils and their colorful sails are quite a sight to see as they pirouette over the wild winter waves; spectating is absolutely free. Call ☎ **808-573-6586** or check www.calendarmaui.com for this year's dates.

✔ **October 31:** Approximately 30,000 people show up to celebrate **Halloween** in Lahaina, an event so festive and popular that some call it the "Mardi Gras of the Pacific." Front Street is closed off from 4 p.m. to 2 a.m. for the costumed revelers and accompanying festivities; a children's parade launches the day. The Great Halloween Costume Contest takes place in Banyan Tree Park at 7 p.m. Lahaina is so gung-ho on Halloween, in fact, that the party starts the week prior to October 31 with haunted houses and other events around town. Call ☎ **888-310-1117** or 808-667-9193 or visit www.visitlahaina.com for this year's events.

✔ **Early to mid-November:** Various locations on Maui host the **Hawaii International Film Festival,** which features filmmakers from Asia, the Pacific Islands, and the United States. Call ☎ **808-528-4433** or point your browser to www.hiff.org.

✔ **Late November:** The annual **Maui Invitational Basketball Tournament** is held at the Lahaina Civic Center. Top college teams from around the nation vie in this annual preseason tournament. Visit www.mauiinvitational.com for more information, including details on how to purchase tickets. Usually held around Thanksgiving.

✔ **Throughout December:** Celebrating **Christmas** on Maui can be quite memorable. Santa arrives for the annual lighting of Lahaina's historic banyan tree, followed by Christmas caroling in Hawaiian. Schedules vary, so call ☎ **888-310-1117** or check www.visitmaui.com. Expect the major resort areas to be decked out in holiday finery all month.

Maximizing Your Time

As you plan your itinerary, keep the following tips in mind:

✔ **Fly directly from the mainland to Maui.** Doing so can save you a two-hour layover in Honolulu and another plane ride on an interisland carrier — a process that can add four or five hours to your total travel time. Multiple direct flights from the mainland serve Maui. However, mainland flights to the neighboring islands can be more expensive and less frequent than those that arrive in Honolulu, so be sure to price compare if money matters.

✔ **Spend a week or ten days vacationing on Maui.** A week or ten days allow you to explore the island at your leisure while still enjoying plenty of time just lazing on the beach. You may enjoy a four- or five-day trip to Maui if you're flying directly from California, but I wouldn't advise anything shorter than a week for folks traveling from farther away. If you want to hop to one or two other Hawaiian islands as well, you really need a full two-week vacation to make it enjoyable.

✔ **Don't overplan your itinerary or try to do everything.** If relaxation is No. 1 on your agenda, work plenty of do-nothing time into your travel plans. Keep your days loose and go with the flow; don't plan up your time the way you would on a sightseeing tour of Europe. A Maui vacation is less about seeing everything and more about letting go with the island flow — and a big part of the experience is just taking things as they come. Don't feel guilty that you're not doing or seeing enough; you do enough the other 50 weeks of the year, don't you? Trust me — everything you miss the first time around will be waiting for you when you get back.

✔ **Leave at least one day to chance.** Don't book a big activity for every day of your vacation. Leave at least one day for whatever strikes your fancy, whether it is sightseeing or shopping or just sitting on your condo's oceanfront lanai, soaking up a beach read and the laid-back vibe. I can't say it enough: A Maui vacation is about leaving the conventions of regular life — including a hard-core commitment to time — behind. Make the most of this carefree week in your life.

✔ **Make mornings your ocean time, if you're dividing your day between land and sea activities.** Beaches tend to be less crowded, and the surf and winds tend to be calmer in the morning hours — especially in winter. Always take the first snorkel and dive cruise of the day, when conditions are calmest and clearest; you'll understand why outfitters offer discounts on their afternoon sails.

✔ **Book extra-special activities before you leave home so that you don't miss out.** Many of Maui's best activities can book up weeks in advance. Do some plan-ahead reading and call to reserve a few select adventures, such as the best luau or a snorkel tour to Lanai you just don't want to miss, before you leave home. After all, you don't get to Maui just every day — and I don't want you to miss out on the best it has to offer. For tips on those activities you may want to book before you arrive, see Chapter 8.

Part II
Planning Your Trip to Maui

The 5th Wave
By Rich Tennant

"That's Maui. You can tell because it resembles a man looking to the right in a panic because he can't find his airline ticket, which his wife wisely packed in their carry-on the night before."

In this part . . .

*I*n this part, I discuss all your travel options: finding the best airfare, working with a travel agent, deciding whether to go the package-tour route, renting a car, and packing smart. I help you work out a realistic budget and show you where you can save and where it makes sense to splurge. I also give you an overview of your options for lodgings so that you can decide whether you want a luxury resort, a condo, or an intimate B&B.

Chapter 4

Managing Your Money

. . . .

In This Chapter

▶ Thinking about your major expenses
▶ Zeroing in on cost-cutting tips
▶ Dealing with a lost or stolen wallet

. . . .

"**S**o, how much is this trip going to cost me, anyway?" It's a reasonable question, no matter where you fall on the income ladder. Vacation can be an expensive proposition, with costs that can add up before you know it — and, as destinations go, Maui is a relatively pricey one. So planning ahead to keep your budget on track is important. In this chapter, I tell you what to expect and offer tips that can help you save big bucks.

Planning Your Budget

The good news is that you can easily structure a Maui trip to suit any budget. Airfare and hotels probably end up being your largest cash outlays. Other items, such as rental cars, are relatively affordable.

Your choice of activities also determines how much you spend: Relaxing on the beach or taking in Maui's natural beauty generally doesn't cost a dime. But guided tours and organized activities — like snorkel trips and helicopter rides during the day and luaus and dinner cruises after dark — can carry surprisingly heavy price tags.

Transportation: Your biggest expense

The cost of your flight to Maui will be one of your top two expenses (right up there with your hotel). Interisland flights are less expensive, but do increase the amount of money you end up spending. The key is to plan ahead and do your research before booking a flight. For details on flying to Maui and getting the best airfare, see Chapter 5.

Transpacific flights

Airfares at any time of year are almost impossible to predict and can change at the drop of a hat. Still, to give you an idea of what to expect, here's a sample of potential fares from season to season: If you're going to Maui in the off-season — say, May or maybe October — you may be able to snag a round-trip ticket for as little as $400 or $500 from San Francisco or Los Angeles, or for $600 to $700 from the East Coast. If you're traveling in the high season (late December to April, or in summer), you'll pay more — probably in the $500 to $800 range from the West Coast and between $700 and $1,400 from back East.

Expect to pay more if you're departing from a city that's not a major airline hub. If you're traveling to Maui over the Christmas holidays, expect to pay full fare. Also, you'll generally pay more for a direct flight to Maui than you will if you're willing to make a connection in Honolulu; however, you should price compare, because fares can vary.

You can score any number of money-saving deals, especially if you consider an all-inclusive package. (See Chapter 5 for more details on travel packages. I tell you more about how to save on airfares in that chapter, too.)

Interisland flights

If you plan to visit more than one island during your stay, you need to take an interisland flight. Fares for one-way trips between the islands, which Aloha Airlines and Hawaiian Airlines operate, average about $106 with tax in the high season.

However, you usually don't need to pay full fare. Numerous sales and special Internet-only fares are frequently available; one-way fares were available for around $70 at press time. (See Chapter 5 for details.)

Car rentals

Rental cars are generally reasonably priced on Maui. You can often get a compact car for as little as $28 to $38 a day, sometimes even less if you hit on a bargain. If you need a family-size car, expect to pay about $35 to $50 per day, depending on where you're staying and the time of year you're booking. Of course, everybody wants a convertible in the islands, so expect to pay upward of $75 a day in season for one. (You can sometimes wheel and deal for one at the rental counter in the low season, when business is slower.) Weekly rates almost always save you a bundle. For more information on car rentals, see Chapter 8.

Do yourself a favor and book a rental car with unlimited mileage. You'll appreciate the freedom, and you don't want to end up paying for your rental on a per-mile basis. Trust me — you'll end up on the short end of this stick. Luckily, most of the major car-rental companies rent on an unlimited-miles basis. Be sure to confirm this policy when you book.

And because you'll probably cover a good deal of ground, don't forget to factor in gas, which is typically more expensive on Maui than on the mainland. Also remember to account for any additional insurance costs, which generally run an extra $10 to $15 a day, depending on the coverage you select. Parking, thankfully, is generally free (although some luxury resorts charge a daily fee for parking; check when you book).

You seldom save by waiting to rent your car; generally, prices only go up as your pick-up date approaches — especially in the busy travel seasons. Book as far in advance as possible for the best rate. Also see the section "Cutting Costs, But Not the Fun," later in this chapter, for additional money-saving tips.

You may not have to worry about shopping around or wrangling a lower rate on a car rental. Often, rental cars and interisland flights are part-and-parcel of a package deal. In many hotel and airline packages, they're thrown in for a nominal fee or for free. See Chapter 5 for more details.

Lodging: Your other big expense

Maui has a wealth of luxury hotels and resorts, but it also offers plenty of affordable choices — especially on the condo market. Still, although you can find decent hotel rooms for $120 or so a night, you really shouldn't expect to pay much less than that. After you start adding on amenities — kitchenettes, room service, ocean views, and so on — expect room rates to climb.

You can score very reasonable rates on a per-person basis if you're travel-ing in a group or with your family. Maui boasts plenty of apartment-style condos that sleep four or more at very reasonable prices — between $100 and $150 per night on the lower end, and $200 or more for quite luxurious digs. Of course, if you stay at a condo, you likely miss out on resort-style amenities and services — concierge, room service, kids' programs, and the like — but it may be worth it if you want to have more room to spread out as well as keep your per-night costs down. For more on rates — including details on how to get the best rate — see Chapter 6.

So that you don't encounter any unwanted surprises at payment time, be sure to account for the 11.42 percent in taxes that will be added to your final hotel bill when planning your budget.

Dining: How to save, when to splurge

Maui has become quite a culinary mecca in the last few years, boasting an increasing number of top-quality restaurants, often charging top-dollar prices. So think about your bottom line. Many of you, no doubt, look forward to indulging in the island's bounty and don't mind paying for the privilege. But if you want to spend your vacation dollars on other activities and attractions, Maui offers plenty of opportunities to dine on the cheap: If you choose carefully, you can spend as little as $5 to $7 for breakfast (a continental breakfast may even be included in your hotel deal), grab a quick-and-easy lunch for around $10, and enjoy a casual dinner for $15 to $20. (Of course, extra niceties like wine or cocktails drive up dinner costs.)

Restaurant bills can add up fast, so if you want to save in this category, I strongly suggest booking a room or condo with kitchen facilities. By preparing a few daytime meals yourself (breakfast, in particular, can be a big money saver, and it's often convenient to make sandwiches to take to the beach), you're in a better position to splurge on a great dinner. Kitchen facilities are a virtual must if you're traveling with kids.

Sightseeing and activities: See it all without going broke

With sightseeing and other activities, the bills can really start to pile up, especially if you're traveling with the family. Ultimately, though, it depends on what you want to do. If you're coming to Maui to simply kick back at the beach and leave your mainland worries behind, you don't have to budget much in this category — going to the beach is free, and even snorkel gear rentals are cheap. See Chapter 12 for more information.

But if you're planning to schedule some organized activities and tours — which I strongly suggest you do — plan ahead to see what your budget can handle because they can get pricey. Expect to pay $60 to $80 a person for your average snorkel cruise, and even more for your average luau. Helicopter rides can easily run more than $100 a head. Budget-minded golfers may want to think twice before they tee up — tee times at Maui's top courses don't come cheap.

This book lists exact prices for activities, entertainment, tee times, admission fees, and the like so that you can budget your money realistically. If you can snag a bargain, I include that information, too.

Shopping and nightlife: Live it up for less

These two areas are the most flexible parts of your budget. Shopping, in particular, is a huge temptation in Maui. But if money is an issue, do yourself a favor and bypass the souvenirs.

What Things Cost in Maui

An average cup of coffee	$1.25
Compact rental car (per day)	$28
Convertible rental car (per day)	$62 to $75
Admission to the Maui Ocean Center	$20

Admission to Haleakala National Park	$10
Trilogy Excursions' snorkel trip	$169 to $229
Helicopter tour	$125 to $280
Greens fees at Kapalua Golf Club	$180 to $225
A day at the beach	Free!
Luxury room for two at the Grand Wailea	$465 to $825
Moderate room for two at the Kaanapali Beach Hotel	$169 to $300
Affordable room for two at the Koa Resort	$85 to $110
Affordable lunch at Maui Tacos	$10
Oceanfront dinner for two at Hula Grill	$75
Ticket to 'Ulalena show	$48 to $75
Old Lahaina Luau	$78.50

Cutting Costs, But Not the Fun

I don't care how much money you have — I know you don't want to spend more than necessary. In this section, I give you tips that can help you save your hard-earned money.

Getting the best airfare is such a huge topic that I dedicate the better part of a chapter to it. Before you even start scanning for fares, see Chapter 5. That chapter also discusses how to find money-saving package deals.

How to avoid paying full price for your hotel room

There's often a huge gap between hotels' official "published" (full-price, or rack) rates and what you actually pay, so don't be scared off at first glance. What's more, savvy travelers can further widen the margin.

More often than not, the best way to score a cheap hotel room is to buy an all-inclusive travel package that includes airfare, hotel, and car, and sometimes other extras, in one low price; for details on scoring a good-value package, see Chapter 5.

The second-best way to avoid paying the full rack rate when booking your hotel is stunningly simple: Just ask the reservation agent for a cheaper or discounted rate. You may be pleasantly surprised — I've been, many times. But you have to take the initiative and ask because no one is going to volunteer to save you money.

Here are a few more potential money-saving tips:

- ✔ **Rates are generally lowest in spring and fall.** The time of year you decide to visit may affect your bargaining power more than anything else. During the peak seasons — basically mid-December through mid-April and summer — when a hotel is booked up, management is less likely to extend heavily discounted rates or package deals. In the slower seasons — generally mid-April through mid-June and September through mid-December — when capacity is down, they're often willing to negotiate. In fact, many places drop rates by 10 to 30 percent automatically in the less busy times of year. If you haven't decided when you want to visit Maui yet, see Chapter 3.

- ✔ **Membership in AAA, AARP, or frequent-flier/traveler programs often qualifies you for discounted rates.** (For details on joining AAA, see "The AAA advantage" sidebar, later in this chapter.) You may also qualify for corporate or student discounts. Attention, seniors: You may qualify for discounts even if you're not an AARP member (although I highly recommend joining; see Chapter 7 for details). Members of the military or trade unions or those with government jobs may also qualify for price breaks.

- ✔ **Inquire about the hotel's own package deals.** Even if you're not traveling on an all-inclusive package (see Chapter 5), you may be able to take advantage of packages offered by hotels, resorts, and condos directly. They often include value-added extras, such as a free rental car, champagne and in-room breakfast for honeymooners, free dinners, discounted tee times or spa treatments, a room upgrade, an extra night thrown in for free (sometimes the fifth, sometimes the seventh), or some other freebie. I note what kinds of discounts are typically available in my hotel reviews. Properties often list these deals on their Web sites, but not always, so it never hurts to ask additional questions about available specials.

- ✔ **If you're booking a hotel that belongs to a chain, call the hotel directly in addition to going through central reservations.** See which one gives you the better deal. Sometimes the local reservationist knows about packages or special rates, but the hotel may neglect to tell the central booking line.

- ✔ **Surf the Web to save.** A surprising number of hotels advertise great packages via their Web sites, and some even offer Internet-only special rates.

  In addition to surfing the hotel's own sites, you may want to try using a general travel booking site like **Expedia.com, Travelocity.com, Hotels.com,** or **Orbitz.com** to book your hotel, or a pay-one-price package that also includes airfare. Acting much like airline consolidators, these sites can sometimes offer big discounts on rooms as well. However, always price compare against the hotel's own Web site; these days, virtually every major hotel chain offers price parity with the online distributors through their own Web sites. Often, you'll save a few bucks through the hotel's own site and/or end up with a better room for the same money, because the hotel doesn't have to pay high distribution fees if you book direct. See Chapter 6 for a more complete discussion of how to use the Web to find a great hotel bargain.

✔ **Ask innkeepers for a break.** B&Bs are generally nonnegotiable on price. Sometimes, however, you can negotiate a discount for longer stays, such as a week or more. You may also score a price break if you're visiting off-season. And some do offer AAA and senior discounts. Remember, it never hurts to ask, politely.

✔ **Look for price breaks and value-added extras when booking condos.** Condos can sometimes be pretty flexible on rates. They tend to offer discounts on multinight stays, and many throw in a free rental car to sweeten the deal. Some condo properties have units handled by multiple management companies; if that's the case, inquire through both companies and see where you get the better deal. You may also want to check with Hawaii Condo Exchange (☎ 800-442-0404 or 323-436-0300; www.hawaiicondoexchange.com), which acts as a consolidator for condo properties throughout the islands.

✔ **Reserve a hotel room with a kitchenette or a condo with a full kitchen and do your own cooking.** You may miss the pampering that room service provides, but you can save plenty of money. Even if you prepare only breakfast and an occasional picnic lunch in the kitchen, you still save significantly in the long run. (I've had some memorable island meals by simply buying fabulous fresh fish in the local supermarket and throwing it on the barbecue grill at an ocean-front condo.) Plus, if the beach is right outside your door, you don't ever have to leave it to go on restaurant runs.

✔ **Skip the ocean views or stay away from the ocean altogether.** Being steps away from the surf is wonderful, but you pay through the nose for the privilege: Oceanview rooms are the most expensive rooms in any hotel, especially those on the upper floors. Mountain or garden views are usually much cheaper — and you probably don't plan on hanging out in your room much, anyway. A stay in a hotel that is located slightly inland from the beach can be even cheaper. For more on this subject, see Chapter 6.

✔ **Ask whether the kids can stay in your room.** Or, better yet, book a condo with a sleeper sofa in the living room or a separate bedroom. A room with two double beds usually doesn't cost any more than one with a king-size bed, and most hotels don't charge an extra-person rate if the additional person is a child. If that's a bit too much togetherness for you, book one of the many one-, two-, or three-bedroom condos that are available on Maui. These full apartments are often no more expensive than your standard hotel room, and they're always cheaper than having to book two or more hotel rooms. Furthermore, they solve the expensive eating-out-at-every-meal problem, too.

The AAA advantage

If you aren't already a member, consider taking a few minutes to join the American Automobile Association (AAA) before you set out for Maui. In addition to providing you with a wealth of trip-planning services, membership can save you big bucks on hotel rates, car rentals, interisland airfares, and even admission to attractions.

The AAA Travel Agency helps you book air, hotel, and car arrangements, as well as all-inclusive tour packages to Maui. Membership in AAA can net you savings on interisland flights with Aloha Airlines and lets you qualify for hotel discounts of 10 percent or more. Discounts and benefits at 3,000 attractions and restaurants and 44,000 retail locations nationwide are available through AAA's Show Your Card and Save program. And don't forget the free maps — they're comprehensive, indispensable, and absolutely free to members.

I hate to sound like a shill, but you really can't go wrong with AAA. Whether it's a discount at an Outrigger hotel or a stress-relieving flat-tire fix, membership pays for itself before you know it. Annual membership fees vary slightly depending on your home region, but you can expect to spend around $55 per individual (primary member) and $25 to $30 for each additional family member.

To find the AAA office nearest your home, look in the phone book under "AAA" or log on to www.aaa.com, where you can link up to your regional club's home page after you enter your home zip code. You can even get instant membership by calling the national 24-hour emergency roadside service number (☎ **800-AAA-HELP**), which can connect you to any regional membership department during expanded business hours (only roadside assistance operates 24 hours a day). If you're a resident of Canada, the Canadian Automobile Association (www.caa.com) offers similar services (plus reciprocal benefits with AAA).

In Hawaii, the only local office is in Honolulu at 1270 Ala Moana Blvd., between Piikoi Street and Ward Centre (☎ **800-736-2886** or 808-593-2221; www.aaa-hawaii.com). The office is open 9 a.m. to 5 p.m. Monday through Friday, and 9 a.m. to 2 p.m. Saturday. Roadside assistance is available on Maui.

Tips for cutting other costs

Here are a few more useful tips to help you enjoy your Maui vacation without breaking the bank:

> ✔ **Consult a reliable travel agent.** A travel agent can often negotiate a better price with certain hotels and assemble a better valued complete travel package than you can get on your own. In fact, in a recent *Condé Nast Traveler* investigation, travel agents could always price out Hawaii resort vacations more cheaply than any other outlet (including airline packagers). Even if you book your own airfare, you may want to contact a travel agent to price out your hotel.

On the other hand, hotels, condos, and even B&Bs are sometimes willing to discount your rate as much as 30 percent — the amount they'd otherwise pay an agent in commissions — if you book direct. It may make sense to base your decision about using a travel agent on time rather than money — think of a travel agent as a convenience. If you do use a travel agent, it makes sense to be an informed consumer, going into the process with a general idea of what things cost so that you know whether you're getting a bargain. A good first step is consulting this book so that you know which hotels appeal to you and their approximate costs. And don't let an agent steer you to a hotel that's not right for you just because he or she might be getting a better commission. If you sense that your agent isn't working hard to line up a trip that really suits your desires, move on and find someone else.

✔ **You don't need much luxury to make Maui feel like paradise.** To find true Hawaii happiness, the rule is always this: The simpler, the better. You won't need 27-inch TVs, 24-hour butler service, or a telephone in the bathroom to be happy. So when reserving your accommodations, don't overdo it by booking a place that taxes your budget too much. Save that extra dough for having fun!

✔ **Surf the Web to save on your rental car, too.** In addition to surfing rental-car agencies' own sites, try comparing rates through a general travel booking site like Expedia.com, Travelocity.com, Orbitz.com, or Sidestep.com. This one-stop-shopping method can save you more than money — it can save you time, too. However, always price compare against the car company's own site, because most companies are now combating online booking agencies with on-par (or lower) pricing.

See Chapter 8 for more money-saving tips to keep in mind while booking your island wheels.

✔ **Don't rent a gas guzzler.** Renting a smaller car is cheaper, and you save on gas to boot (an especially important point, because gas prices are always higher in Hawaii than on the mainland). Unless you're traveling with a large group, don't go beyond the economy size.

✔ **Skip the souvenirs.** I've heard it more than once: "That whale print that looked so right in the art gallery was all wrong back in my living room in Cincinnati." Spend your money on memories, not tchotchkes.

✔ **Look out for the Bargain Alert icon as you read this book.** This icon alerts you to money-saving opportunities and especially good values as you travel.

Handling Money

You're the best judge of how much cash you feel comfortable carrying or what alternative form of currency is your favorite. That's not going to change much on your vacation. True, you'll probably be moving around more and incurring more expenses than you generally do, and you may let your mind slip into vacation gear and not be as vigilant about your safety as when you're in work mode. But those factors aside, the only type of payment that won't be quite as available to you away from home is your personal checkbook.

Using ATMs and carrying cash

The easiest and best way to get cash away from home is from an ATM. **The Cirrus** (☎ **800-424-7787;** www.mastercard.com) and PLUS (☎ **800-843-7587;** www.visa.com) networks span the globe; look at the back of your bank card to see which network you're on and then call or check online for ATM locations at your destination. Be sure you know your personal identification number (PIN) before you leave home and be sure to find out your daily withdrawal limit before you depart.

Also keep in mind that many banks impose a fee every time your card is used at a different bank's ATM. On top of this fee, the bank from which you withdraw cash may charge its own fee. (To compare banks' ATM fees within the U.S., use www.bankrate.com.) To beat these fees (and to avoid wasting precious vacation time running errands), it makes sense to withdraw larger sums rather than relying on lots of smaller withdrawals.

Charging ahead with credit cards

Credit cards are a safe way to carry money: They also provide a convenient record of all your expenses, and for foreign visitors, they generally offer relatively good exchange rates.

You can also withdraw cash advances from your credit cards at banks or ATMs, provided you know your PIN. If you've forgotten yours, or didn't even know you had one, call the number on the back of your credit card and ask the bank to send it to you. It usually takes five to seven business days, though some banks will provide the number over the phone if you tell them your mother's maiden name or some other personal information. But keep in mind that cash advances are a bad idea, only to be used in case of emergency. Your issuing bank will start charging interest from the day you make the withdrawal, usually at significantly higher rates than you're charged on regular purchases.

Some credit-card companies recommend that you notify them of any impending trip so that they don't become suspicious when the card is used numerous times in a new destination and block your charges. Even if you don't call your credit-card company in advance, you can always call the card's toll-free emergency number if a charge is refused — a good reason to carry the phone number with you.

Carrying more than one card with you on your trip is a good idea; a card may not work for any number of reasons, so having a backup is the smart way to go.

Toting traveler's checks

These days, it's so easy to find a 24-hour ATM that traveler's checks are becoming obsolete. Still, if you like the security of traveler's checks, and you don't mind showing identification every time you want to cash one, you may prefer to stick with the tried-and-true.

You can get traveler's checks at almost any bank. **American Express** offers denominations of $20, $50, $100, $500, and (for cardholders only) $1,000. You'll pay a service charge ranging from 1 to 4 percent (which negates any money you may have saved by avoiding fees for using other banks' ATMs while you're on the road). You can also get American Express traveler's checks over the phone by calling ☎ **800-221-7282;** Amex gold and platinum cardholders who use this number are exempt from the 1-percent fee.

Visa offers traveler's checks at Citibank locations nationwide, as well as at several other banks. The service charge ranges between 1.5 and 2 percent; checks come in denominations of $20, $50, $100, $500, and $1,000. Call ☎ **800-732-1322** for information. AAA members can obtain Visa checks without a fee at most AAA offices or by calling ☎ **866-339-3378. MasterCard** also offers traveler's checks. Call ☎ **800-223-9920** for a location near you.

 If you choose to carry traveler's checks, be sure to keep a record of their serial numbers separate from your checks — safely, with a relative or friend back home — in the event that they're stolen or lost. You'll get a refund faster if you know the numbers.

Dealing with a lost or stolen wallet

Be sure to contact all your credit-card companies the minute you discover that your wallet has been lost or stolen and file a report at the nearest police precinct. Your credit-card company or insurer may require a police report number or record of the loss. Most credit-card companies have an emergency toll-free number to call if your card is lost or stolen; they may be able to wire you a cash advance immediately or deliver an emergency credit card in a day or two. Call the following emergency numbers in the United States:

✔ **American Express** ☎ **800-221-7282** (for cardholders and traveler's check holders)

✔ **MasterCard** ☎ **800-307-7309** or 636-722-7111

✔ **Visa** ☎ **800-847-2911** or 410-581-9994

For other credit cards, call the toll-free number directory at ☎ **800-555-1212.**

If you need emergency cash over the weekend when all banks and American Express offices are closed, you can have money wired to you via **Western Union** (☎ **800-325-6000;** www.westernunion.com).

Identity theft or fraud are potential complications of losing your wallet, especially if you've lost your driver's license along with your cash and credit cards. Notify the major credit-reporting bureaus immediately; placing a fraud alert on your records may protect you against liability for criminal activity. The three major U.S. credit-reporting agencies are **Equifax** (☎ **800-766-0008;** www.equifax.com), **Experian** (☎ **888-397-3742;** www.experian.com), and **TransUnion** (☎ **800-680-7289;** www.transunion.com).

Finally, if you've lost all forms of photo ID, call your airline and explain the situation. It may allow you to board the plane if you have a copy of your passport or birth certificate and a copy of the police report you filed.

Chapter 5

Getting to Maui

In This Chapter

▶ Getting the best airfares to and around Maui
▶ Taking advantage of all-inclusive package deals
▶ Stretching your accommodation dollars

*G*etting to Maui may not *really* be half the fun, but it's a necessary step — and a big part of the planning process. How can you beat the high cost of transpacific airfares? Should you reserve a package deal or book the elements of your vacation separately? In this chapter, I give you the information to make the decision that's right for you.

Flying to Maui

Finding a flight to Maui involves more than just picking up the phone. You not only need to book your flight to Maui, but you also need to book any necessary interisland flights. In this section, I help you do both, as well as give you tips to help you get the best deal on all your air travel to and around Maui.

Finding out which airlines fly to Maui

Most transpacific flights arrive at Oahu's Honolulu International Airport, but an increasing number land directly on the bigger neighbor islands — especially Maui.

The following major airlines fly between mainland North America and one or more of Hawaii's major airports:

✔ **Air Canada** (☎ 888-247-2262; www.aircanada.ca) flies from Toronto and Vancouver to Maui's Kahului Airport and also to Oahu's Honolulu International Airport.

✔ **Aloha Airlines** (☎ 800-367-5250; www.alohaair.com), one of Hawaii's two major interisland carriers, flies from Oakland, Sacramento, Burbank (CA), Orange County (CA), Phoenix, Las Vegas, Reno, and Vancouver to Maui, Honolulu, and the Big Island's Kona International Airport. You can also make a connection to any neighbor island on Aloha.

- **American Airlines** (☎ 800-433-7300; www.americanair.com) flies from Chicago, St. Louis, Dallas, San Francisco, San Jose, and Los Angeles to Maui, Honolulu, Kauai, and Kona on the Big Island.

- **American Trans Air (ATA; ☎ 800-225-2995;** www.ata.com) flies from Phoenix, Seattle, Los Angeles, and San Francisco to Maui and Honolulu.

- **Continental Airlines** (☎ 800-525-0280; www.continental.com) is the only airline to fly nonstop from New York (actually Newark) to Honolulu. It also has service from Houston, Seattle, and Los Angeles to Honolulu (where you can hop to Maui on an interisland flight). Continental has a code-sharing relationship with Hawaiian Airlines.

- **Delta Airlines** (☎ 800-221-1212; www.delta.com) flies direct from Atlanta, Houston, Cincinnati, Los Angeles, San Francisco, and Los Angeles to Maui and Honolulu.

- **Hawaiian Airlines** (☎ 800-367-5320; www.hawaiianair.com) flies from Seattle, Portland, Sacramento, Las Vegas, Phoenix, Los Angeles, San Diego, and Ontario, CA (just east of Los Angeles), to Maui and Honolulu, where you can make a Hawaiian Airlines connection to any neighbor island.

- **Northwest Airlines** (☎ 800-225-2525; www.nwa.com) flies from Minneapolis, Detroit, Los Angeles, and Seattle to Honolulu, where you can hop on a quick flight to Maui.

- **United Airlines** (☎ 800-241-6522; www.ual.com) flies direct from Chicago, Los Angeles, and San Francisco to Maui, Honolulu, Kona on the Big Island, and Kauai's Lihue Airport.

Getting the best airfare

Competition among the major U.S. airlines is unlike that of any other industry. Every airline offers virtually the same product (basically, a coach seat is a coach seat is a . . .), yet prices can vary by hundreds of dollars.

Business travelers who need to purchase their tickets at the last minute, change their itinerary at a moment's notice, or get home before the weekend pay the premium rate, known as the *full fare.* Passengers whose travel agenda is more flexible — who can book their tickets far in advance, who don't mind staying over Saturday night, or who are willing to travel on a Tuesday, Wednesday, or Thursday — pay the least, usually a fraction of the full fare. On most flights to Hawaii, even the shortest hops, the full fare is well more than $1,000, but a 7-day or 14-day advance-purchase ticket from the West Coast is often closer to $500 or $600. Obviously, I can't guarantee what fares will be when you book, but you can almost always save by planning ahead.

Keep your eye out in the newspaper, on the Internet, and TV for airfare sales. Sale fares carry advance-purchase requirements and date-of-travel restrictions, but the price is usually worth the restrictions: sometimes no more than $400 for a transpacific flight from the West Coast to Hawaii (even less on some airlines). The sales tend to take place in seasons of low travel volume (usually spring and fall). You'll almost never see a sale around the peak summer vacation months or in the winter high season.

These few tips can help you save on airfares:

✔ **Travel on off days of the week.** Airfares vary depending on the day of the week. Everybody wants to travel on the weekend. If you can travel on a Tuesday, Wednesday, or Thursday, you may find cheaper flights to Maui. When you inquire about airfares, ask whether you can get a cheaper rate by flying on a different day. Remember, too, that staying over on a Saturday night can cut your airfare.

✔ **Reserve your flight well in advance.** Take advantage of advance-purchase fares — or watch the last-minute e-fares online for bargains. (See the upcoming section "Booking through online reservations services" for a discussion of online strategies.)

✔ **Flying direct to Maui may save on interisland airfares.** Maui is served by direct flights from the mainland. (See the list of carriers earlier in this chapter.) Compare the cost of flying to Honolulu plus an interisland fare with the cost of flying directly to Maui. Flying direct also saves you a few hours on each end — and time can be a more valuable commodity than money when your vacation time is limited.

Booking through online reservations services

The "big three" online travel agencies — Expedia (www.expedia.com), Travelocity (www.travelocity.com), and Orbitz (www.orbitz.com) — sell many of the air tickets bought on the Internet. (Canadian travelers should try www.expedia.ca and www.travelocity.ca; U.K. residents can go for expedia.co.uk and opodo.co.uk.) Each has different business deals with the airlines and may offer different fares on the same flights, so shopping around is wise. Expedia and Travelocity also send you an e-mail notification when a cheap fare becomes available to your favorite destination. All these online travel agencies also purport to save you money with pay-one-price packaging — which is really becoming their key business, particularly at Expedia — although I suggest price comparing the separate pieces with the direct service providers before assuming that you're saving.

Of the smaller travel agency Web sites, **SideStep** (www.sidestep.com) receives good reviews from users. It's a browser add-on that purports to "search 140 sites at once," but in reality only beats competitors' fares as often as other sites do.

If you're willing to give up some control over your flight details, use an *opaque fare service* like **Priceline** (www.priceline.com) or Expedia's own **Hotwire** (www.hotwire.com). Both offer rock-bottom prices in exchange for travel on a "mystery airline" at a mysterious time of day, often with a mysterious change of planes en route. The mystery airlines are all major, well-known carriers — and the possibility of being sent from Phoenix to Maui via Tampa is remote. But your chances of getting a 6 a.m. or 11 p.m. flight are pretty high. Hotwire tells you flight prices before you buy; Priceline usually has better deals than Hotwire, but you have to play their "name our price" game. *Note:* In 2004, Priceline added nonopaque service to its roster. You now have the option to pick exact flights, times, and airlines from a list of offers — or you can bid on opaque fares as before.

Great last-minute deals are also available directly from the airlines themselves through a free e-mail service called *E-savers.* Each week, the airline sends you a list of discounted flights, usually leaving the upcoming Friday or Saturday and returning the following Monday or Tuesday. You can sign up for all the major airlines at one time by logging on to **Smarter Living** (www.smarterliving.com), or you can go to each individual airline's Web site. Airline sites also offer schedules, flight booking, and information on late-breaking bargains.

While third-party sites like Expedia and Travelocity sometimes offer the best airfares, never just assume. These days, many major carriers are offering similar — or even cheaper — airfares through their own Web sites in order to avoid paying costly commissions to the online agencies.

Using a consolidator

Consolidators, also known as bucket shops, are a good place to find low fares, often below even the airlines' discounted rates. Basically, these companies are just big travel agents that get discounts for buying in bulk and pass some of the savings on to you.

Bucket shop tickets are usually nonrefundable or rigged with stiff cancellation penalties, often as high as 50 to 75 percent of the ticket price, and some put you on charter airlines with questionable safety records.

Some of the most reliable consolidators include the following:

- ✔ **AirSaver** (☎ 888-346-5795; www.airsaver.com) is an online consolidator that currently specializes in international fares, but it was offering some very good deals on transpacific round-trips at this writing.

- ✔ **Cheap Tickets** (☎ 888-922-8849; www.cheaptickets.com) was originally founded in Honolulu (though it has closed its Hawaii offices since being acquired by Cendant). I almost always do better by calling than I do by pricing out fares on its Web site.

  ✔ **STA Travel** (☎ **800-226-8624** or 800-781-4040; www.statravel.com), the world's leader in student travel, offers good fares for travelers of all ages.

  ✔ **TFI Tours International** (☎ **800-745-8000** or 212-736-1140; www.lowestairprice.com) serves as a clearinghouse for unused seats on most of the world's major airlines.

  ✔ **1-800-FLY-CHEAP** (www.1800flycheap.com) is owned by package-holiday megalith MyTravel and is known for good fares to sunny destinations, so it's worth checking, but I've yet to find an unbeatable fare to Hawaii here.

  ✔ **The TravelHub** (www.travelhub.com) represents nearly 1,000 travel agencies, many of whom offer consolidator and discount fares.

  ✔ **Travel Avenue** (☎ **800-333-3335;** www.travelavenue.com) is an online travel agency willing to rebate part of its commissions to you; this rebate can sometimes save you as much as 7 percent over what you'd pay through another agent.

Some of these consolidators can also save you money on hotels and car rentals as well.

Flying between the Hawaiian Islands

The only way to travel from island to island is by airplane. This trip used to be a relatively simple proposition, because island airports were casual affairs and shuttle-style flights left every 30 or 40 minutes. But since 9/11, there's been a reduction in the number of interisland flights, making it important to book in advance. The airlines request that you show up at least 90 minutes before your flight to allow for security inspections, and I've found that to be good advice.

Two major interisland carriers serve the islands: Aloha Airlines and Hawaiian Airlines. Both offer similar schedules — flights between the major islands every hour or so — at competitive prices.

Aloha Airlines (☎ **800-367-5250** or 808-484-1111; www.alohaairlines.com) employs an all-jet fleet of Boeing 737 aircraft. Aloha's sibling company, **Island Air** (☎ **800-323-3345,** 800-652-6541, or 808-484-2222; www.islandair.com), operates deHavilland DASH-8 and DASH-6 aircraft and serves Hawaii's smaller interisland airports on Maui (Kapalua Airport); Molokai, and Lanai, as well as Kona on the Big Island. Try Aloha first; if you need to take an Island Air flight because there's no accommodating Aloha flight, Aloha can book it for you.

Aloha Airlines is a mileage partner with United Airlines, so you can earn 500 miles in your United Mileage Plus account for every Aloha Airlines interisland segment you fly. Also, I strongly suggest checking Aloha's Web site, where you can join their AlohaPass frequent-flier program for free. Even if you don't plan on flying often enough to rack up miles for a free flight, you'll be entitled to bargain fares (and online booking won you another 10-percent discount as of press time).

Hawaiian Airlines (☎ **800-367-5320,** 800-882-8811, or 808-838-1555; www.hawaiianair.com) offers interisland jet service aboard Boeing 717-200s; the entire fleet was replaced with brand-new aircraft in 2001, making this the youngest fleet in the Pacific.

Hawaiian is mileage partners with Alaska, America West, Northwest, and Virgin Atlantic airlines, which gives you plenty of mileage-earning potential.

At press time, the full interisland fare was about $106 per one-way segment on both airlines, with fares dropping as low as $70 to $75, depending on the dates and routes you wish to fly. Booking more than 14 days in advance gives you the best shot at a bargain fare.

If you're traveling on a package, you probably don't have to worry about any of this — your interisland flights are most likely included in your package deal, on whichever interisland carrier the packager is affiliated with. For more on all-inclusive travel packages, see the next section.

Choosing a Pay-One-Price Package

Comprehensive, pay-one-price travel packages are often the smart way to go when booking your Hawaii vacation. Besides the convenience of having all your travel needs taken care of at once, a package can often save you lots of money. In many cases, a package tour that includes airfare, hotel, and transportation to and from the airport costs less than the hotel alone if you book it yourself.

That's because packages are sold in bulk to tour operators, who resell them to the public. It's kind of like buying your vacation at a buy-in-bulk store — except the tour operator is the one who buys the 1,000-count box of garbage bags and resells them 10 at a time at a cost that undercuts the local supermarket.

Package trips can vary as much as those garbage bags, too. Some offer a better class of hotels than others; others provide the same hotels for lower prices. Some book flights on scheduled airlines; others sell charters. In some packages, your choice of accommodations and travel days may be limited. Some let you choose between escorted vacations and independent vacations; others allow you to add on just a few excursions or escorted daytrips (also at discounted prices) without booking an entirely escorted tour.

Every destination, including Hawaii, usually has a few packagers (tour operators) that are better than the rest because they buy in even bigger bulk. The time you spend shopping around is likely to be well rewarded.

To find package tours, check out the travel section of your local Sunday newspaper or the ads in the back of national travel magazines such as *Travel + Leisure, National Geographic Traveler, Arthur Frommer's Budget Travel,* and *Condé Nast Traveler.* Online, check out **Expedia** (www. expedia.com), **Travelocity** (www.travelocity.com), and **Orbitz** (www.orbitz.com), which are becoming more sophisticated "pay-one-price" packagers every day.

Liberty Travel (call ☎ 888-271-1584 to find the location nearest you; www.libertytravel.com) is one of the biggest packagers in the Northeast and usually boasts a full-page ad in Sunday papers. At press time, Liberty was offering excellent value packages, with or without air, to all the Hawaiian Islands — and its agents are willing to help you construct a multi-island trip. Calling the toll-free number immediately connects you to the Liberty Travel store nearest your home.

Pleasant Hawaiian Holidays (☎ 800-7-HAWAII; www.pleasant holidays.com), the biggest and most comprehensive packager to Hawaii, has more than 40 years of experience in the business and offers tons of package options. At press time, it was offering a high-quality collection of more than 100 condos and hotels to choose from, and booking air travel aboard multiple airlines (as well as on its own charters), which gives you plenty of flexibility if you have an established frequent-flier account with an airline. Pleasant can arrange just about any kind of vacation you want, including fly/drive packages and land-only deals. And because it buys airfares and hotel-room blocks in such bulk, its deals are often excellent (although it offers better deals on some properties than others). Another plus is that Pleasant maintains a local service desk on Maui that can help you book activities and answer any questions you may have. Pleasant can even finance your vacation for you — but that's a bad option due to high interest rates.

SunTrips (☎ 800-SUNTRIPS or 800-357-2400; www.suntrips.com) is committed to arranging affordable and comprehensive Maui vacations, and the majority of the many properties offered are budget and moderately priced hotels and condos. If money is no object, head elsewhere — but if you're looking for a bargain, SunTrips may just be the packager for you.

If you want to work with a travel agency that specializes in booking packaged Maui vacations, offers a more personalized shopping experience, and really knows its stuff, contact Melissa McCoy's Valley Isle–based **Aloha Destinations Vacations** (☎ 800-256-4280 or 808-893-0388; www. alohadestinations.com).

The big three online travel agencies — **Expedia** (www.expedia.com), **Travelocity** (www.travelocity.com), and **Orbitz** (www.orbitz.com) — specialize in pay-one-price vacation packages these days. As with any packager, the best way to cover yourself — to insure that you're really getting the best price — is to price each piece individually and compare against the pay-one-price tag that any online or three-dimensional packager is offering.

Some travel packagers — including Pleasant Hawaiian Holidays and SunTrips — are likely to book you on their own charter flights rather than on commercial flights on major airlines. Flying on a charter doesn't really make a difference, unless you have a particular allegiance to a specific airline (or to collecting miles in a frequent-flier program). Be sure you know what airline you're flying when you book. And if you really do want to fly with a specific airline, that doesn't rule out a packager. In fact, Pleasant has established relationships with major carriers, such as Delta, United, and Hawaiian — and just about any packager will be happy to book you a land-only vacation that lets you book your own airfare separately (even the airline packagers will do this; see the following section).

Many major airlines also offer travel packages to Maui. I always recommend comparison shopping, but you may want to choose the airline that has frequent service to your hometown or the one on which you accumulate frequent-flier miles; you may even be able to pay for your package using miles. The following airlines offer travel packages to Maui as part of their services:

- ✔ **Air Canada Vacations** (☎ 800-662-3221; www.aircanada vacations.com)

- ✔ **American Airlines Vacations** (☎ 800-321-2121; www.aavacations. com), one of the best, after United, in terms of value and range of accommodations

- ✔ **ATA Vacations** (☎ 800-573-3747; www.atavacations.com)

- ✔ **Continental Airlines Vacations** (☎ 800-634-5555; www.cool vacations.com)

- ✔ **Delta Vacations** (☎ 800-872-7786; www.deltavacations.com)

- ✔ **Northwest WorldVacations** (☎ 800-800-1504; www.nwaworld vacations.com)

- ✔ **United Vacations** (☎ 800-328-6877 or 888-854-3899; www.united vacations.com), which is the most comprehensive airline packager to Hawaii and offers the most direct flights to the neighbor islands

Choosing between a travel agent and a packager isn't an either/or proposition; in fact, your travel agent can be your best source in sorting through the various deals that are available. If you're an American Express customer, you may consider going through **American Express Travel Service**, which can book travel packages through various vendors, including

Continental Vacations and Delta Vacations. To locate the office (or official travel-agent representative) nearest you, call ☎ **800-297-3429** or go online to www.americanexpress.com and click "Find a Travel Service Location." You can also use the site's online locator to locate an agent who specializes in Hawaii travel.

Ditto for AAA members, who have access to the **AAA Travel Agency,** which can also book excellent value package deals. Visit www.aaa.com to find the regional office nearest you.

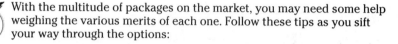

With the multitude of packages on the market, you may need some help weighing the various merits of each one. Follow these tips as you sift your way through the options:

- ✔ **Read up on Maui.** Read through the hotel listings in this book and select the places that sound interesting. Compare the rates that I list with the packagers' prices to best gauge which packagers are really offering a good deal and which have simply gussied up the rack rates to make their full-fare offer sound like a smart buy. Remember that the amount you save depends on both the property and the packager; most packagers can offer bigger savings on some properties than on others. For example, Liberty Travel may give you a better rate on the Grand Wailea than Pleasant Holidays can, but Pleasant may offer you a substantial savings on the condo you want.

- ✔ **Compare apples to apples.** When comparing packages, make sure that you know exactly what's included in the quoted price and what's not. Don't assume anything: Some packagers include everything — including value-added extras like lei greetings, free continental breakfast, and dining discounts — while others don't even include airfare. Additionally, when considering package prices, factor in add-in costs if you're flying from somewhere other than Los Angeles or San Francisco — some packagers price packages directly from your hometown, and some require additional premiums for airfares from your hometown to their Los Angeles or San Francisco gateway.

- ✔ **Before you commit to a package, make sure you know how much flexibility you have.** Some packagers require iron-clad commitments, while others charge only minimal fees for changes or cancellations. Consider the possibility that your travel plans may change, and select a packager with the degree of flexibility that suits your needs. And if you pay up front for a complete vacation package that carries stiff cancellation penalties, consider buying travel insurance that will reimburse you in case an unforeseen emergency prevents you from traveling. (See Chapter 8 for more on this topic.)

- ✔ **Don't believe in fairy tales.** Unfortunately, shady dealers and fly-by-night operations are out there. If a package appears too good to be true, it probably is. Any knowledgeable travel agent can help you determine whether a specific packager is reputable.

If you're booking a last-minute getaway, you may score a stellar deal through **Site 59** (www.site59.com). Site 59 books all-inclusive travel packages as much as 60 percent off what the major packagers charge. The catch? You can only price and purchase your trip between 3 hours and 14 days before your departure, and all destinations aren't available from all departure points. Still, if you're just dying to get away on the spur of the moment, check it out. You may also surf past **TravelHub** (www.travelhub.com) for last-minute package deals.

Joining an Escorted Tour

Pay-one-price discount package tours are one thing, but escorted tours are a different animal altogether. Hawaii is such a foolproof place to visit — and its magic is so dependent on relaxing leisure time — that I strongly recommend traveling on your own rather than signing on to an escorted tour.

If you really prefer to be led around, however, or if you're not able to drive yourself, you may want to consider one.

If you decide to go with an escorted tour, buying travel insurance is a good idea, especially if the tour operator asks you to pay up front. But don't buy your coverage from the tour operator! If the tour operator doesn't fulfill its obligation to provide you with the vacation you paid for, there's no reason to think that they'll fulfill their insurance obligations either. Get travel insurance through an independent agency. (See Chapter 8 for the ins and outs of travel insurance.)

When choosing an escorted tour, along with finding out whether you have to put down a deposit and when final payment is due, ask a few simple questions before you buy:

- ✔ **What is the cancellation policy?** Can they cancel the trip if they don't get enough people? How late can you cancel if you are unable to go? Do you get a refund if you cancel? If they cancel?

- ✔ **How jam-packed is the schedule?** Does the tour schedule try to fit 25 hours into a 24-hour day, or does it give you ample time to relax by the pool or shop? If getting up at 7 a.m. every day and not returning to your hotel until 6 or 7 p.m. at night sounds like a grind, certain escorted tours may not be for you.

- ✔ **How large is the group?** The smaller the group, the less time you spend waiting for people to get on and off the bus. Tour operators may be evasive about giving out this number, because they may not know the exact size of the group until everybody has made reservations, but they should be able to give you a rough estimate.

✔ **What exactly is included?** Don't assume anything. You may have to pay to get yourself to and from the airport. A box lunch may be included in an excursion, but drinks may be extra. How much flexibility do you have? Can you opt out of certain activities, or does the bus leave once a day, with no exceptions? Are all your meals planned in advance?

The escorted trips offered by **Tauck Tours** (☎ 800-788-7885; www.tauck.com) are far more luxurious and far less structured than your average escorted tour; they're pricey, but worth it if you'd rather put someone else in charge of the itinerary. If you're looking for more affordable options, try sister companies **Globus** (☎ 866-755-8581; www.globusjourneys.com) and **Cosmos** (☎ 800-276-1241; www.cosmosvacations.com); Globus offers more luxurious vacations, while Cosmos is more price-savvy. Both are excellent companies. **Perillo Tours** (☎ 800-431-1515; www.perillotours.com) also offers midpriced multi-island tours.

Chapter 6

Booking Your Accommodations

Maui's resort hotels are notoriously expensive. Hotels won't hesitate to charge $300 a night for a partial-oceanview room with little more than a queen-size bed in it. So prepare yourself for the fact that accommodations may take up a larger portion of your total travel budget than you might expect.

That said, don't forsake Kaanapali for the Jersey Shore just yet. Maui boasts plenty of excellent values for every budget if you just know where to look — and I include the best of them in Chapter 10.

Before you book your accommodations, you need to figure out what kind of place you want. You find five types of accommodations on Maui: resorts, hotels, condos, bed-and-breakfasts, and vacation rentals.

Getting to Know Your Options

In Maui, your accommodation options range from ultraposh luxury resorts to no-frills vacation rentals. Your choice depends on your travel needs and your budget — though an expensive resort may be a great option for that romantic getaway, you may much prefer to rent a condo if you have the kids in tow. I list numerous options in each of the following sections below so that you can choose the one which best suits your specific needs. Table 6-1 gives you an idea of what you can expect to pay in each price category.

Table 6-1	Key to Hotel Dollar Signs*	
Dollar Sign(s)	**Price Range**	**What to Expect**
$	Less than $100 per night	Supercheap — a very basic hotel room a distance from the beach
$$	$100 to $175	Still affordable — a midpriced hotel room or condo, possibly on or near the beach
$$$	$175 to $250	Moderate — a good-quality hotel room or condo on or near the beach
$$$$	$250 to $375	Expensive but not ridiculous — a high-quality room in a full-service hotel, or a multibedroom condo, on or near the beach
$$$$$	More than $375 per night	Ultraluxurious — the ultimate in deluxe resort living, generally on the beach

Each range of dollar signs, from one ($) to five ($$$$$), represents the median rack-rate price range for a double room per night. This system applies to each resort, hotel, condo, B&B, or vacation rental.

Relaxing at a resort

Most resorts (or resort hotels) are multi-acre, multibuilding complexes located directly on the beach. Some are sophisticated (sometimes too sophisticated for laid-back Maui), ultraluxury affairs geared to monied adults; others are theme-park-like spreads that cater largely to families with kids. More than a few fall somewhere in between.

A resort (or resort hotel) offers everything that your average hotel offers, plus much more. Every resort hotel is different, of course, but you can expect such amenities as direct beach access with beach cabanas and chairs, and often beach-toy rentals and ocean activities as well; pools (often more than one) and a Jacuzzi, often with poolside bar service; an activities desk; a fitness center and (more and more) a full-service spa; a variety of restaurants, bars, and lounges; a 24-hour front desk; concierge, valet, and bell services; twice-daily maid service (which can come in handy after you've dragged sand in your room and used all your towels by 4 p.m.); room service; tennis and golf (including some world-class courses); a business center; extensive children's programs; and more.

Rooms may be in high-rise towers, but they're often scattered throughout the property in low-rise buildings or clustered cottages. They tend to be done in the same safe, mass-market style throughout the resort — generally, room 101 is going to look exactly like room 1901. As travelers' tastes increasingly demand more, however, many newer properties (and savvy new renovations) are reinventing the resort with smart, high-style concepts that are intended to heighten the resort's own unique setting, concept, or personality. The standards tend to be high, and rooms are usually outfitted with high-quality furnishings and linens. Many luxury resorts also boast an increasing slate of in-room extras, such as CD players and big TVs with Nintendo systems, on-screen Web access, and VCRs (and even DVD players, sometimes).

Being the most well-outfitted, and usually the best located, of Maui's accommodations options, resorts are also the priciest choices on the market, although you can find a few midrange resorts. That said, you can score attractive rates, even at some of the island's most luxurious resorts, especially if you book through a packager (see Chapter 5), but sometimes by just calling or checking a resort's Web site at the right moment and scoring a good deal.

Hanging at a hotel

Hotels tend to be smaller and have fewer facilities than resorts — you may get a swimming pool, but don't expect a golf course or tennis courts, more than one or two restaurants and/or bars, and everything else that comes with a full-fledged resort.

Hotels are often a short walk from the beach rather than actually on the sands. Generally, a hotel offers daily maid service and has a restaurant and/or coffee shop, a bar or lounge, on-site laundry facilities, a swimming pool, and a sundries or convenience-type shop (rather than the shopping arcades that many resorts have these days). Top hotels also have activities desks, concierge and valet services, limited room service, and a business center.

"Boutique hotels" are smaller — maybe 40 or 50 rooms rather than 200 or more — and more intimate than your average Doubletree or Hilton. The rooms are often more stylish, less cookie-cutter, and usually have more amenities. They tend to cater to adults rather than families.

Hotels run the gamut from very expensive to downright cheap. But even the priciest ones (usually boutique hotels) tend to be less expensive than fully outfitted resorts.

Staying in a condo

Condominium apartments make up a large percentage of Maui's accommodations. They're a great option for everyone because they're outfitted like a fully operational home and can accommodate anywhere from two to eight vacationers in one, two, or three bedrooms. You can't pick a better way to travel as a family or in a group, but even couples enjoy the extra space and homestyle amenities.

Condos are usually apartments in either a single high-rise or a cluster of low-rise buildings, often on the beach, though sometimes not. Because they're real apartments, condos almost always come complete with a fully outfitted kitchen, a living room with pullout sofa (which usually means that one-bedroom condos can easily accommodate four guests; two-bedrooms can accommodate six), a private phone line, and a washer/dryer (usually), as well as other homestyle amenities like a TV and VCR in the living room (and usually an extra in the master bedroom). Two-bedroom condos often (but not always) have a second bath; in fact, a good number of one-bedroom condos in Maui also have a second bath. (Never assume anything; always ask when you book.)

On-site you usually find a swimming pool, laundry facilities (if units aren't in the apartments), tennis courts (sometimes), a front desk or property manager to deal with any questions you may have, and some-times an activities desk to book snorkel cruises, luaus, and the like.

 Don't expect the kind of service in a condo complex that you'd get at a hotel. If you prefer room service to your own kitchen, or you want some-body else to schlep your bags or wash your laundry, go with a hotel or resort instead.

More often than not, rental condos are individually owned vacation apartments that the owners use maybe a month or two out of the year. When the apartments aren't owner-occupied (which is most of the time), a management company or agent, which also rents them out, manages and cares for the units. You may book a condo through any number of individuals: an on-site agent or manager, an off-site agent or manager, or an off-site individual owner. Often, at some condo complexes (but not all), more than one manager may represent units at any one time. In this book, I recommend units that are all managed by reputable companies with good track records. (In the cases where more than one agent repre-sents a property, I list the one I feel will give you the best deal and the best service.)

Because they're privately owned homes, condo apartments are almost always individually decorated. However, the management company always requires a certain standard of décor and certain amenities, so the rental agent you use should be able to tell you exactly what to expect.

Condos range in price from bargain basement to ultraluxury, with the majority falling on the affordable end of the continuum. I find that condos are the best values on Maui, hands down, no matter what your price range. You almost always get more for your money than at a comparable resort. Also, because competition between condo properties is so tight, many good properties offer extras, such as a free rental car and the sev-enth night free, to lure you in. Packagers are a great source for bargain rates on condos (see Chapter 5).

Most condos offer some kind of maid service. Some have the kind of full daily service that you get in a hotel; others merely offer a basic weekly linen change. During my own stays, I've found minimal maid service to be just fine, even pleasant — I like not having the daily intrusion, and I don't mind rinsing my own breakfast dishes. But it can be an entirely different story if you're traveling with a big brood. Also, most properties that offer daily or midweek maid service include it in the rate, but a few charge extra for it. Be sure to ask for specifics when inquiring about a condo.

I list some great condo choices in Chapter 10, but many more options exist. For additional choices, contact the **Hawaii Condo Exchange** (☎ **800-442-0404** or 323-436-0300; www.hawaiicondoexchange.com), a Southern California–based agency that acts as a consolidator for condo properties throughout the islands, including a number of excellent choices on Maui. The Exchange works to match you up with the place that's right for you and tries to get you a good deal. In addition, most companies that offer all-inclusive travel packages to Maui can book you into any number of condos, as can your travel agent.

For a complete selection of upscale condos throughout sunny, luxury-minded Wailea, reach out to **Destination Resorts Hawaii** (☎ **877-347-0347** or 808-891-6249; www.destinationresortshi.com). Destination Resorts generally handles first-class properties boasting plenty of deluxe amenities. Prices start as low as $195 per night for a studio and go as high as $1,200 per night for a spacious oceanfront four-bedroom destination.

If you like the sound of the tranquil Kapalua Bay Hotel & Ocean Villas (see Chapter 10), but the luxury hotel rates are out of your league, consider renting an elegant condo or vacation home at **Kapalua Villas** (☎ **800-545-0018** or 808-669-8088; www.kapaluavillas.com). Nightly rates range from $199 for a one-bedroom apartment with a fairway view to $500 for an oceanfront three-bedroom apartment — not bad, considering you enjoy the same delicious perks and spectacular views of your much-higher-paying neighbors (including Kelsey Grammer, who owns his own Kapalua spread). The three- to five-bedroom freestanding luxury vacation homes run from $1,500 to $7,500 nightly. Whether you go large or small, you're sure to be pleased with your first-class accommodation.

Those of you looking for affordable sleeps on the South Maui coast should contact **Bello Realty** (☎ **800-541-3060** or 808-879-3328; www.bellomaui.com). Bello represents affordable condos throughout the Kihei/Wailea area, with prices starting as low as $85 in the low season. Be sure to check out **Koa Resort,** one of Maui's best under-$125 bargains (see Chapter 10). I've received plenty of good feedback from vacationers who've used Bello and come away with an excellent beachfront bargain and good service results, so I'm quite confident about the quality and values that Bello offers.

Condominium Rentals Hawaii (☎ **800-367-5242,** 800-663-2101 from Canada, or 808-879-2778; www.crhmaui.com) also books condos throughout Kihei. The car-and-condo packages and other regular specials can really add to the value to these units.

Maui Beachfront Rentals (☎ **888-661-7200** or 808-661-3500; www.maui beachfront.com) can book you into a range of good apartments along West Maui's condo coast. The studios at the **Napili Bay,** which start as low as $125, are a great value for budget-minded couples. You may even be able to save a few dollars at two of my favorite Kaanapali Beach condo complexes: **The Whaler** and **Kaanapali Alii.** (See Chapter 10 for more on these three properties.)

Enjoying the comforts of a B&B

Staying in a bed-and-breakfast is a nice way to discover Maui's genuine aloha spirit. More often than not, B&Bs offer a more intimate, and often more romantic, setting than your average impersonal resort, and a host who's more than happy to help you get to know Hawaii as it really is. If you want to experience a real slice of island life, B&Bs are the way to go.

B&Bs vary widely in size, style, and services. Generally speaking, they're usually comprised of several bedrooms in a home or several cottages or suites scattered about a property, each of which may or may not have a private bathroom. (All the B&Bs that I recommend in Chapter 10 have units with private baths.)

When you book a B&B, be sure that you fully understand its policies regarding deposits, cancellations, and method of payment. Because a B&B is a small business and has a harder time filling last-minute cancellations than a big hotel would, it may have more rigid policies. Despite the name, B&Bs also vary in whether breakfast is actually included in the rates, so ask ahead of time. And inquire about any other quirks or policies that may matter to you, such as whether smoking is allowed, whether the owners like to have guests take off their shoes when they enter, or whether pets are permitted on the premises.

I recommend contacting one or more of the following agencies if you're considering a stay at a B&B:

- ✔ Tops in the state is **Hawaii's Best Bed & Breakfasts** (☎ **800-262-9912** or 808-985-7488; www.bestbnb.com). The owners and staff personally inspect (and regularly revisit) the B&Bs and inns that they represent, and they're not afraid to say "no" to any property that doesn't meet their exacting standards. You pay $20 on top of the regular nightly rate, and full payment is required well in advance, but it's well worth it to know that you're getting a great B&B. They only represent accommodations with private baths, and all are nonsmoking. Some of their units are free-standing cottages that resemble vacation homes more than B&Bs; they even represent a few really nice condos.

- ✔ **Bed & Breakfast Hawaii** (☎ **800-733-1632** or 808-822-7771; www.bandb-hawaii.com) can also book you into a range of vacation homes and B&Bs throughout the islands, with prices starting at $75 a night.

✔ You won't get the same personal service from the Web, but you can find lots of useful resources there. The **Hawaii Directory of Bed-and-Breakfasts, Country Inns, and Small Hotels** (www.virtualcities.com/ons/hi/hionsdex.htm) offers direct Web links to B&Bs and vacation rentals throughout the state. **InnSite** (www.innsite.com) features B&B listings in all 50 U.S. states, including Hawaii, and around the globe. Find an inn on the island of your choice, see pictures of the rooms, and check prices and availability; text is only included if the proprietor submitted it. (It's free to get an inn listed.) The descriptions are written by the innkeepers, and many listings link to the inn's own Web sites. What's more, you may be able to score an additional discount by booking your reservation through InnSite. Another site that's well worth surfing for Hawaii B&Bs is **BedandBreakfast.com** (www.bedandbreakfast.com).

Making yourself at home in a vacation rental

"Vacation rental" usually means that you have a full cottage or house all to yourself. You may never even see an owner, agent, or manager after you pick up the keys. This option is great for families or people who like their space — but if you prefer a full-service experience, it may not be for you.

The rental may be a studio cottage in a residential neighborhood, a condo, or a huge beachfront multibedroom house — or anything in between. Because vacation rentals are often privately owned homes, they usually have some sort of kitchen facilities, laundry facilities, at least one TV, and at least one phone (ask when booking). Like condos, they usually come outfitted with the basics, such as sheets and towels.

Vacation rentals vary greatly in price depending on their size, location, and amenities. They tend to be much better values than similarly priced resort or hotel accommodations, especially if you're trying to accommodate a group or you plan a long stay (a week or more). Just make sure that you get a 24-hour contact person for those times when the toilet won't flush or you can't figure out how to turn on the air-conditioning.

Both **Hawaii's Best Bed & Breakfasts** and the **Hawaii Directory of Bed-and-Breakfasts, Country Inns, and Small Hotels** are useful sites for statewide vacation rentals. A statewide source that's also worth checking out is **Hawaii Beachfront Vacation Homes** (☎ 808-247-3637; www.hibeach.com).

Contact **Hawaii Condo Exchange** (☎ 800-442-0404 or 323-436-0300; www.hawaiicondoexchange.com), a Southern California–based agency that acts as a consolidator for condo properties throughout the islands. They'll work to match you up with the place that's right for you and try to get you a good deal.

If you'd like a rental house that's slightly off the beaten path — either in Upcountry Maui or in one of the charming communities along the road to Hana — contact **Ohana Maui Vacations** (☎ **808-283-9875;** www.ohana maui.com). While many of Ohana Maui's cottages and rental homes are affordably priced, the agency also represents a number of high-priced executive homes suitable for family reunions, wedding parties, or once-in-a-lifetime vacation splurges. Another option for upcountry rentals is **Hookipa Haven** (☎ **800-398-6284;** www.hookipa.com), which also offers West Maui beach houses for lease.

See **A Maui Vacation Rental Directory** (www.amauivacationrental. com) if you'd like a one-stop-shopping list of vacation rentals available direct from their owners. **Vacation Rentals by Owner** (www.vrbo.com) offers a similar service.

Most companies that offer all-inclusive travel packages to the islands can book you into any number of island condos, as can your travel agent.

Tracking Down the Best Room at the Best Rate

Investing a little time and effort in your hotel search can save you a bundle, so don't neglect to read the following sections for some useful advice.

Finding the best rate

The **rack rate** is the maximum rate a hotel charges for a room. It's the rate you get if you walk in off the street and ask for a room for the night. You sometimes see these rates printed on the fire/emergency exit diagrams posted on the back of your door.

Hotels are happy to charge you the rack rate, but you can almost always do better. Perhaps the best way to avoid paying the rack rate is surprisingly simple: Just ask for a cheaper or discounted rate. You may be pleasantly surprised. Great bargains can be unearthed if you politely ask the hotel's reservations agent to help you find a better rate. But you have to take the initiative and ask, because many hotels bank on the fact that they can get you to accept the first rate you're quoted. You should also chat with the reservations agent about which rooms are the best and which units match your needs. You never know what kind of insider advice or upgrade can be won by just asking a question and turning on the charm.

In all but the smallest accommodations, the rate you pay for a room depends on many factors — chief among them being how you make your reservation. A travel agent may be able to negotiate a better price with certain hotels than you can get by yourself. (That's because the hotel often gives the agent a discount in exchange for steering his or her business toward that hotel.)

Reserving a room through the hotel's toll-free number may also result in a lower rate than calling the hotel directly. On the other hand, the central reservations number may not know about discount rates at specific locations. For example, local franchises may offer a special group rate for a wedding or family reunion, but they may neglect to tell the central booking line. Your best bet is to call both the local number and the toll-free number and see which one gives you a better deal.

Room rates (even rack rates) change with the season, as occupancy rates rise and fall. But even within a given season, room prices are subject to change without notice, so the rates quoted in this book may be different from the actual rate you receive when you make your reservation.

Don't automatically shy away if a hotel's rack rates seem out of your range at first glance. A hotel's official "published" (full-price, or rack) rates usually represent the upper end of what they charge when they're full to capacity, but most hotels routinely offer better prices. And special deals abound in Hawaii, so in each hotel listing throughout this book, I note what kind of bargains you can typically snag.

The best way to get a great deal on a hotel room is to book it as part of an all-inclusive travel package that includes airfare, hotel, and car, and sometimes other extras, in one low price; for details on how to find the best package deals, see Chapter 5.

There's a big list of money-saving strategies in Chapter 4. But here are a few reminders:

- ✔ **Rates are generally lowest in spring and fall.** During peak season — basically winter and summer, and especially around Christmas — demand is high, and you're not going to have much luck fishing for a bargain rate. But in spring and fall, hotels aren't usually full. Not only will you find great deals, but if business is really slow, they'll be willing to negotiate; you might land a room upgrade by playing Let's Make a Deal.

- ✔ **Start by investigating the hotel's own special deals.** Maui's hotels regularly offer a dizzying array of special offers. You might get a free rental car, champagne and in-room breakfast for honeymooners, free dinners, discounted tee times or spa treatments, a room upgrade, an extra night thrown in for free (sometimes the fifth, sometimes the seventh), or some other freebie. Check out the Web site first, but even if you don't find anything on the Internet, ask about any specials when you call.

- ✔ **Membership in AAA, AARP, or frequent-flier programs often qualifies you for discounted rates.** Be sure to mention membership in these organizations and in any corporate rewards programs you can think of — or your Uncle Joe's Elks lodge in which you're an honorary inductee, for that matter — when you call to book. Even Costco membership has been known to pay off. You never know when an affiliation may be worth a few dollars off your room rate.

✔ **Ask innkeepers for a break.** Bed-and-breakfasts are generally nonnegotiable on price. Sometimes, however, you can negotiate a discount for longer stays, such as a week or more. You may also be able to score a price break if you're visiting off-season. And some do offer AAA and senior discounts. It never hurts to ask.

✔ **Look for price breaks and value-added extras when booking condos.** Condo complexes often feature discounts on multinight stays, and many throw in a free rental car to sweeten the deal. Some condo properties have units handled by multiple management companies; if that's the case, price through both companies and see where you get the better deal. You may also want to check with **Hawaii Condo Exchange** (☎ **800-442-0404** or 323-436-0300; www.hawaiicondoexchange.com), which acts as a consolidator for condo properties throughout the islands.

Surfing the Web for hotel deals

Shopping online for hotels is generally done one of two ways: by booking through the hotel's own Web site or through an independent booking agency (or a fare-service agency like Priceline). Internet hotel agencies have multiplied in mind-boggling numbers in the last few years, competing for the business of millions of consumers surfing for accommodations around the world.

The most high-profile of the online agencies is **Expedia,** which offers a long list of special deals and "virtual tours" or photos of available rooms so that you can see what you're paying for (a feature that helps counter the claims that the best rooms are often held back from bargain booking Web sites). **Travelocity** posts unvarnished customer reviews and ranks its properties according to the AAA rating system. Also reliable are **Hotels.com** (a subsidiary of Expedia), **Orbitz.com,** and **Quikbook.com.** Keep in mind that hotels at the top of a site's listing may be there for no other reason than that they paid money to get the placement. All these sites except Quikbook offer pay-one-price travel package services as well.

Always price compare the rate you get through an online travel agency against the hotel's own Web site. These days, virtually every major hotel chain offers price parity with the online distributors through its own Web sites. Often, you'll save a few bucks through the hotel's own site and/or end up with a better room for the same money because the hotel doesn't have to pay high distribution fees (usually a whopping 25 percent of the rate you pay) if you book direct. If you do book through a third-party online agency, don't be surprised if you end up next to the ice machine or with a view of the parking lot. Hotels generally give their best rooms to guests that generate the most revenue for them. This practice shouldn't prevent you from using online agencies; it simply means that, unless you're saving money by booking through a third-party agency, you're likely to be better off booking your room direct with the hotel (or its parent hotel chain).

You might also want to check out **TripAdvisor.com** when you're considering a hotel. TripAdvisor isn't a booking site, per se (although it does offer links to sites that allow you to make bookings), but it does offer untainted, straight-from-the-customer's-keyboard reviews of hotels. Now, I don't recommend putting too much stock in a single review — most people have unrealistic expectations, or just plain-old, bad-luck experiences, now and again — but trends in positive or negative experiences can become apparent.

An excellent free program, **TravelAxe** (www.travelaxe.net), can help you search multiple hotel sites at once, even ones you may never have heard of — and conveniently lists the total price of the room, including the taxes and service charges.

Another booking site, **Travelweb** (www.travelweb), is partly owned by the hotels it represents (including the Hilton, Hyatt, and Starwood chains) and is therefore plugged directly into the hotels' reservations systems — unlike independent online agencies, which have to fax or e-mail reservation requests to the hotel, a good portion of which get misplaced in the shuffle (and more than once, travelers have arrived at the hotel, only to be told that they have no reservation). To be fair, many of the major sites are undergoing improvements in service and ease of use, and Expedia will soon be able to plug directly into the reservations systems of many hotel chains — none of which can be bad news for consumers. In the meantime, it's a good idea to **get a confirmation number** and **make a printout** of any online booking transaction.

In the opaque Web site category, **Priceline** and **Hotwire** (another Expedia subsidiary) are even better for hotels than for airfares; with both, you're allowed to pick the neighborhood and quality level of your hotel before offering up your money. Priceline is much better at getting five-star lodging for three-star prices than at finding anything at the bottom of the scale. On the downside, many hotels stick Priceline guests in their least desirable rooms. Be sure to go to the **BiddingforTravel** Web site (www.biddingfortravel.com) before bidding on a hotel room on Priceline; it features a fairly up-to-date list of hotels that Priceline uses in major cities. For both Priceline and Hotwire, you pay up front, and the fee is nonrefundable. Both sites now offer pay-one-price packaging services, too. *Note:* Some hotels do not provide loyalty program credits or points or other frequent-stay amenities when you book a room through opaque online services.

Reserving the best room

After you make your reservation, asking one or two more pointed questions can go a long way toward making sure that you get the best room in the house. Most Hawaii hoteliers are very friendly and willing to take the time with you, so don't be shy — try to find out which units are the

nicest. If the reservations agent doesn't have any specific recommendations, try asking for a corner room. In some (but not all) cases, they may
be larger and quieter, with more windows and light than standard
rooms, and they don't always cost more.

Also ask whether the hotel is renovating; if it is, request a room away from
the renovation work. Inquire, too, about traffic and the location of the
restaurants, bars, and discos in the hotel — all sources of annoying noise.

And if you aren't happy with your room when you arrive, talk to the
front desk firmly but *nicely*. (Don't get emotional — your mom's old
saying about attracting more flies with honey than with vinegar really
was good advice.) If another room is available, the front desk should be
happy to accommodate you, within reason.

Choosing a room with a view

If you want to see the ocean from your room or condo, expect to pay for
the privilege. Oceanview rooms usually cost substantially more than non-
or partial-view rooms, to the tune of $100, $200, or even $250 higher per
night than the rate for a similar room without the view.

Deciding whether to pay for a view isn't a clear-cut issue. In fact, what
constitutes "oceanview" is far from an agreed-upon industry standard.
Witness these variations on the theme:

- ✔ **Oceanfront rooms:** Only hotels or condo complexes that sit
  squarely on the beach can have oceanfront rooms or apartments.
  Positioned directly over the sand and a stone's throw from the
  waves, these units are the best in the house and usually the most
  expensive. You may still have to walk through the lobby to get to
  the water, but you have an unblocked view of the beach. Keep in
  mind, however, that you hear the waves only from lower-floor
  rooms; these rooms are often my favorites.

- ✔ **Oceanview rooms:** Watch out — some hotels and resorts don't dis-
  tinguish between oceanfront rooms and oceanview rooms, which
  also have a full view of the ocean. Oceanview rooms, however, don't
  have to be directly over the sand. They may sit farther back — or
  even across the street — from the beach, or they may look over the
  rooftops of other buildings. These units are still fabulous, and still
  expensive.

- ✔ **Partial oceanview rooms:** "Partial oceanview" is subject to a whole
  host of interpretations, depending on who's doing the offering. It can
  be almost as good as full oceanview, or it may mean that you see a
  razor-thin slice of blue between two high-rise mountains of concrete.
  Ask plenty of questions about any unit offered as "partial oceanview"
  and know exactly what you're paying for before you book.

✔ **Mountain or gardenview rooms:** Most nonoceanview rooms are called *mountainview,* meaning that they face the island's inland mountains, or *gardenview,* which means they face an inner courtyard or grounds. The view can be good or bad, depending on the location and the layout of the grounds; again, your best bet is to ask plenty of questions when you reserve. These rooms are usually the least expensive in a hotel or condo complex. They're not usually of poorer quality — they just don't have the million-dollar views that those guests on the other side of the building or grounds have (and are paying for!).

The big question, then, is, "Is it worth it to pay for an oceanview room?" Before my first visit to Maui, I was convinced that the answer was cut and dried: No way — too expensive. I'm not going to Maui to hang out in my room, so why should I pay through the nose for the privilege of seeing the water from it?

Then I stayed in an oceanfront room, and I was hooked. Letting the rhythmic sound of the waves and the caress of the ocean breeze lull you to sleep, and waking to gorgeous ocean views, are unforgettable experiences. You know you're in Maui — and that fabulous ocean is why you came all this way in the first place.

I highly recommend staying in an oceanfront (or oceanview) room if you can afford it. But don't blow your whole budget just to make it happen. First, choose the hotel or condo you want based on your needs. Make sure that the style of accommodation suits you, that the space sleeps your travel companions comfortably, and that the property features all the amenities and services you need to be happy. To me, these considerations are much more important than the view. After you choose your property, see whether you can afford to book oceanfront, especially if the hotel or packager is offering you a nice deal on an upgrade. If you can, great! But if staying in an oceanfront room means you have to skip activities or skimp on meals, then go with a cheaper room with a lesser view. Having an oceanview room isn't worth compromising the rest of your trip.

Chapter 7

Catering to Special Travel Needs or Interests

*T*ravelers don't come in a standard package, of course — they come in all ages, sizes, and configurations. You may want to know: How welcoming will Maui be to . . . (pick one or more) a) my kids? b) my senior status? c) my disability? d) my same-sex partner? If so, you've landed in the right chapter. I give you all the details of traveling under any and all of these circumstances.

Plus, if you're looking to plan a dreamy tropical wedding, I tell you the ins and outs of tying the knot on the romantic island of Maui.

Traveling with the Brood: Advice for Families

If you have enough trouble getting your kids out of the house in the morning, dragging them thousands of miles away may seem like an insurmountable challenge. But family travel can be immensely rewarding, giving you new ways of seeing the world through smaller pairs of eyes.

Maui is the perfect *ohana* (family) vacation destination. You and the *keiki* (kids) will love the beaches and the wealth of kid-friendly activities. Lots of families flock to the islands every summer, as well as at holiday time and during the spring break season.

Most hotels and condo complexes, from luxury to budget, welcome the entire family. Virtually all the larger hotels and resorts have great supervised programs for kids 12 and under — which means that you, Mom and

Dad, can have plenty of relaxation time to yourselves, as well as playtime with the kids. Most hotels can also refer you to reliable baby sitters if you want a night on the town sans youngsters.

By Hawaii state law, hotels can accept only children between the ages of 5 and 12 into their supervised activity programs.

Condos are particularly suitable for families who want lots of living space in which to spread out. Parents also appreciate having a kitchen where they can prepare meals for fussy young eaters — and save significantly on dining costs. One drawback of condo complexes is that they typically don't have the extensive facilities (like kids' activities programs) you'd get in big resorts.

If you don't want to cart your own kid stuff across the ocean, **Baby's Away** (www.babysaway.com) rents car seats, cribs, strollers (including jogging strollers), highchairs, playpens, room monitors, and even toys. It serves Maui (☎ **800-942-9030** or 808-875-9030), plus Honolulu (☎ **800-496-6386** or 808-222-6041) and the Big Island (☎ **800-996-9030** or 808-987-9236). Give Baby's Away a call, and it delivers whatever you need to wherever you're staying and picks it up when you're done. I suggest arranging your rentals before you leave home to ensure availability. Unfortunately, there are no locations on Kauai.

You can find good family-oriented vacation advice on the Internet from sites like the **Family Travel Forum** (www.familytravelforum.com), a comprehensive site that offers customized trip planning; **Family Travel Network** (www.familytravelnetwork.com), an award-winning site that offers travel features, deals, and tips; **Traveling Internationally with Your Kids** (www.travelwithyourkids.com), a comprehensive site that offers customized trip planning; and **Family Travel Files** (www.thefamily travelfiles.com), which offers an online magazine and a directory of off-the-beaten-path tours and tour operators for families. **BabyCenter** (www.babycenter.com/travel) has terrific recommendations for planning baby's first trip, and even on traveling while pregnant.

Here are a few tips for family travel planning:

- ✔ **Don't try to do too much.** I can't stress this point too strongly. You'll all consider it the trip from you-know-where if you spend too much time in the car or on interisland flights.

- ✔ **Take it slow at the start.** Give the entire family time to adjust to a new time zone, unfamiliar surroundings, and just being on the road. The best way to do so is to budget a few days in your initial destination without strict itineraries or lots of moving around.

- ✔ **Look for the Kid Friendly icon as you flip through this book.** I use it to highlight hotels, restaurants, and attractions that are particularly welcoming to families traveling with kids. Zeroing in on these listings can help you plan your trip more efficiently.

✔ **Book some private time for Mom and Dad.** Most, if not all, hotels are prepared to hook you up with a reliable baby sitter who can entertain your kids while you enjoy a romantic dinner for two or another adults-only activity. To avoid disappointment, ask about baby-sitting when you reserve. Local visitor centers can also usually recommend licensed and bonded baby-sitting services in their areas; see the Quick Concierge for contact info.

Making Age Work for You: Tips for Seniors

One of the many benefits of getting older is that travel often costs less. Although all the major U.S. airlines except America West have cancelled their senior discount and coupon book programs, many hotels and package-tour operators still offer discounts for seniors. Discounts for seniors are also available at almost all of Hawaii's major attractions, and occasionally at restaurants and luaus. So when you're making reservations or buying tickets, it's always worthwhile to ask about senior discounts. Keep in mind, though, that the minimum age requirement can vary between 50 and 65. (It's usually between ages 55 and 65.) Always carry an ID card with you, especially if you've kept your youthful glow.

The statewide **Outrigger** (☎ **800-OUTRIGGER** or 800-688-7444; www.outrigger.com) and **Ohana** (☎ **800-462-6262;** www.ohanahotels.com) hotel chains offer all travelers over age 50 substantial discounts as well as seriously discounted rental cars through **Dollar Rent a Car** (☎ **800-800-3665;** www.dollar.com).

Members of **AARP** (formerly known as the American Association of Retired Persons), 601 E St. NW, Washington, DC 20049 (☎ **888-687-2277** or 202-434-2277; www.aarp.org), get discounts on hotels, airfares, and car rentals. AARP offers members a wide range of benefits, including *AARP: The Magazine* and a monthly newsletter. Anyone over 50 can join.

YMT Vacations (☎ **800-922-9000;** www.ymtvacations.com) and **White Star Tours** (☎ **800-437-2323** or 610-775-5000; www.whitestartours.com) are just two of the hundreds of travel agencies that specialize in vacations for seniors, including trips to Hawaii. But beware: Many of these outfits are of the tour-bus variety, with free trips thrown in for those who organize groups of 20 or more. If you're the independent type, a regular travel agent may be better for you.

Elderhostel (☎ **877-426-8056** or 978-323-4141; www.elderhostel.org), a nonprofit group that offers travel and study programs around the world, offers excellent low-cost trips to Hawaii for travelers ages 55 and older (plus a spouse or companion of any age). Trips usually include moderately priced accommodations and meals in one low-cost package.

Seniors 62 or older who want to visit Hawaii's national parks — including Haleakala National Park on Maui — can save sightseeing dollars by picking up a **Golden Age Passport** from any national park, recreation area, or monument. This lifetime pass has a one-time fee of $10 and provides free admission to all the parks in the National Parks system, plus 50 percent savings on camping and recreation fees. You can get one at any park entrance as long as you have a proof-of-age ID on hand.

Recommended publications offering travel resources and discounts for seniors include the quarterly magazine *Travel 50 & Beyond* (www.travel50andbeyond.com); *Travel Unlimited: Uncommon Adventures for the Mature Traveler* (Avalon); *101 Tips for Mature Travelers,* available from Grand Circle Travel (☎ **800-221-2610** or 617-350-7500; www.gct.com); *The 50+ Traveler's Guidebook* (St. Martin's Press); and *Unbelievably Good Deals and Great Adventures That You Absolutely Can't Get Unless You're Over 50* (McGraw-Hill), by Joann Rattner Heilman.

Accessing Hawaii: Advice for Travelers with Disabilities

A disability shouldn't stop anyone from traveling. The Americans with Disabilities Act requires that all public buildings be wheelchair accessible and have accessible restrooms. Hawaii is very friendly to disabled travelers. Most hotels throughout the islands are on the newer side and boast wheelchair ramps, extra-wide doorways and halls, and dedicated disabled-accessible rooms with extra-large bathrooms, low-set fixtures, and/or fire-alarm systems adapted for deaf travelers.

Your best bet is to contact the local visitors bureaus. They can provide you with all the specifics on accessibility in the community; see the Quick Concierge at the back of this book for contact info.

The following are excellent resources for information on accessible travel:

✔ An excellent resource for trip-planning assistance is **Access Aloha Travel** (☎ **800-480-1143** or 808-545-1143; www.accessalohatravel.com). This Hawaii-based travel agency has been planning accessible trips for disabled travelers for decades — and it donates half its profits to the disabled community.

✔ Both **Moss Rehab ResourceNet** (☎ **215-456-9900**; www.mossresourcenet.org) and **Access-Able Travel Source** (☎ **303-232-2979**; www.access-able.com) are comprehensive resources for disabled travelers. Both sites feature links to travel agents who specialize in planning accessible trips to Hawaii. Access-Able's user-friendly site also features relay and voice numbers for hotels, airlines, and car-rental companies, plus links to accessible accommodations, attractions, transportation, tours, and local medical resources and equipment repairers throughout Hawaii, making these sites an invaluable resource. **SeniorCitizens.com** also operates a page (www.seniorcitizens.com/accessible/travel.shtml) dedicated to accessible travel, with links to tour organizations that can meet assistive technology needs.

✔ You can join the **Society for the Advancement of Travelers with Handicaps (SATH; ☎ 212-447-7284;** www.sath.org) for $45 a year ($30 for seniors and students), to gain access to its vast network of travel connections. The organization provides information sheets on destinations and referrals to tour operators that specialize in accessible travel. Its quarterly magazine, *Open World*, is full of good information and resources.

✔ The **Hawaii Services on Deafness (☎ 808-946-7300** voice and TTY; www.hsod.org) can provide aid and advice to hearing-impaired travelers, including sign-language interpreters in emergency situations.

✔ Vision-impaired travelers who use a Seeing Eye dog can usually bypass Hawaii's animal quarantine rules (which were dramatically loosened in 2004). You can arrange for your guide or service dog to be inspected in the terminal at Honolulu International Airport (saving the owners a trip to the Airport Animal Quarantine Holding Facility) if you notify **Animal Quarantine (☎ 808-483-7151**) at least seven days in advance. Call or visit www.hawaiiag.org/hdoa for specifics on rules and fees. Contact the **American Foundation for the Blind (☎ 800-232-5463;** www.afb.org) for further travel information.

I highly recommend procuring a copy of the *Aloha Guide to Accessibility.* You can order a copy by phone from the **Disability and Communication Access Board (☎ 808-586-2121** or 808-984-8219) or the **Hawaii Center for Independent Living (☎ 808-522-5400**).

Before you book any hotel room, always ask lots of questions based on your needs. After you arrive, call restaurants, attractions, and theaters to make sure that they're fully accessible.

Consider the following sources for getting around, either on your own or with assistance:

✔ **Avis Rent a Car** has an "Avis Access" program that offers such services as a dedicated 24-hour toll-free number (☎ 888-879-4273; www.avis.com) for customers with special travel needs; special car features such as swivel seats, spinner knobs, and hand controls; and accessible bus service. Many of the big car-rental companies — including Avis, **Hertz (☎ 800-654-3131;** www.hertz.com), and **National (☎ 800-227-7368;** www.nationalcar.com) — rent hand-controlled cars for disabled drivers at Hawaii's major airports. At least 48 to 72 hours advance notice is a must, but do yourself a favor and book further in advance to guarantee availability.

> ✔ **Handicabs of the Pacific** (☎ 808-524-3866) offers taxi services and tours for wheelchair-bound travelers around Honolulu and the rest of Oahu. Its air-conditioned vehicles are specially equipped with ramps and wheelchair lockdowns.
>
> ✔ **Accessible Vans of Hawaii** (☎ 800-303-3750 or 808-871-7785; www.accessiblevanshawaii.com) has wheelchair-accessible vans for rent on Oahu, Maui, Kauai, and in Kona on the Big Island. Its staff can also help arrange accessible accommodations and recommend accessible activities, sightseeing, restaurants, medical equipment rentals, and personal care attendants at no additional charge to you.

Following the Rainbow: Resources for Gay and Lesbian Travelers

Hawaii is extremely popular with same-sex couples due to its long-standing reputation for welcoming all groups.

If you want help planning your trip, **IGLTA,** the **International Gay & Lesbian Travel Association** (☎ 800-448-8550 or 954-776-2626; www.iglta.org), is your best source. IGLTA can link you up with the appropriate gay-friendly service organization or tour specialist; the organization also offers quarterly newsletters and a membership directory that's updated quarterly. Members are kept informed of gay and gay-friendly hoteliers, tour operators, and airline and cruise-line representatives. The IGLTA site links you to other useful Web sites that can help you plan your Hawaii vacation.

If you want assistance in planning a gay-friendly Maui holiday, **Pacific Ocean Holidays** (☎ 800-735-6600 or 808-923-2400; www.gayhawaii.com) is your best resource. The staff can help you arrange a good-value trip that features either gay-friendly hotels serving the general public or those that serve a predominately gay clientele (your choice); you can even book your entire vacation online. Even if you don't want help planning your trip, the Web site is an invaluable resource. Its online island-by-island guide is a terrific community resource directory and guide to gay-owned and gay-friendly businesses throughout Hawaii.

Rainbow Handbook Hawaii, by Big Island resident Matthew Link, is an excellent source for gay and lesbian travelers. To order a copy, call ☎ 800-260-5528 or visit www.rainbowhandbook.com.

Out and About (www.outandabout.com) has been hailed for its "straight" reporting about gay travel. It offers a monthly newsletter packed with good information on the global gay and lesbian scene. Out and About's guidebooks are available at most major bookstores, but the Web site alone is a first-rate resource.

The **Gay and Lesbian Community Center,** 2424 S. Beretania Ave., in Honolulu (☎ **808-951-7000**), offers referrals for nearly every kind of service that you might need. Another great helpline and referral resource for gay-friendly businesses is the Gay and Lesbian Education and Advocacy Foundation's **Gay Community Resource Directory,** which you can find online at www.hawaiigaymarriage.com.

1 Do! 1 Do! Planning a Hawaiian Wedding

No question about it: Maui is the perfect place to get married — which is why so many couples from around the country, and the world, tie the knot here every year. What better way to start your life together? And the members of your wedding party will most likely be delighted because you've given them the perfect excuse for their own island vacation.

For a rundown of the legalities, visit www.hawaii.gov/doh and click Vital Records, where you can find all the details, including a downloadable license form.

A marriage license costs $60 and is good for 30 days from the date of issue. Both parties must be at least 18 years of age (16- and 17-year-olds must have written consent of both parents, legal guardian, or family court) and can't be more closely related than first cousins. You need a photo ID, such as a driver's license; a birth certificate is only necessary if you're 18 or under. No blood tests, citizenship, or residency minimum is required.

Using a wedding planner or coordinator

Wedding planning is a thriving industry in Hawaii. Whether you've got your heart set on a huge formal affair at a luxury resort or an informal beachside ceremony, you won't have any trouble finding assistance.

Many wedding planners are also marriage license agents, which means they can take care of the legalities for you with only minimal effort on your part and then arrange everything else, too — from providing an officiant to ordering flowers. A wedding planner can cost from $500 and up, depending on how involved you want him or her to be and what kind of wedding you want.

Your best bet for finding a reputable wedding planner is to choose one endorsed by the **Hawaii Visitors and Convention Bureau,** whose Web site features a complete list of wedding planners to suit any budget; go to www.gohawaii.com and click Weddings & Honeymoons. You can also call the center for recommendations at ☎ **800-GO-HAWAII,** or — even better — contact the Maui center at ☎ **800-525-6284** or 808-244-3530 (www.visitmaui.com) for local recommendations.

In addition, virtually all the big resorts employ full-time wedding coordinators. Arranging your nuptials directly through a resort may be pricey, but it's a relatively worry-free option. The hotel coordinators are experts, they'll take all the pesky little details off your hands, and they'll usually offer the whole event to you as a pay-one-price wedding package, including accommodations. What's more, the hotels generally offer prime locations for both the ceremony and reception, whether it's for 2 or 200 guests.

Great choices include the Four Seasons Maui, the Grand Wailea, the Fairmont Kea Lani, and the Ritz-Carlton Kapalua (see Chapter 10).

Keep in mind that more affordable hotels and condos, even some B&Bs, can often recommend wedding coordinators that have a proven track record with them. The Kaanapali Beach Hotel, for example, makes a great affordable option (see Chapter 10). The setting is magical, the hotel works with a very reliable local planner, and the on-site food-and-beverage director can arrange a pleasing reception. Don't hesitate to contact any property that strikes your fancy; most have wedding experience or can offer recommendations.

Do-it-yourself planning

After you get to Hawaii, you and your intended must go together to the marriage license agent to get the license (bring cash). You can either go to the nearest Department of Health office (see www.hawaii.gov/doh/about/dho-info.html for locations), or the **Honolulu Marriage License Office,** State Department of Health Building, 1250 Punchbowl St., Honolulu, HI 96813 (☎ **808-586-4545** or 808-586-4544), can direct you to a marriage license agent (basically, a local official who helps you wrap up the legalities) closest to where you'll be staying in the islands.

Local marriage license agents that the office can refer you to are usually friendly, helpful people who can steer you to someone who's licensed by the state of Hawaii to perform the ceremony, whether you're looking for an officiant of a certain denomination or a plain ol' justice of the peace. These marriage performers are great sources of information; they usually know picturesque places to have the ceremony for free or at a nominal fee.

Note that some marriage license agents are state employees, and, under law, they cannot recommend anyone with a religious affiliation; they can give you phone numbers only for local judges to perform the ceremony. Ask first what their limitations are if it matters to you. If you're interested in arranging a church ceremony, inquire with the visitor center to locate an appropriate venue.

You can have a ceremony at any state or county beach or park for free, but keep in mind that you'll be sharing the site with the general public.

For a genuine Hawaiian experience, get married at **Keawali Congregational Church** (☎ **808-879-5557**), a vintage 1831 oceanfront coral-block church in picturesque Makena. The gorgeous grounds — with palm trees and exotic tropical flowers — make a perfect backdrop for your wedding photo.

Another great site is **D.T. Fleming Beach Park,** just north of Kapalua in West Maui. This crescent-shaped beach is generally empty on weekdays, so you can enjoy a quiet wedding on the beautiful beach as sailboats skim along offshore.

Chapter 8

Taking Care of the Remaining Details

- -

In This Chapter

▶ Mastering the ins and outs of renting a car
▶ Buying travel insurance
▶ Staying safe and healthy when you travel
▶ Staying connected while you're on the road
▶ Dealing with airline security
▶ Making reservations before you leave home
▶ Packing what you really need

- -

*T*his chapter helps you shore up the final details — from renting a car to packing the appropriate gear.

Renting a Car

Maui has so many fabulous things to see and do that it would be a real shame for you to miss out. The more you want to see, however, the more you'll be moving around. In order to maximize your time, you need to rent a car.

The following companies rent cars on all the major Hawaiian Islands:

✔ **Alamo:** ☎ **800-GO-ALAMO** (800-462-5266); www.alamo.com

✔ **Avis:** ☎ **800-230-4898;** www.avis.com

✔ **Budget:** ☎ **800-527-0700;** www.budget.com

✔ **Dollar:** ☎ **800-800-4000;** www.dollar.com

✔ **Enterprise:** ☎ **800-325-8007;** www.enterprise.com

✔ **Hertz:** ☎ **800-654-3131;** www.hertz.com

✔ **National:** ☎ **800-CAR-RENT** (800-227-7368); www.nationalcar.com

✔ **Thrifty:** ☎ **800-THRIFTY** (800-847-4389); www.thrifty.com

Be sure to book your rental cars well ahead. Rental cars are almost always at a premium on Kauai, Molokai, and Lanai and may be sold out on all the islands on holiday weekends.

For tips on renting hand-controlled cars or vans equipped with wheelchair lifts, see Chapter 7.

Getting the best deal

Rental cars are quite affordable in Hawaii, although they do vary from island to island and from season to season. Of course, I can't guarantee what you'll pay when you book, but you can often get a compact car for between $160 and $250 a week. If you want a family-size car — or a convertible — expect to pay anywhere from $225 to $400 a week, which is still reasonable.

 Car-rental rates vary even more than airline fares. The price depends on the size of the car, the length of time you keep it, where and when you pick it up and drop it off, where you take it, and a host of other factors. Asking a few key questions may save you hundreds of dollars.

- ✔ **Book your rental car at weekly rates when possible.** Weekly rentals will almost always save you money. Several major rental firms — most notably Hertz and Avis — offer multi-island contracts. For example, if you plan to visit both Oahu and Maui, you can pick up a car in Oahu, keep it for four days, return it, fly to Maui, and then pick up another car for your three days there, all under the same contract. You end up paying for one week at the weekly rate rather than four times the daily rate on Oahu and three times the daily rate on Maui — and that's always much cheaper. Ask when you book.

- ✔ **Mention membership in AAA, AARP, and frequent-flier programs when booking.** These memberships may qualify you for discounts ranging from 5 to 30 percent.

- ✔ **Ask the reservations agency that books your hotel or your interisland air travel if it books rental cars.** Many hotels, condo rental agents, and even B&B owners can book rental cars at seriously discounted rates; ditto for the interisland air carriers, Hawaiian and Aloha (see the beginning of this chapter). Often, you can save as much as 30 percent off the standard rate. And many Maui hotels and condos offer excellent-value room-and-car packages that make your rental essentially free!

- ✔ **Shop online.** As with other aspects of planning your trip, using the Internet can make comparison shopping for a car rental much easier. You can check rates at most of the major agencies' Web sites. Plus, all the major travel sites — **Travelocity** (www.travelocity.com), **Expedia** (www.expedia.com), **Orbitz** (www.orbitz.com), and **Smarter Living** (www.smarterliving.com), for example — have search engines that can dig up discounted car-rental rates. Just enter the car size you want, the pickup and return dates, and location, and the server returns a price. You can even make the reservation through any of these sites.

✔ **If you see an advertised special, ask for that specific rate when booking.** The car-rental company may not offer this information voluntarily. Be sure to remind them; otherwise, you may be charged the standard (higher) rate.

✔ **Consider booking your car as part of a complete travel package.** Package deals not only save you dollars on airfare and accommodations but also on your rental cars, too. This one-stop shopping can help streamline the trip-planning process. For more on package deals, see Chapter 5.

✔ **Don't forget to ask about frequent-flier mileage.** Most car rentals are worth at least 500 miles on your frequent-flier account. Be sure to find out which airlines the rental-car company is affiliated with so that you can earn mileage. Bring your card with you and make sure that your account is credited at pick-up time.

✔ **Join the rental company's preferred customer program.** Most companies offer such promotions (for example, National's Emerald Club). You may be able to snag a bargain rate or have a better shot at an upgrade if you're a member. Some companies make the process of picking up your car more hassle-free for members, too. And membership can work just like the airlines' frequent-flier plans: Renting from the same company several times can land you a free day or other perks.

✔ **Make sure that you're getting free unlimited mileage.** Thankfully, most of the major car-rental companies rent on an unlimited-miles basis, but you should confirm this policy when you book. Even on an island, the miles you drive can really add up.

✔ **Find out whether age is an issue.** Many car-rental companies add on a fee for drivers under 25, while some don't rent to them at all.

In addition to the standard rental prices, other optional charges apply to most car rentals (and some not-so-optional charges, such as taxes). The *Collision Damage Waiver* (CDW), which requires you to pay for damage to the car in a collision, is automatically covered by many credit-card companies. Check with your credit-card company before you leave home so that you can avoid paying this hefty fee (as much as $20 a day). But in any event, make sure that you're covered. (See "Following the rules of the road," later in this chapter; Hawaii is a no-fault state, which has important insurance implications.)

The car-rental companies also offer additional *liability insurance* (if you harm others in an accident), *personal accident insurance* (if you harm yourself or your passengers), and *personal effects insurance* (if your luggage is stolen from your car). Your insurance policy on your car at home probably covers most of these unlikely occurrences. However, if your own insurance doesn't cover you for rentals or if you don't have auto insurance, definitely consider the additional coverage. (Ask your car-rental agent for more information.) Unless you're toting around the Hope diamond — and you don't want to leave that in your car trunk anyway — you can probably skip the personal effects insurance, but driving around without liability coverage is never a good idea. Note that credit cards don't cover you for liability, even if they cover you for collision.

Some companies also offer *refueling packages,* in which you pay for your initial full tank of gas up front and can return the car with an empty gas tank. The prices can be competitive with local gas prices, but you don't get credit for any gas remaining in the tank. If you reject this option, you pay only for the gas you use, but you have to return the car with a full tank or face charges of $4 to $5 a gallon for any shortfall. If you usually run late and a fueling stop may make you miss your plane, you're a per-fect candidate for the fuel-purchase option, but for most people, it's not much of a hardship to top off your tank on the way to the airport.

Hawaii how-to: Renting convertibles

Renting a convertible is a lot like booking an oceanview room. It's a great idea if you can afford it, but not worth it if it's going to put a strain on your budget. The cost of going topless can be double or more what you'd pay for a regular car. Expect to pay between $50 and $80 a day for a convert-ible, compared with $30 or $40 a day for a better-equipped midsize car (with such extras as power windows and power locks that don't usually come with convertibles).

If you really want to rent a convertible for your island driving but you're worried about cost, consider the following:

- ✔ **Rent a convertible for just part of your trip.** If you're going to be visiting two or three islands, book a convertible on just one of them. And Maui is the place to do it — cruising the road to Hana with the top down really is the ultimate Hawaii vacation dream.

- ✔ **Ask about upgrades when you pick up your rental car.** This question may prove especially beneficial if you're visiting in the off-season. Sometimes, if a rental-car branch has a few idle convert-ibles sitting around, it'll offer you an on-the-spot upgrade for just $10 or $15 more a day. If you negotiated a decent compact or midsize rate when you booked, the total should come out to substantially less than the convertible rate offered over the phone.

Following the rules of the road

Know these driving rules and common practices before you get behind the wheel on Maui:

- ✔ **Hawaii is a no-fault insurance state.** If you drive without collision-damage insurance, you're required to pay for all damages before you leave the state, regardless of who is at fault. Your personal auto

policy may provide rental-car coverage; read your policy or check
with your insurer before you leave home, and be sure to bring your
insurance ID card if you decline the rental-car company's optional
insurance. Some credit-card companies also provide collision
damage insurance; check with yours.

✔ **Seatbelts are mandatory for everyone in the car, all the time.**
The law is strictly enforced, so be sure to buckle up. All children
under four years of age must be strapped into car seats.

✔ **You can turn right on red unless a posted sign specifies otherwise.** Make sure that you make a full stop first — no rolling.

✔ **Pedestrians always have the right of way.** This is true even if
they're not on a crosswalk.

✔ **Use your horn judiciously.** Honking your horn to express your
anger at another driver is considered the height of rudeness in
Hawaii. Don't do it. Horns are used to greet friends in Hawaii.

Do *not* use your rental car as a safe in which to store valuables. Don't
leave anything that you don't want to lose in the car or trunk, not even
for a short time. Be especially careful when you park at beaches, where
thieves know that you're going to leave your car for a while (and you're
likely to leave goodies in the glove compartment).

Maui is very easy to negotiate, and all the rental-car companies hand out
very good map booklets on each island. If all you have is what National
or Hertz gives you, you'll do just fine.

Playing It Safe with Travel and Medical Insurance

Three kinds of travel insurance are available: trip-cancellation insurance,
medical insurance, and lost-luggage insurance. The cost of travel insurance varies widely, depending on the cost and length of your trip, your
age and health, and the type of trip you're taking, but expect to pay
between 5 and 8 percent of the cost of the vacation itself. Here is my
advice on all three:

✔ **Trip-cancellation insurance** may make sense if you're paying for
your vacation up front, say, by purchasing a cruise, package deal,
or escorted tour. Coverage will help you get your money back if you
have to back out of a trip, if you have to go home early, or if your
travel supplier goes bankrupt. Allowed reasons for cancellation can
range from sickness to natural disasters to the State Department
declaring your destination unsafe for travel. (Insurers usually don't
cover vague fears, though, as many travelers discovered who tried to
cancel their trips in October 2001 because they were wary of flying.)

A good resource is **"Travel Guard Alerts,"** a list of companies considered high-risk by Travel Guard International (www.travel insured.com). Protect yourself further by paying for the insurance with a credit card — by law, consumers can get their money back on goods and services not received if they report the loss within 60 days after the charge is listed on their credit-card statement.

Note: Many tour operators include insurance in the cost of the trip or can arrange insurance policies through a partnering provider, a convenient and often cost-effective way for travelers to obtain insurance. Make sure that the tour company is a reputable one; however, some experts suggest you avoid buying insurance from the tour or cruise company you're traveling with, saying it's safer to buy from a "third-party" insurer than to put all your money in one place.

✔ For domestic travel, buying **medical insurance** for your trip doesn't make sense for most travelers. Most existing health policies cover you if you get sick away from home — but check before you go, particularly if you're insured by an HMO.

✔ **Lost-luggage insurance** is also not necessary for most travelers. On domestic flights, checked baggage is covered up to $2,500 per ticketed passenger. On international flights (including U.S. portions of international trips), baggage coverage is limited to approximately $9.07 per pound, up to approximately $635 per checked bag. If you plan to check items more valuable than the standard liability, see whether your valuables are covered by your homeowner's policy, get baggage insurance as part of your comprehensive travel-insurance package, or buy Travel Guard's "BagTrak" product. Don't buy insurance at the airport, as it's usually overpriced.

The best advice is simple: Don't pack anything vital in your checked luggage. Be sure to take any expensive or irreplaceable items with you in your carry-on luggage, as many valuables (including books, money, and electronics) aren't covered by airline policies.

If your luggage is lost, immediately file a lost-luggage claim at the airport, detailing the contents. For most airlines, you must report delayed, damaged, or lost baggage within four hours of arrival. The airlines are required to deliver luggage, once found, directly to your house or destination free of charge.

For more information, contact one of the following recommended insurers: **Access America** (☎ 866-807-3982; www.accessamerica.com); **Travel Guard International** (☎ 800-826-4919; www.travelguard.com); **Travel Insured International** (☎ 800-243-3174; www.travelinsured.com); and **Travelex Insurance Services** (☎ 888-457-4602; www.travelex-insurance.com).

Staying Healthy When You Travel

Getting sick will ruin your vacation, so I *strongly* advise against it. (Of course, last time I checked, the bugs weren't listening to me any more than they probably listen to you.)

Talk to your doctor before leaving on a trip if you have a serious and/or chronic illness. For conditions such as epilepsy, diabetes, or heart problems, wear a **MedicAlert identification tag** (☎ **888-633-4298;** www.medicalert.org), which immediately alerts doctors to your condition and gives them access to your records through MedicAlert's 24-hour hotline.

Be sure to consult Chapter 12, which contains lots of important advice on ocean safety and avoiding sunburn.

In the unlikely event that you do get sick in Hawaii, keep the following in mind:

✔ By law, all employers in Hawaii must provide health insurance for their employees, and almost all islanders have insurance. As a result, some doctors simply won't see patients who aren't insured. If you don't have insurance (or you don't have insurance that travels with you) and you need to see a doctor while you're in Hawaii, be sure to inform him or her when you call to make an appointment. Check the "Quick Concierge" section at the back of this book to find a doctor or medical-care clinic that regularly caters to visitors.

✔ Long's Drugs, which has branches throughout the islands, accepts most national prescription cards, such as PCS — so if you have a card, bring it with you. If you get sick and need to fill a prescription during your trip, chances are good that you'll only have to pay a copay, just like back home, instead of the full price for prescribed medicines.

Avoiding "economy-class syndrome"

Deep vein thrombosis, or as it's know in the world of flying, "economy-class syndrome," is a blood clot that develops in a deep vein. It's a potentially deadly condition that can be caused by sitting in cramped conditions — such as an airplane cabin — for too long. During a flight (especially a long-haul flight), get up, walk around, and stretch your legs every 60 to 90 minutes to keep your blood flowing. Other preventative measures include frequent flexing of the legs while sitting, drinking lots of water, and avoiding alcohol and sleeping pills. If you have a history of deep vein thrombosis, heart disease, or other condition that puts you at high risk, some experts recommend wearing compression stockings or taking anticoagulants when you fly; always ask your physician about the best course for you. Symptoms of deep vein thrombosis include leg pain or swelling, or even shortness of breath.

Keeping Clear of Creepy Crawlies

Hawaii is a buggy place. Just like humans, critters love the tropics. Fortunately, most of them won't harm you, but three insects (mosquitoes, centipedes, and scorpions) have pesky stings.

For advice on ocean safety and treating mishaps like jellyfish stings and coral cuts, see Chapter 12.

Mosquitoes

You can't do much about mosquitoes (which aren't native to Hawaii; North Americans brought them via ship, thank you very much), except to apply commercial repellent to keep them off. You can also burn mosquito punk or citronella candles to drive them out of your area, or apply commercial ointments and salves to relieve the itching and swelling after you've been stung. Most bites last anywhere from a few hours to a few days.

Centipedes

These segmented insects with a jillion legs come in two varieties: 6- to 8-inch-long brown ones, and the smaller 2- to 3-inch-long blue guys, who really pack a wallop with their sting. You won't find them hanging out at the beach: Centipedes are generally found in damp, wet places, such as under wood piles or in compost heaps. Wearing closed-toe shoes when hiking can help prevent stings if you happen to accidentally unearth one. If a centipede stings you, the reaction can range from something similar to a mild bee sting to severe pain. Apply ice immediately to prevent swelling and pain. See a doctor if the pain is extreme or if you experience swelling, nausea, or any other severe reaction.

Scorpions

Despite what you may have seen on *The Brady Bunch,* scorpions don't hang out at any of the island's resort areas. Scorpions prefer arid, warm regions. You're highly unlikely to run into one of these critters while you're on Maui, unless you go backpacking into the wild. If you go hiking and camping, shake out your boots before you put them on and check your bedroll before you climb in. Stings can be serious; in the unlikely event that you're stung, apply diluted household ammonia and cold compresses to the area of the sting and seek medical help immediately.

Staying Connected by Cellphone or E-mail

If you'd like to stay connected with your real life while you're in the islands, then the following sections are for you.

Using a cellphone across the U.S.

Just because your cellphone works at home doesn't mean it'll work elsewhere in the country (thanks to our nation's fragmented cellphone system). Take a look at your wireless company's coverage map on its Web site before heading out — T-Mobile, Sprint, and Nextel are particularly weak in rural areas. For example, I've had much better luck with Cingular than Sprint on the neighbor islands. If you need to stay in touch at a destination where you know your phone won't work, **rent** a phone that does from **InTouch USA** (☎ **800-872-7626;** www.intouchglobal. com) or a rental-car location, but beware — you'll pay $1 a minute or more for airtime.

If you're not from the United States, you'll be appalled at the poor reach of our **GSM (Global System for Mobiles) wireless network,** which is used by much of the rest of the world. Your phone will probably work in most major U.S. cities; it definitely won't work in many rural areas. (To see where GSM phones work in the United States, check out www.t-mobile.com/coverage/national_popup.asp). And you may or may not be able to send SMS (text messaging) home — something Americans tend not to do anyway. Assume nothing — call your wireless provider and get the full scoop. In a worst-case scenario, you can always rent a phone; InTouch USA delivers to hotels.

Accessing the Internet away from home

Travelers have any number of ways to check their e-mail and access the Internet on the road. Of course, using your own laptop — or even a pocket computer — gives you the most flexibility. But even if you don't have a computer, you can still access your e-mail and even your office computer from cybercafes.

It's hard nowadays to find a destination that *doesn't* have a few cyber-cafes. Although there's no definitive directory for cybercafes — these are independent businesses, after all — three places to start looking are at www.cybercaptive.com and www.cybercafe.com. Avoid **hotel business centers** unless you don't have another easy option, as you'll probably have to pay high per-minute rates to be online.

Most major airports now have **Internet kiosks** scattered throughout their gates. These kiosks, which you'll also see in shopping malls, hotel lobbies, and tourist information offices around the world, give you basic Web access for a per-minute fee that's usually higher than cybercafe prices. The kiosks' clunkiness and high prices mean that you should avoid them whenever possible.

To retrieve your e-mail, ask your **Internet Service Provider (ISP)** whether it has a Web-based interface tied to your existing e-mail account. If your ISP doesn't have such an interface, you can use the free **mail2web** service (www.mail2web.com) to view and reply to your home e-mail. For more flexibility, you may want to open a free, Web-based e-mail account with **Yahoo! Mail** (http://mail.yahoo.com). (Microsoft's Hotmail is another popular option, but Hotmail has severe spam problems.) Your home ISP may be able to forward your e-mail to the Web-based account automatically.

If you need to access files on your office computer, look into a service called **GoToMyPC** (www.gotomypc.com). The service provides a Web-based interface for you to access and manipulate a distant PC from anywhere — even a cybercafe — provided your "target" PC is on and has an always-on connection to the Internet (such as with Road Runner cable). The service offers top-quality security, but if you're worried about hackers, use your own laptop rather than a cybercafe computer to access the GoToMyPC system.

If you're bringing your own computer, **Wi-Fi** (wireless fidelity) gives you the easiest online access. More and more hotels, cafes, and retailers are signing on as wireless hot spots from where you can get a wireless high-speed connection. You can get a Wi-Fi connection one of several ways. Most laptops sold in recent years have built-in Wi-Fi capability (an 802.11b wireless Ethernet connection). Mac owners have their own networking technology, Apple AirPort. For those with older computers, you can plug an 802.11b/**Wi-Fi card** (around $50) into your laptop. You sign up for wireless access service much as you do cellphone service, through a plan offered by one of several commercial companies that have made wireless service available in airports, hotel lobbies, and coffee shops, primarily in the United States (followed by the U.K. and Japan). **T-Mobile Hotspot** (www.t-mobile.com/hotspot) serves up wireless connections at more than 1,000 Starbucks coffee shops nationwide. **Boingo** (www.boingo.com) and **Wayport** (www.wayport.com) have set up networks in airports and high-class hotel lobbies. IPass providers also give you access to a few hundred wireless hotel lobby setups. Best of all, you don't need to be staying at the Four Seasons to use the hotel's network; just set yourself up on a nice couch in the lobby. The companies' pricing policies can be byzantine, with a variety of monthly, per-connection, and per-minute plans, but in general you pay around $30 a month for unlimited access — and as more and more companies jump on the wireless bandwagon, prices are likely to get even more competitive.

There are also places that provide **free wireless networks** in cities around the world. To locate these free hot spots, go to www.personaltelco.net/index.cgi/WirelessCommunities.

Almost every hotel offers dataports for laptop modems at the very least, and high-speed Internet access using an Ethernet network cable is generally available in chain hotels these days. Access rates range from free to about $15 for each 24-hour period that you're online. **Call your hotel in advance** to see what your options are.

In addition, major ISPs have **local access numbers** around the world, allowing you to go online by simply placing a local call. Check your ISP's Web site or call its toll-free number and ask how you can use your current account away from home, and how much it will cost. If you're traveling outside the reach of your ISP, the **iPass** network has dial-up numbers in most of the world's countries. You'll have to sign up with an iPass provider, who will then tell you how to set up your computer for your destination(s). For a list of iPass providers, go to www.ipass.com and click "Individual Purchase." One solid provider is **i2roam** (www.i2roam.com; ☎ **866-811-6209** or 920-235-0475).

Hotels generally provide all the connection equipment you need. However, you may want to play it safe by bringing a **connection kit** of the right power and phone adapters, a spare phone cord, and a spare Ethernet network cable with you.

Keep in mind that chain hotels are most likely to give you high-speed access. The lower the price point, the less likely it will be available. However, there are some significant exceptions; the affordable Hampton Inn chain, for example, makes wireless access complimentary. On the other hand, you can pretty much expect to have limited access at a bed-and-breakfast. The bottom line: Be sure to check arrangements in advance if high-speed Internet access is important to you.

Keeping Up with Airline Security Measures

Even after the federalization of airport security, security procedures at U.S. airports tend to be uneven. But generally you'll be fine if you arrive at the airport **one hour** before a domestic flight and **two hours** before an international flight. If you show up late, tell an airline employee, and she'll probably whisk you to the front of the line. Be sure to allow extra time if you're traveling on a high-volume holiday getaway day, or if the terrorism alert level has been raised.

It used to be a snap to fly between the Hawaiian Islands; it was a casual procedure to catch shuttle-style flights that left every 30 or 40 minutes. But since 9/11, there's been a dramatic reduction in the number of inter-island flights, making it important to book in advance. The airlines request that you show up at least 90 minutes before your flight to allow for security inspections, and I've found that to be good advice.

Bring a **current, government-issued photo ID,** such as a driver's license or passport. Keep your ID at the ready to show at check-in, the security checkpoint, and sometimes even the gate. (Children under 18 don't need government-issued photo IDs for domestic flights, but they do for international flights to most countries.)

In 2003, the TSA phased out **gate check-in** at all U.S. airports. And **E-tickets** have made paper tickets nearly obsolete. Passengers with E-tickets can beat the ticket-counter lines by using airport **electronic kiosks** or even **online check-in** from your home computer. Online check-in involves logging on to your airline's Web site, accessing your reservation, and printing your boarding pass — and the airline may even offer you bonus miles to do so! If you're using a kiosk at the airport, bring the credit card you used to book the ticket or your frequent-flier card. Print your boarding pass from the kiosk and simply proceed to the security checkpoint with your pass and a photo ID. If you're checking bags or looking to snag an exit-row seat, you'll be able to do so using most airline kiosks. Even the smaller airlines are employing the kiosk system, but always call your airline to make sure that these alternatives are available. **Curbside check-in** is also a good way to avoid lines, although a few airlines still ban curbside check-in; call before you go.

Security checkpoint lines are getting shorter than they were during 2001 and 2002, but some doozies remain. If you have trouble standing for long periods of time, tell an airline employee; the airline will provide a wheelchair. Speed up security by **not wearing metal objects** such as big belt buckles. If you've got metallic body parts, a note from your doctor can prevent a long chat with the security screeners. Keep in mind that only **ticketed passengers** are allowed past security, except for folks escorting disabled passengers or children.

Federalization has stabilized **what you can carry on** and **what you can't.** The general rule is that sharp things are out, nail clippers are okay, and food and beverages must be passed through the X-ray machine — but that security screeners can't make you drink from your coffee cup. Bring food in your carryon rather than checking it, as explosive-detection machines used on checked luggage have been known to mistake food (especially chocolate, for some reason) for bombs. Travelers in the United States are allowed one carry-on bag, plus a "personal item" such as a purse, briefcase, or laptop bag. Carryon hoarders can stuff all sorts of things into a laptop bag; as long as it has a laptop in it, it's still considered a personal item. The Transportation Security Administration (TSA) has issued a list of restricted items; check its Web site (www.tsa.gov/public/index.jsp) for details.

Airport screeners may decide that your checked luggage needs to be searched by hand. You can now purchase luggage locks that allow screeners to open and relock a checked bag if hand-searching is necessary. Look for Travel Sentry certified locks at luggage or travel shops and Brookstone stores. (You can buy them online at www.brookstone.com.) These locks, approved by the TSA, can be opened by luggage inspectors with a special code or key. For more information on the locks, visit www.travelsentry.org. If you use something other than TSA-approved locks, your lock will be cut off your suitcase if a TSA agent needs to hand-search your luggage.

Making Reservations Before You Leave Home

In addition to buying your airfare, booking your accommodations, and reserving a rental car, you may want to make a few plans before you leave home.

In general, you don't have to call ahead to reserve most activities until you arrive on Maui. Most snorkel cruises, guided tours, and the like can be reserved a day or two in advance. Even high-profile restaurants can usually get you in within a few days of the day you call.

Still, planning is never a bad idea. And it's an absolute necessity for certain special events and activities, including the following:

✔ **Luaus:** Maui's **Old Lahaina Luau** is the best luau in the islands — and it always sells out at least a week in advance, often more, as does its sister luau, **The Feast at Lele.** It's never too early to reserve your seats; see Chapter 11 for contact information.

✔ **Snorkel cruises:** Maui's finest snorkel-cruise operator is **Trilogy Excursions.** These cruises are hugely popular, so you may want to book your trip to Molokai or Lanai, both red-hot snorkel spots, before you leave home (see Chapter 12).

✔ **Special events:** Certain special events require advance planning or arrangements, such as the **Hawaii International Jazz Festival** and the **Kapalua Wine & Food Festival.** Check Chapter 3 to see what will be on while you're traveling, and whether it requires advance planning. You may also want to check www.visitmaui.com.

✔ **Special-occasion or holiday meals:** These should always be reserved in advance to avoid disappointment. This is especially true on holidays, when the nicer restaurants are overrun with locals and visitors alike. Take it from me on this one — I couldn't get a same-day table at a decent restaurant on Mother's Day to save my life.

✔ **Scuba classes:** First-time scuba divers may want to look into the various resort courses that are available, because they differ from outfitter to outfitter. See Chapter 12 for reputable local dive instructors.

Consider taking scuba certification classes before you leave home; that way, you don't waste time learning in some resort swimming pool and can dive right in as soon as you get to Maui. A great way to find a local scuba instructor near your home is via the Professional Association of Diving Instructors (PADI) Web site; go online to www.padi.com and click on "Dive Centers and Resorts."

✔ **Tee times:** If you've got your heart set on playing a particular course, it's a good idea to call ahead to book your tee time. This advice is especially true on Lanai, where the two resort courses insist that you reserve *90 days* in advance!

> ✔ **Molokai Mule Ride to Kalaupapa National Historic Park:** Riding a mule down Molokai's towering sea cliffs to visit this remote and poignant site is a once-in-a-lifetime adventure. (Even if you're not planning to stay on Molokai, you can do it on a daytrip from Maui.) It's important to make reservations well in advance of your visit, because space is limited on these unique tours. See Chapter 16 for complete details.

Planning your activities in advance is often the best way to guarantee that you won't miss out on an event or a restaurant that you've been counting on — that way, if there's a sudden rush on tour spots, if a group suddenly decides that it's going to take over a snorkel boat for a full day, or a restaurant is planning to close down for a week to install a new stove in the kitchen, you have the opportunity to amend your plans accordingly. Planning also starts to give useful form to your itinerary, so you'll begin to have an idea of where your busy days and your free days fall. Besides, you don't want to spend your valuable Maui time on the phone in your hotel room, do you?

Packing Smart

To start your packing, set aside everything that you think you need to take. Then get rid of half of it.

Even if the airlines will let you take it all (with some limits), carting loads of stuff around Hawaii is a big fat drag. You really can do without that sixth pair of sandals. Besides, suitcase and duffel-bag straps can be particularly painful on sunburned shoulders — you'll probably spend all day in your bathing suit, anyway. What's more, almost all hotel and condo complexes have on-site laundry facilities, lest you actually run out of clothes or spill a mai tai on your favorite sundress.

Here are the essentials that you should pack:

> ✔ **More than one swimsuit:** Finding out that yesterday's swimsuit isn't dry today is a real bummer. You'll use the extra, I swear.

> ✔ **Sunglasses, a sunhat, and high-SPF sunscreen:** Take SPF 15, at minimum (30 is better); the Hawaiian sun is very strong.

> ✔ **Beach sandals:** I don't want you to scorch your tootsies on the sand. Inexpensive flip-flops do the trick.

> ✔ **A sweater or light jacket:** The evenings can get breezy. Windbreakers come in particularly handy for active travelers.

> ✔ **Good, comfortable walking shoes:** Bring hiking boots if you plan to hike, especially if you're going to visit Haleakala National Park.

- ✔ **A warm jacket and long pants:** You really need these if you plan to visit Haleakala National Park or some other Upcountry location that gets cool even in summer. Basically, count on the temperature dropping 3½ degrees for every 1,000 feet you climb, which means that it can be 35 degrees cooler atop Haleakala's peak than it is at the beach.

- ✔ **Rain gear:** A waterproof jacket with a hood is always a good idea if you're visiting Maui between November and March.

- ✔ **Binoculars:** These come in handy during whale-watching season or to spot dolphins, birds, or other critters at any time of year.

- ✔ **Dramamine or nausea-prevention wristbands:** These can save the day on a snorkel or sunset cruise. (If you plan to rely on Dramamine to prevent car- or seasickness, be sure to take it *before* you set out — because it's too late after you're already on the curving coastal road or rough open seas.)

- ✔ **A cellphone:** It can be an invaluable lifeline in the event that you get a flat or your rental car breaks down.

- ✔ **An extra pair of eyeglasses or contact lenses:** Always a good idea to prevent an inconvenient "Ack — I can't see!" emergency.

Maui is a very easygoing place — so leave the pantyhose and pumps and the jacket and tie at home. A casual dress or a polo shirt and khakis will get you by in most dining rooms in the islands — even the expensive ones. A few ultrafancy resort restaurants require a jacket — but that's all wrong for Maui, so I don't recommend them.

Hawaiian-print aloha wear is acceptable throughout the islands. I tell you where to buy Maui's best-quality and most beautiful aloha clothes in Chapter 14. You say that you'll never wear it again after you get home? You should — aloha wear looks great everywhere!

Bring all your prescription meds, of course, but don't bother hauling a half-dozen bottles of saline solution or 16 rolls of film from home. Maui has a fine collection of drugstores. In fact, if you forget anything, don't panic. You can buy everything you need — and lots of stuff that you don't.

Part III
Settling into Maui

The 5th Wave   By Rich Tennant

In this part . . .

To help orient yourself when you arrive on the Valley Isle, I explain what to do when you land, how to find your bearings, and how to get around. You also find a full listing of Maui's best hotels so that you can book the perfect place to stay. Finally, I give you honest, accurate reviews of Maui's top restaurants in all price categories — from fine dining to down-home local fare.

Chapter 9

Arriving and Getting Around

• •

In This Chapter

▶ Getting from the airport to your hotel without a hassle
▶ Finding your way around Maui and its major resort areas
▶ Getting around without a rental car

• •

*M*aui is slightly more difficult to navigate than the other Hawaiian Islands — instead of circling the island, all the major roads meet and crisscross on the flat land between the island's two volcanoes. Still, getting around isn't overly complicated. With a good map in hand, you're golden.

You'll most likely arrive at the island's centrally located main gateway, Kahului (ka-hoo-*loo*-ee) Airport, in Central Maui.

In this chapter, I give you a quick and easy overview of Maui's geography, with a thumbnail sketch of the island's major hotel districts. This information can help you decide where you want to base yourself.

Arriving at Kahului Airport

Kahului Airport (☎ **808-872-3893;** www.state.hi.us/dot/airports/maui/ogg) is conveniently located 3 miles from the town of Kahului, Maui's main community, at the end of Keolani Place (just west of the intersection of Dairy Road and the Haleakala Highway).

You can easily fly directly between the mainland and Maui. **Aloha Airlines** and **Hawaiian Airlines** provide both interisland and direct mainland service to Kahului. **American, Air Canada, ATA, Delta,** and **United** all serve Kahului directly from the mainland as well. See Chapter 5 for complete details on airline routes and best airfares.

Maui Orientation

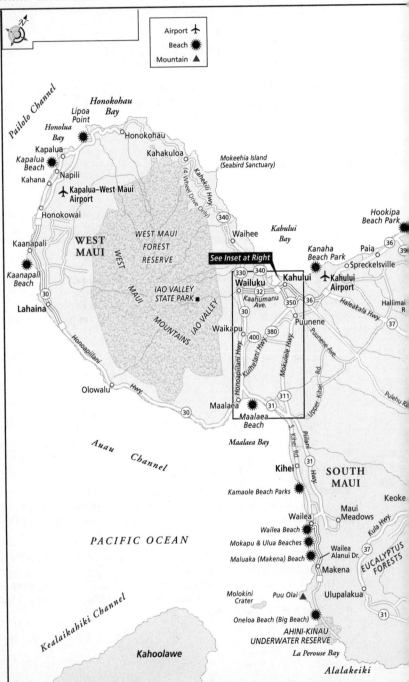

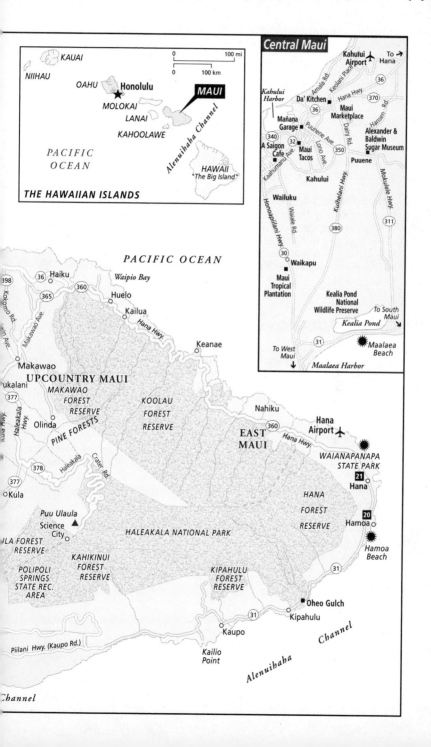

THE HAWAIIAN ISLANDS

KAUAI

NIIHAU

OAHU Honolulu

MOLOKAI
LANAI
KAHOOLAWE

MAUI

PACIFIC
OCEAN

HAWAII
"The Big Island"

Alenuihaha Channel

0   100 mi
0   100 km

Central Maui

Kahului
Airport   To
Hana

Kahului
Harbor   Da' Kitchen   Hana Hwy   36

Amala Rd.
Keolani Place
36   370

Mañana
Garage   Puunene Ave.   Maui
Marketplace

Hansen Rd.

A Saigon
Cafe   32   Maui
Tacos   350   Alexander &
Baldwin
Sugar Museum

340   Lono Ave.   Puunene

Kaahumanu Ave.

Kahului   Kuihelani Hwy.

Mokulele Hwy.

Wailuku

Honoapiilani Hwy.   Waiale Rd.   380   311

30

Maui   Waikapu
Tropical
Plantation   Kealia Pond
National
Wildlife Preserve   To South
Maui

Kealia Pond

To West
Maui   31   Maalaea
Beach

Maalaea Harbor

PACIFIC OCEAN

398   36   Haiku   *Waipio Bay*

365   360   Huelo

Kailua

Hana Hwy.   Keanae

Makawao

UPCOUNTRY MAUI

ukalani   MAKAWAO
FOREST
RESERVE   KOOLAU
FOREST
RESERVE   Nahiku   Hana
Airport

377   Olinda   EAST
MAUI   360   *Hana Hwy.*

PINE FORESTS   WAIANAPANAPA
STATE PARK

378   Haleakala   Crater Rd.   21   Hana

377   Kula   HANA
FOREST
RESERVE   20   Hamoa

Puu Ulaula
Science
City   Hamoa
Beach

LA FOREST
RESERVE   HALEAKALA NATIONAL PARK   31

KAHIKINUI
FOREST
RESERVE   KIPAHULU
FOREST
RESERVE

POLIPOLI
SPRINGS
STATE REC.
AREA   Oheo Gulch

31   Kipahulu

Piilani Hwy. (Kaupo Rd.)   Kaupo

Kailio
Point   *Alenuihaha*   *Channel*

Channel

Open-air Kahului Airport is easy to negotiate. The airport is relatively small, and the route from your gate to the baggage claim is clearly marked.

Nearly all the island's highways are accessible just outside the airport, ready to whisk you to wherever you'll be staying.

After you land at Kahului Airport, stop at the state-operated **Visitor Information Center** while you're waiting for your baggage and pick up a copy of *This Week — Maui, 101 Things to Do on Maui,* and other free tourist publications. If you forget, don't worry — you can find them at malls and shopping centers around the island.

Although nearly everyone arrives at Kahului Airport, Maui does have two single-strip airports served by commercial propeller carriers — one in Kapalua (in West Maui) and another in Hana. If you're interested in avoiding busy Kahului altogether, contact **Island Air** (☎ **800-323-3345,** 800-652-6541, or 808-484-2222; www.islandair.com), a division of inter-island carrier Aloha, or **Pacific Wings** (☎ **888-575-4546** or 808-873-0877; www.pacificwings.com).

Getting from the Airport to Your Hotel

All the major auto-rental agencies have cars available at Kahului, and I suggest that you arrange for one in advance. (For more on this subject, see Chapter 8.) If you'd rather not drive yourself, I give you some alternative transportation options in this section. But if you're willing to drive, having your own rental car is really the way to go.

Driving yourself

Step outside to the curbside rental-car pickup area at the ocean end of the terminal (to your right as you exit the building). Either go over to the counter if your rental company is represented or wait for the appropriate shuttle van — they circle the airport at regular intervals — to take you a half-mile to your rental-car checkout desk.

All the rental-car agencies offer map booklets that are invaluable for getting around the island.

Getting from the airport to your hotel can be a bit of a trial because Kahului is Maui's main business district and Maui's main highways intersect just outside the airport.

If you're heading to **West Maui,** take the Kuihelani (koo-ee-hay-*la*-nee) Highway (Highway 380) to the Honoapiilani (ho-no-ah-pee-ee-*la*-nee) Highway (Highway 30). The Honoapiilani Highway curves around the knob that is West Maui, leading to Lahaina, Kaanapali, Kahana, Napili, and finally Kapalua. To pick up the Kuihelani Highway, exit the airport at Keolani Place and turn left onto Dairy Road, which turns into the highway you want. Expect it to take 30 minutes to reach Lahaina, 40 minutes to reach Kaanapali, and 50 to 60 minutes to reach Kapalua, maybe a little longer if the traffic's heavy.

If you're heading to **South Maui,** exit the airport at Keolani Place, turn left onto Dairy Road, and then left onto Puunene (poo-oo-*nay*-nay) Avenue (Highway 350), which takes you immediately to the Mokulele (mow-koo-*lay*-lay) Highway (Highway 311), which leads directly south. Just north of Kihei, the Mokulele ends; you can choose to continue on the highway — now called Piilani (pee-ee-*la*-nee) Highway (Highway 31) — which takes you through Kihei and to Wailea along the speediest route, with frequent exits along the way. If you're staying at the north end of Kihei, though, exit the Mokulele Highway onto South Kihei Road, Kihei's main drag.

Taking a taxi

As long as you arrive before 10 p.m., you don't need to make arrangements before you leave home to have a taxi pick you up at the airport. Just go out to the well-marked curbside area and hop into the next available cab.

If you do want to arrange for pickup ahead of time, call **Maui Airport Taxi** (☎ **808-877-0907**), **Maui Central Cab** (☎ **877-244-7279** or 808-244-7278; www.mauicab.com), **Kihei Taxi** (☎ **808-879-3000**), or **Wailea Taxi** (☎ **808-874-5000**).

Expect to pay $45 to $70 depending on your West Maui destination, and about $22 to $38 to the Kihei/Wailea area. Don't forget to tack on a 10- to 15-percent tip, of course.

For limousine service, contact **Star Limousine** (☎ 808-875-6900 or 808-669-6900; www.limohawaii.com).

Catching a shuttle ride

If you're not renting a car, the cheapest way to get to your hotel is via airport shuttle. **SpeediShuttle** (☎ **800-977-2605** or 808-875-8070; www.speedishuttle.com) can take you between Kahului Airport and any of the Maui resort areas between 6 a.m. and 11 p.m. daily. Rates vary depending on your destination, but figure on $30 to Wailea (one way) and $41 to Kaanapali. (Rates also vary depending on the number of people riding with you.) You can either set up your airport pickup in advance (which allows you to snag a 10-percent online booking discount on your return trip) or use the courtesy phone in baggage claim to summon a van (dial 65).

When you're ready to leave Maui and fly home, call at least 24 hours before your departure flight to arrange pickup.

Figuring Out the Lay of the Land

The commercial hub of Maui is **Kahului.** Just east of Kahului is **Wailuku,** Maui's appealingly funky county seat (and a burgeoning antiques center). These two Central Maui communities are the island's largest towns, but they're not real vacation destinations.

Instead, most visitors stay on one of the two major resort coasts: West Maui and South Maui. Each one is made up of a series of smaller beach resorts and communities and offers its own distinct personality.

West Maui

Look at a map of Maui — the island faintly resembles the head and shoulders of a person in left profile. If you go with this geographical inkblot test, the West Maui coastline serves as the island's forehead (and Kahului is on Maui's "neck"). In winter, this coast is a little greener — and a little wetter — than the South Maui coast. Some of the best beaches on the island fringe West Maui; eastward, the beautifully jagged mountain peaks of the West Maui Mountains rise in the distance.

Of the coastal communities, only Lahaina is a real town; the others are really just collections of condos and hotels, each targeted to a different audience and anchored by a few fancy resorts or a high-end minimall. The following communities start at the southern end of West Maui and head northward along the **Honoapiilani Highway** (Highway 30):

✔ The historic port town of **Lahaina** isn't really that historic any- more. In fact, it has superseded Waikiki as Hawaii's tacky tourist center. The blocks are lined with bustling waterfront restaurants, tourist-targeted galleries and shops, and aggressive activities cen- ters with employees that catcall onto the street, begging to book your activities (or, if they can, talk you into "sitting through" a time- share presentation). The predominant vibe is that of one big, surf- oriented street party. Some people love the freewheeling ambience, lively energy, and oceanfront setting. Lahaina also has two main advantages: some of Maui's best accommodations values and an extremely convenient location. Lahaina boasts a couple of beaches that will do in a pinch, but expect to drive to reach the best ones.

✔ Three miles north of Lahaina is **Kaanapali** (ka-ah-na-*pa*-lee), Hawaii's first master-planned family resort, and a real favorite of mine. Kaanapali's string of resort hotels and condos fronts a gorgeous golden beach and exudes a nice sense of continuity. A landscaped parkway and a walking path along the sand, with a very nice shopping and dining complex sitting at its midpoint, link them all together. Kaanapali is pricey, but not quite as expensive as Kapalua or Wailea. In fact, it's home to my favorite midpriced resort, the Kaanapali Beach Hotel, and some of Maui's best midrange condos. See Chapter 10 for more details.

✔ Two condo communities, **Kahana** and **Napili,** sit off the highway a few minutes north of Kaanapali, offering great deals for those travelers who want an affordable place to stay and a nice oceanfront setting. Apartment-style units offer a good value for families or anyone who wants homelike amenities that give you the freedom to cook a meal for yourself or wash your own socks. Restaurants and supermarkets also are nearby. The only downside is a lack of personality — expect homogeneous, bulky, and bland condo complexes. (Who can complain, though, when the ocean is just a hop, skip, and a jump away?)

✔ North of Kahana is Hawaii's most beautiful master-planned community, **Kapalua,** the exclusive domain of two gracious luxury hotels, fabulous gold-sand beaches, and world-class golf. Kapalua is a marvelous place to settle in and unwind — if you have the big bucks to do it. But because it's situated at the north end of the Honoapiilani Highway, Kapalua isn't the most convenient base; even Lahaina is a 20-minute drive to the south. Still, the glorious setting can be well worth the tradeoff. Kapalua also tends to get more rain than other Maui resorts, even those a few minutes south on the West Maui coast.

South Maui

South Maui is the island's hottest, driest, and most dependably sunny coast. Actually western-facing, but well-protected from the elements by peninsula-like West Maui, South Maui receives only about 15 inches of annual rainfall, and temperatures stay around 80°F year-round.

If you drive south from Central Maui along **Piilani Highway** (Highway 31) or **Kihei Road** (Highway 310), you first reach Kihei and then Wailea; which one you choose depends entirely on your budget.

✔ Centrally located **Kihei** (*key*-hay) is Maui's bargain coast. Its main drag is South Kihei Road, which is bordered by a continuous string of condos and minimalls on one side and a series of sandy beaches on the other. Kihei isn't charming or quaint — it feels more like Southern California than Hawaii at times, especially when Kihei Road has bumper-to-bumper traffic — but ongoing renovation is improving its appeal somewhat. And what Kihei lacks in physical appeal it more than makes up for in sunshine, affordability, and convenience.

✔ Just a few minutes south of Kihei, **Wailea** (why-*lay*-ah) sits at the opposite end of the budget-deluxe continuum. This ritzy, well-manicured neighborhood is home to Maui's best luxury resort spreads, enough championship golf courses to keep you busy for a week, five outstanding beaches, the elegant Shops at Wailea, and the Wailea Tennis Center (known as Wimbledon West). The strip is well developed and tightly packed, and my favorite Wailea resorts remain worlds unto themselves. Even though Kapalua is unarguably more beautiful, Wailea is no slouch — and I prefer its more accessible location and wider range of hotel choices. You even find some midrange and upscale condos in this appealing neck of the woods.

Upcountry Maui

Cool, inland **Upcountry Maui** puts you away from the beaches (which are a 15- to 30-minute drive away) but closer to Haleakala (ha-lay-ah-*ka*-la) National Park. That proximity can save you hours of sleep if you want to see the sunrise over the crater. You also can visit the park from the beach resort areas, but you have to get up in the middle of the night to make the drive in time for the first rays of dawn.

Upcountry offers a beautiful glimpse into rural Maui. Most accommodations are quiet, intimate, isolated affairs (B&Bs or vacation rentals) that are perfect for those travelers who love solitude, wonderful views, and romance. Upcountry Maui is a little funkier destination than the beach resorts (and more prone to cool weather and rain).

If you want easy access to sun and surf, plenty of action, and tons of services and facilities, Upcountry isn't for you. It is, however, reachable as a daytrip from the West and South Maui resorts — and you may enjoy staying there for a couple of nights after you've had your fill of baking on the sands. Even if you decide not to stay there, I highly recommend that you at least take a drive to Upcountry.

East Maui: Hana

A few visitors also like to stay way out in **Hana,** in easternmost Maui, for the ultimate escape. In Chapter 10, I review a handful of B&Bs and vacation rentals on the road to Hana or in this lovely town itself. In Hana, you can relax in a lush, green, rural setting with access to wonderful beaches. Hana tends to receive more rain than the dry South Maui coast, but as compensation, the vegetation is green, and it boasts a luxuriant rainforest — think giant ferns, vibrant tropical flowers, and swaying palms. Hana is a sleepy area, where the accommodations tend to be intimate and exquisite, but not laden with facilities. If you want to get away, a stay in Hana is just the ticket; if you want to be in the thick of things, stay in West or South Maui.

You can see this beautiful area on a day's drive from the major resort coasts, but that tends to be a rushed experience. I highly recommend doing the drive at a leisurely pace and staying overnight in Hana if you can. It's a wonderful departure from the bustle of South and West Maui — a step back into Hawaii's simpler days before tourism spawned such intense development.

If you're contemplating a visit or a stay either in Upcountry or in Hana, check out Chapter 10.

Finding Information After You Arrive

After you land at Kahului Airport, stop over at the state-operated **Visitor Information Center** while you're waiting for your luggage. Pick up a copy of *This Week Maui, 101 Things to Do on Maui,* and other free tourist publications. If you forget, don't worry — you can find them at malls and shopping centers around the island.

In addition, all the big resort hotels are overflowing with printed info. Even if your hotel or condo doesn't have a dedicated concierge, the staff can point you in the right direction, make recommendations, and give advice. They're usually happy to help — it's part of the spirit of aloha.

The **Maui Visitors Bureau** is located in Central Maui at 1727 Wili Pa Loop, Wailuku (☎ **808-244-3530** or 800-525-6284; www.visitmaui.com), but it's not really designed as a walk-in office. Call before you leave home to order your free Maui travel planner or check the Web site for a wealth of good information.

The *Honolulu Advertiser* (www.honoluluadvertiser.com) and the *Honolulu Star-Bulletin* (www.starbulletin.com) are the two statewide dailies. Maui's own daily paper is the *Maui News* (www.mauinews.com).

Getting around Maui

To really see the Valley Island, you have to drive it yourself. Maui has only a handful of major roads, but they all meet in a complicated web in the island's center, and untangling them can take some effort. Be sure to study a good island map and know exactly where you're going before you set out.

 Maui is growing by leaps and bounds, with new housing developments going up in almost every direction. As a result, traffic can be challenging at times. Try to allow yourself extra time to get where you're going at rush hours, especially in the Central and South Maui areas.

Navigating your rental car around the Valley Isle

 If you get in trouble on Maui's highways and you don't have your wireless phone with you, look for the flashing blue strobe lights on 12-foot poles; at the base are emergency call boxes (programmed to dial 911 as soon as you pick up the handset).

Starting out in Central Maui

Kahului, in Central Maui, is where the major airport is, and where you arrive. Kahului isn't a vacation destination but a real town with Wal-Marts, parking lots, malls, and so on. Still, you may occasionally find yourself in Kahului as you head to other areas of the island because Maui's highways intersect there.

Kahului's main drag is **Kaahumanu** (ka-ah-hoo-*ma*-noo) **Avenue** (Highway 32). If you're heading to the town of Wailuku, either for some antiquing or to visit scenic Iao Valley (see Chapter 13), just follow Kaahumanu Avenue west for about ten minutes and — voilà — you're there.

From Kahului to Haleakala

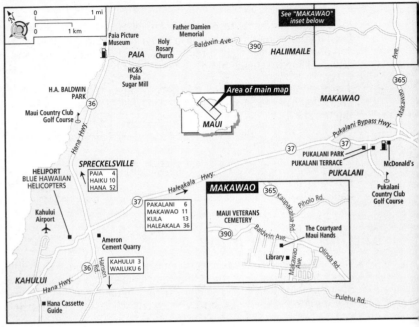

Reaching the West and South Maui resorts

If you're heading to any of Maui's beach resort areas, either in West Maui or South Maui, you first have to head south through the Central Maui corridor (often referred to as Maui's "neck").

To reach West Maui, you take the **Kuihelani Highway** (Highway 380) south from Kahului to the **Honoapiilani Highway** (Highway 30). The Honoapiilani Highway actually starts in Wailuku (it meets up with the end of Kaahumanu Avenue to make a neat inverted "L") and runs directly south to Maalaea (ma-ah-*lay*-ah), a windy harborfront village at the south end of Central Maui — where you may be picking up a snorkel cruise to Molokini or visiting the state-of-the-art Maui Ocean Center aquarium (see Chapter 13 for details). Past Maalaea, the southbound Honoapiilani Highway begins to follow the curve of the land, turning abruptly west and north along the coast toward Lahaina.

West Maui's resort communities lie directly off the Honoapiilani Highway on the ocean side of the road. As you go from south to north, you first reach the old whaling town of Lahaina; then Kaanapali, Hawaii's first master-planned beach resort; then two quiet beachfront condo communities, Kahana and Napili; and, at the end of the road, the Kapalua Resort, a stunning manicured beauty. The road is about 30 minutes of easy highway driving from Lahaina to Kapalua.

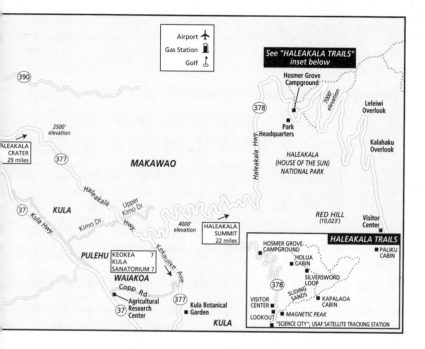

Airport ✈
Gas Station ⛽
Golf ⛳

See "HALEAKALA TRAILS" inset below

Hosmer Grove Campground

390

378

Leleiwi Overlook

2500' elevation

Park Headquarters

Kalahaku Overlook

ALEAKALA CRATER 29 miles

377

MAKAWAO

HALEAKALA (HOUSE OF THE SUN) NATIONAL PARK

Haleakala Hwy

KULA

37

Kula Hwy

Haleakala

Upper Kimo Dr.
Hwy.

Kimo Dr.

4000' elevation

HALEAKALA SUMMIT 22 miles

RED HILL (10,023')

Visitor Center

PULEHU

KEOKEA   7
KULA
SANATORIUM 7

WAIAKOA

Copp Rd.

Agricultural
Research
Center

37   377

Kula Botanical Garden

KULA

HALEAKALA TRAILS

HOSMER GROVE CAMPGROUND

HOLUA CABIN

378

SILVERSWORD LOOP

SLIDING SANDS

KAPALAOA CABIN

VISITOR CENTER

LOOKOUT

MAGNETIC PEAK

PALIKU CABIN

"SCIENCE CITY"; USAF SATELLITE TRACKING STATION

Be extra careful as you drive the Honoapiilani Highway (Highway 30) because the road is rather winding, and drivers who spot whales in the channel between Maui and Lanai sometimes slam on the brakes in awe, precipitating tie-ups and accidents.

From Kahului, you basically drive a straight shot to South Maui, the island's hottest, driest, and sunniest resort coast. The **Mokulele Highway** (Highway 311) heads straight south across the Central Maui corridor from Kahului to the north end of Kihei, west of the Kuihelani Highway, Highway 380.

At the end of the Mokulele Highway, you have two choices. You can pick up South Kihei Road, Kihei's main drag, which is what you should take if you're heading to a destination in the northern portion of Kihei or if you're looking for a supermarket or gas station. If you're on your way to the southern portion of Kihei — to Wailea for a round of golf, or to Makena, farther south, to hang out on a quiet beach or go snorkeling — stick to the right as the Mokulele ends and pick up the **Piilani Highway** (Highway 31), which continues south to Wailea. Near the end of the Piilani Highway, veer right onto the coastal road to reach the Wailea resorts or Makena.

The Mokulele Highway (Highway 311) is often the scene of crashes involving intoxicated and speeding drivers, so be extra careful.

If you're traveling from South Maui to West Maui, or vice versa, you don't need to travel all the way back to Kahului to pick up the appropriate road. **Highway 310** (North Kihei Road) connects the Mokulele Highway (Highway 311, the road to South Maui) to the Honoapiilani Highway (Highway 30, the road to West Maui), running east-west at the south end of Maui's "neck."

Going Upcountry and to East Maui

The giant volcanic crater that dominates the main body of the island is Haleakala (ha-lay-ah-*ka*-la), officially preserved as Haleakala National Park. The road is only about 38 miles from Kahului to the summit of Haleakala, but the drive takes about one and a half hours because of its curving nature and steep ascent (to about 10,000 feet). The drive, naturally, is called the **Haleakala Highway,** which is Highway 37 as it passes through open flatlands, past turnoffs for groovy rural towns like Haliimaile (home to a great restaurant; see Chapter 11) and Makawao (a charming shopping stop). Then, just past Makawao Avenue, the Haleakala Highway becomes Highway 377 — so don't miss the turn for it. After you pass through the little town of Kula, turn onto **Haleakala Crater Road** (Highway 378), which delivers you to the summit.

If you don't take the Haleakala Crater Road turnoff, you continue south on Highway 377, which soon connects up with Highway 37 again, called the **Kula Highway.** If you stay on this road, it eventually takes you all the way to Hana, the small, isolated town at the east end of the island.

But the more popular route to Hana is the **Hana Highway** (Highway 360), which hugs the north cliffs of Maui for about 52 miles east of Kahului. The Heavenly Road to Hana, as it's often called, is a winding drive that borders on treacherous in each direction, crossing more than 50 one-lane bridges in the process. Still, the drive is one of the most spectacular scenic drives you'll ever take in your life. I guide you through it, mile by mile, in Chapter 13. Even if you don't head all the way to Hana, consider making a visit to charming Paia (pa-*ee*-ah), a hip little surf town about ten minutes east of Kahului that has two main draws: some hip and artsy boutiques, and the best windsurfing beach in the world, Hookipa Beach Park, which I cover in Chapter 12.

The south route to Hana is officially Highway 31, but most folks call it the **Kaupo** (*cow*-po) **Road.** I discuss this route in Chapter 13, but some warnings about it bear repeating here, too. Although the road has been considerably improved in recent years, it's still a risky route. Before you set out on it, check with your hotel regarding current road conditions. The road is usually fine if the weather has been clear — but stay away if it has been raining because unpaved sections of the road can wash out. And check with your rental-car company before you set out; many rental contracts actually *forbid* customers to drive their car on Kaupo Road — so if you get stuck, the cost of the tow will be your responsibility.

Getting around without wheels

Your options are limited if you're not going to rent a car, because the island has no islandwide public transportation system.

Holo Ka'a Public Transit is a public/private partnership that recently began to offer economical and air-conditioned shuttle-bus service in Central, West, and South Maui. The costs range from $1 for routes in Kaanapali-Lahaina or along South Kihei Road, $2 for routes in Kapalua-Kaanapali, up to $5 for stops from Wailea to Maalaea. For more information, call ☎ **808-879-2828** or visit www.akinatours.com.

Words you want to know

Yes, everyone speaks English in Hawaii. However, a few Hawaiian and Pidgin (a native mixture of English and other languages, similar to Creole) words and phrases are used regularly in everyday conversation in the islands. For example, don't be surprised if a waiter asks you "Are you pau?" (*pau* means "done" in Hawaiian).

By far, the two most important words are **aloha** (a-*lo*-ha), which serves as an all-purpose greeting (hello or goodbye), and **mahalo** (ma-*ha*-low), which means "thank you." Know those two, and you'll get by just fine. But take a moment to study this short list and get a head start on all the other *malihini* (first-time visitors).

hale (*ha*-lay): house or building

haole (*how*-lay): foreigner, Caucasian

heiau (heh-*ee*-ow): Hawaiian temple or place of worship

hula (*hoo*-lah): native dance

kamaaina (ka-ma-*eye*-nah): local person

keiki (*keh*-kee): child

lanai (*lah*-nigh): porch or veranda

lei (lay): garland

luau (*loo*-ow): feast

makai (ma-*kah*-ee): a direction, toward the sea

malihini (ma-li-*hee*-nee): stranger, newcomer

mauka (*mow*-kah): direction, toward the mountains

pau (pow): finished, done

Maui does have islandwide taxi service. The meter can run up fast, but a taxi can get you where you need to go if you don't have your own wheels. Call **Alii Cab** (☎ **808-661-3688** or 808-667-2605), **Maui Central Cab** (☎ **877-244-7279** or 808-244-7278; www.mauicab.com), **Kihei Taxi** (☎ **808-879-3000**), or **Wailea Taxi** (☎ **808-874-5000**). If you want to be shuttled around in style, call **Star Limousine** (☎ **808-875-6900** or 808-669-6900; www.limohawaii.com).

If you're going to skip renting a car on Maui, a good bet is to base yourself in Lahaina, where restaurants, shops, and attractions are right at hand. Your beach enjoyment will be limited, though, because even though Lahaina has a beach, it's not the greatest.

An even better alternative for auto-free visitors is basing yourself in Kaanapali — the beach is excellent, and restaurants and shops are right at hand in Whaler's Village. A free resort shuttle connects hotels, golf, and other attractions within the resort, but most of Kaanapali's attractions are within walking distance of one another. What's more, Kaanapali is an easy place to pick up the $1 or $2 shuttle van services to destinations all along the coast. Ask your hotel's concierge or front desk staff for details; everyone in Kaanapali is well versed on the shuttle.

Kapalua and Wailea also have local resort shuttles that you can rely on to transport you between destinations within the resort — to the golf course, to local restaurants, and to resort shops. This option is, however, very limited.

If you're coming to Maui and not renting a car, ultimately your best bet may be to call your hotel's concierge before you leave home. He or she can give you a clear heads-up on how convenient the hotel or resort is to nearby restaurants, shopping, and the beach, as well as what kinds of transportation are readily available for you to get to other destinations on the island. See Chapter 13, which fills you in on taking bus tours that can pick you up and drop you off at your hotel.

Chapter 10

Checking In at Maui's Best Hotels

● ●

In This Chapter

▶ Deciding where to stay

▶ Discovering a fabulous romantic getaway

▶ Uncovering the best family-friendly options

▶ Finding an affordable choice

● ●

*M*aui boasts a terrific crop of resorts. But it's such a popular destination that resort hotels and condos can — and do — garner ridiculously high rack rates.

But take heart: You can find some good bargains, especially in the condo market. I describe some of the best values in this chapter. You can find an even wider array of additional condo options by also going through one of the rental agencies listed in Chapter 6.

In fact, Chapter 6 has lots of advice geared to help you book the hotel of your dreams on Maui. It includes a handy overview of the various lodging types available on the island that can help you choose the option that's right for you. It also features the best money-saving strategies and a discussion about whether to splurge on a room with a view.

You may save a bundle on Maui by purchasing an all-inclusive package deal, especially if you're looking for an upscale vacation. In this case, Maui's popularity may work in your favor: Packagers scoop up huge numbers of Maui hotel rooms, and because they're buying rooms in bulk, they can negotiate substantial price breaks — passing the savings on to you. Of course, I can't guarantee what the prices will be when you book, but checking out what's available is worth the extra effort, even if you're booking the rest of your vacation on your own. (Some packagers can arrange land-only vacations if you already have your plane tickets covered.) See Chapter 5 for tips on finding the package deal that's right for you. An all-inclusive package can save you big bucks on both accommodations and airfare, and sometimes car rentals and activities, too.

Maui's Best Accommodations

In the following listings, each resort hotel, condo, or B&B name is followed by a number of dollar signs, ranging from one ($) to five ($$$$$). Each represents the median rack-rate price range for a double room per night, as follows:

Symbol	Meaning
$	Supercheap — less than $100 per night
$$	Still affordable — $100 to $175
$$$	Moderate — $175 to $250
$$$$	Expensive but not ridiculous — $250 to $375
$$$$$	Ultraluxurious — more than $375 per night

You almost never *need* to pay the asking price for a hotel room. Check out Chapter 6 for tips on how to avoid paying the *rack rate,* or listed full price for hotel rooms.

Don't forget that the state adds 11.42 percent in taxes to your hotel bill.

Aston at the Maui Banyan
$$–$$$ South Maui (Kihei)

Skip the standard hotel rooms, if you can, and go straight for a condo unit — which offers much more value for your dollar — at this very nice apartment-like complex situated across Kihei Road from Kamaole (kam-a-*oh*-lay) Beach Park II. The roomy, open-plan one- and two-bedroom units are all nicely outfitted and well maintained; a few three-bedroom units are also available. They've all been recently renovated and feature comfy, contemporary island-style furniture, full kitchens with a microwave, washer/dryer, and furnished lanai. Light daily maid service is included, and two pools, tennis courts, and a Jacuzzi are on-site. The building sits perpendicular to the coast, so partial ocean views are the best you can do — most upper units overlook the parking structure or the building next door. Still, this condo is a great value, especially if you can score one of the many price breaks.

See map p. 125. 2575 S. Kihei Rd., Kihei. ☎ *800-822-4409, 800-922-7866, or 808-875-0004. Fax: 808-874-4035.* www.aston-hotels.com. *Parking: Free! Rack rates: $150–$200 double, $190–$280 1-bedroom, $250–$375 2-bedroom, $395–$510 3-bedroom. Deals: Excellent opportunities for discounts. Internet-only ePriceBreaker rates as low as $104 double, $129 1-bedroom, $169 2-bedroom at press time. Ask for AAA, senior (50-plus), and corporate discounts; packages that include airfare; and other special rate programs. AE, DC, DISC, MC, V.*

Accommodations in West Maui: Kapalua, Napili, and Kahana

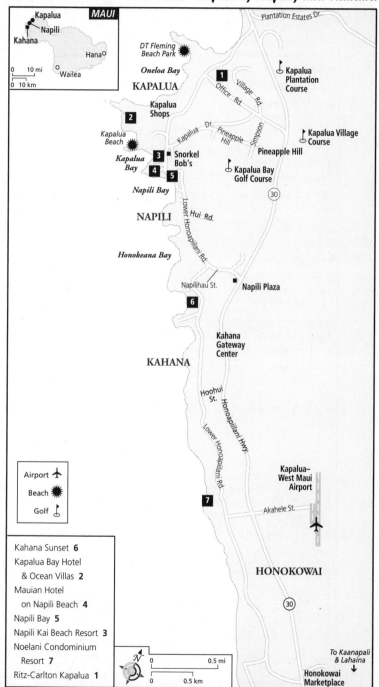

Accommodations in West Maui: Lahaina and Kaanapali

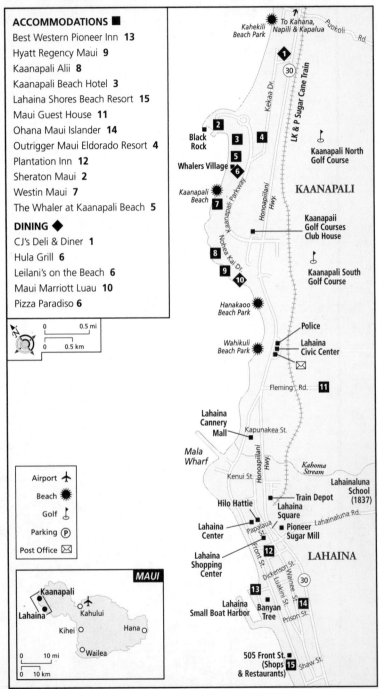

ACCOMMODATIONS ■
Best Western Pioneer Inn **13**
Hyatt Regency Maui **9**
Kaanapali Alii **8**
Kaanapali Beach Hotel **3**
Lahaina Shores Beach Resort **15**
Maui Guest House **11**
Ohana Maui Islander **14**
Outrigger Maui Eldorado Resort **4**
Plantation Inn **12**
Sheraton Maui **2**
Westin Maui **7**
The Whaler at Kaanapali Beach **5**

DINING ◆
CJ's Deli & Diner **1**
Hula Grill **6**
Leilani's on the Beach **6**
Maui Marriott Luau **10**
Pizza Paradiso **6**

Airport ✈
Beach ✸
Golf ⛳
Parking ℗
Post Office ✉

MAUI
Kaanapali
Lahaina
Kahului
Kihei
Hana
Wailea

0   10 mi
0   10 km

Accommodations in South Maui

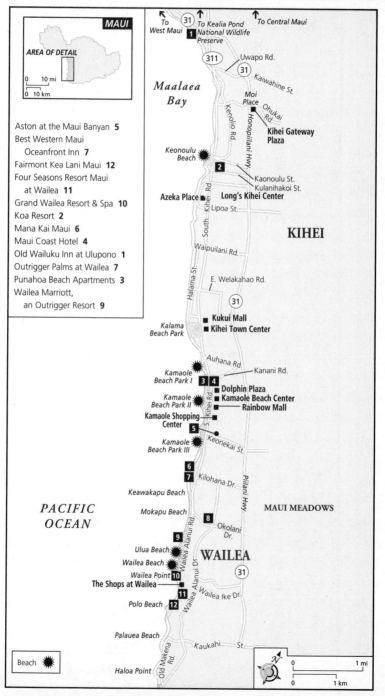

Aston at the Maui Banyan **5**
Best Western Maui
  Oceanfront Inn **7**
Fairmont Kea Lani Maui **12**
Four Seasons Resort Maui
  at Wailea **11**
Grand Wailea Resort & Spa **10**
Koa Resort **2**
Mana Kai Maui **6**
Maui Coast Hotel **4**
Old Wailuku Inn at Ulupono **1**
Outrigger Palms at Wailea **7**
Punahoa Beach Apartments **3**
Wailea Marriott,
  an Outrigger Resort **9**

Accommodations in Upcountry and East Maui

0 ____ 2 mi
0 ____ 2 km

Pauwela Point

Opana Point

Uaoa Bay

Maliko Bay

Hookipa Beach County Park
Paia Kuau
Paia Bay
Paia
1
36
364
Hamakua

Haiku

Twin Falls
2
36
360
3 →
To Hana →

Ulumalu
365

Sugar Mill
← To Spreckelsville

Baldwin Ave.

398

Kaupakalua

390

ACCOMMODATIONS ■
Huelo Point Flower Farm **3**
The Inn at Mama's Fish House **1**
Maluhia Hale **2**
Olinda Country Cottages & Inn **4**

Haliimaile
371

Kokomo

Haleakala Highway
37

Makawao
365

394

Pukalani

390

377

4
Olinda

37

372

Kula Highway

Haleakala Highway

370

Omaopio

Pulehu

Crater Road

Waiakoa

378

378

Kula

HALEAKALA NATIONAL PARK

MAUI

Beach ✸

Kula Highway
Waiohuli

POLIPOLI STATE PARK

378

Best Western Maui Oceanfront Inn
$$ **South Maui (Kihei)**

Want to stay on the beach without paying the exhorbitant prices that usually tag oceanfront hotels? This freshly renovated small hotel is an excellent option. Like the neighboring Mana Kai Maui (see review later in this chapter), the Oceanfront Inn is located at the quietest south end of Kihei, just north of ritzy Wailea, on the golden sands of Keawakapu Beach, which offers excellent snorkeling and swimming. The Oceanfront Inn offers smaller rooms and suites than the Mana Kai's roomy apartments — making this a better choice for couples than families — but it compensates with like-new everything thanks to a 2002 renovation. Standard hotel rooms offer a queen bed with minifridge, coffeemaker, and individually controlled A/C; ceramic tile floors, plantation shutters, and tropical-style ceiling fans add a gentle island flair. The two-room suites add a pleasing tropical-style sitting room and a microwave; the extra space is well worth the cost if you can afford it. Sarento's on the Beach offers a splurge-worthy dining experience, especially for romance-seeking couples (see Chapter 11). Blue Hawaii Water Sports offers all the water toys and dive equipment you need — including PADI-certified instruction and boat dives — making this an excellent choice for wallet-watching divers and snorkelers. On-site laundry adds to the convenience.

See map p. 125. 2575 S. Kihei Rd., Kihei. ☎ *800-263-3387 or 808-879-7744. Fax: 808-874-0145.* www.mauioceanfrontinn.com *or* www.bestwestern.com. *Parking: Free! Rack rates: $99–$159 double, $159–$259 2-room suite. Deals: Excellent opportunities for discounts, including BestRates, AAA discounts, and senior rates. AE, DC, DISC, MC, V.*

Best Western Pioneer Inn
$$ **West Maui (Lahaina)**

This delightfully restored 1901 whaler's inn overlooking Lahaina Harbor blends a genuine old-time ambience with proven Best Western comforts, and it's a winning combination. Rooms are small and on the dark side, but they're cool, pretty, and comfortable, with new curtains and carpets, modern tiled baths, and coffeemakers. Deluxe rooms also have wet bars with minifridge, and suites add an additional Murphy bed. The quietest rooms face the garden courtyard pool or the massive banyan tree next door; a few have harbor views that heighten the maritime experience. Front Street–facing rooms are noisy, but shaded and furnished lanais give you a ringside seat for the sidewalk party. The hotel has an appealing indoor-outdoor restaurant and bar; the beach is a drive away, but the town couldn't be more convenient. All in all, the Best Western Pioneer Inn isn't Maui's roomiest or quietest place to stay, but it's a real charmer.

See map p. 124. At Lahaina Pier, 658 Wharf St. (at Front Street), Lahaina. ☎ *800-457-5457 or 808-661-3636. Fax: 808-667-5708.* www.pioneerinnmaui.com *or* www.bestwestern.com. *Parking: $4 in lot 2 blocks away. Rack rates: $115–$135 standard double, $150–$185 deluxe double, $165–$200 suite. Deals: Discounts for AAA and AARP members as well as seniors (55-plus); inquire about family rates and other special packages. AE, DC, DISC, MC, V.*

Fairmont Kea Lani Maui
$$$$–$$$$$ **South Maui (Wailea)**

Now under the guiding hand of the fabulous Fairmont hotel chain, this fanciful Moorish palace is just as pricey as Maui's other luxury resorts, but it gives you so much more room for your money. Spread out and enjoy a giant one-bedroom suite, complete with a gorgeous living room with full entertainment center — VCRs and CD and DVD players, plus a second TV in the bedroom — and a wet bar with coffeemaker and microwave; a mammoth marble bath with a soaking tub big enough for two, double sinks, separate shower, and terrific toiletries; and a furnished lanai that's ideal for an alfresco breakfast. The villas are even more luxurious, each boasting a gourmet kitchen, a gas barbecue and plunge pool on the private patio, and a prime on-the-sand location. Amenities include three swimming pools and two Jacuzzis, an excellent spa (second only to the neighboring Grand Wailea's), a fitness center, a full beach activities center, a wealth of daily activities and kids' programs, and excellent dining, including one of my favorite Maui restaurants, Nick's Fishmarket (see Chapter 11). It's a first-rate choice on every level. The cherry on the cake: The beach out front is simply divine.

See map p. 125. 4100 Wailea Alanui Dr., Wailea. ☎ *800-441-1414, 800-882-4100, or 808-875-4100. Fax: 808-875-1200.* www.kealani.com. *Parking: Free. Rack rates: $345–$785 suite, $1,400–$2,200 2- or 3-bedroom villa. Deals: Many available specials, including golf and spa packages, and deals that throw in a rental car or a fifth night free. Be sure to check the Web site or ask. AE, DC, DISC, MC, V.*

Staying off the beaten path

Situated at the far east end of the winding Hana Highway (Highway 36/360) and isolated from the rest of the island by a three-hour drive, Hana makes a dreamy place to kick back and stay awhile, surrounded by little but lush natural beauty. One of Maui's most popular attractions is the drive along the winding 50-plus-mile route to Hana, one of the most beautiful scenic drives in the world. (I describe the drive in detail in Chapter 13.)

Most people drive to Hana and back again in a day, which is an entirely doable trip. But it makes for a seriously long day — the curving highway has 50 or so one-lane bridges. Furthermore, because the drive boasts so many wonderful stops, simply getting there can turn into an all-day event. So consider booking a place to stay at the end of the road in lush and lovely Hana for a couple of nights. Staying in Hana is good idea, except for a few downsides: Many of the area's B&Bs and rentals require a two-night minimum stay (sometimes longer), and your dining options are pretty limited.

If you want to stay in Hana itself, I recommend the **Hotel Hana-Maui,** the **Heavenly Hana Inn,** and **Hana Oceanfront Cottages** as my absolute local favorites. (I review all in this chapter.)

Other wonderful one-of-a-kind options are available in the wonderful rural territory along the road to Hana. Elsewhere in this chapter, I review my favorites: the **Huelo Point Flower Farm,** the **Inn at Mama's Fish House,** and **Maluhia Hale.**

As an alternative to Hana, some folks who want to get away from life's stresses like to stay in Maui's cool, misty upland, on the slopes of the sleeping volcano at Maui's core. Basing yourself here gives you easy extended access to magical, barren Haleakala National Park. In this chapter, I review the Olinda Country Cottages & Inn, an Upcountry choice that offers fantastic views.

If you'd like to stay off the beaten path, a great resource is **Hawaii's Best Bed & Breakfasts** (☎ **800-262-9912** or 808-885-4550; www.bestbnb.com), which has a wonderful selection of B&Bs, inns, and vacation rentals that are inspected and approved in all the locations I've just mentioned. Hawaii's Best holds all the innkeepers it represents to a very high standard, so you can be assured of quality lodgings if you book with it. Some properties worth inquiring about in the Hana area include **Ekena,** an elegant 1,700-square-foot apartment on the lower level of a gorgeous country home right in Hana, and the oh-so-romantic, Balinese-style **Hamoa Bay Bungalow.**

Bed & Breakfast Honolulu (☎ **800-288-4666** or 808-595-7533; www.hawaiibnb.com) also offers vacation rentals in Hana, in Kula on the slopes of Haleakala, and around the island. **Bed & Breakfast Hawaii** (☎ **800-733-1632** or 808-822-7771; www.bandb-hawaii.com) can also book you into a range of vacation homes and B&Bs throughout the islands, with prices starting at $75 a night.

If you prefer not to use a third-party agency, the **Hawaii Directory of Bed-and-Breakfasts, Country Inns, and Small Hotels** (www.virtualcities.com/ons/hi/hionsdex.htm) offers direct Web links to B&Bs and vacation rentals throughout the island of Maui. Other sites that are well worth surfing for Hawaii B&Bs are **Bedand Breakfast.com** (www.bedandbreakfast.com) and **InnSite** (www.innsite.com).

For an off-the-beaten-path vacation rental — an entire house for you and the family — visit **Ohana Maui Vacations** (☎ **808-283-9875;** www.ohanamaui.com) and **Hookipa Haven** (☎ **800-398-6284;** www.hookipa.com).

For more information on bed-and-breakfasts and vacation rentals around the island, be sure to check out Chapter 6.

Four Seasons Resort Maui at Wailea
$$$$$ South Maui (Wailea)

Averaging an extra-large 640 square feet (though they're still not quite as spacious as the Fairmont Kea Lani's suites), the guest rooms are done in soft, warm yellows and feature cushy furnishings, grand and gorgeous bathrooms (among the best in Hawaii), and big lanais. About 80 percent have ocean views, but beware of those rooms that overlook the driveway — they're a real mood killer. You're better off with a gardenview room overlooking the lovely sculpture gardens and waterfalls (and most of these rooms have a bit of ocean view anyway). At $345, the mountainview rooms are a good value for pricey Maui, considering the cream-of-the-crop quality of the accommodations and service. The gorgeous grounds overflow with first-rate facilities — including the only Hawaii branch of Wolfgang Puck's legendary Spago restaurant and a sublime spa offering yoga, Pilates, and a wide variety of pampering treatments. The beach is one of Maui's finest. If you prefer to lounge poolside, you can recline in comfort under a shaded cabana or on a grassy lawn; a pool attendant even brings you chilled towels and sprays you with Evian if you break a sweat. The kids are duly pampered in an excellent activities program.

I prefer the excitement of the Grand Wailea (see the next entry in this chapter) and the spacious suites and island-style elegance of the Fairmont Kea Lani, but you can't argue with the Four Seasons's unrivaled service and star power. I find it to be a tad generic compared to, say, its spectacular sister property on the Big Island, but this Four Seasons is still a fabulous hotel — just ask the many young, hotter-than-hot celebs (like Kirsten Dunst and Britney Spears) who've made it their prefered Maui base.

See map p. 125. 3900 Wailea Alanui Dr., Wailea. ☎ *800-334-6284 or 808-874-8000. Fax: 808-874-6449.* www.fourseasons.com/maui. *Rack rates: $345–$775 double, $800–$6,500 suite. Parking: Free! Deals: Multiple package deals almost always on offer, including room-and-car, bed-and-breakfast, golf, spa, and others. Also ask about fifth-night-free deals and special family rates. AE, DC, DISC, MC, V.*

Grand Wailea Resort & Spa
$$$$$ South Maui (Wailea)

I didn't want to love this outrageous resort, but it's just too glorious to deny. This monument to monied excess won me over with its lush, art-filled grounds (boasting works by such masters as Botero, Legér, Picasso, and Warhol) and its exclusive tropical-theme-park vibe. The sigh-inducing 50,000-square-foot Spa Grande is the island's ultimate temple to the pampered life. Best of all, the grounds feature Hawaii's best water playground, a fantasy of falls, rapids, slides, grottos, hidden hot tubs and swim-up bars — the world's only water-powered elevator merely puts the finishing touch on the ultimate pool complex. If you manage to make it out to the beach, you'll find that it's one of Maui's best (equal to the sands at the Four Seasons). Rooms are huge and elegantly appointed, with luxurious marble baths. Stay in the Napua Tower if you can afford it; this exclusive 100-room hotel-within-a-hotel offers personalized concierge service plus free continental breakfast. Restaurants, shops, and lounges abound, and the high-tech Tsunami nightclub is the place to hit the dance floor in South Maui. Furthermore, both food and service are first rate, making the Grand Wailea the place to stay if you can afford to live large. And bring the kids — they'll think they've died and gone to heaven, especially after they see the whopping 20,000-square-foot kids' camp. This elegant fantasyland is an ideal place to tie the knot, too, because it's home to a picture-perfect seaside wedding chapel. Minimalists, on the other hand, should book elsewhere.

See map p. 125. 3850 Wailea Alanui Dr., Wailea. ☎ *800-888-6100 or 808-875-1234. Fax: 808-874-2442.* www.grandwailea.com. *Valet parking: $12. Rack rates: $465–$825 double, $1,650–$10,850 suite. Mandatory $15-per-night "resort fee" for "free" self-parking, "free" local and toll-free calls, in-room coffee, daily fitness classes, and other resort extras. Deals: Numerous packages are usually available, including room-and-car, bed-and-breakfast, spa, golf, kids, and more. AE, DC, DISC, MC, V.*

Hana Oceanfront Cottages
$$$ Hana

Housed in two new plantation-style buildings built by friendly California refugees Dan and Sandi Simoni, these two marvelous one-bedroom units are fully outfitted for Hana living. Each comes complete with a living room, a fully appointed kitchen (no worrying about that pesky where-to-dine problem), new, supercomfortable furniture (including beautifully made beds), a full bath, and a big lanai with ocean views. Brand-new in 1999, the property now boasts lush, mature tropical grounds. Best of all, paradise-like Hamoa Beach, East Maui's finest swimming beach — which James Michener called "the most beautiful beach in the world" — is just steps away. Say hello if you see Dan and Sandi's next-door neighbor — Oprah Winfrey recently purchased the adjacent 4 acres.

See map p. 126. Hana Highway, Hana. ☎ _**808-248-7558.**_ www.hanaoceanfront cottages.com. _Parking: Free. Rack rates: $225–$250. Discounts available for weeklong stays; 3-night minimum. MC, V._

Heavenly Hana Inn
$$$ Hana

This gorgeous Japanese-style inn was originally built in the 1950s and completely renovated in the '90s — with no dollar or attention to detail spared. It's utterly beautiful, luxuriously comfortable, and totally serene. Every room exhibits stunning woodwork and the impeccable taste of the innkeepers. The suites boast sitting rooms, little lanais, big baths with deep soaking tubs, and platform beds adorned in lavish textiles and deep, cushy futons. The two outside acres are landscaped Japanese-style with a bamboo fence, tiny bridges over a meandering stream, and lava-rock paths. The $16 two-course continental breakfast is an expanded gourmet feast served _kaiseki_ style (a Japanese feast featuring dish after dish of artfully displayed foods), and picnic lunches and afternoon tea service can be prepared to order with advance notice. Note that no children under age 15 are accepted.

See map p. 126. Hana Highway, Hana. ☎ _/Fax: **808-248-8442.**_ www.heavenlyhana inn.com. _Parking: Free! Rack rates: $190–$260 suite. Full gourmet breakfast available for $15 per person. Ask about special rates. 2-night minimum stay. AE, DISC, MC, V._

Hotel Hana-Maui
$$$$$ Hana

The best news to come out of Maui — and maybe all of Hawaii — in years is the rebirth of the Hotel Hana-Maui, a breathtaking oceanfront property that had languished in disrepair for too many years. It's now being managed by the same folks behind Big Sur's impeccable Post Ranch Inn and Fiji's Jean-Michel Cousteau Fiji Islands Resort. And sure enough, this new team has transformed the Hotel Hana-Maui into one of Maui's most magical resorts. It's reason enough alone to cruise to the end of the road to Maui's remote eastern shore.

It's a small hotel, with just 66 rooms and suites nestled in one-story Hawaiian-style cottages on meticulously landscaped grounds that slope gently to glorious Hana Bay. The expansive grounds allow for plenty of privacy and quiet relaxation, and both the setting and warmhearted staff exude an old-Hawaii feeling. Accommodations, on the other hand, boast only the most luxe comforts: Warm and welcoming interiors featuring indigenous island materials, textiles, and patterns; all of the generously apportioned units are at once designer-stylish and sigh-inducingly comfortable. The duplex Sea Ranch cottages are the most luxurious, with cathedral ceilings, gorgeous oversized bathrooms, and private lanais; about half have patio Jacuzzis. But you can't go wrong with the low-rise Bay View suites a little farther up the slope if your wallet is tighter. A lack of TVs, radios, and air-conditioning (you don't need it out here) suits the mood perfectly; no one travels to the end of the road in Hana to watch *The Sopranos* or CNN. (The common Club Room has a giant screen TV, VCR, and Internet access if you really need a fix.) A wealth of marvelous outdoor activities will keep you content — from cultural walks and horseback riding to sunbathing at Hamoa Beach, which James Michener once called the most beautiful beach in the world — as will the utterly pampering and peaceful spa.

See map p. 126. At Hana Ranch, Hana Highway, Hana. ☎ *800-321-HANA [4262] or 808-248-8211. Fax: 808-248-7202.* www.hotelhanamaui.com. *Valet parking: Free! Rack rates: $375–$425 Bay cottage for two, $495–$845 Sea Ranch cottage for two, $1,195–$2,000 2-bedroom suite or Plantation guest house. Deals: Numerous value-added packages available; call or check Web site for current offers. AE, DC, DISC, MC, V.*

Huelo Point Flower Farm
$$–$$$ East Maui (On the Road to Hana)

The Huelo Point Flower Farm is a romantic little gem on a spectacular, remote 300-foot sea cliff near a waterfall. This 2-acre estate overlooking Waipio Bay has two guest cottages, a guesthouse, and a main house available for rent. The studio-sized Gazebo Cottage has a glass-walled ocean front, a koa-wood captain's bed, a TV, a stereo, a kitchenette, a private ocean-side patio, a private hot tub, and a half-bathroom with outdoor shower. The new 900-square-foot Carriage House apartment sleeps four and has glass walls facing the mountain and sea, plus a kitchen, a den, decks, and a loft bedroom. The two-bedroom main house contains an exercise room, a fireplace, a sunken Roman bath, cathedral ceilings, and other extras. On-site is a natural pool with a waterfall and an oceanfront hot tub. You're welcome to pick fruit, vegetables, and flowers from the extensive garden, and you can use an on-site washer/dryer. Homemade scones, tree-ripened papayas, and fresh-roasted coffee start your day. Despite its seclusion, off the crooked road to Hana, you can drive to Kahului in 30 minutes or in about 20 minutes to Paia's shops and restaurants.

See map p. 126. Off Hana Highway, between mile markers 3 and 4. ☎ *808-572-1850.* www.mauiflowerfarm.com. *Parking: Free! Rack rates: $160 cottage (sleeps 2); $190 carriage house (sleeps up to 4); $350 2-bedroom guesthouse; $450 3-bedroom* *main house. All rates are for two people; extra person $20–$35. Two-night minimum stay (7-night minimum stay for main house). Deals: Discounts on weeklong stays. No credit cards.*

Hyatt Regency Maui Resort & Spa
$$$$–$$$$$ West Maui (Kaanapali)

If you like the idea of a fantasy megaresort but can't swing the price tag at the Grand Wailea, also consider this often-less-expensive alternative, located on 40 oceanfront acres at the quieter south end of appealing Kaanapali Beach. This opulent fantasyland is dotted with a riot of tropical foliage, rushing waterfalls, sparkling lagoons, and exotic wildlife. While not quite as fab as the Grand Wailea's, the half-acre pool complex is no slouch here, either; there's a lava tube slide and a rope bridge for the kids, and even a man-made beach in case the spectacular sands out front are too crowded.

The spacious guest rooms are warmly decorated in rich colors, floral prints, and Asian accents (a welcome change from the chain-standard beiges that often plague Hawaii resorts), and feature separate sitting areas and furnished lanais. The Hyatt is an excellent choice for restless vacationers, because activities include a rooftop astronomy program, tennis, world-class golf within walking distance, beach and ocean activities, and a nightly luau complete with fire dancers. When it's time to relax, give yourself over to the soothing Spa Moana, Hawaii's only oceanfront spa. The Swan Court offers very good Pacific Rim–accented continental cuisine in an ultraromantic setting for couples. Although it's not exactly an intimate experience — how could it be with 806 guest rooms? — it's a very satisfying choice nonetheless.

See map p. 124. 200 Nohea Kai Dr., Kaanapali. ☎ *800-233-1234 or 808-667-4440. Fax: 808-667-4497.* www.maui.hyatt.com. *Valet parking: $10. Self-parking: Included in $15-per-night resort fee, which also includes free local and toll-free calls, in-room coffee, health club access, and other extras. Rack rates: $345–$575 double, from $650 suite. Deals: Special deals (including fifth night free) and packages galore. AE, DC, DISC, MC, V.*

The Inn at Mama's Fish House
$$$ East Maui (On the Road to Hana)

These tropical cottages on one of Maui's most gorgeous oceanfront lots are ideal for those who want a quiet but central location. Nestled in a coconut grove on secluded Kuau Cove — just a ten-minute drive from the airport — six charming vacation rentals feature rattan furnishings, lovely local artwork, terra-cotta floors, and complete kitchens (even dishwashers). Extras like big TVs with VCR, CD players, Weber gas barbecues, laundry facilities, and tons of beach toys make this a great place to stay with friends or family. The one-bedrooms can sleep up to four — Mom and Dad on the queen bed in the bedroom, two kids on the sleeper sofa. The two-bedrooms can sleep up to six: one bedroom has a queen bed, and the second has a full bed or two twin beds, plus a sleeper sofa in the bedroom. Two-bedrooms also benefit from a prime beachfront location, while the one-bedrooms are just steps from the beach nestled in colorful tropical foliage. The divine Mama's Fish House — my favorite Maui restaurant (see Chapter 11) — is next door, and inn guests benefit from discounts at lunch and dinner. Just down the road is hip-as-can-be Paia, the fun 'n' funky surf town that serves as the gateway to the road to Hana.

See map p. 126. 799 Poho Place (off the Hana Highway in Kuau), Paia. ☎ *800-860-HULA [4852] or 808-579-9764. Fax: 808-579-8594.* www.mamasfishhouse.com. *Parking: Free! Rack rates: $175 1-bedroom unit; $475 2-bedroom unit. Three-night minimum stay. AE, DISC, MC, V.*

Kaanapali Alii
$$$$$ West Maui (Kaanapali)

If you want luxury living and condo conveniences, this high-rise beachfront complex is the place for you. These condos are Maui's finest (and priciest), but they're worth it. Each is privately owned, so décor varies, but owners are held to a high standard. The one- and two-bedroom apartments are universally large (between 1,500 and 1,900 square feet) and come with a fully equipped gourmet kitchen, huge living room and dining room, two TVs and VCR, two full baths (even in the one-bedrooms), washer/dryer, and private lanais. The luxuriant grounds feature a fitness room, tennis facilities, a heated pool with hot tub and poolside snack service plus a separate kids' pool, a beach activities center, and poolside gas grills for fun family outings. Among the resortlike amenities are daily maid service; concierge, bell, valet, and room service; complimentary kids' club activities in summer; and even grocery delivery and a resident tennis pro.

See map p. 124. 50 Nohea Kai Dr., Kaanapali. ☎ *800-642-6284 or 808-661-3339. Fax: 808-667-1145.* www.classicresorts.com. *Parking: Free. Rack rates: $350–$525 1-bedroom, $475–$740 2-bedroom. Three-night minimum stay. Deals: Numerous deals are usually on offer, including fifth-night-free, seventh-night-free, room-and-car, and romance packages. AE, DC, MC, V.*

Kaanapali Beach Hotel
$$$ West Maui (Kaanapali)

The Kaanapali Beach Hotel is the last hotel left in Hawaii that gives you a real resort experience in this price range. It's older, and it's not luxurious, but it boasts a genuine spirit of aloha that's absent in so many other hotels. Set beachfront around a wide, grassy lawn with a whale-shaped pool, three low-rise wings house spacious, well-maintained rooms. Still rather motel-like, they're nevertheless perfectly comfortable and feature all the conveniences, plus lanais overlooking the pretty yard or beach. Tiki torches, hula, and music create an irresistible Hawaiian ambience every evening, and the service is some of the friendliest around. An extensive Hawaiian program goes beyond the standard hula lessons to include lauhala weaving, lei making, and cultural tours. A kids' program, three good restaurants, and coin-op laundry are also on-site. It's one of my all-time favorites. *Travel + Leisure* agrees with me: The magazine has dubbed this Hawaii's top hotel for value, and second-best hotel in the world for less than $200 a night.

See map p. 124. 2525 Kaanapali Pkwy., Kaanapali. ☎ **800-262-8450** *or 808-661-0011. Fax: 808-667-5978.* www.kaanapalibeachhotel.com. *Self-parking: $5. Valet parking: $7. Rack rates: $169–$300 double, $255–$610 suite. Deals: Free breakfast, free car, free night, golf, and romance packages are almost always available, as well as senior (50-plus) and corporate discounts and Internet specials. AE, DC, DISC, MC, V.*

Kahana Sunset
$$–$$$ West Maui (Kahana/Napili)

These oceanfront condos are an excellent value, one of Maui's best. The attractive wooden complex stair-steps down pretty terraced grounds to a petite but perfect white-sand-fringed swimming cove. The apartments are roomy enough to accommodate families (especially if you book one of the two-bedroom units, which boast two full bathrooms). Every unit has nice island-style furniture; a complete kitchen with dishwasher, microwave, and a refrigerator with an ice maker; washer/dryer; A/C and ceiling fans; VCR and sleeper sofa in the living room; and a big lanai with a terrific view. Nestled between the coastline and the road above, the complex is much more private than many on this condo coast. On-site are a lovely heated pool and Jacuzzi, a separate kids' pool, barbecues, and beach showers. Furthermore, daily maid service (not a given in condos) makes it actually feel like you're on vacation.

See map p. 123. 4909 Lower Honoapiilani Hwy., at the northern end of Kahana (8 miles north of Lahaina). ☎ **800-669-1488**, *800-367-7052, or 808-669-8011. Fax: 808-669-9170.* www.kahanasunset.com *or* www.premier-hawaii.com. *Parking: Free. Rack rates: $130–$240 1-bedroom, $195–$375 2-bedroom. Three-night minimum. Deals: Car-and-condo packages, special rates, and Internet offers often available, so always search for discounts. AE, MC, V.*

Kapalua Bay Hotel & Ocean Villas
$$$$$ West Maui (Kapalua)

The standard rooms are just a step above dowdy, but a downright phenomenal setting and an open, airy island feeling brings loyal guests coming back for more. Sprawling over 18 oceanfront acres, the lush grounds command gorgeous views in every direction. The beach cove (named "Best in America" more than once) is virtually private and excellent for swimming, and golf and tennis facilities don't get any better. Additional perks include two pools, a fitness center, a full-service beach activities desk, a great kids' program, and easy access to classes at the Kapalua Golf Academy and Kapalua Art School. The amenity-laden one- and two-bedroom Bay Villas — freestanding luxury homes with full kitchen, washer/dryer, and multiple lanais — make a great choice for families who have the necessary cash. Bay Villa guests also enjoy three private pools. For the ultimate in Kapalua luxury, score a stay in one of the new Coconut Grove Villas, where a mere $4,500 a night scores you a three-bedroom luxury oceanfront condo (at this price, it *better* be luxurious) with round-the-clock butler service.

See map p. 123. 1 Bay Dr., Kapalua. ☎ **800-782-9488** *or 808-669-5656. Fax: 808-669-4694.* www.kapaluabayhotel.com *or* www.luxurycollection.com. *Valet parking: $15. Rack rates: $390–$630 double; suites and villas $540–$4,500. Mandatory "resort fee" of $13 per day for welcome lei, local and toll-free phone calls, use of fitness center, lobby coffee and tea, in-room safe, incoming faxes, resort shuttles, self parking, and daily newspaper. Deals: Excellent package deals often include unlimited golf, activity, and romance options, so be sure to inquire. AE, DC, MC, V.*

Koa Resort
$–$$ South Maui (Kihei)

These nice condos sit right across the street from the ocean and make a good choice for active families on tight budgets: On-site are two tennis courts, a very nice swimming pool, a hot tub, and an 18-hole putting green. The spacious, privately owned one-, two-, and three-bedroom units are fully equipped and have plenty of room for even a large clan. Each comes with a full kitchen — complete with dishwasher, microwave, and coffeemaker — and a large lanai with ceiling fans, and washer/dryer. The majority of two- and three-bedroom units have multiple bathrooms. The smaller units have showers only, so ask for one with a tub if it matters to you. Also, for maximum peace and quiet, ask for a unit removed from Kihei Road.

See map p. 125. 811 S. Kihei Rd. (between Kulanihakoi Street and Namauu Place), Kihei. Reservations c/o Bello Realty (Maui Beach Homes). ☎ **800-541-3060** *or 808-879-3328. Fax: 808-875-1483.* www.bellomaui.com. *Parking: Free! Rack rates: $85–$110 1-bedroom, $100–$130 2-bedroom, $135–$180 3-bedroom. AE, MC, V.*

Lahaina Shores Beach Resort
$$$ West Maui (Lahaina)

This pleasant plantation-style complex of studios and one-bedroom suites sits right on the sand at the quiet end of Lahaina, within easy walking distance of restaurants, shopping, and entertainment, but nicely out of the noisy fray. The hotel isn't exactly what you'd call stylish, but the pastel-hued units are comfortable and well-outfitted — and the price is right, especially considering the on-the-beach location. Even the smallest unit is a spacious 550 square feet. Every one comes with a fully equipped, like-new kitchen with a microwave, sitting and dining areas, and a furnished lanai. Obviously, those units overlooking the waves and the island of Lanai across the channel are best, but the mountain views aren't shabby. Outside is a lovely grassy lawn with a small pool, hot tub, and lounge chairs; just beyond it is a narrow stretch of swimming beach (first-time surfers often learn on the low-riding waves). Other amenities include on-site laundry facilities and tennis courts just across the street.

See map p. 124. 475 Front St. (near Shaw Street), Lahaina. ☎ **800-642-6284** *or 808-661-3339. Fax: 808-667-1145.* www.lahainashores.com *or* www.classicresorts.com. *Parking: $3. Rack rates: $180–$215 studio, $250–$280 1-bedroom. Deals: Fifth-night-free specials offered at press time. Also ask about room-and-car packages, romance packages, and other available discounts. AE, MC, V.*

Maluhia Hale
$$ East Maui (On the Road to Hana)

My heart just sings when I think of Maluhia Hale (ma-loo-*he*-ah *ha*-lay); it's one of the most magical places I've ever stayed. The sole guest accommodation is an open-plan cottage with a wall of windows and a simple but gracious old Hawaiian vibe. A sense of peace reigns there: You enter through an open and airy screened veranda, which leads to a glassed-in sitting room with a TV, a king bed impeccably made up in lacy white linen, a stocked kitchenette with nostalgic charm, and a traditional Hawaiian bathhouse with an old clawfoot tub and a wonderfully romantic indoor/outdoor shower. Innkeeper Diane Garrett has filled the cottage with a beautiful selection of antiques that make it feel cozy rather than formal. She also leaves charming notes throughout (like "Bang the top of the TV twice if the reception is bad"), which make the cottage just that much more darling. Diane does light housekeeping daily; at the end of the day, you return to a softly lit place filled with sweet-smelling flowers. Not fancy, but idyllic through and through — you'll remember this place forever.

Situated up a dirt-road turnoff part way down the Hana Highway, Maluhia Hale isn't the most convenient place to stay on Maui, but its remoteness adds to its romance. Pristine waterfall pools are just a walk away.

*See map p. 126. Off Hana Highway, Haiku. ☎/Fax: **808-572-2959**. Parking: Free! Rack rates: $110–$145 cottage (holiday rates slightly higher). Rates include continental breakfast. Three-night minimum stay. No credit cards.*

Mana Kai Maui
$–$$$ South Maui (Kihei)

Situated on a beautiful white-sand beach with excellent snorkeling, this eight-story hotel-condo hybrid is one of my favorite affordable choices. About half of the units are hotel rooms, which are smallish but offer great value. The larger apartments feature full like-new kitchens, nice island-style furnishings, well-maintained baths, and open living rooms that lead to small lanais with ocean views. These are older units, but they're clean and comfortable, thanks to daily maid service. A coin-op laundry is located on each floor, a restaurant and lounge is downstairs, and a nice pool and a grassy lawn with beach chairs complement that fabulous beach. Management is friendly and conscientious. But the Mana Kai's real ace in the hole is its location: It lies on Wailea's doorstep, on the prettiest, most quiet end of Kihei, away from the strip-mall fray.

*See map p. 125. 2960 S. Kihei Rd., Kihei (just before Wailea). ☎ **800-367-5242** (800-663-2101 from Canada) or 808-879-2778. Fax: 808-879-7825. www.crhmaui.com. Parking: Free. Rack rates: $95–$135 double hotel room, $175–$245 1-bedroom, $220–$300 2-bedroom. $25 reservation fee added to every booking. Deals: Excellent car-and-condo packages usually on offer; also ask about other available specials. Discounts available on monthly stays. AE, MC, V.*

Maui Coast Hotel
$$–$$$ South Maui (Kihei)

After a $2.5-million renovation a couple of years back, I recommend this affordable hotel for its fresh feel, great package deals, and its central (if rather unpretty) location — about a block from the beach and a walk away from restaurants, shopping, and nightlife. This hotel isn't the Four Seasons, so don't expect luxury — but the nicely designed rooms feature good-value extras, including sitting areas, coffeemakers, minifridges, Nintendo game systems, and furnished lanais. Add a pretty good restaurant, room service, free use of laundry facilities, two pools (one for the kids) with poolside service, two Jacuzzis, a restaurant, and tennis courts (with lights for night play), and you end up with a full-service hotel at a bargain price. The suites offer families excellent value, especially if you can find a package to suit you.

See map p. 125. 2259 S. Kihei Rd. (at Ke Alii Alanui Drive), Kihei. ☎ *800-895-6284, 800-663-1144, or 808-874-6284.* www.mauicoasthotel.com *or* www.westcoast hotels.com. *Parking: Free! Rack rates: $165–$185 double, $215 alcove suite, $255 1-bedroom suite. Deals: Inquire about golf and romance packages; room-and-car and fifth-night-free packages from $185 at press time. AE, DC, DISC, MC, V.*

Mauian Hotel on Napili Beach
$$–$$$ West Maui (Kahana/Napili)

These studio units have a pleasing old-fashioned Hawaiian style. The family-run Mauian is perched above a beautiful half-mile-long, white-sand beach with great swimming and snorkeling. It has a pool with lounge chairs, umbrellas, and tables on the sun deck, and the verdant grounds are bursting with tropical color. The rooms feature hardwood floors, Indonesian-style furniture, fridges, coffeemakers, and big lanais with great sunset views. The rooms don't have phones or TVs (this place really is about getting away from it all), but the large *ohana* (family) room does have a TV with a VCR and an extensive library of videos. Complimentary coffee, coin-op washer/dryers, and phones and fax service are available. Great restaurants are just a five-minute walk away, and Kapalua Resort is up the street.

See map p. 123. 5441 Lower Honoapiilani Rd., Napili. ☎ *800-367-5034 or 808-669-6205. Fax: 808-669-0129.* www.mauian.com. *44 units. Parking: Free! Rack rates: High season $165–$195 double; low season $145–$180 double. Rates include continental breakfast. Extra person $10. Children under 5 stay free in parent's room. Deals: Check for Internet specials, which were as low as $99 double at press time. AE, DISC, MC, V.*

Maui Guest House
$$ West Maui (Lahaina)

This appealing and professionally run bed-and-breakfast is an excellent value and offers more amenities than many of the "full-service" hotels just down the road in Kaanapali. The spacious home offers four guest accommodations, all mostly suited to couples looking for romance at a budget rate. All rooms have queen beds (three have an extra twin bed if you're traveling with a child or a friend), plus a private bathroom, TV with DVD player, a fridge, and — the coup de grace — a private lanai with its own private Jacuzzi. You're welcome to make yourself at home throughout the house, which boasts parquet floors, floor-to-ceiling windows, a large and lovely swimming pool with comfortable lounging chairs and a hammock, a well-outfitted kitchen for your use, a 300-plus DVD library, and laundry facilities (no quarters needed). The house even has a wireless network throughout for laptop toters, plus a computer you can use if you just want to check your e-mail once or twice during your trip. A generous continental breakfast is laid out each day, and the owners can help you arrange just about every island activity. The nearest beach is about a block away.

See map p. 124. 1620 Ainakea Rd. (off Fleming Rd.), Lahaina. ☎ *800-621-8942 or 808-661-8085.* www.mauiguesthouse.com. *Parking: Free! Rack rates: $129 double. AE, DC, DISC, MC, V.*

Napili Bay
$$ West Maui (Kahana/Napili)

You can find this excellent bargain right on Napili's beautiful half-mile white-sand beach. This small, two-story complex is perfect for an affordable romantic getaway; the sound of the waves creates a comfortable and relaxing atmosphere. The studio apartments are definitely small, but still, you have a full kitchen (with fridge and coffeemaker), a comfortable queen bed, a queen sleeper sofa that lets you sleep two more (if you don't mind lots of togetherness), a TV with VCR, and a spacious lanai where you can sit and watch the sun set. Louvered windows and ceiling fans keep the units cool during the day. You have plenty of restaurants and a convenience store within walking distance, you're about 10 to 15 minutes away from Lahaina and some great golf courses. The coin-op washer/dryers and a barbecue are also nice features. The beach right out front is one of the best on the coast, with great swimming and snorkeling right outside your door. Book early because this place fills up fast. Attention, Internet addicts: A few units have high-speed Internet access, so ask for one if you want it.

See map p. 123. 33 Hui Dr. (off Lower Honoapiilani Highway, in Napili). Bookings handled by Maui Beachfront Rentals, 256 Papalaua St., Lahaina. ☎ *888-661-7200 or 808-661-3500. Fax: 808-661-5210.* www.mauibeachfront.com. *Parking: Free! Rack rates: $125–$145 studio. Five-night minimum stay. Deals: 10 percent discount for stays of 21 days or more (lucky you!). MC, V.*

*If Napili Bay is booked — or you need a larger unit — inquire with **Maui Beachfront Rentals** (☎ **888-661-7200** or 808-661-3500;* www.mauibeachfront.com*), which offers good-value condo rentals throughout West Maui and in Maalaea, the appealing harbor town situated on the "neck" of Maui, on the way to Kihei.*

Napili Kai Beach Resort
$$$–$$$$ **West Maui (Kahana/Napili)**

Make yourselves right at home at this terrific complex of bright one- and two-story units embracing its own wonderful, white-sand snorkeling beach. All but a handful of basic hotel rooms have lovely tropical-modern décor, a large lanai, and top-notch kitchenettes (all with a microwave, some with a dishwasher); the hotel rooms have minifridges and coffeemakers. The one-bedrooms have sleeping accommodations in both rooms — usually a king bed in one room, two twin beds in the other — making this configuration great for families; some even have a second bathroom. The two-bedrooms can sleep as many as six or seven, and all have a second bath. The Kehaka suites unite two or three adjoining hotel rooms or studios in one value-priced package for families or shares. Most, but not all, units offer A/C, so ask if you want it (you only need it in summer); otherwise, ceiling fans do the trick.

The complex has a nice restaurant and bar, a beach pagoda serving daytime snacks and drinks and doling out snorkel gear for your free use, daily maid service, four pools and a hot tub, barbecues, a fitness room, dry cleaning as well as self-serve laundry, two putting greens (great for practicing your tee-offs for nearby Kapalua's championship greens), and the Makai Massage and Bodywork Center for Hawaiian *lomi lomi* massages, European facials, and more. During family seasons — Easter, summer, and Christmas — kids 6 to 12 can enjoy the supervised Keiki Club, with two to three hours of activities daily (except Sunday). Help yourself to free coffee every morning and tea every afternoon. This place has a very loyal following, so book way in advance.

See map p. 123. 5900 Honoapiilani Rd., Napili (at the extreme north end of Napili, next to Kapalua). ☎ *800-367-5030 or 808-669-6271. Fax: 808-669-0086.* www.napilikai.com. *Parking: Free. Rack rates: $190–$245 double, $220–$325 studio, $360–$515 1-bedroom or 2-room Keaka suite, $525–$735 2-bedroom or 3-room Keaka suite. Deals: Ask about room-and-car, bed-and-breakfast, fifth-night-free, and spa packages. AE, MC, V.*

Making yourself at home: Condos

Condominium apartments are one of Maui's most appealing and cost-effective accommodations options, because they're outfitted like a full-service home and can accommodate anywhere from two to eight vacationers in one, two, or three bedrooms. You can't pick a better way to travel as a family or in a group, but even couples enjoy the extra space and homestyle amenities.

In addition to the excellent options already listed — including **Aston at the Maui Banyan, Kaanapali Alii,** and **The Whaler on Kaanapali Beach,** just to name a few — a number of booking agencies offer one-stop shopping for condo rentals all over the island.

The **Hawaii Condo Exchange** (☎ 800-442-0404 or 323-436-0300; www.hawaiicondo exchange.com) is a Southern California–based agency that acts as a consolidator for condo properties throughout the islands, including a number of excellent choices on Maui. The Exchange works to match you up with the place that's right for you and tries to get you a good deal.

For a complete selection of upscale condos throughout sunny, luxury-minded Wailea, reach out to **Destination Resorts Hawaii** (☎ 877-347-0347 or 808-891-6249; www.drhmaui.com). Destination Resorts generally handles first-class properties boasting plenty of deluxe amenities. Prices start as low as $180 for a studio and go as high as $1,200 per night for a spacious oceanfront four-bedroom destination. High-speed Internet access is available for virtual surfers.

If you like the sound of the tranquil Kapalua resort but the luxury hotel rates are out of your league, consider renting an elegant condo or vacation home at **Kapalua Villas** (☎ 800-545-0018 or 808-669-8088; www.kapaluavillas.com). Nightly rates range from $199 for a one-bedroom apartment with a fairway view to $500 for an oceanfront three-bedroom apartment — not bad, considering you enjoy the same delicious perks and spectacular views of your much-higher-paying neighbors (including Kelsey Grammer, who owns his own Kapalua spread). The three- to five-bedroom freestanding luxury vacation homes run from $1,500 to $7,500 nightly. Whether you go large or small, you're sure to be pleased with your first-class accommodation.

Bello Realty (☎ 800-541-3060 or 808-879-3328; www.bellomaui.com) specializes in affordable sleeps on the South Maui coast: Koa Resort (reviewed earlier in this chapter) is just one of many good bargains. Bello represents affordable condos throughout the Kihei/Wailea area, with prices starting as low as $85 in the low season. I've received plenty of good feedback from vacationers who've used Bello and come away with an excellent beachfront bargain and good service results, so I'm quite confident about the quality and values that Bello offers.

Condominium Rentals Hawaii (☎ 800-367-5242, 800-663-2101 from Canada, or 808-879-2778; www.crhmaui.com) also books condos throughout Kihei. The car-and-condo packages and other regular specials can really add to the value of these units.

Maui Beachfront Rentals (☎ 888-661-7200 or 808-661-3500; www.mauibeachfront.com) can book you into a range of good apartments along West Maui's condo coast. The studios at the Napili Bay, which start as low as $125, are a great value for budget-minded couples. You may even be able to save a few dollars at two of my favorite Kaanapali Beach condo complexes: The Whaler and Kaanapali Alii (reviewed in this chapter).

Most companies that offer all-inclusive travel packages to Maui can book you into any number of condos, as can your travel agent; see Chapter 5 for details on booking a pay-one-price travel package.

For more insight on the pros and cons of opting for a condo — or even a full-service vacation rental home — on Maui, see Chapter 6.

Noelani Condominium Resort
$$ West Maui (Kahana/Napili)

I stand by all my recommendations — but that doesn't mean I didn't get a teensy bit nervous when my old boss said that she was going to take me up on one. So I was thrilled when she came home from Maui confirming my own observations — that this top-notch oceanfront condo is a stellar value and a great place to stay. All the well-maintained apartments sport kitchens, VCRs, ceiling fans (no A/C), and spectacular ocean views; all but the studios have dishwashers and washer/dryers, too. (Laundry is available for studio dwellers.) Best is the Antherium building, where apartments have ocean-facing lanais just 20 feet from the surf. Concierge and midweek maid service, two freshwater pools (one heated for night swimming), and an oceanfront Jacuzzi round out the good value. You're invited to a continental breakfast orientation on the first day of your stay, and mai tai parties in the evenings, while oceanfront barbecues are ideal for family outings. Next door is a sandy cove that's popular with snorkelers, but you may find yourself driving to a prettier beach; at these prices, you won't mind.

See map p. 123. 4095 Lower Honoapiilani Rd., Kahana. ☎ 800-367-6030 or 808-669-8374. Fax: 808-669-7904. www.noelani-condo-resort.com. *Rack rates: $107–$142 studio, $157–$165 1-bedroom, $237 2-bedroom, $297 3-bedroom. Three-night minimum stay. Parking: Free! Deals: Check for 5 percent Internet booking discount, 10 percent discount on monthly stays, weekly discounts for seniors and AAA members, and honeymoon specials. AE, MC, V.*

Ohana Maui Islander
$$ West Maui (Lahaina)

Run by Outrigger, the value-minded, Hawaii-based hotel chain, this well-managed plantation-style complex offers one of Maui's best deals. A few hotel rooms (with coffeemaker and minifridge) are available, but most of the spacious units are apartment-style studios and one- and two-bedrooms (some of which can be linked to form a three-bedroom), all with fully outfitted kitchens (some with microwaves). In the last couple of years, all the rooms have been renovated and brightened. The grounds are tropically lush and feature coin-op laundry, tennis courts, barbecues, and a pool. The larger units are perfect for families; your kids will love the heart-of-Lahaina location, and you'll appreciate the tranquil ambience that results from a peaceful side-street location (a rarity in Lahaina). The complex is very quiet in general, but ask for a unit away from the highway for minimum intrusion. Rack rates are high, but discounts and stellar package deals abound.

See map p. 124. 660 Wainee St. (between Dickenson and Prison streets), Lahaina. ☎ 800-462-6262 or 808-667-9766. Fax: 808-661-3733. www.ohanahotels.com. *Parking: $5. Rack rates: $149 double, $179 studio, $209 1-bedroom, $299 2-bedroom. Deals: Better-than-average discounts for AAA and AARP members and seniors (50-plus), plus corporate, government, and military discounts. Ask about heavily discounted SimpleSaver rates and first-night-free, bed-and-breakfast, room-and-car, and other package deals. AE, DC, DISC, MC, V.*

Old Wailuku Inn at Ulupono
$$ Central Maui (Wailuku)

If you're charmed by the notion of old-time Hawaii, book into this 1920s home, located in the historic town of Wailuku. Innkeepers Tom and Janice Fairbanks have restored the house (a cross between Craftsman and plantation style) very nicely, although a few negatives — such as yellow safety tape on the hardwood stairs — undermine the ambiance. Janice has used her impeccable eye to fill the home with island-style bamboo and Asian antiques. Each of the seven guest rooms in the main house is decorated with a Hawaiian heirloom quilt and top-quality everything, including an oversize luxury bathroom; unfortunately, housekeepers took the gorgeous quilt off the bed the first time they made up my room, folded it inside out and stored it for the duration of my week's stay, so I never got to enjoy it. Though the bathrooms are large, they tend to lack storage space. Still, the furnishings are oversized, cushy, and invite you to kick back and make yourself at home.

In 2002, the inn added three new units in a modern annex called the Vagabond's House (named to honor Don Blanding, the "vagabond poet laureate" of Hawaii). Sig Zane, Hawaii's premier fabric designer, created custom linens inspired by Hawaiian flowers for each of these wonderful new rooms. These units are a better option for light sleepers, because noise can travel a bit in the main house. The beach is a drive away, but the central location puts Maui within easy reach — plus, for people in an acquisitive mood, Wailuku is lined with antiques shops.

See map p. 125. 2199 Kahookele St. (at High Street), Wailuku. ☎ *800-305-4899 or 808-244-5897. Fax: 808-242-9600.* www.mauiinn.com. *Parking: Free! Rack rates: $120–$180 double. Rates include full gourmet breakfast. Two-night minimum stay. AE, DC, DISC, MC, V.*

Olinda Country Cottages & Inn
$$ Upcountry

On a lush protea farm, this enchanting B&B on the slopes of Haleakala is surrounded by 35,000 acres of ranch lands (with miles of great hiking trails). This huge and beautifully furnished home has large windows with incredible panoramic views of Maui. Upstairs are two guest rooms with antique beds, private full bathrooms, TVs, fridges, and separate entrances. Connected to the main house but with its own private entrance, the Pineapple Suite has a full kitchen, an antiques-filled living room, a full bathroom, and a separate bedroom. A separate 1,000-square-foot cottage is the epitome of cozy country luxury, with a fireplace, a queen bedroom, cushioned window seats (with great sunset views), and cathedral ceilings. The 950-square-foot Hidden Cottage features three decks, a full kitchen, a washer/dryer, and a private hot tub for two.

Restaurants are a 15-minute drive away in Makawao, and beaches are another 15 minutes beyond that. You'll truly be away from civilization at this charming inn.

See map p. 126. 2660 Olinda Rd., a 15-minute drive from Makawao. ☎ **800-932-3435** *or 808-572-1453. Fax: 808-573-5326.* www.mauibnbcottages.com. *Parking: Free! Rack rates: $140 double (includes continental breakfast); $140 suite (includes first morning's breakfast in fridge); $195–$245 cottage for 2 (includes first morning's breakfast in fridge). Extra person $25. Two-night minimum stay for rooms and suite, three-night minimum for cottages. No credit cards.*

Outrigger Maui Eldorado Resort
$$$ West Maui (Kaanapali)

These spacious condos — all with full kitchens, washer/dryers, and daily maid service — were built back in the good old days when land in Kaanapali was cheap, contractors took pride in their work, and visitors expected spacious accommodations with views from every window. It may be of late-'60s vintage, but the Outrigger chain keeps quality and maintenance high. This resort is a wonderful choice for families, with big, comfy units, grassy areas that are perfect for running off all that excess kid energy, and a shoreline that's usually safe for swimming. Three pools, barbecue areas, shops, and a coin-op laundry round out the appeal.

See map p. 124. 2661 Kekaa Dr., Kaanapali. ☎ **800-688-7444** *or 808-661-0021. Fax: 808-667-7039.* www.outrigger.com. *Parking: Free! Rack rates: $195–$240 studio double, $245–$295 1-bedroom (sleeps up to 4), $355–$425 2-bedroom (up to 6). Deals: The Outrigger chain is the king of package deals, including fifth-night-free, frequent-flier, and room-and-car packages. Discounts available for seniors and military personnel. AE, DC, DISC, MC, V.*

Outrigger Palms at Wailea
$$$ South Maui (Wailea)

This freshly renovated villa-style apartment complex is an excellent choice if a sunny Wailea location appeals to you but you just don't want to shell out for one of those ridiculously expensive resorts. The smart, upscale complex boasts contemporary Southwestern-style buildings spread over tidy greens. The modern apartments are quality furnished and feature all the expected amenities, including a fully outfitted kitchen, fully furnished lanai, VCR, and washer/dryer. A very nice pool and hot tub are on-site, and championship Wailea golf and tennis facilities are right at hand. Daily maid service and concierge-style desk service are part of the package. Guests have easy access to excellent Ulua Beach, located just across the street.

See map p. 125. 3200 Wailea Alanui Dr., Wailea. ☎ **800-688-7444** *or 808-879-5800. Fax: 808-874-3723.* www.outrigger.com. *Parking: Free! Rack rates: $235–$265 1-bedroom, $279–$305 2-bedroom. Deals: Better-than-average discounts for AAA* *and AARP members and seniors (50-plus), plus corporate, government, and military discounts. Fifth-night-free, bed-and-breakfast, and room-and-car packages regularly on offer. AE, DC, DISC, MC, V.*

Plantation Inn
$$–$$$ West Maui (Lahaina)

This charming Victorian-style hotel in the heart of Lahaina offers both in-town convenience and old-fashioned romance. It's actually of 1990s vintage, but those modern extras — like soundproofing (a plus in downtown Lahaina), VCRs, fridges, and private bathrooms (some with shower only) — don't detract from the period appeal. Deluxe rooms have lanais, and a few have kitchenettes. No. 17 is a standout for romantics, with a writing desk and a canopy bed, while light and spacious No. 20 features a terrific kitchen and makes an excellent family suite. The inn wraps around a nice, large tiled pool and deck with a hot tub. On-site are coin-op laundry facilities and Gerard's, a top-notch French restaurant. The staff is excellent. You have to drive to a good beach, but Lahaina Harbor is a walk away (great for early-morning snorkel cruises).

See map p. 124. 174 Lahainaluna Rd. (between Wainee and Luakini streets), Lahaina. ☎ **800-433-6815** *or 808-667-9225. Fax: 808-667-9293.* www.theplantationinn. com. *Parking: Free! (A rarity in Lahaina.) Rack rates: $157–$215 double, $220–$255 suite. Rates include continental breakfast. Deals: 10 percent discounts for long stays (7 nights or more). $10 discounts for AAA members, military personnel, and seniors over 50. Ask about gourmet, honeymoon, rental-car, and other packages, and check for great Internet specials. AE, DC, DISC, MC, V.*

Punahoa Beach Apartments
$–$$ South Maui (Kihei)

With the best location in Kihei, this friendly little complex is a bona fide beachfront bargain. The setting — off noisy, traffic-congested Kihei Road, on a quiet side street that faces the ocean — is fabulous: A grassy lawn extends down to the sand, where great offshore snorkeling awaits, and a popular surfing spot sits just next door. Coin-op laundry is on-site, and markets and restaurants are a stroll away. The apartments aren't fancy, but they're nicer than you'd expect for the money; each has a fully equipped kitchen and a lanai with great ocean views. Only one unit has A/C, but ceiling fans draw in the trade winds. Guests keep coming back, so reserve your bargain unit as far in advance as possible.

See map p. 125. 2142 Iliili Rd. (off S. Kihei Road, near Kamaole Beach Park I), Kihei. ☎ **800-564-4380** *or 808-879-2720. Fax: 808-875-9147.* www.punahoabeach.com. *Parking: Free! Rack rates: $94–$130 studio, $130–$200 1-bedroom, $160–$220 2-bedroom. Five-night minimum stay. Deals: 10 percent discount on stays of 10 nights or more Apr–Nov; 15 percent discount on stays of 21 nights or more year-round. AE, DC, DISC, MC, V.*

Ritz-Carlton Kapalua
$$$$–$$$$$ West Maui (Kapalua)

Situated at the end of the road in glorious Kapalua, Maui's most gorgeous planned resort development, the Ritz is a destination resort by default alone. But you won't need to hop in the car every day in search of fun, because everything is right at hand. You find a small but fabulous beach and activities galore, including Kapalua's 54 holes of world-class, tournament-quality golf, plus the resort's justifiably renowned art school for vacationers who want to feed a creative appetite. The natural setting — on 50 terraced oceanfront acres, surrounded by century-old Norfolk pines and ironwood trees — is breathtaking. The spacious and tropically gorgeous rooms live up to the chain's usual high standard, with heavenly featherbeds and extra-large marble baths. The dining is excellent (especially the superb sushi bar), the amenities are extensive (including a full-service spa and the outstanding Ritz Kids program, so bring 'em along), and the service is unsurpassed. Designed to look like a grand plantation house, the hotel is airy and graceful, with a gracious pool area, two hot tubs, and a professional croquet lawn. You get what you pay for at this spectacular resort — and, frankly, it's less overpriced than so many of Maui's resorts are these days. You may find it worthwhile to spend a few extra dollars for a club-level room; club guests enjoy individualized concierge service and five — yes, five — complimentary food presentations throughout the day, including a generous morning continental spread.

See map p. 123. 1 Ritz-Carlton Dr., Kapalua. ☎ *800-241-4333 or 808-669-6200. Fax: 808-665-0026.* www.ritzcarlton.com. *Self-parking: Free! Valet parking: $10. Rack rates: $340–$500 double, suites from $610. Mandatory $15-per-night "resort fee" covers such amenities as shuttle service, use of fitness center, kids' program, and other extras. Deals: Romance, golf, room-and-car, and other packages often available. AE, DC, DISC, MC, V.*

Sheraton Maui
$$$$–$$$$$ West Maui (Kaanapali)

This expansive resort hotel boasts the best location on Kaanapali Beach: on a spectacular stretch of sand at the foot of Black Rock, one of Maui's best offshore snorkel spots. This Sheraton is ideal for people who don't care for the forced formality or over-the-top excesses that often go hand-in-hand with resort vacations. The Sheraton Maui has an easygoing, open style, and great facilities for families and active types, including a nice fitness center and an open-air spa. After a recent renovation, the resort is looking great, with a new lagoonlike pool that features lava-rock waterways, wooden bridges, and an open-air whirlpool. You're greeted with a lei upon arrival, and then the valet takes you and your luggage straight to your room so that you don't stand in line. The big rooms are simple yet comfortable (with nice extras like minifridges and coffeemakers). A class of oversized two-room suites is dedicated to families. Restaurants and bars, a nightly torch-lighting and cliff-diving show, a terrific year-round kids' program, tennis courts, and plenty of other extras add to the appeal.

See map p. 124. 2605 Kaanapali Pkwy., Kaanapali. ☎ *800-782-9488 or 808-661-0031. Fax: 808-661-0458.* www.sheraton-maui.com. *Valet parking: $5. Rack rates: $350–$630 double, family suite $750, luxury suites from $850. Mandatory "resort fee" of $14 per day for "free" self-parking, newspaper delivery, local and toll-free phone calls, in-room coffee, and fitness center access. Deals: Special rates and/or package deals are almost always available, including family, romance, and rental-car deals. Also ask for AAA-member and senior discounts and look for Internet specials. AE, DC, DISC, MC, V.*

Wailea Marriott, an Outrigger Resort
$$$$–$$$$$ South Maui (Wailea)

This is the oldest and least glamorous of Wailea's resorts, but it's the most authentically Hawaiian of the bunch. The open-air 1970s-style hotel is airy, comfortable, and roomier than its younger neighbors, and a $25-million upgrade in 2000 added a dash of contemporary tropical luxury to an already-appealing property. Eight buildings, all low-rise except for an eight-story tower, are thoughtfully spread over 22 gracious acres, with lots of open park-like space and a half-mile of prime oceanfront. Minifridges, hair dryers, and lanais come standard in the spacious rooms. The resort offers a comprehensive kids' program for *keiki* ages 5 to 13, plus three pools — including a kid-friendly water activities playground complete with a pair of water slides — and a terrific beach out front. A good indoor/outdoor restaurant and nightly Hawaiian entertainment, coin-op laundry, a newly renovated fitness center, and the full-service Mandara Spa and salon make life easier for the grownups in your group, too.

See map p. 125. 3700 Wailea Alanui Dr., Wailea. ☎ *800-688-7444 or 808-879-1922. Fax: 808-874-8331.* www.outriggerwailea.com. *Parking: Free! Rack rates: $340–$525 double, $650–$3,000 suite. Deals: Better-than-average discounts for AAA and AARP members and seniors (50-plus), plus corporate, government, and military discounts. Fifth-night-free, bed-and-breakfast, room-and-car, and spa packages regularly on offer. AE, DC, DISC, MC, V.*

Westin Maui
$$$$$ West Maui (Kaanapali)

This hotel isn't quite as fabulous as the Grand Wailea (see earlier in this chapter), but it's considerably cheaper, and your kids will be in water-hog heaven here, too, thanks to an 87,000-square-foot "Aquatic Playground" complete with swim-through grottos, waterfalls, and a 128-foot water slide. Rooms are on the smallish side, but they're stylishly contemporary in the W Hotels mode, and each and every one boasts a truly celestial Heavenly

Bed, which keeps me coming back to Westin every time. The Heavenly Shower adds to the luxury in the bathroom, while your youngest ones can enjoy Westin's own plush-as-can-be Heavenly Cribs. A prime stretch of Kaanapali Beach and a wealth of facilities are on hand, including a well-outfitted fitness center, a brand-new 13,000-square-foot spa, and a full children's program. The stylish Tropica restaurant isn't the best on Maui, but the innovative fare is just fine, and the oceanfront setting is both designer-sleek and romantic at the same time. Beware the timeshare salesperson in the lobby — and if you get suckered in, don't say I didn't warn you.

See map p. 124. 2365 Kaanapali Pkwy., Kaanapali. ☎ *866-500-8313 or 808-667-2525. Fax: 808-661-5764.* www.westinmaui.com. *Valet parking: $10. Rack rates: $370–$680 double, $900–$3,000 suite. Mandatory "resort fee" of $15 per day for "free" self-parking, newspaper delivery, local and toll-free phone calls, in-room coffee, and fitness center access. Deals: Inquire about family, golf, wedding and honeymoon, and other packages, as well as special promotions that may include a sixth night free and/or resort credits. Promotional rates from $279 at press time. AE, DC, DISC, MC, V.*

The Whaler on Kaanapali Beach
$$$–$$$$$ West Maui (Kaanapali)

Not only would I stay at this beachfront midrise condo complex again, but also I'd *move* there if I could. The Whaler was built in the '70s and still sports a few "Me Decade" hallmarks, but in a good way — it feels like the kind of place where Jack Lord would keep his neighbor-island bachelor pad. The relaxing atmosphere starts in the clean-lined, open-air lobby and continues in the impeccably kept apartments. They're privately owned and individually decorated, but all have a fully equipped kitchen, VCR, marble bath, and big, blue-tiled lanai. Many one-bedrooms have two full bathrooms, making them great for small families or shares. Most units have some kind of ocean view, but the garden views are also pleasant. Luxuries include daily maid service, plus bell and concierge services. The grounds are private and well-manicured, and on-site extras include an oceanfront pool and spa, an exercise room, and great dining and shopping at neighboring Whaler's Village. Both property managing agents are reliable, so go with the best rate.

See map p. 124. 2481 Kaanapali Pkwy., Kaanapali. ☎ *808-661-4861. Fax: 808-661-8315. Parking: Free! Rack rates: $235–$255 studio, $330–$485 1-bedroom, $600–$700 2-bedroom. Deals: Car-and-condo packages and other bargains often available through both booking agents, so always mine for specials and off-season discounts. Internet-only ePriceBreaker rates from $180 at press time. Ask for AAA, senior (50-plus), and corporate discounts, and other special rate programs. AE, DC, MC, V. Reserve through either one of the following companies:* **Premier Resorts:** ☎ *888-211-7710,* www.the-whaler.com; **Aston Resorts:** ☎ *877-997-6667,* www.aston-hotels.com.

Accommodation Indexes

This section presents listings of hotel recommendations by location and by price. Use the maps in this chapter to get a more specific fix on where each hotel is located in relation to what you want to see and do while you're in Maui.

Accommodations Index by Location

South Maui (Wailea)
Fairmont Kea Lani Maui ($$$$–$$$$$)
Four Seasons Resort Maui at Wailea ($$$$$)
Grand Wailea Resort & Spa ($$$$$)
Outrigger Palms at Wailea ($$$)
Wailea Marriott, an Outrigger Resort ($$$$–$$$$$)

South Maui (Kihei)
Aston at the Maui Banyan ($$–$$$)
Best Western Maui Oceanfront Inn ($$)
Koa Resort ($–$$)
Mana Kai Maui ($–$$$)
Maui Coast Hotel ($$–$$$)
Punahoa Beach Apartments ($–$$)

West Maui (Lahaina)
Best Western Pioneer Inn ($$)
Lahaina Shores Beach Resort ($$$)
Maui Guest House ($$)
Ohana Maui Islander ($$)
Plantation Inn ($$–$$$)

West Maui (Kaanapali)
Hyatt Regency Maui Resort and Spa($$$$–$$$$$)
Kaanapali Alii ($$$$$)
Kaanapali Beach Hotel ($$$)
Outrigger Maui Eldorado Resort ($$$)
Sheraton Maui ($$$$–$$$$$)

Westin Maui ($$$$$)
The Whaler at Kaanapali Beach ($$$–$$$$$)

West Maui (Kahana/Napili)
Kahana Sunset ($$–$$$)
Mauian Hotel on Napili Beach ($$–$$$)
Napili Bay ($$)
Napili Kai Beach Resort ($$$–$$$$)
Noelani Condominium Resort ($$)

West Maui (Kapalua)
Kapalua Bay Hotel & Ocean Villas ($$$$$)
Ritz-Carlton Kapalua ($$$$–$$$$$)

Central Maui (Wailuku)
Old Wailuku Inn at Ulupono ($$)

Upcountry
Olinda Country Cottages and Inn ($$)

East Maui (On the Road to Hana)
Huelo Point Flower Farm ($$–$$$)
The Inn at Mama's Fish House ($$$)
Maluhia Hale ($$)

Hana
Hana Oceanfront Cottages ($$$)
Heavenly Hana Inn ($$$)

Hotel Hana-Maui ($$$$$) Accommodations Index by Price

$$$$$

Four Seasons Resort Maui at Wailea
(South Maui/Wailea)
Grand Wailea Resort & Spa
(South Maui/Wailea)
Hotel Hana-Maui (Hana)
Kaanapali Alii (West Maui/Kaanapali)
Kapalua Bay Hotel & Ocean Villas
(West Maui/Kapalua)
Westin Maui (West Maui/Kaanapali)

$$$$–$$$$$

Hyatt Regency Maui Resort and
Spa ($$$$–$$$$$)
Fairmont Kea Lani Maui (South Maui/
Wailea)
Ritz-Carlton Kapalua (West Maui/
Kapalua)
Sheraton Maui (West Maui/Kaanapali)
Wailea Marriott, an Outrigger Resort
(South Maui/Wailea)

$$$–$$$$$

The Whaler on Kaanapali Beach
(West Maui/Kaanapali)

$$$

Hana Oceanfront Cottages (Hana)
Heavenly Hana Inn (Hana)
The Inn at Mama's Fish House
(East Maui: On the Road to Hana)
Kaanapali Beach Hotel (West Maui/
Kaanapali)
Lahaina Shores Beach Resort
(West Maui/Lahaina)
Napili Kai Beach Resort (West Maui/
Napili)
Outrigger Maui Eldorado Resort
(West Maui/Kaanapali)
Outrigger Palms at Wailea
(South Maui/Wailea)

$$–$$$

Aston at the Maui Banyan
(South Maui/Kihei)
Huelo Point Flower Farm (East Maui:
On the Road to Hana)
Kahana Sunset (West Maui/Kahana)
Maui Coast Hotel (South Maui/Kihei)
Mauian Hotel on Napili Beach
(West Maui/Napili)
Plantation Inn (West Maui/Lahaina)

$$

Best Western Maui Oceanfront Inn
(South Maui/Kihei)
Best Western Pioneer Inn (West Maui/
Lahaina)
Maluhia Hale (East Maui: On the Road
to Hana)
Mana Kai Maui (South Maui/Kihei;
$–$$$)
Maui Guest House (West Maui/
Lahaina)
Napili Bay (West Maui/Napili)
Noelani Condominium Resort
(West Maui/Kahana)
Ohana Maui Islander (West Maui/
Lahaina)
Old Wailuku Inn at Ulupono
(Central Maui/Wailuku)
Olinda Country Cottages & Inn
(Upcountry)

$–$$

Koa Resort (South Maui/Kihei)
Punahoa Beach Apartments
(South Maui/Kihei)

Chapter 11

Dining and Snacking in Maui

· ·

In This Chapter

▶ Choosing among Maui's best restaurants
▶ Finding the finest luaus if you're in the hula mood

· ·

Maui's dining scene is excellent, with amazing scope and innovation. The lovely and charismatic Valley Isle has attracted so many top chefs from around the globe that choosing among their outposts can be a trying business.

But be prepared to pay for the privilege of dining on Maui. The island is overflowing with restaurants, so choice isn't a problem — but you have to navigate a minefield of overpriced, mediocre-quality restaurants in order to get value for your dollar. The listings in this chapter offer a recommendable course of action, whether you're looking for a splurge-worthy special-occasion restaurant or a satisfying casual meal that relieves the pressure on your wallet.

Lahaina, on Maui's west shore, is the heart of the island's dining scene. Luckily, it's quite convenient — no more than a half-hour drive or so from any of the beach resorts (45 minutes from Wailea). Many of its restaurants — even the affordable ones — boast front-row, on-the-water seats for spectacular sunset-watching. But nowhere is the minefield of mediocrity more explosive, so choose carefully.

Chapter 18 gives you a fun and easy overview of Maui's dining scene, with tips on local specialties and the astounding variety of seafood on island menus.

Maui's Best Restaurants

In the restaurant listings that follow, each restaurant name is followed by a number of dollar signs, ranging from one ($) to five ($$$$$). The dollar signs are meant to give you an idea of what a complete dinner for one person — with appetizer, main course, a drink, tax, and tip — is likely to cost. The price categories go like this:

Dollar Sign(s)	Price Range
$	Cheap eats — less than $15 per person
$$	Still inexpensive — $15 to $25
$$$	Moderate — $25 to $40
$$$$	Pricey — $40 to $70
$$$$$	Ultraexpensive — more than $70 per person

Of course, how much you spend depends on how you order, so stay away from the surf and turf or the north end of the wine list if you're watching your wallet. To give you a better idea of how much you can expect to spend, I also include the price range of main courses in the listings. (Prices can change at any time, of course, but restaurants usually don't raise their prices by more than a dollar or two at any given time.)

The state adds 4 percent in sales tax to every restaurant bill. A 15- to 20-percent tip for the server is standard, just like back home.

At the end of the chapter, I index the restaurants in three different ways: by location, cuisine, and price. Also, use the maps in this chapter to get a more specific fix on where each restaurant is located in relation to your accommodation.

Aloha Mixed Plate
$ West Maui (Lahaina)   Local Hawaiian

This charming, inexpensive patio restaurant specializes in traditional foods of Hawaii: great *saimin* (ramen noodle soup), teriyaki chicken, finger-lickin' Korean-style barbecue ribs, coconut shrimp, mahimahi sandwiches, stir-frys, and other local staples, plus burgers (both garden and beef). Most dishes are served as complete meals (a style called "plate lunch"), accompanied by "two scoops" rice and a scoop of macaroni salad for a sumo-sized starchfest, making them a real bargain in the process. Brought to you by the people behind the Old Lahaina Luau (the top luau in the islands), this colorful place serves up the best local food around. Don't expect gourmet — this restaurant is Hawaii's version of paper-plate eats. Still, Aloha Mixed Plate offers real value — and in an oceanfront setting to boot! You can even settle at the bar, celebrating the sunset with a tropical cocktail or washing down your hearty meal with an ice-cold beer.

See map p. 157. 1285 Front St. (across from Lahaina Cannery Mall), Lahaina. ☎ *808-661-3322.* www.alohamixedplate.com. *Reservations not necessary. Pupus, burgers, salads, and noodles $3.25–$8; plate lunches $7–$14. MC, V. Open: Lunch and dinner daily.*

Cakewalk Paia Bakery
$ Central Maui (Paia)   Bakery/Sandwiches

This delightful bakery in the heart of funky Paia is my favorite place to pick up a gourmet-quality picnic lunch for a drive to Hana or a day at the beach. It's little more than a storefront with a walk-up counter, but the service is friendly, and fresh-baked breads and pastries perfume the air. Start the day with a celestial cinnamon roll, muffins bursting with blueberries, or fresh-from-the-oven coffee cake, accompanied by an aromatic brew from the full-service espresso bar. Sandwiches are freshmade, hearty, healthy, and universally yummy; think moist turkey breast with butter lettuce, upcountry tomatoes, and housemade aioli; curried chicken salad; or bountiful roast beef. The Cakewalk folks can pack you one to go, accompanied by thick kettle chips and a fresh-baked cookie, as early as 7 a.m. (8:30 a.m. on Sundays). On the island to celebrate? There's no better place to order a specialty cake — or stop in to celebrate any day with a decadent slice of cheesecake for dessert.

See map p. 218. Baldwin Avenue at Hana Hwy., Paia. ☎ *808-579-8870.* www.cakewalk maui.com. *Reservations not taken. Pastries, sandwiches, and picnic lunches $2–$8. Open: Breakfast and lunch daily.*

Capische?
$$$$–$$$$$ South Maui (Wailea)   Mediterranean-Italian

Nestled in a little-known hilltop resort that caters largely to Japanese guests, this dreamy hideaway is one of Maui's best-kept secrets. Capische? boasts majestic coastal views, an ultraromantic ambiance, service that's both friendly and professional, and a menu bounteous with the culinary delights of the Mediterranean. Book a table on the view-endowed lanai and come for sunset to maximize your enjoyment. Start with a delectable quail saltimbocca wrapped in apple-smoked bacon, or a garden-fresh caprese salad of buffalo mozzarella, sweet baby basil, and Big Island tomatoes. Follow with a seafood-rich cioppino, a gorgonzola-crusted filet mignon with Maui onion jus, or one of the delightful daily specials. Join the select few who delight in this hidden gem, where a pianist often adds to the ambiance.

See map p. 158. In the Diamond Resort, 555 Kaukahi St., Wailea. ☎ *808-879-2224.* www.casanovamaui.com. *Reservations recommended. Main courses: $28–$39. AE, DC, MC, V. Open: Dinner daily.*

Dining in Maui

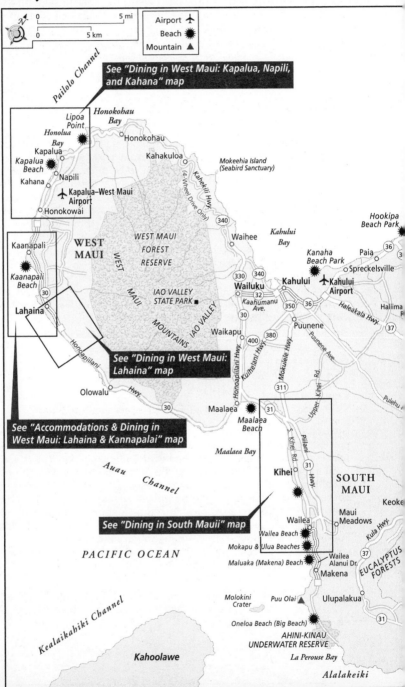

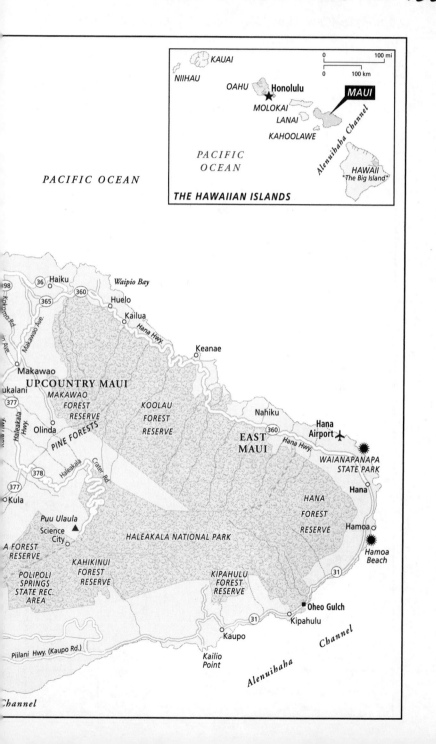

THE HAWAIIAN ISLANDS

Dining in West Maui: Kapalua, Napili, and Kahana

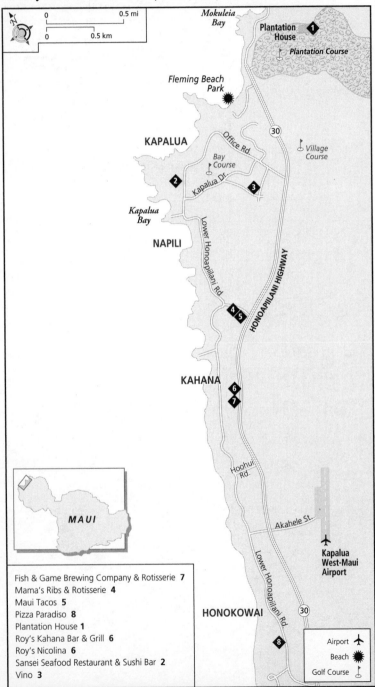

Fish & Game Brewing Company & Rotisserie **7**
Mama's Ribs & Rotisserie **4**
Maui Tacos **5**
Pizza Paradiso **8**
Plantation House **1**
Roy's Kahana Bar & Grill **6**
Roy's Nicolina **6**
Sansei Seafood Restaurant & Sushi Bar **2**
Vino **3**

Dining in West Maui: Lahaina

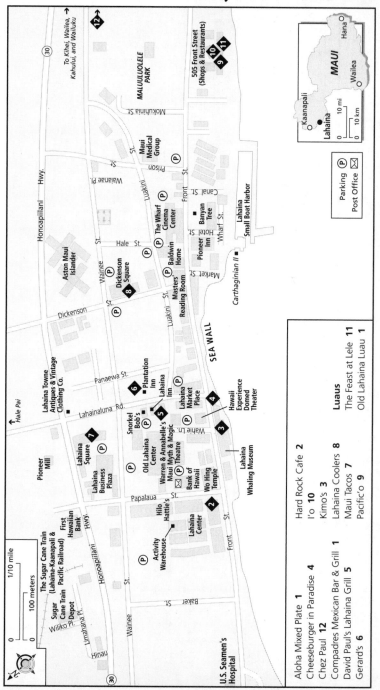

Dining in South Maui

Capische? **13**
Cheeseburger in Paradise **9**
Da' Kitchen **6**
Ferraro Bar e Ristorante **11**
Joe's Bar & Grill **10**
Maalea Waterfront Restaurant **1**
Maui Tacos **7**
Nick's Fishmarket **12**
Peggy Sue's **4**
Roy's Kihei **2**
Sansei Seafood Restaurant
  & Sushi Bar **5**
Sarento's on the Beach **8**
Spago **11**
Stella Blues Cafe & Deli **3**
Tommy Bahamas Tropical Cafe **9**

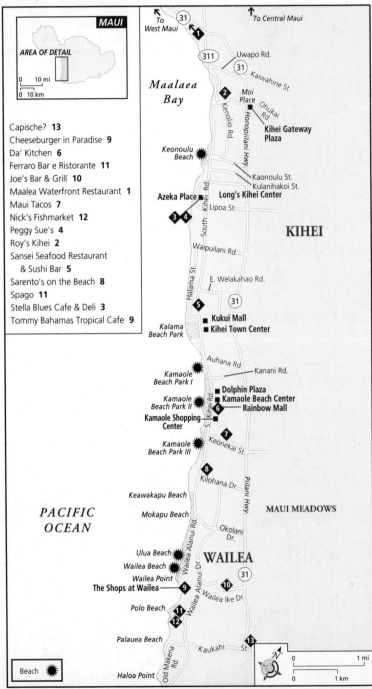

Casanova
$$–$$$ Upcountry Maui Italian

Located in the town of Makawao, Casanova is a hip, casual spot with terrific food and music. Look for a tiny veranda with a few stools in front of a deli at Makawao's busiest intersection. The restaurant contains a stage, dance floor, and bar; it's the setting for some of Maui's liveliest nightlife Wednesday through Saturday nights. (Friday evenings bring live Latin sounds, while Saturdays feature some surprisingly big names, from the top talents on the contemporary Hawaiian music scene to visiting celebrities like Los Lobos. Expect a cover charge ranging from $5 to $15, depending on the entertainment.)

The pasta is homemade, and the selections are first-rate — try the zesty spaghetti fradiavolo, the spinach gnocchi in a fresh tomato-Gorgonzola sauce, or the tagliolini al salmone (thin pasta sautéed in a saffron cream sauce with naturally smoked salmon, leeks, and green peas). Other choices include a huge pizza selection; grilled lamb chops in an Italian mushroom marinade; fresh Kula spinach sautéed with butter, pine nuts, and Parmesan cheese; a fabulous polenta with radicchio, mushrooms, and cream sauce; and Maui's best tiramisu.

See map p. 218. 1188 Makawao Ave., Makawao. ☎ *808-572-0220.* www.casanova maui.com. *Reservations recommended for dinner. Main courses: $12–$24; 12-inch pizzas $10–$18. DC, MC, V. Open: Lunch Mon–Sat, dinner daily. Dancing Wed–Sat evenings until 1 a.m., lounge open nightly until 12:30 a.m. or 1 a.m. Deli open daily 8 a.m.–6:30 p.m.*

Charley's Restaurant & Saloon
$$ Central Maui (Paia) American/International

Before I set out on any drive to Hana, I always make time for breakfast at Charley's. This restaurant is my favorite breakfast place on Maui, thanks to overstuffed breakfast burritos, fluffy omelets, mac-nut pancakes, and eggs Benedict with perfectly puckery hollandaise. Lunch and dinner bring burgers, kiawe-smoked ribs and marlin, calzones baked fresh to order, and a variety of vegetarian delights, from veggie lasagna to bounteous salads and stir-frys. Expect nothing in the way of ambience, but service is friendly and prices are low, making Charley's worth the half-hour drive from Kihei for an affordable and unpretentious meal, even if you're not heading to Hana. The adjacent roadhouse-style bar serves up a good selection of microbrews.

See map p. 218. 142 Hana Hwy. (at Baldwin Avenue), Paia. ☎ *808-579-9453. Reservations not taken. Main courses: $6–$12 at breakfast and lunch, $12–$25 at dinner. AE, DC, DISC, MC, V. Open: Breakfast, lunch, and dinner daily.*

Cheeseburger in Paradise/Cheeseburgers, Mai Tais & Rock 'n' Roll
$–$$ West Maui (Lahaina)/South Maui (Wailea) American

This oceanfront burger joint is a perennial favorite thanks to an always-lively atmosphere, consistently terrific food, and million-dollar views, all at bargain-basement prices. At the original Lahaina location — the first in the burgeoning minichain — the second-level open-air room offers a prime ocean view from every seat. The Wailea outpost is set back farther from the surf, but an upstairs location gives it its own terrific ocean vistas, and the retro-hip décor sets just the right mood. No matter which location you choose, the tropical-style burgers are first class all the way — big, juicy mounds of natural Angus beef, served on fresh-baked buns and guaranteed to satisfy even the most committed connoisseur. Chili dogs, fish and chips, crispy onion rings, and spiced fries broaden the menu. Dieters and vegetarians can opt for the excellent garden and tofu burgers, a lean chicken breast sandwich, or a meal-size salad. Two full bars boast a festive, first-rate menu of tropical drinks (including one of the best piña coladas in the islands). There's lively music every night to round out the party-hearty appeal at both locations. You can even launch your day oceanside with hearty omelets, French toast, eggs Benedict, and other morning faves.

In Lahaina: 811 Front St. (oceanside near the end of Lahainaluna Road), Lahaina. ☎ *808-661-4855.* www.cheeseburgermaui.com. *See map p. 157. In Wailea: At the Shops at Wailea, 3750 Wailea Alanui Dr., second floor.* ☎ *808-874-8990.* www.cheeseburgerwailea.com. *See map p. 158. Reservations not taken. Main courses: $8–$17 (burgers less than $10). AE, DISC, MC, V. Open: Breakfast, lunch, and dinner daily.*

Chez Paul
$$$$–$$$$$ **West Maui (Lahaina)**   **Provençal French**

Boasting cozy country-style décor, luscious French cuisine that could hold its own in Paris, and career waiters who care more about your needs than tomorrow's surf report, Chez Paul is a real original in a sea of chic island hot spots. Under the guiding hand of Patrick Callarec, Chez Paul is better than ever. Locally grown veggies and the freshest catches of the day make copious appearances, but preparations are single-mindedly rich and classic. Witness such winning dishes as out-of-the-shell Kona lobster served in a delicate saffron-basil cream sauce, crispy duck roasted with exotic island fruits and bathed in sweet-tart pineapple juice, and a brilliant filet mignon in tricolor peppercorn sauce. Save room for dessert, because the delicious sweet treats (such as a classic vanilla crème brulée served in a Maui pineapple shell) are beautifully presented. Be prepared for a tab that's heftier than it needs to be — but if you're willing to pay for quality, you won't be disappointed.

See map p. 157. 1 Olowalu Village, Honoapiilani Hwy., Olowalu (4 miles south of Lahaina, on the mountain side of the highway). ☎ *808-661-3843.* www.chezpaul.net. *Reservations highly recommended. Main courses: $29–$39. AE, MC, V. Open: Dinner nightly.*

CJ's Deli & Diner
$ **West Maui (Kaanapali)**   **American**

"Comfort food at comfort prices" — that's the motto at CJ's, and this cheap-chic diner does a great job of delivering on its promise. An extensive chalkboard menu hangs from the brightly colored wall above the open-air kitchen; the friendly staff stands behind the counter, just waiting to cook up your order. The menu runs the gamut: farmer-style breakfasts, hearty veggie-packed salads, half-pound burgers, classic reubens, roasted chicken, and fresh-grilled fish. There's a pleasing local flair to the offerings. Don't miss the hot *malasadas,* a light and flaky sweet pastry, sort of like a pow-dered-sugar-covered donut hole, that's one of the islands' favorite sweet treats; CJ's version can be downright addictive. Food can be prepared for takeout or plated to enjoy in the casual, colorful dining room. There's even an Internet-connected computer on hand so that you can check your e-mail while you wait. Stop by for a box lunch if you're heading to Hana, Haleakala, or the beach. There's also a kids' menu on hand.

See map p. 124. At the Kaanapali Fairway Shops, 2580 Keka'a Dr. (facing Honoapiilani Hwy., on the access road), Kaanapali. ☎ *808-667-0968. Reservations not accepted. Main courses: $6–$13. MC, V. Open: Breakfast, lunch, and early dinner daily.*

Compadres Mexican Bar & Grill
$$ West Maui (Lahaina)   Mexican

This big, airy, comfortable, and lively restaurant serves up high-quality south-of-the-border fare and the best margaritas on the island. The monster menu features all your Mexican favorites, including eight kinds of enchi-ladas, a half-dozen quesadillas, and four variations on the chile relleno. The fish tacos are always first-rate (you can even get them to go at a new takeout window), and you can't go wrong with the huevos rancheros at any time of day. The chips are light and greaseless, the guacamole is fresh and chunky, and the combos are big enough to satisfy even Hungryman appetites, making Compadres an excellent value in an overpriced restaurant town.

See map p. 157. In the Lahaina Cannery Mall, 1221 Honoapiilani Hwy. (on the Front Street side of the mall, facing Aloha Mixed Plate), Lahaina. ☎ *808-661-7189. Reservations accepted. Main courses: $10–$20 (most less than $15). AE, DC, DISC, MC, V. Open: Breakfast, lunch, and dinner daily.*

Da' Kitchen
$ South Maui (Kihei)/Central Maui (Kahului)   Local Hawaiian

Just ask any local: Da' Kitchen is the place to come for the most authentic local grinds on the island. The simple but comfortable Kihei closet is the original; come for the food, not the mood. Place your order at the counter and then grab one of the handful of tables to chow down on the extra-hearty eats. All the classic Hawaiian plate lunches come with two scoops of rice, plus potato *and* macaroni salad (you can request a green salad instead) — trust me, you don't leave hungry. Top-notch choices include pulled kalua pork, slow-cooked until tender and seasoned with Hawaiian salt; chicken katsu, breaded in panko crumbs and served with Japanese barbecue sauce; and loco moco, a hamburger patty grilled, topped with two fried eggs, and smothered in gravy (a dieter's delight!). You can also choose a yummy lemon chicken and a couple of teriyaki dishes for more-mainstream tastes, plus big Asian-style noodle bowls, hamburgers, and a better-than-you'd-expect Chinese chicken salad. The Kahului location is more cafe-style, with full table service.

Reservations not taken. In Kihei: In Rainbow Mall, 2439 S. Kihei Rd. (at the south end of town). ☎ 808-875-7782. See map p. 158. Open: Late breakfast (from 9 a.m.), lunch, and dinner daily. In Kahului: In Triangle Square, 425 Koloa St. (off Dairy Road). ☎ 808-871-7782. See map p. 218. Open: Lunch and dinner Mon–Fri, lunch only Sat, closed Sun. At both locations, most items $6–$12, plate lunches $7–$13. No credit cards.

David Paul's Lahaina Grill
$$$$–$$$$$ West Maui (Lahaina) New American/Hawaii Regional

David Paul's is a bastion of quiet sophistication in ticky-tacky, party-hearty Lahaina, racking up numerous awards and stellar ratings from dining bible *Zagat's*. Both locals and visitors regularly name it as their Maui favorite. It's definitely one of mine, and I'm relieved that it has maintained its quality even after the departure of star chef David Paul Johnston. The dining room is stylish yet delightfully homey, with pressed-tin ceilings, butter-yellow walls, original art, and a black-and-white tile floor. The kitchen excels at distinctive flavors that are bold without being overpowering. Johnston's signature dishes remain the stars of the menu, including "kalua" duck bathed in reduced plum wine sauce — rich, fork-tender, and greaseless. I'm also fond of the Kona coffee–roasted rack of lamb dressed in a light Cabernet demi-glace. The wine list is excellent, and the all-pro wait staff offers welcome relief from Lahaina's usual surfer style.

See map p. 157. In the Lahaina Inn, 127 Lahainaluna Rd. (1 block inland from Front Street), Lahaina. ☎ 808-667-5117. www.lahainagrill.com. *Reservations highly recommended. Main courses: $25–$42. Chef's tasting menu: $85 or $125. AE, DC, DISC, MC, V. Open: Dinner nightly.*

Fish & Game Brewing Company & Rotisserie
$$$ West Maui (Kahana) Steak/Seafood

This restaurant has all the style of a bad toupee, but I really like it anyway — part brewpub, part sports bar (with live nightly music), part fish market, and part clubby restaurant. The kitchen's got it going on, despite the schizophrenic ambience and straight-outta-the-'80s décor. The fare is straight-ahead seafood and grill fare. Start with a half-dozen oysters on the half-shell, or maybe the *kiawe-* (mesquite-) grilled brewer's sausage and then move on to a first-rate fresh catch or something meatier, if you've eaten your fill of seafood in Hawaii. The kitchen prepares fish to your taste, one of four ways: blackened Cajun style, habañero cornmeal crusted, seven spiced with soy mirin glaze, and "just plain" grilled. Beware of the seven spices — five of them are peppers. I like the "just plain" best because it lets the quality of the fish shine. The 10-ounce kiawe-smoked prime rib is a steal at $20, especially considering the cut's high quality. The rotisserie also produces a lovely herb-rubbed chicken with a golden crust. All the housemade beers are terrific — particulary the amber-hued Plantation Pale Ale and the dark, robust Wild Hog Stout — and I found the service to be an ideal combination of easygoing and attentive. A kids' menu is on hand for family meals, plus a late-night menu of casual bar fare in case the munchies strike between 10:30 p.m. and 1 a.m.

If you're staying in a nearby condo, stop by Fish & Game to visit the seafood market at the back of the store, where you can choose from a wide range of unprepared fresh catches and flown-in-fresh shellfish to throw on the stove or the grill back at your vacation rental.

See map p. 156. In the Kahana Gateway Shopping Center, 4405 Honoapiilani Hwy. (Highway 30), Kahana. ☎ **808-669-3474.** www.fishandgamerestaurant.com. *Reservations recommended. Main courses: $7–$14 at lunch, $18–$33 at dinner (most less than $25; steak-and-lobster combo $46). AE, DC, DISC, MC, V. Open: Lunch and dinner daily.*

Gerard's
$$$$–$$$$$ West Maui (Lahaina) New French

Chez Paul's has a slight edge cuisine-wise, but Gerard's boasts an even more romantic setting, especially for couples who prefer to swoon in an alfresco setting. A regular winner of the *Wine Spectator* Award of Excellence and named "Maui's little French jewel" by *Bon Appetit* magazine, Gerard's offers refined cuisine that never disappoints. Gerard Reversade excels at seeking out the freshest local ingredients and preparing them in traditional Gallic style. My favorite among the starters is the shiitake and oyster mushrooms in puff pastry, but the foie gras terrine is a must for those people who indulge. A wealth of meat and poultry dishes is at hand (including a terrific rack of lamb in mint sauce), plus divine daily fresh fish preparations that depend on what the boats bring in. Inventive desserts provide a memorable finale, unless you opt for a cheese plate, served with toasted country bread and poached pears. Service is appropriately attentive.

See map p. 157. In the Plantation Inn, 174 Lahainaluna Rd. (between Wainee and Luakini streets), Lahaina. ☎ **877-661-8939** *or 808-661-8939.* www.gerardsmaui.com. *Reservations highly recommended. Main courses: $30–$40. AE, DC, DISC, MC, V. Open: Dinner nightly.*

Haliimaile General Store
$$$$ Upcountry Maui Hawaii Regional

This simple but attractive plantation-style restaurant is a nice choice for those people who prefer to sample top-quality island-style cooking in a refreshingly casual and pretentious-free setting. Star chef Bev Gannon presents a heartier-than-average Hawaii Regional menu full of American home-style favorites prepared with an island spin. Look for such signature satisfiers as succulent barbecued pork ribs, long-simmering coconut fish and shrimp curry, pumpkin-seed-crusted scallops accompanied by a roasted-veggie enchilada in mole sauce, and New Zealand rack of lamb prepared Hunan style. The desserts — created by Bev's daughter Teresa Gannon, now a well-known chef in her own right — are better than Mom used to make; I never miss the light and tangy lilikoi (passion fruit) tart.

Prices have crept higher than they should have, and it can get noisy at times, but it's still worth the 45-minute drive (but if you're in South Maui, head to sibling restaurant Joe's Bar & Grill first; see review later in this chapter).

See map p. 218. 900 Haliimaile Rd., Haliimaile (ha-lee-ee-my-lee). From the Hana Highway (Highway 36), take Highway 37 for 4½ miles to Haliimaile Road (Highway 371); turn left and drive 1½ miles to the restaurant. ☎ *808-572-2666.* www.haliimaile generalstore.com. *Reservations recommended. Main courses: $10–$20 at lunch, $22–$32 at dinner. AE, DC, MC, V. Open: Lunch Mon–Fri, dinner nightly.*

Hotel Hana-Maui Main Dining Room
$$$$ Hana   Continental-Island Fusion

This formerly dowdy luxury resort has been reborn — and, thankfully, so has the dining room. Now under the guiding hand of executive chef (and Hawaii native) Larry Quirit, it's once again the best restaurant in Hana. Quirit has crafted a fresh new menu that matches island-style ingredients and regional island influences with contemporary techniques and flavors. Expect lots of local fresh fish, meats, and crisp Maui-grown greens in elegant and pleasing preparations. It's a perfect match for the freshly remade dining room, with its elegant island-style blend of traditional materials, ocean views, and original island-inspired art that includes the breathtaking *Red Sails* painting, with its imagery of the first Hawaiians voyaging to the islands. Come for dinner on Friday to enjoy live island-style music and dance.

If you're coming for dinner or cocktails in the adjacent Paniolo Lounge, please adhere to the restaurant's dress code: collared shirts and slacks or dress shorts for men, skirts or slacks for women.

Hana's other option is the more casual, affordable, and freshly renovated **Hana Ranch Restaurant** ($–$$$), in town on the mountain side of Hana Highway (☎ **808-248-8255**). At lunchtime, choose between the informal takeout window, serving up local fare like teriyaki chicken and hot dogs that you can enjoy at outdoor picnic tables, or the indoor all-you-can-eat lunch buffet ($11–$15). The restaurant is also open for pizza on Wednesday evenings and a sit-down dinner on Friday and Saturday for somewhat higher priced fare as New York steaks and grilled fish (reservations required).

See map p. 218. In the Hotel Hana-Maui, Hana Highway, Hana. ☎ *808-248-8211. Reservations recommended for dinner. Main courses: $10–$20 at breakfast and lunch, $18–$33 at dinner. AE, DC, MC, V. Open: Breakfast, lunch, and dinner daily.*

Rock 'n' roll, tropical style

The **Hard Rock Cafe Maui**, at 900 Front St. (at Papalaua Street) in Lahaina (☎ **808-667-7400**), has to be the best-located Hard Rock Cafe on the planet. Boasting a prime position just across the street from the water, it's oft rewarded with light trade winds and great sunset views. Expect the standard Hard Rock rock 'n' roll atmosphere and eats, this time with a tropical bent.

Hula Grill
$–$$$ **West Maui (Kaanapali)   Steak/Seafood**

My favorite Kaanapali restaurant features a killer beachfront setting and a
midpriced island-style steak-and-seafood menu brought to you from Big
Island star chef Peter Merriman and the people behind Waikiki's renowned
Duke's Canoe Club. Kissed by the trade winds, the patio is the ideal setting
for sunset-watchers, and tiki torches make for after-dark magic. The wide-
ranging menu has something for everyone, including superb wood-grilled
or macadamia-crusted fresh island fish, yummy barbecued pork ribs in
mango barbecue sauce, and steamed Alaskan king crab legs (with a side
of top sirloin, if you like). Those travelers on a budget can stick to the bar
menu, which features Merriman's famous *poke* rolls (filled with seared
fresh ahi), kiawe- (mesquite-) fired pizzas, and creative salads and sand-
wiches. Hawaiian music, hula dancing at sunset, and well-blended tropi-
cal drinks dressed up with umbrellas round out the carefree island vibe. If
you want a patio table, request one when you book. The more casual
Barefoot Bar invites you to sit with your toes in the sand while you enjoy
burgers, fish, pizza, and salads.

See map p. 124. In Whaler's Village, 2435 Kaanapali Pkwy., Kaanapali Beach. ☎ *808-
667-6636.* www.hulapie.com. *Reservations recommended for dinner. Main courses:
$20–$29 at dinner (most less than $25). Barefoot Bar menu (served all day): $8–$16.
AE, DISC, MC, V. Open: Lunch and dinner daily.*

I'o
$$$$ **West Maui (Lahaina)   New Pacific**

You can't get closer to the ocean than I'o's alfresco tables, some of which
sit just feet from the surf (request one when you book). Overseen by
award-winning chef James McDonald, I'o is a multifaceted joy, with win-
ningly innovative fusion cuisine, first-rate service, and a top-notch wine
list that has won the *Wine Spectator* Award of Excellence. The seafood-
heavy menu features copious Pacific Rim accents, plus a few creative
twists courtesy of the Western Hemisphere: The tropical seafood cocktail
gets a chipotle tomatillo sauce for zest; Maine lobster tails are stir-fried
and served with sweet potatoes flambéed in a dark rum and mango Thai
curry sauce; the grilled lamb tenderloin lies on a bed of wasabe-spiced
mashed potatoes; and the fresh catch gets a crust of foie gras for the ulti-
mate decadence. Each dish is paired with a recommended wine for easy
ordering. Skip the silken purse appetizer, though — it's an overrated sig-
nature. A full, friendly bar (including a tempting array of specialty martinis)
makes this restaurant an all-around terrific choice.

See map p. 157. 505 Front St. (on the ocean at Shaw Street), Lahaina. ☎ *808-661-8422.*
www.iomaui.com. *Reservations recommended. Main courses: $23–$34 ($59 for
4 lobster tails). AC, MC, V. Open: Dinner nightly.*

Joe's Bar & Grill
$$$$ South Maui (Wailea)   New American/Hawaii Regional

I prefer Joe's over its more widely lauded sister restaurant, the Haliimaile General Store (see earlier in this chapter). It's a little slicker than its Upcountry sibling and serves a similarly pleasing menu of American home cooking with an island-regional twist, this time without the strong Asian influence. Top choices include the signature grilled applewood salmon, smoky and sublime; a creamy lobster and seafood potpie with a light and flaky crust; and innovative preparations of such classics as meatloaf, rack of lamb, and center-cut pork chops. The wood-paneled room is casual and welcoming, rock 'n' roll memorabilia lines the walls (Joe Gannon managed Alice Cooper for years), and open-air views take in the tennis action below. At night, low lighting and well-spaced tables make for a surprisingly romantic ambience, but the room takes on a laid-back liveliness after it fills up. The service is top-notch.

See map p. 158. At the Wailea Tennis Center, 131 Wailea Ike Place (between Wailea Alanui Drive and Piilani Highway), Wailea. ☎ **808-875-7767.** *Reservations recommended. Main courses: $18–$32. AE, DC, DISC, MC, V. Open: Dinner nightly.*

Kimo's
$$$ West Maui (Lahaina)   Steak/Seafood

This casual waterfront restaurant boasts a winning combination of affordable prices, good food, and great ocean views. The menu isn't quite as innovative as that of sister restaurant Hula Grill, but it still offers a reliable and satisfying selection of fresh fish preparations (you can choose from a good half dozen), hefty sirloins served with garlic mashed potatoes, and island favorites like koloa pork ribs with plum barbecue sauce. With Caesar salads and sides included, dinners make for a very good deal, and there's nightly entertainment to boot. Dessert lovers should save room for Kimo's own Hula Pie, macadamia-nut ice cream in a chocolate-wafer crust with fudge and whipped cream — a decadent island delight.

See map p. 157. 845 Front St., Lahaina. ☎ **808-661-4811.** www.kimosmaui.com. *Reservations recommended for dinner. Main courses: $7–$12 at lunch; $17–$26 at dinner, including Kimo's Caesar salad. AE, MC, V. Open: Lunch and dinner daily.*

Lahaina Coolers
$$ West Maui (Lahaina)   American/Eclectic

Billing itself as "The *Cheers* of the Pacific," this lively, friendly spot serves up affordable eats at breakfast, lunch, and dinner that are a step above the standard. Despite its side-street location, this happy-hour favorite maintains an appealingly laid-back tropical vibe. Start the morning with an overstuffed breakfast burrito with black beans and rice or fluffy Portuguese sweetbread french toast. Lunch on one of the tropical pizzas (I love the Evil Jungle Pizza, with grilled chicken and spicy Thai peanut sauce), or perhaps a grilled portabello mushroom sandwich on focaccia bread. The famous fresh fish tacos or the homemade pastas are excellent dinner choices, especially if you start with $1.75 drafts and crispy calamari to munch on. The full dinner menu is served until midnight (tropical cocktails until 2 a.m.), making Lahaina Coolers a Hawaii late-night rarity. Live music — often blues, sometimes folk or rock — adds to the lively atmosphere on Saturdays and on the occasional weeknight.

See map p. 157. 180 Dickenson St. (between Front and Wainee streets), Lahaina. ☎ *808-661-7082.* www.lahainacoolers.com. *Reservations accepted. Main courses: $7.50–$11 at breakfast and lunch, $10–$22 at dinner (most less than $15). AE, DC, DISC, MC, V. Open: Breakfast, lunch, and dinner daily.*

Leilani's on the Beach
$$$ West Maui (Kaanapali)   Steak/Seafood

I like Hula Grill (see the review earlier in this chapter) better, but its next-door sister restaurant, Leilani's on the Beach, makes a good choice for reliable steak-and-seafood fare — the burgers, in particular, are terrific — and an equally lovely oceanfront setting. The Beachside Grill serves an affordable all-day menu similar to that at the Hula Grill's Barefoot Bar.

See map p. 124. Whaler's Village, Kaanapali. ☎ *808-661-4495.* www.hulapie.com. *Reservations recommended for dinner. Main courses $6.95–$13 at Beachside Grill; $15–$26 for dinner at Leilani's. AE, DC, DISC, MC, V. Open: Beachside Grill lunch and dinner daily; Leilani's dinner only daily.*

Maalaea Waterfront Restaurant
$$$$ South Maui/Kihei   Continental/Seafood

Family-run for many years, this decidedly unhip seafooder is a traditionalist's delight. The European-style wait staff, which serves every dish with a professional flourish, regularly wins the annual "Best Service" and "Best Seafood" awards from the *Maui News*. A half-dozen fresh catches are usually on hand, and you can choose the preparation you'd prefer. Your choices include *à la meuniere* (baked and stuffed with Alaskan king crabmeat), Provençal style (sautéed with olives, peppers, and tomatoes in garlic and olive oil); and Cajun spiced. But my absolute favorite is the *en Bastille,* in which the fish is "imprisoned" (get it?) in grated potato and sautéed, and then crowned with scallions, mushrooms, tomatoes, and meuniere sauce — yum! Meat and poultry are on hand for nonseafood-eaters, including a well-prepared steak Diane. The bread comes with a delectable beer cheese spread (how retro is that?), and your server prepares your Caesar salad tableside if you ask. Book a table on the lanai before sunset for pretty harbor views.

See map p. 158. In the Milowai Condominium, 50 Hauoli St., Maalaea (north of Kihei). ☎ *808-244-9028.* www.waterfrontrestaurant.net. *Reservations recommended. To get there: From Highway 30, take the second right into Maalaea Harbor, then turn left. Main courses: $18–$38. AE, DC, DISC, MC, V. Open: Dinner nightly.*

Going for a post-Haleakala-sunrise breakfast

Rising at o'dark thirty to drive two hours Upcountry to catch the glorious sunrise from atop Haleakala Crater is one of Maui's greatest pastimes (see Chapter 13). But the real treat comes after, in the form of a hearty, country-style breakfast. Two wonderful breakfast stops sit at the base of the mountain, in a tiny town called Kula that you can't help but drive through on your way back to the beach.

Kula Sandalwoods Restaurant ($), on Haleakala Highway (Highway 377; ☎ 808-878-3523), is a family-run restaurant that starts serving home-baked pastries, omelets prepared with fresh-from-the-chicken-coop eggs and garden-fresh veggies, and eggs Benedict topped with hollandaise sauce (made from scratch) every day at 6:30 a.m. All the home-style breakfasts and lunches are hearty and delicious; I especially like the French toast made from home-baked Portuguese sweetbread. You can choose to eat in the large dinerlike room or out on the lanai if it's not too chilly.

For slightly more upscale dining, head down the road to **Kula Lodge & Restaurant** ($$; ☎ 808-878-1535), whose cozy lodgelike dining room features a big stone fireplace; breakfast is served from 6:30 a.m. Picture windows with lush panoramic views on three sides let the outside in as you enjoy eggs scrambled with bacon and sausage or the justifiably famous banana-macadamia-nut pancakes.

Mama's Fish House
$$$$$ Central Maui (Paia)   Seafood

Despite pay-through-the-nose prices and a touch of touristiness, Mama's is my favorite choice on Maui and one of my all-time favorite Hawaii restaurants — and one of its most popular, too. The tiki-room setting is an archetype of timeless Hawaii cool. The beachhouse dining room has ambience in excess, with lavish tropical floral arrangements, sea breezes ruffling the tapa tablecloths, soft lighting, and gorgeous views galore. Fresh island fish simply doesn't get any better than this; it's all caught locally, with the provenance indicated on the menu. ("Opakapaka caught by Earle Kiawi bottomfishing outside his homeport of Hana Bay.") The day's catches are the stars of the show, and you choose from four preparations. My favorite is the Pua Me Hua Hana, two of the day's fresh catches steamed gently and served traditional luau style with purple Molokai sweet potato, baked banana, fresh island fruit, and a fresh young coconut — plates just don't get prettier than this. The service is sincere if a bit serious ("And what will the lady have?"), but somehow it suits the mood. A lengthy list of tropical drinks (dressed with umbrellas, of course) completes the tropical-romantic picture. A kids' menu is on hand for families. A real island-style delight!

See map p. 218. 799 Poho Place, Paia (just off the Hana Highway, 1½ miles past Paia town). ☎ **808-579-8488.** www.mamasfishhouse.com. *Reservations recommended for lunch, required for dinner. Main courses: $22–$32 at lunch, $32–$49 at dinner. AE, DC, DISC, MC, V. Open: Lunch and dinner daily.*

Mama's Ribs & Rotisserie
$ West Maui (Honokowai)   Barbecue

This simple, family-owned storefront specializes in freshly prepared, quick, and affordably priced home-style barbecue. The take-out cafe is bright and clean, with a few cafe tables and chairs outside. The rotisserie chicken (prepared traditional, teriyaki, or teriyaki citrus style) is moist and delicious, as are the slow-cooked pork ribs — not greasy or fatty, painted with tangy, but not spicy, house-special sauce. All dinners come with your choice of two sides: steamed rice, macaroni salad, or divine barbecue baked beans. The only misstep is the cole slaw made with raisins and apples — yuck! The polite, friendly staff is happy to pack your plated meal in a styrofoam box, which makes it perfect for a beach lunch or take-home dinner back at the condo.

See map p. 156. Napili Plaza, 5095 Napilihau St. (at Honoapiilani Highway), Napili. ☎ **808-665-6262.** *Plated meals: $5–$12 (full rib rack $19). No credit cards. Open: Lunch and early dinner (to 7 p.m.) Mon–Fri.*

Mañana Garage
$$ Central Maui (Kahului)   Latin American

Locals and visitors alike flock here for the winning indoor-outdoor setting and creative, nicely prepared Latin American cuisine that scores on all fronts. The boldly colored restaurant can be described as retro-industrial — it's cute and fun, but the groovy patio is the place to be. Paying for chips and salsa is a drag ($5, $7.50 with guacamole!), but all is forgiven after the basket arrives with its trio of zesty "samba" salsas. Everything just gets better. At lunchtime, I like the adobo barbecued duck and sweet potato quesadilla, mildly spiced with delicate green chiles, and the classic pressed Cuban sandwich. At dinner, you may start with green tomatoes, fried just right with smoked mozzarella and slivered red onions, or the *arepas con queso* — cornmeal and cheese griddle cakes topped with smoked salmon "pastrami," caper tobiko relish, and wasabi sour cream that manage to meld pan-continental flavors and textures without a hitch. For your main course, consider the pumpkin-crusted shrimp, a black-pepper-rubbed New York strip steak grilled in roasted pepper butter, or the seafood-rich paella. You can't go wrong with anything on the menu; every pan-Latin dish sings with flavor. Live entertainment adds to the cha-cha ambience Tuesday through Saturday evenings. A real winner!

See map p. 218. 33 Lono Ave. (at Kaahumanu Avenue), Kahului. ☎ **808-873-0220.** *Reservations recommended, especially for Fri–Sat dinner. Main courses $7–$13 at lunch, $13–$26 at dinner. AE, DC, DISC, MC, V. Open: Lunch and dinner Mon–Sat, dinner only Sun.*

Maui Tacos

$ **Central Maui/West Maui (Lahaina, Napili)/South Maui (Kihei) Island/Mexican**

This growing Maui chain (which now has several mainland locations) serves up high-quality, island-accented Mexican with a healthy bent in a fast-food format. All menu items are prepared using top-quality produce, lean steak, skinless chicken, light sour cream, and vegetable oil and stocks only (no lard). Chips, beans, and guacamoles are all made fresh on the premises, making Maui Tacos a terrific choice for a quickie meal that you won't regret later. Each location has a big bar offering a half dozen or so homemade salsas. The pineapple salsa's just silly, but the top-notch tomatillo salsa is perfectly zested with the just-right touch of lime and vinegar. Go with one of the generously stuffed big surf burritos for maximum satisfaction — and take it to the beach for the ultimate setting.

Central Maui: In Kahukui Kaahumanu Center, 275 Kaahumanu Ave., Kahului. ☎ *808-871-7726. See map p. 218.* *West Maui: In Lahaina Square, 840 Wainee St. (at Lahainaluna Road), just off Honoapiilani Hwy., Lahaina.* ☎ *808-661-8883. See map p. 157 Also in Napili Plaza, 5095 Napilihau St. (at Honoapiilani Highway) Napili.* ☎ *808-665-0222. See map p. 156.* *South Maui: In Kamaole Beach Center, 2411 S. Kihei Rd. (across from Kamaole Beach II), Kihei.* ☎ *808-879-5005.* www.mauitacos.com. *See map p. 158. Main courses: $4–$8. AE, DISC, MC, V. Open: Lunch and dinner daily.*

Milagros Food Co. Maui

$$ **Central Maui (Paia)   Southwestern**

This charmingly artsy indoor/outdoor place is a great stop for innovative island-style riffs on South-of-the-Border fare, top-shelf margaritas, and more. The fish tacos — flavored with secret sauce — are fabulous, as are the chile rellenos with grilled ahi and Kula greens. But the chef reaches beyond the standard, offering a nightly fresh ahi creation and other Southwestern specialties with a local flair. The outdoor patio is a nice place to start your day or wind up the drive to Hana with a late afternoon plate of piled-high nachos and a beer. This place draws a Gen-X crowd, so expect to be surrounded by laid-back surfer dudes and other Paia hipsters.

See map p. 218. 3 Baldwin Ave. (at Hana Highway), Paia. ☎ *808-579-8755. Main courses: $6–$17. MC, V. Open: Lunch and dinner daily.*

Nick's Fishmarket

$$$$$ **South Maui (Wailea)   Mediterranean/Seafood**

Wow! This expensive Mediterranean-accented seafooder gets everything just right: food, wine list, setting, and service. Nick's isn't on the beach, but the ambience is romantic to the max anyway. I prefer the vine-covered terrace, but the gorgeous, dimly lit dining room doesn't disappoint, either. The straightforward preparations let the clean, fresh flavor of the top-quality seafood shine. Kona-raised lobster is perfectly steamed and shelled at your table. Mahimahi is kiawe- (mesquite-) grilled and dressed with a sweet corn relish and aged balsamic vinegar, and an elegant *opakapaka* (pink snapper) is sautéed with meaty rock shrimps and lightly dressed with lemon butter and capers. The young, elegantly dressed servers have been schooled as pros, and it shows; you'll want for nothing here. The wine list is pricey, but excellent. A nice kids' menu (with dinners priced at $13) is at hand if an upscale family dinner is in your plans.

See map p. 158. In the Fairmont Kea Lani Maui, 4100 Wailea Alanui Dr., Wailea. ☎ *808-879-7224.* www.tri-star-restaurants.com. *Reservations highly recommended. Main courses: $27–$46. AE, DC, DISC, MC, V. Open: Dinner nightly.*

Pacific'o
$$$$ West Maui (Lahaina)   New Pacific

I'o (see the review earlier in this chapter) has an equally divine, equally pricey, and equally well-situated sister restaurant. Star chef James McDonald also oversees Pacific'o. I don't know which of the two restaurants you'll like better; frankly, they're not all that different. I'o is the more post-modern in terms of décor, while Pacific'o is more middle-of-the-road contemporary. Pacific'o's menu has become more distinctly Asian-influenced of late, and features more red-meat and fowl dishes for nonfish eaters. The Hapa/Hapa Tempura is a don't-miss for ahi tuna lovers.

See map p. 157. 505 Front St., Lahaina. ☎ *808-667-4341.* www.pacificomaui.com. *Reservations recommended. Main courses: $9–$16 at lunch, $24–$36 at dinner. AE, DC, MC, V. Open: Lunch and dinner daily.*

Peggy Sue's
$ South Maui (Kihei)   American

Step back in time to the fabulous '50s at this gleaming retro-style diner. Cherry cokes, egg creams, beefy burgers, and old-fashioned shakes are the order of the day. This place is old-fashioned all the way, and I love it. But it's not just about nostalgia: The burgers are juicy, the fries crispy, and the malts as creamy as they come. It's a good choice for a satisfying, affordable, all-American meal. Don't miss the opportunity to spin some vintage tunes on the genuine Wurlitzer jukebox!

See map p. 158. In Azeka Mauka Shopping Center, 1279 S. Kihei Rd. (at the north end of South Kihei Road), Kihei. ☎ *808-875-8944. Main courses: $6–$12. DC, MC, V. Open: Lunch and dinner daily.*

Pizza Paradiso
$ West Maui (Honokowai, Kaanapali)   Italian

This sit-down pizzeria serves up top-quality pies that manage to wow even skeptical New Yorkers (really!). In addition to a long list of create-your-own traditional toppings, Pizza Paradiso also offers a variety of theme pies, from the Maui Wowie (with ham and pineapple) to the Clam Slam (with juicy clams and tons of garlic), plus pastas, fresh, bounteous salads, and surprisingly good desserts (including a lovely homemade tiramisu). It's a terrific choice for bargain-hunting families, or anybody who needs a break from high-priced ahi for awhile. The Kaanapali location is an express take-out joint, but you can enjoy your pie at a table in the adjacent Whaler's Village food court. Both locations offer free delivery in the immediate area.

In Honokowai: In the Honokowai Marketplace (next to the Star Market), 3350 Honoapiilani Rd., Honokowai (south of Kahana). ☎ *808-667-2929. See map p. 156. In Kaanapali: At Whaler's Village, 2435 Kaanapali Pkwy., Kaanapali Beach.* ☎ *808-667-0333.* www.pizzaparadiso.com. *See map p. 124. Full-size pizzas: $13–$26. Pastas and sandwiches: $6–$12. MC, V. Open: Lunch and dinner daily.*

Plantation House
$$$$ West Maui (Kapalua)   Hawaii Regional/Mediterranean

Overlooking luxuriant golf greens and the stunning Kapalua coastline, the absolutely wonderful Plantation House may have the most glorious set-ting on Maui. Chef Alex Stanislaw and his team have crafted a one-of-a-kind Asian-Mediterranean fusion menu that changes frequently to take advan-tage of fresh seasonal produce. Expect to find dishes like scallop skewers with apple-smoked bacon and honey glaze; macadamia nut and goat cheese salad with Kula greens, Kalamata olives, and passionfruit vinai-grette; or roasted Molokai pork tenderloin with caramelized Maui onions. Fresh-caught island fish is the star of the menu, with several preparations available, including the divine Rich Forest option. (The fish is pressed with bread crumbs and porcini mushroom powder, sautéed, and nestled in garlic-braised spinach and mashed potatoes.) Chef Alex even lends his descriptive thoughts to the impressive wine list, one of the finest on the island. Book a terrace table and come at sunset for maximum enjoyment.

See p. 156. In the Plantation Course Clubhouse, 200 Plantation Club Dr., Kapalua. ☎ *808-669-6299.* www.theplantationhouse.com. *Reservations highly recom-mended for dinner. Main courses: $8.50–$16 at breakfast and lunch, $16–$39 at dinner ($54 for surf and turf). AE, DC, MC, V. Open: Breakfast, lunch, and dinner daily.*

Roy's Kahana Bar & Grill/Roy's Nicolina Restaurant/Roy's Kihei
$$$–$$$$ West Maui (Kahana)/South Maui (Kihei)   Hawaii Regional

Roy Yamaguchi is the most famous name in Hawaii Regional Cuisine. His island restaurants have always been terrific, and they continue to shine. You won't notice any striking difference between these two bustling side-by-side siblings, which share the same executive chef and the same basic menu. Roy's Kahana has an open kitchen and a livelier atmosphere, while Roy's Nicolina is quieter, a tad more sophisticated, and boasts outdoor dining on the lanai. Thanks to an oversized menu of dim sum, appetizers, and imu-baked pizzas, you can easily eat affordably in either dining room. The daily menu revolves around a few standards, such as sublime Szechuan baby-back ribs and blackened ahi with a delectable soy-mustard butter. The service is always attentive, and Roy's well-priced private-label wines are an excellent value (though you might be tempted to sample the out-standing private-label sakes instead). Roy's newest location, in Kihei, makes a wonderful addition to the South Maui dining scene.

In the Kahana Gateway Shopping Center, 4405 Honoapiilani Hwy. (Highway 30), Kahana. **Roy's Kahana:** ☎ **808-669-6999. Roy's Nicolina:** ☎ **808-669-5000.** *See map p. 156.* **Roy's Kihei:** *In the Piilani Shopping Center, 303 Piikea Ave., Kihei.* ☎ **808-891-1120.** www.roysrestaurant.com. *See map p. 158. Reservations highly recommended. Appetizers and pizzas: $8–$14. Main courses: $16–$33. AE, DC, DISC, MC, V. Open: Dinner nightly.*

A Saigon Cafe
$$ Central Maui (Wailuku) Vietnamese

This family-run restaurant in decidedly untouristy Wailuku serves up out-standing Vietnamese cuisine that's worth seeking out, especially if you're looking for a high-quality culinary return on your dollar. The wide-ranging menu features a dozen different soups (including a terrific lemongrass ver-sion), a complete slate of hot and cold noodle dishes, and numerous wok-cooked Vietnamese specialties starring island-grown produce and fresh-caught fish. Expect a taste sensation no matter what you order; every authentic dish bursts with piquant flavor. Ambience is minimal, but the quality of the food, low prices, and caring service more than compensate.

See map p. 218.1792 Main St. (between Kaniela and Nani streets), Wailuku. To get there: Take Kaahumanu Avenue (Highway 32) to Main Street; it's the white building under the bridge. ☎ **808-243-9560.** *Reservations recommended for 4 or more. Main courses: $7.50–$17. DC, MC, V. Open: Lunch and dinner daily.*

Sansei Seafood Restaurant & Sushi Bar
$$$ West Maui (Kapalua)/South Maui (Kihei) Japanese/
Pacific Rim Seafood

Both of sushi chef D.K. Kodama's Maui sushi palaces offer some of the best dining on the island — especially for sushi lovers. Composed primarily of pan-Asian seafood dishes with multicultural touches, Sansei's innovative menu has won raves from fans around the globe. Entrees are available, but I recommend assembling an adventurous family-style meal from the sushi rolls and small plates: The rock shrimp cake in ginger-lime chili butter, topped with crispy Chinese noodles, and Thai ahi carpaccio in a red pepper-lime sauce are both standouts. You really can't go wrong with any-thing. I love the beautifully presented flower sushi; don't miss it if you're a fishhead. For premier sushi service, cozy up to the bar at the bustling Kihei location; you won't be disappointed. Even the desserts are divine at this low-key, Japanese-style place. Book in advance so that you don't miss out. Take advantage of late-night dining and live karaoke from 10 p.m. to 1 a.m. on Thursdays and Fridays, and early-bird and late-night specials can take the sting out of the bill. A real winner!

In Kapalua: *In the Shops at Kapalua, 115 Bay Dr.* ☎ *808-669-6286. See map p. 156.* **In Kihei:** *Kihei Town Center (near Foodland), 1881 S. Kihei Rd.* ☎ *808-879-0004.* www . sanseihawaii.com. *See map p. 158. Reservations highly recommended. Sushi and sashimi: $3–$17. Main courses: $19–$38. AE, DISC, MC, V. Open: Dinner nightly.*

Sarento's on the Beach
$$$$–$$$$$ **South Maui (Kihei)   Italian/Mediterranean**

The Maui outpost of a Honolulu special-occasion favorite has won over well-dressed couples in droves with its first-class service and its gorgeous setting, which seamlessly fuses white-linen elegance and white-sand romance. The sophisticated Italian-Mediterranean cuisine more than lives up to the rest of the package. The stellar Greek salad is a Sarento's signature, and an excellent way to begin any meal. Veal lovers rave without fail about the osso buco, served on a bed of saffron risotto. I love the swordfish "saltimbocca," dressed with prosciutto and porcinis, and the seafood fra diavolo, with Kona lobster, diver scallops, and Manila clams. If you don't want to splurge on dinner, go to the sexy bar to revel in a perfectly poured cocktail and stupendous sunset views.

See map p. 158. At the Maui Oceanfront Inn, 2980 S. Kihei Rd. (at the south end of Kihei, just north of Kilohana Street), Kihei. ☎ *808-875-7555.* www.tri-star-restaurants.com. *Reservations highly recommended. Main courses: $13–$18 at lunch, $26–$40 at dinner. AE, DC, DISC, MC, V. Open: Lunch and dinner daily.*

Spago
$$$$$ **South Maui (Wailea)   Hawaii Regional/Pacific Rim**

America's first celebrity chef, Wolfgang Puck, goes Hawaiian. Puck's signature cutting-edge California style showcases fresh, local Hawaii ingredients. The fabulous dining room is a sleek, modern, open-air setting overlooking the blue Pacific. The menu features a heavenly coconut soup with local lobster, keffir, chili, and galangal; a whole steamed fish served with chili, ginger, and baby choy sum; and an incredible Kona lobster with sweet-and-sour banana curry, coconut rice, and dry-fried green beans. Spago has an extensive and thoughtful wine list. Save room for dessert (perhaps a warm chocolate truffle purse with Big Island vanilla bean ice cream). Be prepared for super-high prices and a sleek, L.A.-inspired attitude.

If you're in the mood for an elegant dinner in South Maui but suspect that Spago is a bit too style-conscious for you, opt instead for the Four Seasons' sister restaurant, **Ferraro's Bar e Ristorante** ($$$$; ☎ **808-874-8000**). South Maui's only outdoor beachside restaurant turns into a twinkle-lit seaside paradise in the evening. Ferraro's has built a deserved buzz with authentic Italian *cucina rustica* (the scrumptious focaccia is baked over a wood fire). It's a gorgeous sunset setting, with live evening entertainment. Casual poolside fare dominates during the daytime.

See map p. 158. In the Four Seasons Resort Maui, 3900 Wailea Alanui Dr., Wailea.
☎ *808-879-2999.* www.wolfgangpuck.com. *Reservations required well in advance.*
Main courses: $27–$42. AE, DC, DISC, MC, V. Open: Dinner nightly.

Stella Blues Cafe

$$–$$$ South Maui (Kihei)   New American

Stella Blues has moved down the street — and uptown in a big way. This
former Deadhead-themed deli has done a great job of reinventing itself as
a stylish and sophisticated grown-up restaurant. The rock-and-roll memorabilia still dresses the walls, but now it adds a pleasingly funky touch to
an airy dining room dressed in rich colors and warm woods, with an open
stainless-steel kitchen and a big, backlit bar. Tiki torches add romance to
the outdoor patio after dark. But the great thing about Stella Blues is that
it's still friendly, unpretentious, and affordable; you'd be hard-pressed to
find another restaurant in the islands that offers this much panache and
good cooking at such affordable prices.

Start your day with a hearty create-your-own omelette and then move on
to a french dip or another hefty sandwich at lunch. The place really comes
alive at dinner: Start with the surprisingly good Caesar salad, the delectable homemade hummus served with hot pita, or the funky nachos (blue
and yellow corn chips layered with mahimahi, ahi, jalapeños, jack cheese,
and guacamole). Choose from a range of creative pizzas, pastas, and big
plates for your main course; the New York steak (homegrown by the Maui
Cattle Company) is as good as most cuts of beef that are twice the price.
Late-night dining (until midnight weekdays, to 1:30 a.m. Friday and
Saturday nights) is another plus. Good job, Stella — you go, girl!

*See map p. 158. In Azeka Mauka Shopping Center, 1279 S. Kihei Rd. (at the north end
of Kihei).* ☎ *808-874-3779.* www.stellablues.com. *Reservations not necessary.
Main courses: $6–$10 at breakfast, $7–$10 at lunch, $11–$22 at dinner. DISC, MC, V.
Open: Breakfast, lunch, and dinner daily.*

Tommy Bahama's Tropical Cafe

$$$ South Maui (Wailea)   Caribbean

Housed in the Tommy Bahama's fashion emporium at the Shops at Wailea,
this delightful restaurant perfectly embodies the tropical haberdasher's
breezily sophisticated style. The open-air room is a mélange of bamboo,
rattan, and tropical prints that come together in a postmodern tropical-
plantation style. The restaurant actually looks more expensive than it is
— much like Tommy Bahama's delightful tropical-print wear. I love Tommy
Bahama's for lunch, when the menu focuses on Caribbean-inspired sand-
wiches and bounteous entree-sized salads. Pleasing choices include the
Habana Cabana pulled-pork sandwich, finished with the restaurant's own
blackberry brandy barbecue sauce, and the South Seas spinach salad,

tossed in a warm bacon balsamic vinaigrette and garnished with goat cheese, hardboiled egg, crispy fried onions, and shrimp or chicken (your choice). Dinner brings more substantial fare, like char-grilled baby back ribs, and pan-seared sashimi-grade ahi crusted in cilantro and lemongrass.

As good as the food is, Tommy Bahama's Tropical Cafe is really about soaking up the carefree mood, along with a few fruity cocktails. Come early for dinner because the second-level setting enjoys gorgeous sunset views.

See map p. 158. At the Shops at Wailea, 3750 Wailea Alanui Dr., second floor. ☎ **808-875-9983**. *Reservations recommended. Main courses: $8–$17 at lunch, $22–$35 at dinner (most less than $30). AE, MC, V. Open: Lunch and dinner daily.*

Vino
$$$ West Maui (Kapalua)   Italian

This first-class addition to the Maui dining scene also happens to be a great value, too. Vino is the brainchild of chef D.K. Kodama of the celebrated Sansei restaurants (see listing earlier in this chapter) and master sommelier Chuck Furuya — and their expertise makes this place shine. Kodama may be better known for his sushi, but it doesn't matter — this is world-class Italian fare (with the requisite island flair, of course). Highlights of the pasta-heavy menu (all are housemade) include delicately fried calamari dressed with a delicate lemon aioli and a side of spicy marinara; "silk handerchiefs," squares of egg pasta tossed with a light pesto (made with fresh-grown basil) and oven-roasted roma tomatoes, toasted almonds, and romano cheese; and a grilled half chicken "under a brick," stuffed with fennel and fresh herbs and grilled — well, you know where — for a delightful finish. I didn't find any dish that took a wrong turn here; everything was delightful. Furuya's wine list is equally captivating, with a good selection of well-priced choices by the glass accompanied by candid descriptions that let you pair easily. The high-ceilinged plantation-style room is outfitted with generous wood tables and open to the tropical breeze, setting the perfect stage for an enjoyable and casually sophisticated dining experience. Vino is a real value and a real find!

See map p. 156. In the Kapalua Village Course Golf Club House, 2000 Village Rd., Kapalua. ☎ **808-661-8466**. *Reservations recommended. Main courses: $13–$25. AE, DISC, MC, V. Open: Lunch and dinner daily.*

Luau!

Maui is Hawaii's hands-down winner in the luau department. These lavish feasts are a splurge, but they're an only-in-Maui experience.

You need reservations for the luaus that I list in this section. Make reservations as far in advance as possible — preferably before you leave home — because all these first-rate beach parties are often fully booked a week or more in advance, sometimes two.

Don't give up if you're trying to make last-minute plans, though; it never hurts to call and ask whether a few spots have opened up due to cancellations. Also, if you're booking at the last minute or you want more island luaus to choose from, check with **Tom Barefoot's Cashback Tours** (☎ **888-222-3601;** www.tombarefoot.com), a very reliable Maui-based activities center that can hook you up with a number of other luaus on Maui, and sometimes even save you a few bucks in the process.

Old Lahaina Luau

Old Lahaina Luau is Hawaii's most authentic and acclaimed luau, and my absolute favorite. The oceanfront luau grounds provide a stunning setting, both the luau feast and riveting entertainment serve as a wonderful intro-duction to genuine island culture, and the staff exudes aloha. When you book, choose between Hawaiian-style seating on mats and cushions set at low tables at the foot of the stage or traditional seating at generously pro-portioned common tables with comfortable wooden chairs; all tables have great views, but earlier bookings garner the best seats.

You're welcomed with a fresh flower lei (the yellow plumeria is the fragrant one) and greeted with a tropical cocktail. Arrive early so that you have plenty of time to stroll around the grounds — watching craftspeople at work and taking in the gorgeous views — before the imu ceremony, in which the luau pig is unearthed from the underground oven. The traditional buffet spread is excellently prepared and well labeled, so you know what you're eating (although the sit-down Feast at Lele, which I describe later in this section, should be the choice for gourmands).

Following dinner, the luau's excellent show begins, featuring authentic hula and traditional chants accompanied by an intelligent narrative charting the history of Hawaii from the first islanders to modern day. Don't mistake this narrative for a deadly dull history lesson — it's compelling entertain-ment, and both the male and female dancers are first-rate performers. (Don't expect fire dancers, though, because ancient Hawaiians didn't play with fire.) It's well worth the money, and a joy from start to finish — and an excellent choice for families, groups, and couples alike.

See map p. 157. 1251 Front St. (on the ocean side of the street, across from Lahaina Cannery Mall), Lahaina. ☎ *800-248-5828 or 808-667-1998.* www.oldlahainaluau. com. *Times: Nightly at 5:45 p.m. (at 5:15 p.m. Oct–Mar). Admission: $86 adults, $54 kids 2–12. Prices include cocktails.*

The Feast at Lele

This partnership between the folks behind the stellar Old Lahaina Luau and star chef James McDonald of I'o and Pacific'o (see earlier in this chapter) is a winning concept. It's ideal for those diners who don't mind paying extra for a more intimate oceanfront setting and a private table. An excellent five-course meal is prepared by a skilled chef and served at your own table (no standing in line at an all-you-can-eat buffet). You'll experience a lovely flower-lei greeting but no traditional imu ceremony or craft demonstrations (as at the Old Lahaina Luau). The performance troupe is smaller, but they're held to the same exacting standards.

This feast celebrates not only Hawaii but also three more Polynesian islands — Tonga, Tahiti, and Samoa — so the structure diverges from your standard luau. Each course is dedicated to an island culture — comprised of gourmet versions of foods from the native cuisine, followed by a native song and dance performance. Not only does this creative approach offer you the opportunity to sample plenty of well-prepared dishes — steamed *moi* (island trout) from Hawaii; lobster, octopus, and ogo salad from Tonga; steamed chicken and taro leaf in coconut milk from Tahiti; and so on — but also it highlights the nuances among the unique but related Polynesian groups. Furthermore, because Samoa is represented, the dazzling show can both stay culturally correct and feature crowd-pleasing fire-knife dancers.

Although the Feast at Lele welcomes all visitors, it tends to cater to a more sophisticated, kid-free, grown-up crowd than most luaus, making it an ideal choice for romance-seeking couples or anyone wanting a more refined experience. You can choose from a full wine list and tropical cocktail menu in addition to the included well cocktails, and you can expect your two dedicated servers to be friendly, knowledgeable, and attentive.

See map p. 157. 505 Front St. (on the ocean at Shaw Street), Lahaina. ☎ 808-667-5353. www.feastatlele.com. *Times: Nightly at 6 p.m. (at 5:30 p.m. Oct–Mar). Admission: $99 adults, $68 kids 2–12. Cocktails are included, but tips are not..*

Maui Marriott Luau

Marriott's nightly luau may not be quite the triumph that Old Lahaina's is, nor as innovative as the Feast at Lele (see earlier listings), but it's fabulous fun nonetheless if you can't get into one of the other two luaus. It's a glitzy affair set beachside in Kaanapali that starts with the traditional imu ceremony and culminates in a full-scale, Vegas-style Polynesian revue complete with traditional hula and a kid-wowing finale starring three fire-knife dancers. You're greeted with a shell lei, and you can learn traditional coconut husking and tiki carving before you line up to fill your plate from the satisfying all-you-can-eat luau spread. Take advantage of those bottomless mai tais, and you'll be doing the Hukilau (Hawaii's version of the Hokey Pokey) before you know it. Expect a rollicking good time.

See map p. 124. At the Maui Marriott, 100 Nohea Kai Dr. (on Kaanapali Parkway), Kaanapali. ☎ 800-745-6997. www.luaus.com. *Times: Nightly (except Monday) at 5:30 p.m. Admission: $80–$100 adults, $40–$60 kids 3–12, kids under 3 free. Prices include cocktails.*

Restaurant Indexes

The following section presents a listing of restaurant recommendations by location, cuisine, and price. Use the maps in this chapter to get a more specific fix on where each restaurant is located in relation to your accommodation.

Index of Restaurants by Location

South Maui (Wailea)

Capische? (Mediterranean-Italian, $$$$–$$$$$)
Cheeseburger in Paradise (American, $–$$)
Ferraro's Bar e Ristorante (Italian, $$$$)
Joe's Bar & Grill (New American/ Hawaii Regional, $$$$)
Nick's Fishmarket (Mediterranean Seafood, $$$$$)
Spago (California/Hawaii Regional/Pacific Rim, $$$$$)
Tommy Bahama's Tropical Cafe (Caribbean, $$$)

South Maui (Kihei)

Da' Kitchen (Local Hawaiian, $)
Maalaea Waterfront Restaurant (Continental/Seafood, $$$$)
Maui Tacos (Island/Mexican, $)
Peggy Sue's (American, $)
Roy's Kihei (Hawaii Regional, $$$–$$$$)
Sansei Seafood Restaurant & Sushi Bar (Japanese/Pacific Rim Seafood, $$$)
Sarento's on the Beach (Italian/ Mediterranean, $$$$–$$$$$)
Stella Blues Cafe (American, $$–$$$)

West Maui (Lahaina)

Aloha Mixed Plate (Local Hawaiian, $)
Cheeseburger in Paradise (American, $–$$)
Chez Paul (Provençal French, $$$$–$$$$$)
Compadres Mexican Bar & Grill (Mexican, $$)
David Paul's Lahaina Grill (New American/Hawaii Regional, $$$$–$$$$$)
The Feast at Lele (Luau, $$$$$)
Gerard's (New French, $$$$–$$$$$)
Hard Rock Cafe (American, $$)
I'o (New Pacific, $$$$)
Kimo's (Steak/Seafood, $$$)
Lahaina Coolers (American/ Eclectic, $$)
Maui Tacos (Island/Mexican, $)
Old Lahaina Luau (Luau, $$$$$)
Pacific'o (New Pacific, $$$$)

West Maui (Kaanapali)

CJ's Deli & Diner (American, $)
Hula Grill (Steak/Seafood, $–$$$)
Leilani's on the Beach (Steak/ Seafood, $$$)
Maui Marriott Luau (Luau, $$$$$)
Pizza Paradiso (Italian, $)

West Maui (Kahana/Napili)

Fish & Game Brewing Company & Rotisserie (Steak/Seafood, $$$)
Mama's Ribs (Barbecue, $)
Maui Tacos (Island/Mexican, $)
Pizza Paradiso (Italian, $)
Roy's Kahana Bar & Grill/Roy's Nicolina Restaurant (Hawaii Regional, $$$–$$$$)

West Maui (Kapalua)

Plantation House (Hawaii Regional/Mediterranean, $$$$)
Sansei Seafood Restaurant & Sushi Bar (Japanese/Pacific Rim Seafood, $$$)
Vino (Italian, $$$)

Central Maui

Cakewalk Paia Bakery (Bakery/Sandwiches, $)
Charley's Restaurant & Saloon (American/International, $$)
Mama's Fish House (Seafood, $$$$$)
Mañana Garage (Latin American, $$)
Maui Tacos (Island/Mexican, $)

Milagros Food Co. Maui (Southwestern, $$)
A Saigon Cafe (Vietnamese, $$)

Hana

Hotel Hana-Maui Main Dining Room (Continental/Island Fusion, $$$$)
Hana Ranch Restaurant (American, $–$$$)

Upcountry

Casanova (Italian, $$–$$$)
Haliimaile General Store (Hawaii Regional, $$$$)
Kula Lodge & Restaurant (Breakfast, $$)
Kula Sandalwoods Restaurant (Breakfast, $)

Restaurant Index by Cuisine

American

Charley's Restaurant & Saloon (Central Maui/Paia, $$)
Cheeseburger in Paradise (South Maui/Wailea, also in West Maui/ Lahaina; $–$$)
CJ's Deli & Diner (West Maui/Kaanapali; $)
Hana Ranch Restaurant (Hana, $–$$$)
Hard Rock Cafe (West Maui/ Lahaina, $$)
Lahaina Coolers (West Maui/ Lahaina, $$)
Peggy Sue's (South Maui/Kihei, $)
Stella Blues Cafe (South Maui/Kihei, $$–$$$)

Bakery/Sandwiches

Cakewalk Paia Bakery (Central Maui/ Paia, $)

Barbeque

Mama's Ribs & Rotisserie (West Maui/ Napili)

Breakfast

Cakewalk Paia Bakery (Central Maui, $)
Charley's Restaurant & Saloon (Central Maui, $$)
Kula Lodge & Restaurant (Upcountry, $$)
Kula Sandalwoods Restaurant (Upcountry, $)

Caribbean

Tommy Bahama's Tropical Cafe (South Maui/Wailea, $$$)

Continental

Hotel Hana-Maui Main Dining Room (Hana, $$$$)
Maalaea Waterfront Restaurant (South Maui/Kihei, $$$$)

French

Chez Paul (West Maui/Lahaina, $$$$–$$$$$)
Gerard's (West Maui/Lahaina, $$$$–$$$$$)

Hawaii Regional

David Paul's Lahaina Grill (West Maui/Lahaina, $$$$–$$$$$)
Haliimaile General Store (Upcountry, $$$$)
Joe's Bar & Grill (South Maui/Wailea, $$$$)
Plantation House (West Maui/Kapalua, $$$$)
Roy's Kihei (South Maui/Kihei, $$$–$$$$)
Roy's Kahana Bar & Grill/Roy's Nicolina Restaurant (West Maui/Kahana , $$$–$$$$)
Spago (South Maui/Wailea, $$$$$)

Italian

Capische? (South Maui/Wailea, $$$$–$$$$$)
Casanova (Upcountry, $$–$$$)
Ferraro's Bar e Ristorante (South Maui/Wailea, $$$$)
Pizza Paradiso (two West Maui locations: Kaanapali and Kahana/Napili, $)
Sarento's on the Beach (South Maui/Kihei, $$$$–$$$$$)
Vino (West Maui/Kapalua, $$$)

Japanese

Sansei Seafood Restaurant & Sushi Bar (West Maui/Kapalua and in South Maui/Kihei, $$$)

Latin American

Mañana Garage (Central Maui, $$)

Local Hawaiian

Aloha Mixed Plate (West Maui/Lahaina, $)
Da' Kitchen (South Maui/Kihei, $)

Luau

The Feast at Lele (West Maui/Lahaina, $$$$$)
Maui Marriott Luau (West Maui/Kaanapali, $$$$$)
Old Lahaina Luau (West Maui/Lahaina, $$$$$)

Mediterranean

Capische? (South Maui/Wailea, $$$$–$$$$$)
Nick's Fishmarket (South Maui/Wailea, $$$$$)
Plantation House (West Maui/Kapalua, $$$$)
Sarento's on the Beach (South Maui/Kihei, $$$$–$$$$$)

Mexican/Southwestern

Compadres Mexican Bar & Grill (West Maui/Lahaina, $$)
Maui Tacos (South Maui/Kihei, Central Maui, and two West Maui locations in Lahaina and in Kahana/Napili; $)
Milagros Food Co. Maui (Central Maui, $$)

New American

David Paul's Lahaina Grill (West Maui/Lahaina, $$$$–$$$$$)
Joe's Bar & Grill (South Maui/Wailea, $$$$)

Pacific Rim

I'o (West Maui/Lahaina, $$$$)
Pacific'o (West Maui/Lahaina, $$$$)
Sansei Seafood Restaurant & Sushi Bar (West Maui/Kapalua and in South Maui/Kihei, $$$)
Spago (South Maui/Wailea, $$$$$)

Seafood

Maalaea Waterfront Restaurant (South Maui/Kihei, $$$$)
Mama's Fish House (Central Maui/Paia, $$$$$)
Nick's Fishmarket (South Maui/Wailea, $$$$$)
Sansei Seafood Restaurant & Sushi Bar (West Maui/Kapalua and in South Maui/Kihei, $$$)

Steak/Seafood

Fish & Game Brewing Company & Rotisserie (West Maui/Kahana, $$$)

Hula Grill (West Maui/Kaanapali, $-$$$)

Kimo's (West Maui/Lahaina, $$$)

Leilani's on the Beach (West Maui/Kaanapali, $$$)

Vietnamese

A Saigon Cafe (Central Maui, $$)

Restaurant Index by Price

$$$$$

The Feast at Lele (West Maui/Lahaina, Luau)

Mama's Fish House (Central Maui/Paia, Seafood)

Maui Marriott Luau (West Maui/Kaanapali, Luau)

Nick's Fishmarket (South Maui/Wailea, Mediterranean/Seafood)

Old Lahaina Luau (West Maui/Lahaina, Luau)

Spago (South Maui/Wailea, Hawaii Regional/Pacific Rim)

$$$$-$$$$$

Capische? (South Maui/Wailea, Mediterranean-Italian)

Chez Paul (West Maui/Lahaina, Provençal French)

David Paul's Lahaina Grill (West Maui/Lahaina, New American/Hawaii Regional)

Gerard's (West Maui/Lahaina, New French)

Sarento's on the Beach (South Maui/Kihei, Italian/Mediterranean)

$$$$

Ferraro's Bar e Ristorante (South Maui/Wailea, Italian)

Haliimaile General Store (Upcountry, Hawaii Regional)

Hotel Hana-Maui Main Dining Room (Hana, Continental/Island Fusion)

I'o (West Maui/Lahaina, New Pacific)

Joe's Bar & Grill (South Maui/Wailea, New American/Hawaii Regional)

Maalaea Waterfront Restaurant (South Maui/Kihei, Continental/Seafood)

Pacific'o (West Maui/Lahaina, New Pacific)

Plantation House (West Maui/Kapalua, Hawaii Regional/Mediterranean)

$$$-$$$$

Roy's Kahana Bar & Grill/Roy's Nicolina Restaurant (West Maui/Kahana , Hawaii Regional)

Roy's Kihei (South Maui/Kihei, Hawaii Regional)

$$$

Fish & Game Brewing Company & Rotisserie (West Maui/Kahana, Steak/Seafood)

Kimo's (West Maui/Lahaina, Steak/Seafood)

Leilani's on the Beach (West Maui/Kaanapali, Steak/Seafood)

Sansei Seafood Restaurant & Sushi Bar (West Maui/Kapalua and in South Maui/Kihei, Japanese/Pacific Rim Seafood)

Tommy Bahama's Tropical Cafe (South Maui/Wailea, Caribbean)

Vino (West Maui/Kapalua, Italian)

$$–$$$
Casanova (Upcountry, Italian)
Stella Blues Cafe (South Maui/Kihei, American)

$$
Charley's Restaurant & Saloon (Central Maui/Paia, American/International)
Compadres Mexican Bar & Grill (West Maui/Lahaina, Mexican)
Hana Ranch Restaurant (Hana, American)
Hard Rock Cafe (West Maui/Lahaina, American)
Hula Grill (West Maui/Kaanapali, Steak/Seafood)
Kula Lodge & Restaurant (Upcountry, Breakfast)
Lahaina Coolers (West Maui/Lahaina, American/Eclectic)
Mañana Garage (Central Maui, Latin American)
Milagros Food Co. Maui (Central Maui, Southwestern)
A Saigon Cafe (Central Maui, Vietnamese)

$–$$
Cheeseburger in Paradise (South Maui/Wailea, also in West Maui/Lahaina; American)

$
Aloha Mixed Plate (West Maui/Lahaina, Local Hawaiian)
Cakewalk Paia Bakery (Central Maui/Paia, Bakery/Sandwiches)
CJ's Deli & Diner (West Maui/Kaanapali, American)
Da' Kitchen (South Maui/Kihei, Local Hawaiian)
Kula Sandalwoods Restaurant (Upcountry, Breakfast)
Mama's Ribs & Rotisserie (West Maui/Napili, Barbecue)
Maui Tacos (South Maui/Kihei, Central Maui, and two West Maui locations in Lahaina and in Kahana/Napili; Island/Mexican)
Peggy Sue's (South Maui/Kihei, American)
Pizza Paradiso (two West Maui locations: Kaanapali and Kahana/Napili; Italian)

Part IV
Exploring Maui

The 5th Wave   By Rich Tennant

THE ISLAND EXPERIENCE

Your glass of water...

In this part . . .

This part is just what you need for your introduction to Maui's famous beaches. I show you how to enjoy the waves, with the lowdown on the best watersports, snorkel spots, cruises, and much more. You also discover the island's top adventures: watching the mystical sunrise at Haleakala National Park, cruising the Heavenly Road to Hana, and splashing in tropical waterfalls along the way. (Don't worry, duffers; I have all the best golf courses listed here, too.) I show you where to shop, where to toast the perfect sunset, and where to party the night away. As if this weren't enough, a whole world of adventure is waiting for you on Maui's closest neighbors, Molokai and Lanai. I talk you through it step by step.

Chapter 12

Enjoying Maui's Best Beaches and Watersports

In This Chapter

▶ Locating Maui's best beaches
▶ Playing in the waves: Dive trips, snorkel cruises, and much more
▶ Watching whales
▶ Staying safe while you enjoy the water

*F*or people who love spending time outdoors, Maui is practically paradise. Even if you have no intention of sampling every activity that it has to offer, the bounty of choice will wow you — and you may have trouble deciding on exactly what you want to do. This action-packed island has something for everyone — and then some — so staying active and happy won't be a problem on Maui. Your biggest dilemma likely may be just trying to fit everything into your vacation calendar.

In this chapter, I help you maximize your outdoors time on Maui. I show you where the best beaches are, and I also direct you to the companies that schedule dive trips, snorkel cruises, whale-watching tours, and so much more. No matter how you want to spend your time on Maui, the island is ready and waiting for you. Don't waste another minute!

See Chapter 13 for detailed information on land sports, including golf, hiking, horseback riding — and even mountain biking down a volcano!

Taking the Plunge: Knowing Where to Start

In order to begin your fabulous Maui adventure, you may need a little help from your new island friends. Several companies offer reliable personal assistance that can help you choose the activities that are right for you. The best and most reliable activity booker on Maui is

Tom Barefoot's Cashback Tours, in the heart of Lahaina at 834 Front St., near Lahainaluna Road (☎ **888-222-0350** or 808-661-8889; www.tombare foot.com). Unlike most other so-called "activity centers" on Maui, this professional operation has nothing to do with timeshares — activities are their business, and their reps are pros who really know their stuff. I've found the salespeople's recommendations to be consistently good ones. Their office is filled with pictures and descriptive information on all the activities they represent.

Furthermore, Tom Barefoot's offers a 10-percent discount on select activities when you pay with cash, personal check, or traveler's checks, as well as a 7-percent discount if you pay by credit card. However, if you tell Tom Barefoot's that you want the top-of-the-line snorkel cruise or luau, they'll freely recommend and book you with Trilogy or Old Lahaina, even though they can't offer you a savings and won't make a dime — because they figure that a happy customer is a returning customer. You can book discounted activities before you leave home via their Web site or toll-free number.

Another recommendable activity booker is **Trilogy Ocean Sports,** which maintains a kiosk on Kaanapali Beach in front of the Kaanapali Beach Hotel (☎ **808-661-7789**). A sister business to Trilogy Excursions — which is universally regarded as the finest snorkel-sail operator on Maui (read more about Trilogy Excursions' offerings later in this chapter) — Trilogy Ocean Sports can book you not only onto Trilogy cruises but also with other activity providers they endorse, whether you're looking for a backcountry four-wheeling excursion or a beginning surfing lesson. They've handpicked a top-flight group of activity providers to represent, and I've found their recommendations to be terrific.

Do yourself a favor and avoid those activities bookers that are trying to sell you a timeshare. Believe me — you don't want to spend a half-day of your precious vacation time warding off a salesperson's hard-sell advances to buy a timeshare you don't need in exchange for a "free" snorkel cruise on a cut-rate operator.

Hitting the Beaches

Maui's fabulous beaches (even those in front of exclusive resorts) are open to the public. Hawaii state law requires all hotels to offer public right-of-way access (across private property) to the beach, along with public parking. So just because a beach fronts a hotel doesn't mean that you can't enjoy the water. However, the hotel may restrict certain areas of private property for hotel guests' use only. Generally, hotels welcome nonguests to their facilities (though they frown on nonguests using the beach chairs reserved for guests), and they're happy to rent you beach gear or sell you refreshments.

Never leave valuables in your rental car while you're at the beach. Knowledgeable thieves like to prey on tourists, and they know how to get into your interior, trunk, and glove box in no time flat. Be especially diligent about leaving your stuff behind at your condo or in your hotel safe when you're heading off to a remote beach.

Also, if you see a red flag hoisted at any beach, don't venture into the water because it indicates that conditions are unsafe for swimmers. Even if the waves look placid, trust the warning. Turn to the end of this chapter for more detailed tips on water safety.

In West Maui

Following are some beaches to check out in West Maui.

Honolua/Mokuleia Bay Marine Life Conservation District

Snorkelers love this gorgeous cove for its smooth surf, clear waters (which are protected as a marine-life conservation district), excellent coral formations, and abundance of tropical fish, especially on the west side of the bay. The beige-sand crescent is lovely, and never too crowded. In winter, stay out of the water — it's too rough and dangerous. Instead, come to watch daredevil surfers ride some of the finest breaks in the islands. Sorry, this sight has no facilities. If you're in this area and you want a beach with facilities, you can find restrooms, showers, picnic tables, and barbecue grills at nearby **D.T. Fleming Beach Park.** This quiet, crescent-shaped cove north of the Ritz-Carlton starts at the 16th hole of the Kapalua golf course (Makaluapuna Point) and rolls around to the sea cliffs at the other side. Ironwood trees provide shade. The waters are generally calm enough to offer good swimming and snorkeling.

See map p. 190. At the northernmost end of Honoapiilani Highway (Highway 30), about 2 miles past Office Road (the turnoff for Kapalua); park with the other cars in the available spaces or along the roadside and walk 200 yards down the stairs and to the beach.

Kapalua Beach

This gorgeous, golden crescent bordered by two palm-studded points is justifiably popular for sunbathing, swimming, and snorkeling. The sandy bottom slopes gently to deep water that's so clear you can see where the gold sands turn to green, and then deep blue. Well-protected from strong winds and currents, Kapalua's calm waters are usually great for swimmers of all ages and abilities year-round, and waves come in just right for easy riding. The rocky points offer good fish-communing opportunities for both snorkelers and offshore divers. The beach is also great for offshore whale-watching in winter, too. A shady path and cool lawns edge the beach's inland side. Facilities include showers, restrooms, a rental shack, and outdoor showers. The small parking lot is limited to about 30 spaces, so arrive early.

Maui's Best Beaches and Watersports

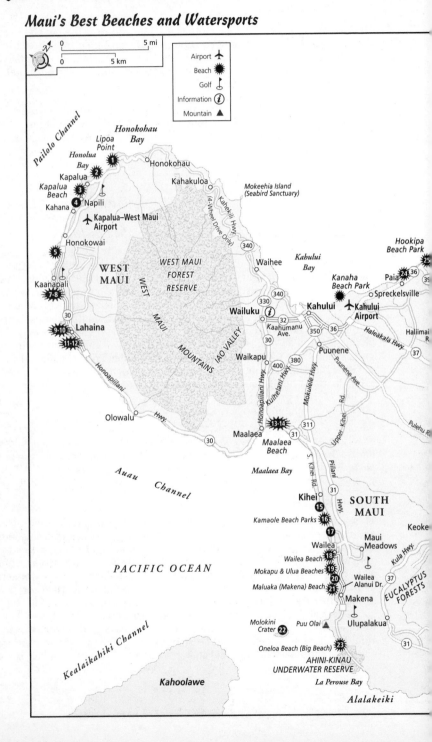

Airport ✈
Beach ✹
Golf ⚑
Information ⓘ
Mountain ▲

Pailolo Channel

Honokohau Bay

Lipoa Point

Honolua Bay

Kapalua

Kapalua Beach

Kahana

Napili

Honokohau

Kahakuloa

Mokeehia Island (Seabird Sanctuary)

Kahekili Hwy. (4-Wheel Drive Only)

Kapalua–West Maui Airport

Honokowai

WEST MAUI

WEST MAUI FOREST RESERVE

340

Waihee

Kahului Bay

Hookipa Beach Park

Kanaha Beach Park

Paia

Spreckelsville

Kaanapali

WEST MAUI MOUNTAINS

330

340

Wailuku ⓘ

Kahului

Kahului Airport

Lahaina

32

Kaahumanu Ave.

350

36

Haleakala Hwy.

Hallimai R

37

Honoapiilani

IAO VALLEY

Waikapu

30

400

380

Puunene

Puunene Ave.

Olowalu

Hwy.

Maalaea

30

Maalaea Beach

311

31

Upper Kihei

Mokulele Hwy.

Kuihelani Hwy.

Pulehu R

Auau Channel

Maalaea Bay

Kihei

31

15

SOUTH MAUI

Keoke

Kamaole Beach Parks

16

17

Wailea

Maui Meadows

PACIFIC OCEAN

Wailea Beach

18

Mokapu & Ula Beaches

19

20

Maluaka (Makena) Beach

21

Wailea Alanui Dr.

Kula Hwy.

EUCALYPTUS FORESTS

37

Makena

Ulupalakua

Molokini Crater

22

Puu Olai ▲

31

Kealaikahiki Channel

Oneloa Beach (Big Beach)

23

AHINI-KINAU UNDERWATER RESERVE

La Perouse Bay

Kahoolawe

Alalakeiki

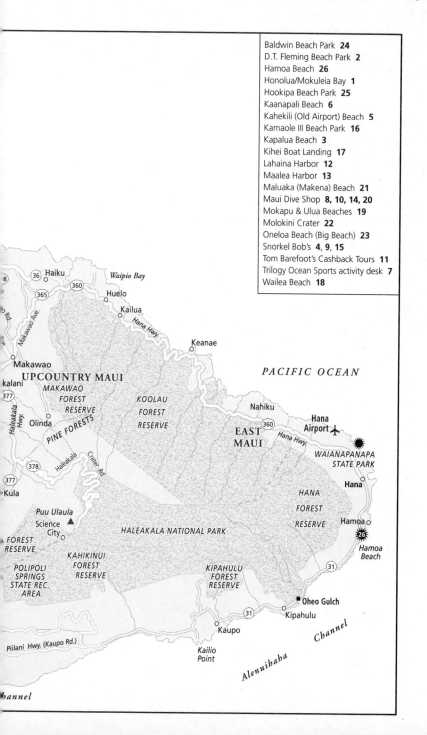

Baldwin Beach Park **24**
D.T. Fleming Beach Park **2**
Hamoa Beach **26**
Honolua/Mokuleia Bay **1**
Hookipa Beach Park **25**
Kaanapali Beach **6**
Kahekili (Old Airport) Beach **5**
Kamaole III Beach Park **16**
Kapalua Beach **3**
Kihei Boat Landing **17**
Lahaina Harbor **12**
Maalea Harbor **13**
Maluaka (Makena) Beach **21**
Maui Dive Shop **8, 10, 14, 20**
Mokapu & Ulua Beaches **19**
Molokini Crater **22**
Oneloa Beach (Big Beach) **23**
Snorkel Bob's **4, 9, 15**
Tom Barefoot's Cashback Tours **11**
Trilogy Ocean Sports activity desk **7**
Wailea Beach **18**

See map p. 190. On Lower Honoapiilani Road at the south end of Kapalua, just before the Napili Kai Beach Club. To get there: From Honoapiilani Highway, turn left just past mile marker 30, go 1/10 mile to Lower Honoapiilani Road, turn left, and go 9/10 mile to the access point.

Kahekili (Old Airport) Beach

This smallish but extremely attractive beach is one of Maui's best snorkel spots for beginners and families with small kids because waters are shallow, clear, and well protected by an expansive offshore reef that teems with colorful fish. Its nice facilities — including very clean restrooms with showers, plus picnic tables — make it a good place to come and spend the day. Don't be surprised if you see groups of divers, because Kahekili is a popular instructional dive spot.

See map p. 190. Off Honoapiilani Highway (Highway 30) at the north end of Kaanapali, just across from the Sugar Cane Train. To get there: From Honoapiilani Highway, turn left at the northernmost access to Kaanapali; look for public beach access and parking on your right.

Kaanapali Beach

Maui's first resort developers chose this beach to start building on because it's absolutely fabulous. Hotels and condos (almost approaching the density of Waikiki) now line Kaanapali's 4 miles of grainy, gold sand, but the not-too-wide beach tends to be populated only in pockets; you can usually find an uncrowded area to spread out your towel even when the hotels are at capacity. Swimming and wave jumping are excellent, but beware of the rough winter shorebreak (where the waves break on the shore), which can really kick up. At the beach's north end, in front of the Sheraton, is Black Rock, the best offshore snorkel spot on Maui. The water is clear, the reef is well-protected, and the clouds of tropical fish are used to finned folks.

A paved beach walk links the hotels and the open-air Whaler's Village shopping and dining complex — a great place to cure the midday munchies or slurp down a tropical cocktail. Lifeguards and beachboys from the resorts man the beach, beach-gear rental shacks are set up right on the sand, and most hotels have outdoor showers (and sometimes restrooms) you can use; restrooms are also available at Whaler's Village. The only downside is that you likely have to pay for parking if you're not staying there, but the few bucks for such prime beachgoing are worth it. (A few free spaces are available, but good luck snaring one — I've never been able to.)

See map p. 190. Kaanapali Parkway, off Honoapiilani Highway (Highway 30), Kaanapali.

Along the South Maui Coast

The South Maui Coast offers several popular beaches.

Sunburn: Just say no

I don't know whether it's the hole in the ozone, but tanning just ain't what it use to be. Hawaii's Caucasian population has the highest incidence of deadly skin cancer (malignant melanoma) in the United States. But people of all skin types and races fry when exposed to the sun too long — and I can't think of a worse way to ruin a perfectly good vacation.

Every time I visit Hawaii, I see vacationers burned to a painful red crisp. I don't want you to fry, so use these helpful tips on how to tan safely and painlessly:

- ✔ **Always wear a strong sunscreen.** Use a sunscreen with a sun-protection factor (SPF) of 15 or higher; people with light complexions should use at least 30. Apply sunscreen as soon as you get out of the shower in the morning. Don't skimp — really slather it on and reapply every two hours and after swimming, even if the bottle says it's waterproof.

- ✔ **Read the fine print before you leave the store.** To avoid developing allergies to sunscreens, avoid sunscreens that contain para-amino benxoic acid (PABA). Look for sunscreens with zinc oxide, talc, or titanium dioxide, because they reduce the risk of developing skin allergies.

- ✔ **Wear a big floppy hat and sunglasses.** The hat should have a wide brim (all the way around, to cover not only your face but also the sensitive back of your neck). Make sure that your sunglasses have UV filters.

- ✔ **Don't expect a T-shirt to protect you.** Believe it or not, that old T-shirt you put over your bathing suit only has an SPF of 6. If you're going to rely on your clothing to protect you, make sure that it has been specifically manufactured to block UV rays.

- ✔ **Avoid the sun during peak midday hours.** Seek the shade during peak hours from 11 a.m. to 2 p.m. And a beach umbrella won't do ya, either; with the reflection from the water, the sand, and even the sidewalk, some 85 percent of the ultraviolet rays are still bombarding you.

- ✔ **Cover kids well and keep infants out of the sun altogether.** Older babies need zinc oxide to protect their fragile skin. Slather children with sunscreen every hour. The burns that children get today predict what their future with skin cancer will be tomorrow. Keep infants under 6 months out of the sun.

- ✔ **If you start to turn red, get out of the sun immediately.** You don't have to turn red to tan — if your skin is red, it's burned, and that's serious. The full force of that burn may not appear for 24 to 36 hours. During that time, you can look forward to pain, itching, and peeling.

The best remedy for sunburn is to stay out of the sun until all the redness is gone. Aloe vera, cool compresses, cold baths, and anesthetic benzocaine may also help with the pain.

Kamaole III Beach Park

Three popular beach parks — Kamaole I, II, and III — face the waves across from South Kihei Road in mid-Kihei. The biggest and best is Kamaole III (or Kam-3, as the locals call it), which boasts a playground and a grassy lawn that meets the finely textured, golden sand. Swimming is generally safe, but parents should make sure that little ones don't venture too far out because the bottom slopes off quickly. Families may prefer the beach's grassy end with shade trees, where the ocean bottom has a fairly gentle slope. Both the north and south ends have rocky fingers that are great for snorkelers, and the winter waves attract bodysurfers. This west-facing beach is also an ideal spot to watch the sun go down or look for whales offshore in winter. Facilities include restrooms, showers, picnic tables, barbecues, volleyball nets, and lifeguards. Food and beach-gear rentals are available at the malls across the street — but be careful crossing busy Kihei Road!

See map p. 190. On South Kihei Road, just south of Keonekai Street (across from the Maui Parkshore and Kamaole Sands condos), Kihei.

Mokapu and Ulua Beaches

Situated at the north end of Wailea, these lovely side-by-side sister beaches boast pretty, golden sand, grassy areas for sandless picnicking, and clean facilities, including restrooms and a freshwater shower pole. The ocean bottom is shallow and gently slopes down to deeper waters, making swimming generally safe; snorkelers find Wailea's best snorkeling at the rocky north end. When the surf kicks up, the waves are excellent for bodysurfers. Although these beaches are popular with the nearby upscale condo crowd, the sand rarely gets too crowded. The parking lot is tiny, though, so come early.

See map p. 190. On Wailea Alanui Road at Hale Alii Place, just south of the Renaissance Wailea (across from the Palms at Wailea condos), Wailea.

Wailea Beach

The ultrafine gold-sand beach is long, wide, and protected on both sides by black lava points with a sandy and sloping bottom, making the clear waters excellent for swimming (and okay for snorkeling, too). The year-round waves are just right for easy board-riding or bodysurfing, but trade winds can kick up in the afternoon, so come early. The view out to sea is gorgeous, with the islands of Kahoolawe and Lanai framing the view. This site is ideal to watch for humpback whales in winter. This stretch of shoreline may feel like it belongs to the ultradeluxe resorts that line it, but it doesn't; just look for the blue "Shoreline Access" signs for easiest access. Restrooms and showers are available.

See map p. 190. Fronting the Grand Wailea and Four Seasons resorts, Wailea. To get there: The blue "Shoreline Access" sign is between the two resorts on Wailea Alanui Drive.

Maluaka (Makena) Beach

This wonderful beach park offers a pleasing off-the-beaten-path experience for people in search of a first-rate snorkel experience, or anybody who wants a break from Maui's ever-present crowds. Short, wide, and palm-fringed, this unspoiled crescent of golden, grainy sand is set between two protective lava points and bounded by big, grassy sand dunes. Snorkelers find surprisingly colorful coral and an impressive array of vibrantly hued reef fish at the beach's rocky south end, past the lava point. Sunbathers and casual swimmers stick to the beautiful strand closer to the hotel, which is virtually empty on weekdays. Facilities include restrooms and showers.

See map p. 190. Makena Alanui Drive, Makena (south of Wailea). To get there: Follow Wailea Alanui Drive south through Wailea to Makena, and look for the "Shoreline Access" sign near the Maui Prince Hotel; turn at the "Dead End" sign past the hotel for public access parking.

Oneloa Beach (Big Beach)

Oneloa means "long sand" in Hawaiian, and locals call it Big Beach. It comes by its name honestly, for this lovely stretch of sand is 3,300 feet long and more than 100 feet wide. Oneloa is a beautiful spot for swimming, sunbathing, surfing, body boarding, and strolling along the shore. Snorkeling is good around the north end at Puu Olai, a 360-foot cinder cone. In winter storm season, beware of fierce waves and a strong rip current that sweeps the sharp drop-off. The area has no facilities except portable toilets, but plenty of parking is available.

See map p. 190. South of Makena. To get there: Drive past the Maui Prince Hotel to the second dirt road, which leads to the beach.

Central and East Maui

Three beaches in particular stand out in Central and East Maui.

Baldwin Beach Park

Despite the beauty of this gorgeous beach park — a long ribbon of powdery white sands backed by swaying palms and fringed by white-crested turquoise waves — this north shore is almost never crowded. The beach stretches for a good mile, so it has plenty of room for everybody, especially because only locals and intrepid visitors generally end up here. This is a terrific spot for swimmers and body boarders, because the water is silky, warm, and gorgeous. But be careful before venturing into the water and always heed the lifeguard, because the undercurrent can be strong at times — and it's best to stay out of the water altogether in the rough winter months. When it's rough, the water's not for inexperienced swimmers — but everybody can enjoy the beautiful setting at any time of the year. Facilities include restrooms and showers.

See map p. 190. On the Hana Highway (Highway 36), just east of Paia. To get there: Drive past the Maui Prince Hotel to the second dirt road, which leads to the beach.

Hookipa Beach Park

Possibly the most famous windsurfing beach in the world, this small, gold-sand beach at the foot of a grassy cliff attracts top windsurfers and wave jumpers from around the globe with hard, constant winds and endless waves that result in near-perfect wave-riding conditions. Come on weekday afternoons to watch the local experts fly over the waves with their colorful sails; winter weekends host regular competitions. When the winter waves die down, snorkelers and divers explore the reef. Even then, be extremely careful because these waters are rough year-round; summer mornings are best. Facilities include some rustic restrooms and showers, plus pavilions, picnic tables, and barbecues. The lower parking lot is generally reserved for windsurfers and their equipment, so park in the upper lot (see the following directions), where the high, grassy bluff offers a better perch for watching the action anyway.

See map p. 190. Off Hana Highway (Highway 36), 2 miles east of Paia, about 6 miles east of Haleakala Highway (Highway 37). To get there: Drive past the park and turn left at the entrance at the far side of the beach, at the Hookipa Lookout sign.

Hamoa Beach

This remote, half-moon-shaped beach near the end of the Hana Road is one of the most breathtakingly lovely in Hawaii, celebrated in writing by no less than James Michener for its singular beauty. The Hotel Hana-Maui likes to maintain the beach as its own — but it has to share, so feel free to march right down the steps from the lava-rock lookout point and stake out a spot on the open sand. Even if you don't want to swim or sunbathe, come to peek at this stunner from above: You find surf that's the perfect color of turquoise, golden-gray sand, and luxuriant green hills serving as the postcard-perfect backdrop. The beach is generally good for swimming and wave-riding in the gentle seasons, but stick close to the shore because you're in open, unprotected ocean. Stay out of the water entirely in winter. The hotel maintains minimal facilities for nonguests, including a restroom.

See map p. 190. Off the Hana Highway (Highway 36), about 2½ miles past Hana town. To get there: Turn at the small white sign that says "Hamoa Beach" and go about 1½ miles to the lava-rock lookout point; you can park on the roadside or in the dirt area across the road. The stairs are just beyond the lookout point. (If you reach the steep service road to the beach, you've gone too far.)

Discovering Water Fun for Everyone

If your hotel or condo doesn't provide beach gear or beach toys, you won't have a problem finding a place to rent these items. In addition to offering top-quality snorkel gear, **Snorkel Bob's** (see contact information in the next section) rents boogie boards and beach chairs at its three Maui stores. Rental shacks on popular beaches like Kaanapali and Kapalua can hook you up with whatever you need. You can also rent gear — beach chairs, picnic coolers, boogie boards, surfboards, ocean kayaks, and the like — at very reasonable prices from **Duke's Surf Shop,** 578 Front St. (at Prison Street), Lahaina (☎ **808-661-1970**).

Snorkeling

Maui is justifiably famous for its snorkel cruises to Molokai and Lanai, both of which offer first-class fish-spotting, some of the best in the state (see Chapters 16 and 17 for more information). But anybody who's already perused the "Hitting the Beaches" section earlier in this chapter knows that Maui offers a wealth of terrific snorkel spots that are accessible from shore. Probably the best of these spots is Black Rock at the north end of **Kaanapali Beach;** also excellent are **Honolua Bay,** north of Kapalua; **Mokapu and Ulua beaches,** in Wailea; and one of my lesser known favorites, **Maluaka (Makena) Beach,** south of Wailea in Makena.

For the most comprehensive guide to the best snorkel spots around the island, stop into the **Maui Dive Shop** and pick up a copy of the free publication *Maui Dive Guide.* In the centerfold of the magazine-style guide is a map to all of the best snorkel spots, with information on level of difficulty, best water access points, facilities information, and all the details you need to get there. Maui Dive Shop has four locations in West Maui, including the Lahaina Cannery Mall (☎ **808-661-5388**) and Whaler's Village at Kaanapali (☎ **808-661-5117**), and four locations in South Maui, including Maalaea Harbor Village (☎ **808-244-5514**) and the Shops at Wailea (☎ **808-875-9904**). To find the location nearest you, call ☎ **800-542-3483** (from the mainland United States and Canada), ☎ **808-661-6166** (Lahaina), or ☎ **808-879-3388** (Kihei), or visit www.mauidiveshop.com.

Snorkeling without getting your hair wet

You can see Maui's spectacular underwater world even if you don't swim: Take a submarine ride with **Atlantis Submarines** (☎ 800-548-6262 or 808-661-1210; www.goatlantis.com/hawaii). From Lahaina Harbor's Pier No. 18, you go 130 feet beneath the surface in one of Atlantis's state-of-the-art subs to see a whole new world of sea critters, including — if you're lucky — humpback whales in season. The 90-minute tours cost $80 for adults, $40 for kids (children must be at least 36 inches tall). You may be able to save a few bucks by booking your submarine tour online.

Note: The ride is perfectly safe, but skip it if you suffer from serious claustrophobia. On the other side of the coin: If you're a swimmer — even if you just have basic paddle skills — you may want to skip this expensive adventure, don a mask and snorkel, and hit the waves instead for a primo underwater experience.

If you want to take advantage of Maui's offshore snorkeling opportunities, you probably need to rent some gear. My favorite rental-gear supplier in Hawaii is **Snorkel Bob's;** they rent the best-quality gear, with friendly service and a refreshing dose of snarky humor thrown in for good measure. Snorkel Bob's maintains four Maui locations, with two in West Maui. One is at 1217 Front St. in Lahaina, at the town's north end near the Old Lahaina Luau (☎ **808-661-4421**); look for the landmark "Jesus Coming Soon" sign. The other West Maui store is almost to Kapalua in Napili Village, 5425 Lower Honoapiilani Hwy. (☎ **808-669-9603**). In South Maui, find Bob's at Azeka Place 2, 1279 S. Kihei Rd., #310 (☎ **808-875-6188**), and at the Kamaole Beach Center at Kihei Marketplace, 2411 S. Kihei Rd., between Rainbow Mall and Dolphin Plaza, across from Kamaole I Beach Park (☎ **808-879-7449**).

The basic set of snorkel gear — mask, snorkel, and fins — is $9 a week, but I recommend going with the "Ultimate Truth" package for $30 a week. (Reasonable daily rates are available, too.) Do yourself a favor and rent the highest-quality gear. Spending the extra bucks is worth getting a mask that doesn't leak and a snorkel that doesn't clog. If you're nearsighted, you can rent a prescription mask (for an additional $10) that allows you to actually *see* the fish; wetsuits and life vests are also available. The shops are open daily from 8 a.m. to 5 p.m. You don't need to reserve gear in advance, but you're welcome to book your gear online at www.snorkelbob.com.

When you rent gear from Snorkel Bob's, you can pick up a set of snorkel gear at the start of your trip, carry it with you as you travel throughout the islands, and then return it to another Snorkel Bob's location on Oahu, the Big Island, or Kauai. (All shops offer 24-hour gear return service.)

 Any snorkel cruise or kayak outfitter supplies you with gear, but I highly recommend renting your own set and bringing it aboard. Free gear is almost universally bad — and can you think of anything worse than not being able to see sea turtles or other cool creatures because of a crappy mask? Spending the few extra dollars to rent a quality mask and snorkel and fins that fit is worth every penny.

 Keep these snorkel tips in mind as you don your fins and head into the water:

- ✔ Make mornings your offshore snorkel time on Maui, because the winds often start to kick up around noon, making surf conditions rougher and less conducive to fish-spying.

- ✔ Always snorkel with a friend and keep an eye on each other.

- ✔ Look up every few minutes to get your bearings, check your position in relation to the shoreline, and check for any boat traffic.

- ✔ If you're not a strong swimmer, don't be embarassed to don a life jacket while you snorkel.

🖝 Don't touch anything. Not only can your fingers and feet damage coral, but also the coral can give you nasty cuts. Moreover, camouflaged fish and spiny shells may surprise you.

🖝 Before you set out, check surf conditions by calling one of the local dive or snorkel shops, such as Snorkel Bob's, which can give you the latest on local conditions and recommend alternative spots if the prime ones are too rough for snorkeling.

Trilogy Excursions

Book these trips in advance, because Trilogy — the Mercedes of Maui snorkel-sail operators — offers the island's best and most popular snorkel-sail trips, hands down. They're the most expensive, too, but they're worth every penny. The trips feature first-rate catamarans, top-quality equipment, great food, and the best crew in the business. Furthermore, Trilogy is the only Lanai cruise operator that's allowed to land on the island's Hulopoe Beach, a terrific marine preserve that's one of the best snorkel and dolphin-watching spots in Hawaii, for a fun-filled day of sailing and snorkeling. Trilogy Excursions also is the only one to offer an island ground tour. If you really want a genuine Lanai experience, don't book with anyone else. Trilogy also offers terrific half-day snorkel-sail trips to Molokini and unique late-morning snorkel-sail trips off Kaanapali Beach, plus sunset sails and overnighters to Lanai.

No matter which trip you take, you'll find that the Trilogy crews are fun and knowledgeable (they always have a naturalist on board), and the state-of-the-art boats are comfortable, well-equipped, and meticulously maintained. All trips include a continental breakfast (with home-baked cinnamon buns) and a very tasty barbecue lunch (shipboard on the half-day trip, ashore on the Lanai trip). You should know, however, that they may make you wear a flotation device no matter how good your swimming skills are; if wearing a life jacket is going to bother you, ask when you book.

Scuba upgrades are available for both first-timers and certified divers on most Trilogy excursions for beginning and certified divers alike ($49 to $75). Also inquire about additional Lanai-trip upgrades, including a guided two-hour island Jeep safari ($60 per person) and a 1½-hour high-speed Zodiac cruise in search of spinner dolphins (and whales, in season; $60).

See map p. 190. Departures from Maalaea Harbor (at the Highway 30/130 junction), Maalaea; Lahaina Harbor, on Front Street, Lahaina; or Kaanapali Beach, Kaanapali, depending on cruise. ☎ **888-225-6284** *or 808-661-4743.* www.sailtrilogy.com. *Full-day Lanai cruises: $169 adults, $85 kids 3–15, including continental breakfast, BBQ lunch, and island tour. (Deluxe "Ultimate Adventure" version with Jeep safari and champagne return sail $229 adults, $115 kids.) 5½- to 6½-hour Molokini or Kaanapali cruise: $95 adults, $48 kids. Shorter Kaanapali sunset cruise $59 adults, $30 kids; 2-hour Kaanapali whale-watching cruise $39 adults, $20 kids. Lanai overnighters from $320 per person. Ten-percent online advance-booking discounts available at press time.*

Paragon Sailing Charters

Paragon is noted for its state-of-the-art, high-performance catamarans, intimate gatherings (only 24 to 38 passengers, depending on the trip), and landing rights at Manele Bay, which give the Lanai trip a special edge. (Trilogy is the only other outfitter that lands on Lanai, and the only one that takes you on an island tour.) This quality outfitter is a nice choice if you want to embark on a Molokini cruise or a champagne sunset sail, too.

Departures from Maalaea Harbor (at the Highway 30/130 junction), Maalaea, and Lahaina Harbor, on Front Street, Lahaina, depending on cruise. ☎ *800-441-2087 or 808-244-2087.* www.sailmaui.com. *Cruises (which include drinks and hors d'oeuvres or full meals, depending on the outing you choose): $51–$85 adults, $29–$43 kids ages 4–12. Fifteen-percent online advance-booking discount available at press time.*

Scuba diving

Molokini is one of Hawaii's top dive spots thanks to calm, clear, protected waters and an abundance of marine life at every level, from clouds of yellow butterfly fish to white-tipped reef sharks to manta rays. This crescent-shaped crater has three tiers of diving: a 35-foot plateau inside the crater basin (used by beginning divers and snorkelers), a wall sloping to 70 feet just beyond the inside plateau, and a sheer wall on the outside and backside of the crater that plunges 350 feet below the surface.

Other top dive spots include the pristine waters off the island of **Lanai,** whose south and west coasts are a dream come true for divers looking for a one-of-a-kind setting.

You need to book a dive boat to get to Molokini or Lanai. **Lahaina Divers** (☎ **800-998-3483** or 808-667-7496; www.lahainadivers.com) is a five-star PADI facility that publications like *Scuba Diving* magazine have lauded as one of Hawaii's top dive operators. The company can take certified divers to Molokini or Lanai aboard one of its big, comfortable dive boats for two- to four-tank dives ranging in price from $119 to $179; West Maui dives start at $99. Instruction is available for divers of all experience levels, and the "Discover Scuba" package for beginners starts at just $129 (check for Internet specials). Full open-water training packages are also available, as well as specialty training in deep diving, underwater photography, and more. Lahaina Divers is happy to take divers with disabilities, too.

Or contact **Ed Robinson's Diving Adventures** (☎ **800-635-1273** or 808-879-3584; www.mauiscuba.com/erd1.htm), which caters to certified divers from a South Maui base. A widely published underwater photographer, Ed is one of Maui's best; most of his business is repeat customers. Ed offers personalized two-tank dives, three-tank adventures, Lanai trips, and sunset and night dives; prices start at $110. Custom dives are also available, plus discounts for multiday dives.

For two-tank boat dives to Molokini and nearby Maui waters, I also recommend **Mike Severns Diving** (☎ **808-879-6596;** www.mikeseverns diving.com), which takes 12 divers at a time out from Kihei in two groups of six for a quiet and crowd-free experience. The price is $120, with discounts available if you have your own equipment or schedule multiday dives.

If you've never been scuba diving before but want to discover how, contact either Lahaina Divers or **Bobby Baker's Maui Sun Divers** (☎ **877-879-3337;** www.mauisundivers.com). This outfit specializes in training beginners, and it offers a whole slate of introductory dives (for around $110) and multiday starter and certification programs.

Ocean kayaking

Whether you already paddle or you want to discover how, Maui's a great place to hit the waves in a kayak. Riding low on the turquoise water not only puts you at one with the ocean, but also allows you to visit snorkel spots where the big boats just don't go. (I've had my finest sea-turtle-spotting experiences while kayaking Maui's waters.)

Maui's best kayaking outfitter for beginners and accomplished kayakers alike is **South Pacific Kayaks & Outfitters,** in the Rainbow Mall, 2439 S. Kihei Rd., Kihei (☎ **800-776-2326** or 808-875-4848; www.southpacific kayaks.com). It offers a range of kayak tours that launch from both South and West Maui and incorporate whale-watching in winter. The excellent guides are knowledgeable and ecofriendly. You meet at their office, where you can stow valuables (instead of leaving them in your car — always a no-no) and choose your equipment before you load it (another big plus). Tour prices run from $55 to $89 per person, with custom options available.

If you're an experienced kayaker capable of setting out on your own, South Pacific can rent you single or double kayaks for $30 or $40 a day, respectively, and point you to good launching areas. Weekly rates and islandwide delivery (for an additional charge) are also available.

Winter whale-watching

From January through April, the world's largest mammals migrate from frigid Alaska to balmy Hawaii. More than any other Hawaiian Island, Maui is your best perch for spotting Pacific humpback whales in winter. Because whales prefer water depths of less than 600 feet, these endangered gentle giants come in relatively close to shore. You can see them regularly from the beach in prime season, spouting and *spyhopping* (peeking above the waterline to "spy" on what's going on). They often prefer the west, or leeward, sides of the islands.

Virtually all boats that operate from Maui combine whale-watching with their regular adventures from December through April, and a good number, most notably the **Pacific Whale Foundation Eco-Adventures** (☎ 800-942-5311 or 808-249-8811; www.pacificwhale.org), offer dedicated whale-watching cruises in season. This nonprofit has been at the forefront of Maui-based whale research, education, and conservation since the 1970s — and it also happens to host very fine cruises. Its first-rate modern catamaran fleet offers some of the best tours of Molokini and offshore Lanai. The five and a half hour Lanai snorkel sail takes in the island's less visited bays and includes a search for wild dolphins in its regular itinerary. The five-hour Molokini trip is as fine as any and includes a visit to a second snorkel spot, Turtle Arches. Not only does each tour always have at least one naturalist on board, but also the entire crew is knowledgeable, ecoconscious, and friendly; the boats (each of which carry 100 people maximum), even burn ecofriendly fuel. Furthermore, the cruises are great for beginning snorkelers, because guides lead fish talks and reef tours, and a wide variety of flotation devices are available. The winter whale-watching cruises are unparalleled, of course. You simply can't go wrong with these folks.

You have numerous ways to save significant bucks on Pacific Whale Foundation cruises. You save 10 percent if you book by phone or online at least seven days in advance. Or you can save 15 percent (and snag yourself a groovy T-shirt in the process) by becoming a PWF member, which costs $35 dollars, but still puts you ahead if you book a snorkel cruise for two (and it's tax-deductible because the foundation is a nonprofit).

Departures are from Maalaea Harbor (at the Highway 30/130 junction), Maalaea and Lahaina Harbor, on Front St., Lahaina, depending on the cruise. Prices (cruises: $20 to $75 adults, $15 to $38 kids ages 4–12) include continental breakfast and/or deli lunch, depending on the cruise. Cruise times range between 90 minutes and 5½ hours, depending on the cruise chosen.

You don't have to shell out the bucks for a pricey cruise to see whales. In season, you can spot them right from shore. Just look out to sea — just about any west-facing beach offers you a prime whale-watching opportunity.

Follow these tips to increase your humpback-spotting chances:

✔ **After you see a whale, keep watching in the same vicinity.** They travel in groups and often stay down for 20 minutes or so and then pop back up to take in some air and play a little. Be patient, and you're likely to see several.

✔ **Bring your binoculars from home.** You see so much more with a little magnification.

 ✔ **Pick a spot nearly anywhere along the West Maui coast for whale-watching.** Whales love to frolic in the channel separating the Valley Isle from Molokai and Lanai. A great place to park yourself is **McGregor Point,** a scenic lookout at mile marker 9 on the Honoapiilani Highway (Highway 30), on the way to Lahaina from Maalaea. Another good West Maui whale-watching perch is the straight part of Honoapiilani Highway between McGregor Point and Olowalu (where Chez Paul is). However, do yourself — and everybody else — a favor and pull over to the side of the road before you look out to sea because whale-spotting along the highway has caused more than a few accidents.

 ✔ The nonprofit Pacific Whale Foundation operates a **Whale Information Station** on McGregor Point staffed by friendly naturalists daily from 8:30 a.m. to 3:30 p.m. from December through April. Just stop by — you can even use the high-powered binoculars there — or call ☎ **800-WHALE-1-1** (800-942-5311) or 808-249-8811 for further details.

Catching a wave

Book your surfing or windsurfing lesson for early in your stay. That way, if conditions aren't right on your scheduled day, you have plenty of time to reschedule.

Figuring out how to surf

If you've always wanted to surf, Maui is a great place to fulfill the dream. Surfers know Maui has the easiest surf in all Hawaii, making it the spot where many first-timers take lessons.

The motto at the **Nancy C. Emerson School of Surfing** (☎ **808-244-7873;** www.surfclinics.com) is, "If a dog can surf, so can you!" — a dubious challenge, but a surprisingly comforting one, too. A pro international surfing champ, an instructor since 1973, a stunt performer in movies like *Waterworld,* and a surf teacher to such celebs as Kiefer Sutherland and Beau Bridges, Nancy has pioneered the technique of teaching completely unskilled folks to surf in one two-hour lesson. You can, really — I've seen it happen firsthand. The instructors are professional and personable; you'll probably have your lesson on the beach behind 505 Front St. in Lahaina, where the surf breaks are big enough for beginners but not overwhelming. A beginning lesson starts at $100 per person for a one-hour private lesson, $70 per person for two hours with a group; I recommend going for the group option. Experienced surfers can take full- and multi-day private lessons and group clinics with Nancy's skilled instructors (or Nancy herself, whose time is worth top dollar; check the Web site or call for rate schedules).

Action Sports Surf School (☎ 808-871-5857; www.actionsportsmaui. com) offers everything from kids' lessons to extreme tow-in and strap surfing lessons for experienced board riders. **Hawaiian Island Surf and Sport,** 415 Dairy Rd., Kahului (☎ 800-231-6958 or 808-871-4981; www.maui.net/hisurf), also offers lessons for beginners and kids, as well as intermediate and advanced surfers looking to take their skills and experience to the next level. The average lesson is $79 from both of these companies.

For experienced surfers only

Expert surfers visit Maui in winter when the surf's really up. The best surfing beaches include **Honolua Bay,** north of Kapalua; **Maalaea,** just outside the breakwall of the Maalaea Harbor; and **Hookipa Beach Park** in Paia, where surfers get the waves until noon, when the windsurfers take over. If you have a bit of experience but don't want a serious challenge, head to the **505 Front Street Beach,** next to Lahaina Harbor in Lahaina, where even long-surfing locals regularly catch the easy waves.

Second Wind Surf, Sail & Kite, 111 Hana Hwy. (between Dairy Road and Hobron Avenue), Kahului (☎ 800-936-7787 or 808-877-7467; www.second windmaui.com), has the best fleet of rental boards on the island ($18 per day, or $105 for a week), and friendly service to boot.

For daily reports on wind and surf conditions, call the **Wind and Surf Report** at ☎ 808-877-3611.

Windsurfing and kiteboarding

Expert windsurfers may want to head to Paia's world-famous **Hookipa Beach,** known all over the globe for its brisk winds and excellent waves in the afternoons. When the winds turn northerly, **Kihei** is the spot to be; some days you can see whales in the distance behind the windsurfers. The northern end of Kihei is best. At **Ohukai Park,** the first beach along South Kihei Road, the winds are good, the water is easy to access, and a long strip of grass is available on which to assemble your gear. If you have enough experience to head out on your own but you want manageable waves, head to **Kanaha Beach Park** near the airport in Kahului, which is where all the top schools take their students.

Endorsed by Robbie Naish, Hawaii's most famous windsurfer (who has his own windsurfing school on Oahu), **Hawaiian Island Surf and Sport,** 415 Dairy Rd., Kahului (☎ 800-231-6958 or 808-871-4981; www.maui. net/hisurf), offers beginning 2½-hour windsurfing lessons for $79 (plus equipment), as well as instruction in shortboard sailing for those ready to move to the next level. The island's best assortment of quality gear rentals is available as well.

You can find top-quality rental gear for windsurfing and kitesurfing from **Second Wind Surf, Sail & Kite,** 111 Hana Hwy. (between Dairy Road and Hobron Avenue), Kahului (☎ **800-936-7787** or 808-877-7467; www.second windmaui.com or www.mauikitesurfing.com). The company is also an excellent contact if you want to arrange windsurfing lessons, for beginners and experienced windsurfers alike, as well as kiteboarding lessons for experienced wave riders. **Action Sports Maui** (☎ **808-871-5857;** www.actionsportsmaui.com) also offers lessons in windsurfing and kiteboarding, as well as paragliding for high-soaring adventurers.

Sportfishing

Are you ready to head out on the open waves in search of big-game fish like marlin, tuna, and wahoo? **Sportfish Hawaii** (☎ **877-388-1376** or 808-396-2607; www.sportfishhawaii.com) can book a first-class charter for you out of Maalaea or Lahaina harbors on Maui. Half-day private charters start at $600.

Playing Safely in the Ocean

Even people with ocean experience should know a few things before they plunge into Maui's waters.

Ocean safety

Keep the following tips in mind while enjoying the water on your Maui vacation:

✔ **Never, ever, turn your back to the ocean.** Big waves can come seemingly out of nowhere and travel far upshore in a matter of minutes. Always keep one eye on the waves, even if you're just beachcombing or taking a casual stroll along the water's edge. Never let a younger child go into the ocean alone and always keep an eye on your older children.

✔ **Get out of the water when the swells come.** Ocean conditions can change in a few hours. Surf that was placid and safe for swimming one day can be dangerous the next.

✔ **Use the buddy system.** Always swim with a partner.

✔ **Swim at beaches with lifeguards.** When swimming at an unfamiliar beach, ask the lifeguard about the current conditions, and where the safest place to swim is. If the beach doesn't have a lifeguard, ask other beachgoers, some of whom are likely to be locals. If no one is around to ask, stay out of the water: Hidden rip currents, undertows, and submerged rocks may turn a pleasant dip into a disaster.

Shark!

Sharks aren't a big problem in Hawaii. In fact, they're so seldom seen that locals actually *look forward* to spotting one. Since records have been kept — starting in 1779 — Hawaii has only had about 100 shark attacks, around 40 of which have been fatal. The greatest number of attacks occurred after someone fell into the ocean from a cliff or a boat; in these cases, the sharks most likely attacked after the person was dead.

Still, just to be on the safe side, use these good shark-avoidance tips:

✔ **Don't swim at sunrise, sunset, or where the water is murky —** sharks may mistake you for lunch.

✔ **Don't swim where bloody fish are in the water.** Surprise, surprise: Sharks become aggressive around blood.

Avoiding things that sting

Most people manage to hang out in tropical waters without incident. But if you do happen to run into a jellyfish, the pointy spine of a sea urchin, or some sharp coral, take the following advice.

According to Hawaiian folklore, in order to treat certain ocean injuries, the injured party should — I'm not making this up — urinate on the wound. Contrary to popular wisdom, however, urinating on any sort of ocean wound (or probably any wound, for that matter) won't help, so don't let anybody talk you into it.

Portuguese man-of-war

Portuguese man-of-war stings are painful and a nuisance but rarely harmful; fewer than one in a thousand requires medical treatment. The best prevention is to watch for these jellyfish as you snorkel or swim: They're a bluish-purple floating bubble with a long tail (look for the hanging tentacles below the surface). Get out of the water if anyone near you spots one because they tend to hang out in clusters. Also pay attention when walking near the water because even beached man-of-wars can deliver a nasty sting.

Reactions to stings range from mild burning and reddening to severe welts and blisters. Pick off any visible tentacles with a gloved hand, a stick, or anything handy, rinse the sting with salt or fresh water, and apply ice to prevent swelling and fight pain. Most man-of-war stings disappear in 15 to 20 minutes. If pain persists or a rash or other symptoms develop, see a doctor. Skip folk remedies, such as vinegar, meat tenderizer, baking soda, alcohol, and the aforementioned urine — they don't work.

Box jellyfish

These transparent, square-shaped bell jellyfish are nearly impossible to see in the water. Fortunately, they seem to follow a monthly cycle: Eight to ten days after the full moon, they appear in the waters on the *leeward* side (the side away from the wind) of each island and hang around for about three days. Also, they seem to sting more in the morning hours, when they're on or near the surface. The best prevention is to get out of the water if you spot one.

Stings range from no visible marks to red hivelike welts, blisters, and pain (a burning sensation) lasting from ten minutes to eight hours. To treat a sting, start by pouring regular household vinegar on the affected area; this action stops additional burning. Don't rub the area with anything. Then pick off any vinegar-soaked tentacles with a stick and apply an ice pack for pain. Most box jellyfish stings disappear by themselves without any treatment, but see a doctor if you experience shortness of breath, weakness, palpitations, muscle cramps, or any other severe symptoms.

Punctures

Most sea-related punctures come from stepping on or brushing against the needlelike spines of sea urchins. Be careful when you're in the water; don't put your foot down (even if you have booties or fins on; the sea urchin's spines can puncture a wetsuit) if you can't clearly see the bottom.

A sea-urchin sting can result in burning, aching, swelling, and discoloration (black or purple) around the area where the spines broke off. Pull any protruding spines out; the body absorbs any spines within 24 hours to 3 weeks, or the remainder of the spines will work themselves out. Again, if people recommend vinegar or urine, ignore them.

Cuts

The most common cuts are from corals. Take any cut you get in the ocean seriously. Contrary to popular belief, coral can't grow inside your body; however, bacteria can — and very often does. The best way to prevent cuts is to wear a wetsuit, gloves, and reef shoes. **Never, under any circumstances, should you touch coral. And *never* walk on coral, even when you are wearing reef shoes.** Not only can you cut yourself, but also you can damage a living organism that took decades to grow.

The symptoms of a coral cut can range from a slight scratch to severe welts and blisters. Gently pull the edges of the skin open and remove any embedded coral or grains of sand with tweezers. Rinse the cut well with fresh water (*not* ocean water). If the cut is bleeding, press a clean cloth against it until it stops. If bleeding continues or the edges of the injury are jagged, find a doctor.

Landlubbers' curse: Seasickness

You're not alone: Some 90 percent of the population tends toward sea-sickness. The waters in Maui can range from calm as a lake to downright frightening (in stormy conditions), but they usually fall somewhere in between. Generally, expect rougher conditions in winter than in summer. Afternoon seas in particular can be very choppy; the channel between Maui and Lanai has caused at least a few snorkelers to upchuck their barbecue lunch.

If you've never been out on a boat before, or if you've found yourself seasick in the past, take the following precautions:

The day before . . .

- ✔ Avoid alcohol, caffeine, and citrus and other acidic juices, as well as greasy, spicy, or other hard-to-digest foods.

- ✔ Get a good night's sleep.

That day . . .

- ✔ Use whatever seasickness prevention works best for you — pills, a patch, an acupressure wrist band, ginger-root tea or capsules, or any combination — *before* you board. After you set sail, using these preventive measures generally isn't going to help.

- ✔ After you're onboard, stay as low and as near the center of the boat as possible. Avoid the fumes (especially if it's a diesel boat); stay in the fresh air and watch the horizon. Don't read.

- ✔ If you start to feel queasy, drink clear fluids like water and eat something bland, such as a soda cracker.

Chapter 13

Exploring the Island

In This Chapter

▶ Watching the magical sunrise at Haleakala National Park
▶ Cruising the Heavenly Road to Hana
▶ Sightseeing via tour, on foot, or by helicopter
▶ Discovering Maui's history
▶ Golfing, horseback riding, and playing tennis

*M*aui is home to two of Hawaii's most renowned attractions: Haleakala National Park, a remarkable, otherworldly crater at the heart of the island that offers an incredible, mystical view of the sunrise (not to mention one-of-a-kind hiking and biking fun); and the Heavenly Road to Hana, one of the most scenic drives in the United States.

Visiting Haleakala National Park

Haleakala (*ha*-lay-ah-*kah*-la) — the House of the Sun — is the massive 10,023-foot-high mountain that forms the core of Maui. It's also Hawaii's second largest national park (after the Big Island's Hawaii Volcanoes National Park), designated as such in 1961, and Maui's biggest natural attraction. About 2 million people drive to the summit of Haleakala to peer down into the crater of the world's largest dormant volcano. (Its official status is "active but not currently erupting," even though Haleakala has remained dormant since 1790.) The crater is impressive. At 3,000 feet deep, 7½ miles long by 2½ miles wide, and encompassing 19 square miles, it could hold half of Manhattan. More than anything, it resembles a barren moonscape.

Haleakala is best known for its mystical sunrise vistas. Crowds of visitors drive here in the dark pre-dawn hours to watch the spectacle of dawn breaking over the crater. If you decide to join the early-morning crowds, stick around after sunrise for some excellent hiking opportunities. Or do what a lot of people do: Hop on a bike and coast down the switchbacked road to the base of the mountain, enjoying magnificent views as you go.

Haleakala National Park

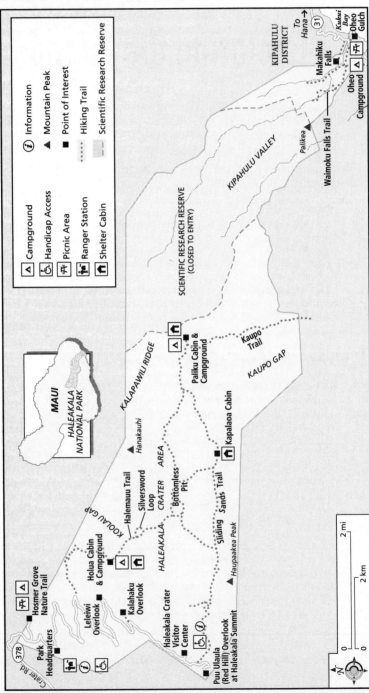

The park actually contains two separate and distinct destinations: Haleakala Summit and the Kipahulu Coast. Lush, green, and tropical, Kipahulu is a world apart from the summit — and accessible only from the east side of the island, near Hana. No road links the summit and the coast, so Hana is a completely separate outing. I concentrate on the summit-related info in the following sections. For a discussion of Kipahulu and its biggest attraction, Oheo Gulch, see "Driving the Heavenly Road to Hana," later in this chapter.

Among the rare endangered species that call Haleakala home are the *nene* (*nay*-nay), a gray-brown Hawaiian goose that doesn't migrate, prefers rock-hard lava beds to lakes, and is now protected as the state bird, and the silvery-green, porcupiney *silversword* plant, which grows only in Hawaii, lives for about 50 years, blooms once in a beautiful purple bouquet, and dies.

Nene like to hang out around park headquarters, so you can spot one or two there — if you don't hear their distinctive call ("nay! nay!") first. Kalahaku Overlook (see the "Driving back down the mountain" section, later in this chapter) is a good place to see silverswords. Please don't feed the nene and leave the silverswords where you see them.

Haleakala is never more stunning than at sunrise. It's a truly awesome, you've-never-really-seen-a-sunrise-until-now Technicolor sight from this lofty perch. However, locals know that sunset is nearly as spectacular, and it's one that doesn't require you to rise at o'dark thirty. The best photo ops are in the afternoon, when the sun illuminates the crater and clouds are few. Stargazing from the summit can be spectacular, so consider bringing your binoculars (or renting a pair) and making the ascent if the sky is clear.

Preparing for your visit to Haleakala

For information before you go, contact **Haleakala National Park** at ☎ **808-572-4400** for information on the Haleakala-summit (main) area of the park (dial ☎ **808-248-7375** for information and the ranger station at the park's Kipahulu district, near Hana, which is a completely separate outing I discuss in the section "Driving the Heavenly Road to Hana," later in this chapter). Or point your Web browser to the park's official Web site at www.nps.gov/hale. You can call to have camping and hiking information sent to you in advance. You also can find plenty of useful information at an unofficial but excellent site, www.haleakala.national-park.com.

For the sunrise time and viewing conditions at Haleakala summit, call ☎ **808-877-5111.**

The summit of Haleakala is 37 miles, or about a one and a half hour drive, from Kahului in Central Maui. To get there, take the Haleakala Highway (Highway 37 and then Highway 377) to wiggly Haleakala Crater Road (Highway 378), the heavily switchbacked road that leads you to the 10,000-foot summit. Allow two hours to reach the summit if you're driving from Lahaina or Kihei, 2½ hours if you're arriving from Wailea or Kaanapali, and 15 minutes more if you're coming from Kapalua.

Admission to the park is $10 per car, which allows you to come and go as you please for seven days.

Keep these tips in mind as you plan your visit to Haleakala National Park:

- ✔ **If Maui is the first Hawaiian Island you're visiting, schedule your sunrise visit for the first full day of your trip.** Your body clock won't be on Hawaii time yet, so it shouldn't be too hard to get up at 3 a.m. — because your body will still think that it's anywhere from 5 to 9 a.m. if you're from the mainland. If Maui is the last island on your itinerary, schedule your sunrise visit for the final day of your trip, because you need to start reacclimating yourself to your at-home hour anyway.

- ✔ **Dress warmly, in layers, no matter what time of year you visit.** Temperatures at the summit usually range between 40 and 65°F but can drop below freezing any time of year after you factor in the wind chill, especially in the pre-dawn hours. Wear a hat and sturdy shoes and bring a blanket if you don't have a warm jacket. The weather is unpredictable at the summit, so be prepared for wind and rain in winter no matter what the time of day. Don't be fooled by the coastline conditions. Call ☎ **808-877-5111** for the summit forecast.

- ✔ **Bring drinking water.** You need plenty of water on hand — especially if you plan on hiking.

- ✔ **Remember that this locale is a high-altitude wilderness area.** The thinness of the air makes some people dizzy; you may also experience lightheadedness, shortness of breath, nausea, headaches, and dehydration. The park recommends that pregnant women and people with heart or respiratory problems consult a doctor before ascending to high elevations.

- ✔ **Fill up your gas tank before you head to Haleakala.** The last gas station is 27 miles below the summit at Pukalani. Fill up the night before if you're going for sunrise, because finding an open gas station at 4 a.m. is nearly impossible.

Those of you who want to explore the park thoroughly may consider booking a Haleakala day hike with **Hike Maui** or **Maui Hiking Safaris;** see the section "Enjoying Guided Nature Hikes," later in this chapter. If you're interested in a stay near the park for a few nights so that you can explore it more fully, I list some accommodations that fit the bill in Chapter 10.

Arriving at the park and making the drive to the summit

About a mile from the entrance is **Park Headquarters,** open daily from 7:30 a.m. to 4 p.m. The headquarters is a great place to pick up park information, including the latest schedule of guided walks and ranger talks. If, however, you arrive before dawn, the around-the-clock restrooms are the only facilities open; the restrooms there are much nicer than the ones at the summit, so I highly recommend making a pit stop on the way up. Drinking water is also available.

Traveling along Haleakala Crater Road, you pass two scenic overlooks on the way to the summit. Stop at the one just beyond mile marker 17, **Leleiwi Overlook,** if only to get out, stretch, and get accustomed to the heights. From the parking area, a short trail leads to a panoramic view of the lunarlike crater. (The other overlook, Kalahaku, is most easily accessible on the descent. Check out the "Driving back down the mountain" section, later in this chapter.)

Continue on, and you'll soon reach **Haleakala Visitor Center,** 11 miles from the park entrance (open daily from sunrise to 3 p.m.), which offers spectacular views and some bare-bones restrooms. Park rangers also offer excellent, informative, and free naturalist talks daily at 9:30, 10:30, and 11:30 a.m. (Call ahead to confirm the next day's schedule to avoid disappointment.)

The actual summit — and the ideal sunrise-viewing perch — is beyond the turnoff for the visitor center, at **Puu Ulaula Overlook** (Red Hill). At Puu Ulaula, a triangular glass building serves as a windbreak and the best sunrise-viewing spot. After the spectacle of sunrise, you can often see all the way to the snowcapped summit of Mauna Kea on the Big Island if it's clear. Haleakala Observatories (nicknamed Science City), which isn't open to the public, is also located there.

Hitting the park's trails

If you want to hike the park, I strongly suggest going with a guide. The park is an outlandishly huge, empty place. You can view it better with someone who can lead you in the right direction and help you understand what you're seeing. Park rangers offer a range of free guided hikes; call for the latest schedule (☎ 808-572-4400) and to find out what to wear and bring. (Sturdy shoes and water are musts.) Also consider taking one of the guided Haleakala Crater hikes offered by Hike Maui and Maui Hiking Safaris; see the section "Enjoying Guided Nature Hikes," later in this chapter.

If you don't want to bother with a serious hike but just want a glimpse of the park's peculiar brand of natural beauty, take a half-hour walk down the half-mile **Hosmer Grove Nature Trail,** which anybody can do. The trail is well-marked, with placards that point out what you're seeing along the way. Ask the ranger at the visitor center to direct you to the trailhead.

If you want to strike out on your own along the park's more serious trails, you can preview your options online at www.haleakala.national-park.com (click on "Hiking Guide") or call ahead; the rangers will be happy to send you complete trail information.

Driving back down the mountain

Put your rental car in low gear on the way down so that you don't ride your brakes.

Around mile marker 24 is **Kalahaku Overlook,** the best place to spot the spiky, alienlike silversword plant, and to take in some fabulous panoramic views.

At the mountain's base, where you turn onto Haleakala Crater Road from the Haleakala Highway, is **Kula,** the closest resemblance to a gateway town that Haleakala has. Kula is most notable for its two restaurants, Kula Sandalwoods and the Kula Lodge, both of which serve great post-sunrise breakfast and lunch. (See Chapter 11 for more information.)

Biking down the volcano

Another great way to experience Haleakala is to cruise down it, from summit to base, on a bicycle. The guided ride is quite an experience, with stunning views the entire way. And you don't need to be an expert cyclist to do it; you just have to be able to ride a bike. In fact, you barely have to pedal — you'll coast down at a nice, leisurely pace. (The constant switchbacks keep you from picking up too much speed.)

A number of companies offer these trips with minor variations — some offer midday tours, others have go-at-your-own-pace options — but they generally work like this: A van picks you up at your hotel or condo anywhere between 2 and 3:30 a.m. and transports you to headquarters, where they'll outfit you with a custom-fitted bike (with a comfy seat and good brakes), a helmet, rain gear, and any other equipment you'll need for the downhill cruise. You and your fellow bikers then reboard the van, which takes you (and the bikes on an attached trailer) up to Haleakala's summit.

Just after the miracle of sunrise, you mount your bike and start down Haleakala Crater Road, usually riding single file behind a guide on the right shoulder of the road so that you don't interfere with traffic. The group generally stops for photo ops along the way. By about 10 a.m., you've come 22 miles to the end of Haleakala Crater Road. Some tours end with breakfast in Kula, while others break for breakfast and then proceed the rest of the way down the hill, to sea level.

Generally, riders have to be at least 12 and at least 4 feet 10 inches tall. Younger kids and pregnant women can usually ride along in the van.

Maui's oldest downhill company is **Maui Downhill** (☎ **800-535-BIKE** or 808-871-2155; www.mauidownhill.com). Maui Downhill offers a variety of guided Haleakala bike "safaris" at both sunrise and midday that run $150 per person.

Other reliable companies include **Maui Mountain Cruisers** (☎ **800-232-6284** or 808-871-6014; www.mauimountaincruisers.com), whose tours run $125 to $130 per person (book online, and you save $35). **Mountain Riders** (☎ **800-706-7700** or 808-242-9739; www.mountainriders.com) charges $115 for the sunrise trip, $115 for the daytrip, and also offers a self-paced option for about $70 per rider. Book online for a 15-percent discount.

At press time, you could save a bundle on most of these tours by booking online at the companies' own Web sites. (For example, Maui Downhill was offering $48 per person discounts!) But if you're already on the island and don't have access to a computer, Maui's most reliable activity booker, **Tom Barefoot's Cashback Tours,** 834 Front St., near Lahainaluna Road in Lahaina (☎ **888-222-3601** or 808-661-8889; www.tombarefoot.com), may save you a few bucks with the companies I mention.

If you prefer a more independent — and more affordable — downhill ride, contact **Haleakala Bike Company** (☎ **888-922-2453** or 808-575-9575; www.bikemaui.com). Haleakala Bike Company outfits you with all the gear and takes you up to the top, but, after a little initial guidance, leaves you to proceed down the mountain at your own pace. Tours are $75 to $85 per person, with no hotel pickup or meal included (you meet at their Upcountry bike shop), and gear is available for kids as young as 8. The company also offers straight bike rentals of newer model Gary Fisher mountain bikes for $45 a day, including gear.

Coasting down Haleakala can be an incredible ride, and thousands of people come home from Maui every year claiming that it was the highlight of their trip. Still, you should know a few things before you book one of these trips. I'm not trying to discourage you, by any means; I just want you to know exactly what to expect:

✔ Virtually all the outfitters advertise these trips as safe, no-strain bicycle rides that anyone can do, even Grandma. However, these downhill bike tours do require some stamina, particularly in winter. Conditions can be harsh, and you have to stay in line and keep pace with the other riders as cars go by. (Drivers are usually quite respectful, so you don't have to worry about dodging traffic.) The entire trip makes for a very long day.

✔ Summer and fall — when drive conditions and relatively mild temperatures usually prevail — are the best seasons for Haleakala downhill rides. Even though the better outfitters provide you with slick jumpsuits and headgear to protect you from the rain you'll almost inevitably encounter at some point, count on getting cold and wet in winter and spring.

The legend behind the House of the Sun

The name *Haleakala* actually means "House of the Sun." The story of how this wild-looking volcano got such a magnificent name goes like this: One day, a mom complained that the sun sped across the sky so quickly that her tapa cloth didn't have enough time to dry. So in the pre-dawn hours of the next morning, her thoughtful son, the demi-god Maui, climbed to the top of the volcano. When the sun rose above the horizon, Maui lassoed it, bringing it to a halt in the sky. The sun begged Maui to let go. Maui said he would, on one condition: That the sun slow its trip across the sky to give the island more sunlight. The sun agreed. In honor of the agreement, islanders dubbed the mountain "House of the Sun."

Driving the Heavenly Road to Hana

 No road in Hawaii is more celebrated than the Hana Highway (Highway 36), the supercurvaceous, two-lane highway that winds along Maui's northeastern shore, offering some of the most scenic natural sightseeing in the entire state.

The Hana Highway winds for approximately 52 miles east from Kahului, in Central Maui, crossing more than 50 one-lane bridges, passing greener-than-green taro patches, magnificent seascapes, gorgeous waterfalls, botanical gardens, and rainforests before passing through the little town of Hana and ultimately ending up in one of Hawaii's most beautiful tropical places: the Kipahulu section of Haleakala National Park. Kipahulu is home to Oheo (oh-*hay*-oh) Gulch, a stunning series of waterfall pools that tumble down to the sea. (See the section "Venturing beyond Hana: Hamoa Beach and Oheo Gulch," later in this chapter.)

Despite the draws at the end of the road, this drive is about the journey — *not* the destination. The drive from end to end takes at least three hours, but allow all day for it. If you race along just to arrive in Hana as quickly as you can, you'll be as perplexed as so many others who just don't understand all the hype. Start out early, take it slow and easy, stop at the scenic points along the way, and let the Hana Road work its magic on you. It will — I promise.

 Take these points into consideration as you plan your Hana Road trip:

> ✔ **Leave early.** Get up just after dawn, have an early breakfast (Charley's in Paia opens at 7 a.m.; see Chapter 11), and hit the road by 8 a.m. If you wait until midmorning to leave, you'll get stuck in bumper-to-bumper Hana Road traffic, you won't have enough time to enjoy the sights along the way, and you'll arrive at Oheo Gulch too late in the day to take a hike or a dip. To make the most of the daylight hours, leave early, particularly in the winter when days are shortest.

✔ **Consider booking a place to stay in Hana if you really want to take your time.** If you book a room, you can head out to Hana against the traffic in the afternoon, stay for a couple of nights so that you have a full day to enjoy East Maui's attractions (including an abundance of peace and quiet), and meander back at your own pace (once again avoiding the traffic) on the morning of the third day. See Chapter 10 for recommendations.

✔ **Fill up on gas before you set out.** If all else fails, make sure that you stop in Paia, just east of Kahului, because the next gas station is in Hana — 44 miles, 50-some bridges, and 200-plus hairpin turns down the road.

✔ **Don't bother if it's been raining heavily.** The Hana Highway is well paved and well maintained but can nevertheless be extremely dangerous when wet — and you can easily get stuck in muddy shoulders and pull-offs.

✔ **Bring your bathing suit in warm weather.** You find a number of waterfall pools along the way that are ideal for a refreshing dip, and folks love to swim in Oheo Gulch's placid summer pools.

✔ **Only enter waterfall pools in the calmest ranger-approved conditions.** A mainland visitor was washed away to sea during a seemingly innocuous Oheo Gulch photo op in 2002. Always check with the rangers before you go in the pools. And if water seems to be running between the pools at all, stay out.

✔ **Bring mosquito repellent.** Lush East Maui is a buggy place.

✔ **Leave your mainland road rage on the mainland.** Practice aloha as you drive the Hana Road: Give way at the one-lane bridges. Wave at passing motorists. Let the locals who drive this road with jaw-dropping speed and who pass on blind curves have the right-of-way. If the guy behind you blinks his lights, let him pass. And don't honk your horn — it's considered rude in Hawaii.

There's one exception to the no-horn-honking rule: If you reach a blind curve, *do* honk your horn to indicate that you're coming around the bend — and proceed slowly.

If you want some narration to accompany what you're seeing along the road to Hana, pick up a **Hana Cassette Guide** on your way out of town. The 90-minute tape or CD is $20 at the **Hana Cassette Guide Shop** in Kahului on Dairy Road (Highway 380), next to the Shell Service Station just before the Hana Highway (☎ **808-572-0550**). I highly recommend using it in tandem with the text in this chapter because it covers many more sights and gives much more background than I have the space to include. Along with the recorded tour, you get a Hana Road map and flower guide, and the shop even lends you a cooler or a tape player for free (with refundable $7 deposit) if your rental car doesn't have one. The Hana Cassette Guide Shop also has a recorded guide to Haleakala available for $10, and opens daily at 3 a.m. to accommodate the earliest risers.

The Heavenly Road to Hana

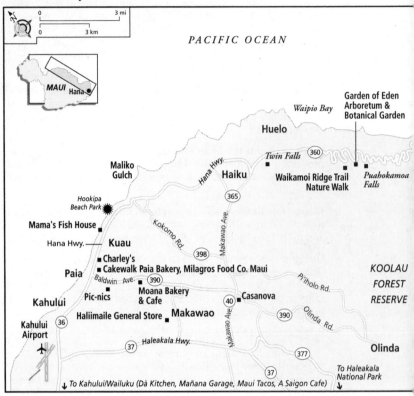

To avoid traffic, consider one of these two route-reversal strategies (While both have problems, you may prefer these options if the crowded roads distract you from enjoying the drive.):

✔ Drive directly to Oheo Gulch, at the end of the road, without stopping. Explore Hana and Oheo Gulch in the morning. Head out of Hana right after lunch and do your meandering on the way home, against traffic. The disadvantage of this strategy is that, for some, the gorgeous scenery can lose some of its magic by afternoon: You're tired, and you've been in the car a long time — you know how it goes.

✔ If conditions allow, drive out along the south route, which most Mauians call the Kaupo (*cow*-po) Road. After you're done exploring Kipahulu and Hana, drive home along the Hana Highway. This strategy, however, has the same tired-of-being-in-the-car problem that

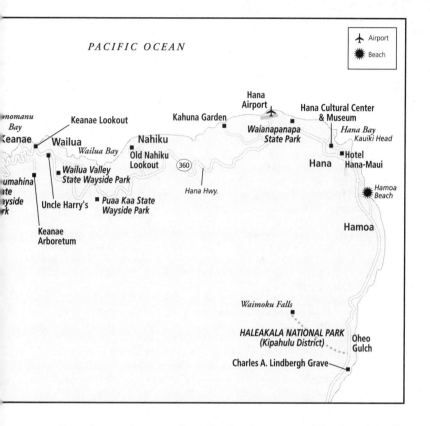

PACIFIC OCEAN

Airport

Beach

Hana Airport

Hana Cultural Center & Museum

Kahuna Garden

Hana Bay
Kauiki Head

Waianapanapa State Park

Keanae Lookout

Nahiku

Hana Hwy.

Old Nahiku Lookout

Hotel
Hana Hana-Maui

Wailua Bay

360

Wailua

Hamoa Beach

Keanae

Wailua Valley State Wayside Park

Hamoa

nomanu Bay

Uncle Harry's

Puaa Kaa State Wayside Park

umahina ate ayside rk

Keanae Arboretum

Waimoku Falls

HALEAKALA NATIONAL PARK (Kipahulu District)

Oheo Gulch

Charles A. Lindbergh Grave

the previous one does. Furthermore, a good 7 miles of the Kaupo Road remains unpaved; not only is it impassable in bad weather, but many rental-car contracts forbid you from driving on it. Lastly, if you set out on this route too late in the day (after lunch), the traffic you encounter on the narrow road as you near Kipahulu will make you feel like you're heading the wrong way on a one-way street — quite unnerving. Read the section, "Heading back to the resorts," later in this chapter, which discusses the Kaupo Road more fully.

If you want to see the Hana Road but you just don't want to drive it yourself, consider taking a guided van or bus tour. See the section called "Taking a guided van or bus tour on the road to Hana," later in this chapter, for recommended tour operators.

Setting out from Kahului

A half-dozen miles east of Kahului on the Hana Highway is Paia (pa-*ee*-ah), a former mill town that's now a neohippie, boutique-dotted surf spot. **Charley's,** at Baldwin Avenue in the heart of town, makes an ideal stop for a hearty breakfast (see Chapter 11). Afterward, you can bop around the corner to 30 Baldwin Ave., where **Pic-nics** (☎ **808-579-8021**) can put together a picnic for you to take on the road.

On my last visit, I fell in love with the **Cakewalk Paia Bakery,** just around the corner from the Hana Highway on Baldwin Avenue (☎ **808-579-8870;** www.cakewalkmaui.com). Pick up a muffin or ask for a gourmet lunch to go — the sandwiches are *very* yummy; see Chapter 11 for a more detailed review of Cakewalk. Another excellent stop for a morning muffin, coffee, or a lunch to take with you is **Moana Bakery & Cafe,** 71 Baldwin Ave. (☎ **808-579-9999**). I enjoy the heavenly mango-blueberry scones here, but the whole Moana menu is delightful.

After you leave Paia, the road bends into an S-turn, where you see the entrance to **Mama's Fish House,** depicted by a restored boat with Mama's logo on the side. Mama's is one of my favorite Maui restaurants (though it's pricey); see the review in Chapter 11. Mama's also has an inn (see Chapter 10).

Just beyond Paia is **Hookipa Beach Park,** one of the greatest windsurf-ing spots on the planet; see Chapter 12. World-championship contests are held there, but on nearly every windy afternoon, you can watch dozens of colorful windsurfers dancing in the breeze. To watch them, don't stop on the highway, but go past the park and turn left at the entrance on the beach's far side. You can either park on the high, grassy bluff or drive down to the sandy beach and park alongside the pavilion. The park also has restrooms, a shower, picnic tables, and a barbecue area.

The road narrows to one lane in each direction and starts winding around mile marker 3. But at mile marker 16, the curves really begin, one right after another. Slow down and enjoy the bucolic surroundings.

Following the road to Hana

After mile marker 16, the highway number changes from 36 to 360 and the mile markers start again at 0 (I have no idea why). I follow suit and include the 0 in this section.

At mile marker 2: The first great place to stop is **Twin Falls,** on the road's inland side; the Twin Falls Fruit Stand marks the spot. Hop over the short ladder on the right side of the red gate and walk about 3 to 5 minutes to the waterfall off to your left or continue on another 10 to 15 minutes to the second, larger waterfall. You may notice a "No Trespassing" sign at the gate, but the sign doesn't seem to bother the crowds. If it bothers you, skip Twin Falls altogether; you have plenty more to see that's not so marked farther down the road.

Just before mile marker 4: On a blind curve, look for a double row of mailboxes on the left-hand side by the pay phone. Down the road lies the remote, rural community of **Huelo,** embraced by Waipo and Hoalua bays. This fertile area was once home to a population of 75,000. Today, only a few hundred live in this serene small town, where you find a few B&Bs and vacation rentals (see Chapter 10).

After mile marker 4: The vegetation grows lusher as you head east. This area is the edge of the **Koolau Forest Reserve,** where the branches of 20- to 30-foot-tall guava trees are laden with green (not ripe) and yellow (ripe) fruit, and introduced eucalyptus trees grow as tall as 200 feet.

The upland forest gets 200 to 300 inches of rainfall annually, so you begin to see waterfalls around just about every turn as you head east from here. The one-lane bridges start, too, so drive slowly and yield to oncoming cars.

After mile marker 6: Just before mile marker 7 is a forest of waving bamboo. The sight is so spectacular that drivers are often tempted to take their eyes off the road, so be very cautious. Just after mile marker 7, you can pull over at the **Kaaiea Bridge,** which offers a terrific view of the bamboo grove.

At mile marker 9: The sign says Koolau State Forest Reserve, but the real attraction is the **Waikamoi Ridge Trail,** an easy and well-marked ¾-mile loop. This place is great to stretch your legs; look for the turnout on the right.

Between mile markers 10 and 11: At the halfway point, on the road's inland side, is the **Garden of Eden Arboretum and Botanical Garden** (☎ 808-572-9899; www.mauigardenofeden.com), with more than 500 exotic plants, flowers, and trees from around the Pacific (including several wild ginger plants and an impressive palm collection) on 26 acres. You can drive through the garden in about five minutes, walk its main loop in about 20 minutes, or stay a bit longer and follow any number of nature trails. The garden is open daily from 8 a.m. to 3 p.m., and admission is $7.50 per person. A fruit and smoothie stand offers refreshments at the gate.

At mile marker 11: Park at the bridge and take the short walk up the stone wall-lined trail to 30-foot **Puohokamoa Falls,** tucked away in a fern-filled amphitheater surrounded by banana trees, colorful helico- nias, and fragrant ginger. The gorgeous pool is a great place to take a plunge.

As you continue on the Hana Highway, the road winds through banana patches, cane grass blowing in the wind, vibrant ferns, and forests of guava trees, avocados, kukui trees, palms, and Christmas berry.

Just beyond mile marker 12: Kaumahina State Wayside Park has portable toilets and picnic tables at the large parking area, plus a gorgeous view of the rugged coastline across the road.

Just beyond mile marker 14: One of my favorite stops on the entire drive is **Honomanu Bay,** a stark rocky beach popular with net fishermen that faces a beautiful bay. Tear your eyes away, and you find incredible golden-green cliffs forming an intense backdrop as you look inland and up. The turnoff is on the left, at the stop sign just after the mile marker; don't attempt the rutted and rocky road if it has been raining recently. Swimming is best in the stream inland from the ocean because of strong rip currents offshore.

Between mile markers 16 and 17: Farther along the winding road, between mile markers 16 and 17, is a cluster of bunkhouses composing the YMCA Camp Keanae (☎ **808-242-9007**). A quarter mile down is the **Keanae Arboretum,** where the region's botany is divided into three parts: native forest; introduced forest; and traditional Hawaiian plants, food, and medicine. You can swim in the pools of Piinaau Stream or walk a mile-long trail into Keanae Valley, where a lovely tropical rainforest waits at the end.

If you have time to spare, the old Hawaiian village of **Keanae** stands frozen in time, one of the last coastal enclaves of native Hawaiians. They still grow taro in patches and pound it into poi (the staple of the old Hawaiian diet), pluck *opihi* (limpet) from tide pools along the jagged coast, and cast throw nets at schools of fish. The turnoff to the Keanae Peninsula is on the left, just after the arboretum. The road passes by farms and banana bunches as it hugs the peninsula. Where the road bends, you notice a small beach where fishermen gather to catch dinner. A quarter mile farther is the **Keanae Congregational Church,** built in 1860 of lava rocks and coral mortar, standing out in stark contrast to the green fields. Beside the church is a small beachfront park, with false kamani trees against a backdrop of black lava and a rolling turquoise ocean.

Just beyond mile marker 17: Keanae Lookout is a wide spot on the road's ocean side where you can see the entire Keanae Peninsula jutting out into the sea, with its checkerboard pattern of green taro fields and its ocean boundary etched in black lava. If time is precious, though, wait to stop after mile marker 19, where the view from the **Wailea Valley** viewpoint is even better.

At mile marker 18: The road widens, and fruit and flower stands begin to line the road. Many of these operate on the honor system: You select your purchase and leave your money in the basket. I recommend stopping at **Uncle Harry's,** just beyond Keanae School on the ocean side of the road. Harry Kunihi Mitchell was a legend in his time, an expert in native plants who devoted his life to the Hawaiian-rights and nuclear-free movements.

A quarter mile after mile marker 19: For the best view of the **Wailua Peninsula,** stop at the lookout and parking area on the road's ocean side, where sun-dappled picnic tables serve up great views.

A bit farther down the road, just before the bridge on the inland side, is a pretty waterfall view.

Between mile markers 22 and 23: At **Puaa Kaa** (poo-*ah*-ah *ka*-ah) **State Wayside Park,** the splash of waterfalls provides the soundtrack for a small park area with restrooms and a picnic area. On the opposite side of the road from the toilets is a well-marked and paved path that leads through a patch of sweet-smelling ginger to the falls and a swimming hole.

After mile marker 25: After the mile marker, turn toward the ocean at the steep turnoff just before the one-lane bridge and follow the well-paved but winding road 2½ miles down to the **Old Nahiku Lookout,** one of the very few points along the entire route that lets you get close to the ocean, and the finest picnic spot on the entire route. A small, grassy lawn faces rocky lava points and crashing turquoise surf for a breathtaking, up-close view. Don't swim there, but you can walk down to the rocky beach at the backside of the parking lot.

At mile marker 31: Turn toward the ocean on Ulaino Road and go a half mile to **Kahanu Garden,** one of four National Tropical Botanical Gardens in Hawaii (☎ **808-248-8912;** www.ntbg.org). Surrounded by a native pandanus forest (the leaf that *lauhala* products are woven from), the garden features a remarkable collection of ethno-botanical plants from the Pacific islands (with a particular concentration on plants of value to the people of Polynesia and Micronesia), plus the foundation of Poolanihale Heiau, the largest Hawaiian temple in Hawaii. The self-guided walking tour is $10 and takes 30 to 40 minutes to complete; open Monday through Friday from 10 a.m. to 2 p.m. The road that leads to the garden entrance is rough and unpaved, but not bad; still, don't bother if it has been raining.

At mile marker 32: The turnoff for 122-acre **Waianapanapa** (why-*ah*-na-pa-na-pa) **State Park** leads to shiny black-sand **Waianapanapa Beach,** whose bright-green jungle backdrop and sparkling cobalt water make for quite a stunning view. On hand are picnic pavilions, restrooms, trails, and fruit stands lining the road, so come down to take a peek. The beach isn't for swimming, though. A blowhole appears when the winter surf kicks up. This natural hole in the rocks is configured so that when harsh surf kicks up, water shoots through the hole like a spout — quite an interesting sight.

Arriving in Hana

Postage stamp–sized Hana is a lush and charming little hamlet, but frankly, the town doesn't have much to see. As I state elsewhere in this chapter, the drive to Hana is more about the *drive* and less about *Hana.*

The few attractions include the **Hana Coast Gallery,** on the Hana Highway adjacent to the Hotel Hana-Maui (☎ **808-248-8636**), an excellent showcase for island-made products hewn by master craftspeople, including gorgeous woodworks. The quirky **Hasegawa General Store** (☎ **808-248-8231**) is worth stopping in for kicks (look for the Spam sushi vending machine near the entrance) or to use the ATM, but the prices on practical items and munchies are better across the road and up the hill at the **Hana Ranch Store** (☎ **808-248-8261**). If you want a meal, you have two choices: the casual **Hana Ranch Restaurant** or the **Hotel Hana-Maui Dining Room;** for details, see Chapter 11.

History buffs may want to head toward Hana Bay; overlooking the bay is the **Hana Cultural Center and Museum,** 4974 Uakea Rd. (☎ **808-248-8622;** www.hookele.com/hccm), open daily from 10 a.m. to 4 p.m. (most of the time). This charming museum is dedicated to preserving the history of Hana, with exhibits showcasing traditional Hawaiian quilts and such implements of life as poi boards and fish hooks carved out of the tusks of wild pigs. Also on-site is the Old Hana Courthouse and Jailhouse and four *hale* (living structures) where you can see what it was like to live in the style of Hana's earliest settlers.

If you want to see more of what's available in town, pick up a copy of the **Hana Visitors Guide,** a foldout map and pamphlet that's available free around town. If you don't run across one, stop into Hasegawa's to pick one up.

For those of you spending some time in these parts, a number of active adventures are available:

- ✔ **Hang Gliding Maui** (☎ **808-572-6557;** www.hanggglidingmaui.com), offers tandem instructional flights aboard its engine-powered ultralight aircraft. Prices are $115 for a 30-minute lesson, $190 for an hour-long lesson.

- ✔ If you want to explore the lush Kipahulu District on horseback, reach out to **Maui Stables** (☎ **808-248-7799;** www.mauistables.com), which offers a taste of real island culture as you explore the gorgeous scenery. Choose a morning or afternoon half-day tour; prices are $150 per person, including a deli lunch. Reservations are a must.

- ✔ **Maui Cave Adventures** (☎ **808-248-7308;** www.mauicave.com) offers cave-exploring hikes for every age and ability, including kids as young as 7, through Kaeleku Caverns; prices run $29 to $69 per person, depending on the length and difficulty of your tour.

Hana

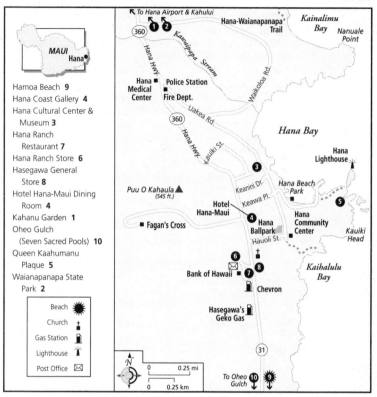

MAUI
Hana•

Hamoa Beach **9**
Hana Coast Gallery **4**
Hana Cultural Center &
　Museum **3**
Hana Ranch
　Restaurant **7**
Hana Ranch Store **6**
Hasegawa General
　Store **8**
Hotel Hana-Maui Dining
　Room **4**
Kahanu Garden **1**
Oheo Gulch
　(Seven Sacred Pools) **10**
Queen Kaahumanu
　Plaque **5**
Waianapanapa State
　Park **2**

Beach
Church
Gas Station
Lighthouse
Post Office

To Hana Airport & Kahului
360
Hana-Waianapanapa
Trail
Kainalimu Bay
Nanuale Point
Hana Hwy.
Kanaipapa Stream
Waikoloa Rd.
Hana
Medical
Center
Police Station
Fire Dept.
Uakea Rd.
360
Hana Hwy.
Kauiki St.
Hana Bay
Hana
Lighthouse
Puu O Kahaula (545 ft.)
Keanini Dr.
Hana Beach Park
Keawa Pl.
Hotel
Hana-Maui
Fagan's Cross
Hana
Ballpark
Hana
Community
Center
Kauiki Head
Hauoli St.
Bank of Hawaii
Kaihalulu Bay
Chevron
Hasegawa's
Geko Gas
31
N
0　　0.25 mi
0　　0.25 km
To Oheo
Gulch

Taking a guided van or bus tour on the road to Hana

If you've rented a car and can get around easily on your own, driving around the island is definitely the preferable way to go. But, if your mobility is limited, or if you're traveling alone and you don't want to make the drive to Hana on your own, or if you just want to kick back and let somebody else take the driver's seat, you may want to hook up with a guided tour.

Remember that with a guided tour, you have little or no control over where you go and how long you stay, and your time communing with nature at some of Hawaii's finest natural spots may be limited. Still, for some people, a guided tour is the best way to see Haleakala National Park or take in the glories of the Heavenly Road to Hana.

For small-scale, local-led van tours of the Heavenly Road to Hana and Haleakala National Park, book your guided trip with family-owned **Ekahi Tours** (☎ **888-292-2422** or 808-877-9775; www.ekahi.com). Its Hana tour is a circle island tour; you not only drive the road to Hana, but you also experience the otherworldly desert landscape of the little-traveled back road on the return trip, which takes you along the south coast and around the back side of the Haleakala Volcano (weather permitting). Ekahi takes you to Hana and also to hidden Kahakuloa, a half-day tour that offers an insightful look at Maui's ancient past and rural present. Ekahi tour prices range from $70 to $95 adults, $50 to $70 kids under 12, depending on the tour you choose; prices include a deli lunch.

Now offering guided bus tours statewide, **Polynesian Adventure Tours** (☎ **800-622-3011** or 808-877-4242; www.polyad.com) offered the very first guided tours along the Heavenly Road to Hana and is still going strong. In addition to the Hana option, it offers both Haleakala sunrise and Iao Valley tours in minivans, big-windowed minicoaches, and full-size luxury buses. Prices run $60 to $79 for adults, $35 to $50 for kids 3 to 11.

Book your Polynesian Adventure Tour online to get a 10-percent price break.

If you choose to visit Haleakala National Park on a guided tour, remember to dress warmly, because it gets cold at 10,000 feet.

Venturing beyond Hana: Hamoa Beach and Oheo Gulch

About 2½ miles past Hana is the turnoff for **Hamoa Beach,** one of the most gorgeous beaches in all Hawaii — and great for swimming, to boot (in summer, anyway). For details, see Chapter 12.

About 10 luxuriant miles past Hana along the highway is **Oheo** (oh-*hay*-oh) **Gulch,** a dazzling series of waterfall pools cascading into the sea that some folks call Seven Sacred Pools, even though it has more like two dozen. This area is the Kipahulu district of Haleakala National Park, and a **ranger station** located at the back of the unpaved parking lot (☎ **808-248-7375**) is staffed daily from 9 a.m. to 4:30 p.m. Restrooms are available, but no drinking water, so pick some up in Hana if you're out. You don't have to pay a fee to visit the park.

The easy, half-mile **Kuloa Point Loop Trail** leads to the lower pools, where you can take a dip when the weather is warm and the water is placid. This well-marked 20-minute walk is a must for everyone.

Stay out of the Oheo Gulch pools in winter or after a heavy rain, when the otherwise placid falls can wash you out to sea in an instant, to the waiting sharks below. (No kidding — they actually do hang out in the brackish water at the foot of the falls.) No matter what the season, if you do take a dip, always be extra vigilant — keep an eye on the water in the streams. Even when the sky is sunny near the coast, upland rain can cause floodwaters to rise in minutes, so if the water seems to be running between the pools at all, stay out. Always check with the rangers before you go in the pools.

The 2-mile (each way), moderate **Pipiwai Trail** leads upstream to additional pools and 400-foot Waimoku Falls. The often muddy but rewarding uphill trail leads through taro patches and bamboo, guava, and mango stands to the magnificent falls. The trail is unmarked but relatively easy to follow. Wear sturdy shoes, bring water, and don't attempt the trek in the rain.

A mile past Oheo Gulch on the road's ocean side is **Lindbergh's Grave.** First to fly across the Atlantic Ocean, Charles Lindbergh found peace in Hana, where he died of cancer in 1974. The famous aviator is buried under river stones in a seaside graveyard behind the 1857 **Palapala Hoomau Congregational Church,** where his tombstone is engraved with his favorite words from the 139th Psalm: "If I take the wings of the morning and dwell in the uttermost parts of the sea. . . ."

Heading back to the resorts

Most visitors head back to Kahului the way they came, along the Hana Highway. But if the weather is good, you have an alternative. The Hana Highway continues past Kipahulu around Maui's southern coast, becoming the Piilani Highway (Highway 31) as it traverses the empty desert that meets the southern sea along a route that's informally but universally known as the **Kaupo** (cow-po) **Road.** The Kaupo Road ultimately meets up with Highway 37 (the Kula/Haleakala Highway), which takes you back to Central Maui and the resorts. The route is no shorter or less time-consuming than the Hana Road — just different.

Be aware of the Kaupo Road — and consider the route very carefully — before you set out on it. First, you find nothing there, except for a few lone cows, some desert scrub, and amazing ocean views — no structures at all, let alone any modern conveniences. Those who appreciate desert beauty find the landscape striking, but anyone else may feel like they've arrived in Mad Max territory.

Seven miles of road remain unpaved, but the entire stretch between mile markers 39 and 23 (the markers run west to east) is dreadful. In fact, the unpaved portion is an improvement over the other pitted 9 miles, whose pavement is so lumpy that it doesn't deserve to be called pavement.

While the Kaupo Road is fine for average cars in dry weather, the road washes out with a little rain, so don't go near it if the weather has been poor. Ask around, both at your hotel and in Hana; news on the current conditions gets out. And check with your rental-car company before you set out because many rental contracts forbid you from taking their car on this road. If you get stuck, you pay a hefty tow charge — but that will be the least of your problems, because you'll be stuck in the middle of nowhere, where other cars may not pass by for hours.

Maui's Top Attractions

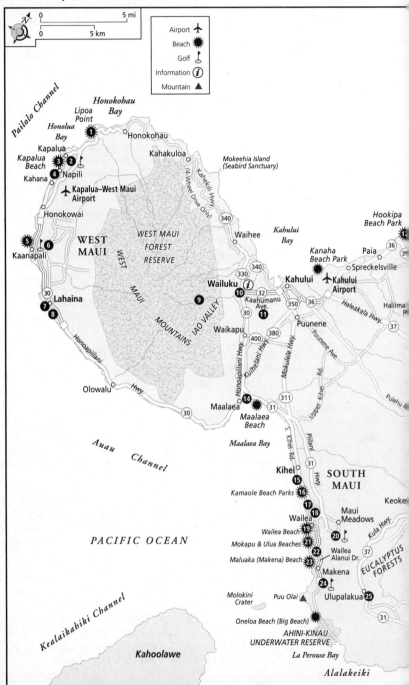

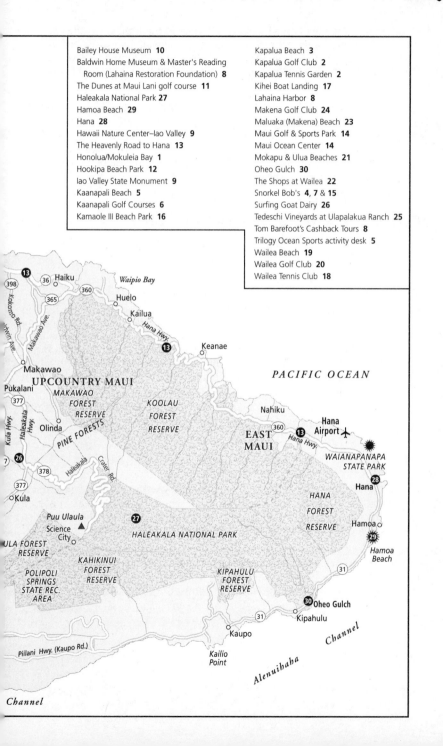

After warning you, I love the Kaupo Road and the little-seen side of Maui it shows. Still, before you consider it, take all my warnings and recommendations extremely seriously. And if one person tells you that conditions aren't good and advises you against it, skip it — go back the way you came.

Before departing Hana, don't forget to check your gas gauge no matter which road west you're traveling because neither route has a place for you to fill up on your way back to civilization. If you need gas, stop at one of the town's two service stations, Chevron and Hasegawa's Hana Geko Gas, which sit nearly side by side on the right side of the Hana Highway as you leave town.

Seeing the Sights in Central Maui

You can find the following attractions in Wailuku, the charming county seat directly west of Kahului, Maui's main city.

Bailey House Museum

This 19th-century missionary and sugar planter's home — built in 1833 on a royal Hawaiian site — is a treasure trove of Hawaiiana that includes a notable collection of precontact Hawaiian artifacts as well as items from post-missionary times. Excellently curated, island-themed, temporary exhibits are also part of the mix. This little museum is well worth a half-hour stop for history buffs. It boasts lovely gardens and a wonderful gift shop, too, neither of which require admission.

2375-A Main St., just west of the Kaahumanu Avenue/Honoapiilani Highway (Highway 32/30) intersection, Wailuku. ☎ *808-244-3326.* www.mauimuseum.org. *Admission: $5 adults, $4 seniors, $1 kids 7–12. Open: Mon–Sat 10 a.m.–4 p.m.*

Hawaii Nature Center — Iao Valley

Before heading into Iao Valley, families may want to stop into this small, kid-centered interactive science center, which features great hands-on exhibits and displays relating to the park's natural history. The center also has a nice gift shop if you're in the market for nature-themed toys.

Call ahead to reserve a spot on Hawaii Nature Center's daily Rainforest Walk through Iao Valley, offered at 11:30 a.m. and 1:30 p.m.; your guide can offer historical, cultural, and natural insight that you just can't gain on a self-guided tour. The price is $25 for adults, $23 for kids ages 8 to 12.

At the gateway to Iao Valley State Monument, 875 Iao Valley Rd. ☎ *808-244-6500.* www.hawaiinaturecenter.org. *Admission: $6 adults, $4 kids under 12. Open: Daily 10 a.m.–4 p.m.*

Iao Valley State Monument

As you head west to Iao (*ee*-ow) Valley, the transition between town and wild is so abrupt that most people who drive up into the valley don't realize they're suddenly in a rainforest. The walls of the canyon rise, and a 2,250-foot needle pricks gray clouds scudding across the blue sky. The Iao Needle is an erosional remnant of rock. This is Iao Valley, a place of great natural beauty and a haven for Mauians and visitors alike.

You can see everything in an hour or two, though it's a lovely place to bring a picnic and linger. Two paved walkways loop the 6-acre park; a leisurely half-mile loop walk takes you past lush vegetation and lovely views of the fabulously impressive Iao Needle. An architectural park of Hawaiian heritage houses — including a Japanese teahouse with a lovely koi pond, a Chinese pagoda, a New England–style mission house, a Hawaiian *hale,* and a Portuguese garden — stands in harmony by Iao Stream at Kepaniwai Heritage Garden, near the park's entrance; it makes an excellent place for a picnic because tables are at hand. You'll see ferns, banana trees, and other native and exotic plants in the streamside botanic garden.

On Iao Valley Road (at the end of Main Street), Wailuku. To get there: From Kahului, follow Kaahumanu Avenue east directly to Main Street and the park entrance. Admission: Free! Open: Daily 7 a.m.–7 p.m.

Exploring Lahaina Town

You may not believe it, seeing today's Lahaina overrun with contemporary tourist schlock, but anyone who has read James Michener's *Hawaii* knows that back in the whaling and missionary days, Lahaina was the capital of Hawaii and the Pacific's wildest port. Now Lahaina is a party town of a different kind and has lost much of its historic vibe, but history buffs with an interest can unearth a half-day's worth of historic sites.

Your best bet is to start at the **Baldwin Home Museum,** a beautifully restored 1838 missionary home at the corner of Front and Dickenson streets, where the **Lahaina Restoration Foundation** (☎ **808-661-3262;** www.lahainarestoration.org) is headquartered in the adjacent Master's Reading Room. Stop in any day between 10 a.m. and 4:30 p.m. to pick up the free self-guided walking tour brochure and map of Lahaina's most historic sites. All are within easy walking distance of one another. Stops include the **Brig *Carthaginian II,*** a replica of the 19th-century whaling ship that brought the first missionaries to Hawaii, docked at Lahaina Harbor; the **banyan tree,** planted as a sapling in 1873 and now a massive 60 feet high and spanning two-thirds of an acre; an 1850s prison, the inside of which the rowdiest whalers no doubt saw on a regular basis; and a number of other interesting sites, including some lovely Buddhist missions and temples.

Lahaina

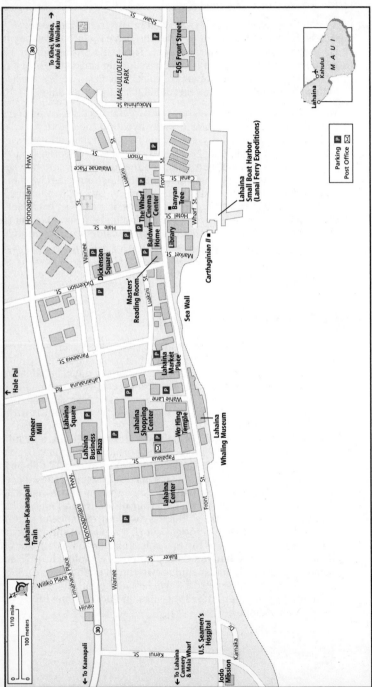

History aside, Lahaina is the real center of tourism on the island, with hotels, B&Bs, restaurants, T-shirt shops, and a gallery on nearly every block. Expect the town to be rather congested and expect to battle for a parking spot.

Touring South Maui

Check out the following sites when you explore South Maui.

Maui Ocean Center

This state-of-the-art aquarium is too pricey for its own good — it's no Monterey Bay Aquarium, after all — but it's still a cool place. All exhibits feature the creatures that populate Hawaii's waters, which makes this place great to visit before you set out on a snorkel cruise.

Start at the surge pool, where you'll see shallow-water marine life like spiny urchins and cauliflower coral, and then move on to the reef tanks and a turtle lagoon (where you'll meet some wonderful green sea turtles). A "touch" pool features tidepool critters, and a stingray pool is populated by graceful bottom dwellers; the whale discovery exhibit (no live creatures) is disappointing, though. Then you get to the star of the show: the 600,000-gallon main tank, which features tiger, gray, and white-tip sharks, as well as tuna, surgeon fish, triggerfish, and other large-scale tropicals. The neatest thing about the tank is that it's punctured by a clear acrylic tunnel that lets you walk right through it, giving you a real idea of what it might be like to stand at the bottom of the deep blue sea. Allow about two hours for your visit.

In Maalaea Harbor Village, 192 Maalaea Rd. (at the triangle between Honoapiilani Highway (Highway 31) and Maalaea Road), Maalaea. ☎ *808-270-7000.* www.maui oceancenter.com. *Admission: $20 adults, $17 seniors, $13 kids 3–12. Open: Daily 9 a.m.–5 p.m. (July–Aug, daily 9 a.m.–6 p.m.).*

Maui Golf & Sports Park

Maui's coolest new attraction may be this first-class miniature golf playland, whose two courses have been designed with both fun and duffing precision in mind. It also has bumper boats with water cannons (great on a hot day), a rock climbing wall, and an "xtreme" trampoline; all activities carry separate charges, or you can bundle them into a package deal. Tiki torches set the mood after dark, and the staff is very friendly. The park is ideal for both family fun and an after-dinner date.

In Maalaea Harbor Village (at the triangle between Honoapiilani Highway [Highway 31] and Maalaea Road; the entrance is on Maalaea Road), Maalaea. ☎ *808-242-7818. Activity prices: $13 for adults, $10 kids for 18 holes of golf (add $5 for a second round); other activities $8 adults, $6 kids. Package rates available. Open: Daily 10 a.m.– 10 p.m.*

Going Upcountry

The biggest attraction in Upcountry (the area on the slopes of Maui's 10,000-foot Haleakala volcano) is, of course, **Haleakala National Park,** which is so huge that it's discussed in a separate section at the beginning of this chapter. The rural Upcountry also has a handful of other appealing features, most notably Maui's only commercial winery (see the listing later in this section) and the cowboy-turned-boutique-town of **Makawao** (see "Off the Beaten Path: Paia, Makawao, and Kula" in Chapter 14 for more information).

Surfing Goat Dairy

This delightful place is a must on any foodie's tour of the Valley Isle. German ex-pats Thomas and Eva Kafsak came to Maui, purchased 42 verdant acres on the sunny slopes of Haleakala volcano, and opened the finest goat dairy in the Pacific. Surfing Goat Dairy is now a thriving business with a herd of 80 goats that Eva and Thomas care for as if they were their children; the result is some of the finest goat cheese you'll ever taste. Eva and Thomas open their blissful farm to visitors, who come to learn about the practice of goat farming and the craft of artisan goat cheese making — and, above all else, to pet the utterly charming goat kids, each of whom have their own personalities and cute names. The casual 20-minute tour is offered on weekends; just show up during the open hours, and Eva will show you around, give you a brief overview of the process, and introduce you to the goats; the fun culminates in a cheese tasting. Eva likes to take a minimum of four people on the tour, but my husband and I had no problem hooking up with another couple on our visit. For a more detailed experience — including an opportunity to feed and milk the goats and an extended play period with the kids — sign on for the two-hour Grand Tour, which is available on most Saturdays by appointment. You can also enjoy a simple farm-style lunch while you're at the farm, and/or order some of the gourmet goat cheeses — which come in a variety of hard, soft, and herb-infused flavors — to carry out or send home. Don't miss this wonderful spot if you can manage it; if you can't, you can also order cheeses online.

3651 Omaopio Rd., Kula. ☎ *08-878-2870.* www.surfinggoatdairy.com. *To get there: From the Hana Highway (Highway 36), turn south on Pulehu Road (Highway 370), and then turn left on Omaopio Road (Highway 372); the entrance will be about 1½ miles on your right. Twenty-minute tours: $4 (minimum 4 people): Sat 10 a.m.–4 p.m., Sun 10 a.m.–1 p.m. 2-hour tour: $12 (reservations required); call for schedule. Custom group tours also available.*

Tedeschi Vineyards at Ulupalakua Ranch

Maui's only winery is worth visiting less for its wines — which aren't going to cause the Napa Valley to worry about the Hawaii competition anytime soon — and more for the stunning mountain drive it takes to get there, and the pretty pastoral view you find after you arrive. Sitting on the little-visited south slopes of Haleakala at 2,000 feet elevation, these rolling, golden-hued ranchlands are like no other place you'll find on the island. The ranch dates back to the mid-19th century (the tasting room is housed in a lovely 1874 stone cottage built for a visit by King David Kalakaua), so it has a wonderful historic feeling and well-established grounds that are fine for picnicking; buy a bottle — red, white, or sparkling — to accompany lunch, but skip the silly pineapple wine. Allow an hour each way for the drive from most resorts. Free tastings and guided tours (daily at 10:30 a.m. and 1:30 p.m.) make this destination surprisingly popular.

On the Kula Highway (Highway 37), Ulupalakua. ☎ **877-878-6058.** www.mauiwine. com. *To get there: Follow the Haleakala Highway south to the Kula Highway; after you reach Keokea, go 5 miles past the Henry Fong Store. Admission, tastings, and tours: Free! Open: Daily 9 a.m.–5 p.m.*

Hitting the Links: Maui's Best Golf

If you love golf, don't miss the opportunity to play on Maui. The Valley Isle boasts a wealth of championship courses designed to make 18-hole memories.

Always book your tee times well in advance (a week or even more) on popular Maui, especially in high season. Weekdays are best for avoiding the crowds and securing the tee times you want. Note that golf carts are required on all Maui golf courses.

The **Maui Golf Shop,** 357 Huku Lii Place, Kihei (☎ **800-981-5512** or 808-875-4653; www.golf-maui.com), can book discounted tee times for you at many of Maui's finest courses (including, at press time, the Dunes, Kaanapali, and Makena, all in the following section). If you want to schedule your tee times before you leave home, you can even submit your discount requests online (where you also find information and insider tips on playing a wealth of Maui links). After you arrive, the shop is the best place on the island to rent clubs and stock up on gear; you can find it just off the Piilani Highway (Highway 31) at Ohukai Road (behind Tesoro Gas Express).

Play in the afternoon, when discounted twilight rates are in effect. I can't guarantee that you'll get 18 holes in, especially in winter when it's dark by 6 p.m., but you'll have an opportunity to experience these world-famous courses at half the usual fee. I note discount times in the following listings.

A terrific guide to all of Maui's golf courses is available from the Maui Visitors Bureau. Just call ☎ **800-525-MAUI** and request a copy of *Maui's Golf Coast.* You can also request a copy at www.visitmaui.com.

The Dunes at Maui Lani

This dramatic British links-style course — new to Maui in 1997 — plays like an old pro. Inspired by the old-growth links of Ireland, Honolulu-based course architect Robin Nelson built this public course on the former home of a sand-mining operation, which has allowed the fairways to mature in record time. Several blind and semiblind shots give this all-around, enjoyable course an edge. Considering the course's quality, the rates are a veritable bargain. Private lessons and half-day schools at the PGA pro-taught golf school even make improving your swing a comparatively affordable endeavor.

1333 Mauilani Pkwy., Kahului. ☎ *808-873-0422.* www.dunesatmauilani.com. *Greens fees: $98, $60 after 2 p.m.*

Kaanapali Golf Courses

Both of these popular, rolling resort courses pose a challenge to all golfers, from high handicappers to near-pros. The par-71, 6,136-yard Tournament North Course is home to the Senior PGA Tour, and a true Robert Trent Jones, Jr., design, with an abundance of wide bunkers, several long, stretched-out tees, the largest, most contoured greens on Maui, and one of Hawaii's toughest finishing holes. The par-71, 6,067-yard Resort South Course is an Arthur Jack Snyder design that, although shorter than the North Course, requires more accuracy on the narrow, hilly fairways. The 18th hole has a tricky water hazard, so don't tally up your scorecard until you sink your final putt. Facilities include a driving range, putting green, clubhouse, and comprehensive golf academy.

2290 Kaanapali Pkwy. (off Highway 30), Kaanapali. ☎ *808-661-3691.* www.kaanapali-golf.com. *Greens fees: $142–$160 ($117–$130 for Kaanapali resort guests); $85 at noon, $74–$77 after 2 p.m.*

Kapalua Golf Club

These three spectacularly sited championship courses are worth the sky-high greens fees for the views alone. Resort golf hardly gets finer — *Hawaii* magazine regularly names the Bay and the Plantation courses two of the top nine courses in Hawaii. An Arnold Palmer/Francis Duane design, the par-72, 6,600-yard Bay Course is a bit forgiving thanks to generous and gently undulating fairways, but even the pros have trouble with the 5th, which requires a tee shot over an ocean cove. The breathtaking — and breathtakingly difficult — Ben Crenshaw/Bill Coore–designed Plantation Course is prime for developing your low shots and precise chipping; this 7,263-yard, par-73 showstopper is home to the PGA's annual Mercedes Championship. The par-71, 6,632-yard Village Course, a Palmer/Ed Seay design and the most scenic of the three courses, suits beginners and pros alike, but winds can make for a challenging day among the Cook and Norfolk pines. Facilities include locker rooms, driving range, and restaurant.

The first-rate **Kapalua Golf Academy** (☎ **808-669-6500**) just may be Hawaii's best place to improve the swing of beginner and almost-pro alike.

Check for money-saving seasonal specials and golf packages at Kapalua's Web site.

Off Honoapiilani Highway (Highway 30), Kapalua. ☎ *877-527-2582 or 808-669-8044.* www.kapaluamaui.com. *Greens fees: $180–$225 ($125–$140 for Kapalua resort guests); $80–$90 after 1:30 p.m.*

Makena Golf Club

Robert Trent Jones, Jr., was in top form when he designed these 36 holes. The par-72, 7,017-yard oceanside South Course is considered the more forgiving of the two but has a couple of holes you'll never forget: Running parallel to the ocean, the par-4 16th has a two-tiered green that slopes away from the player, while the par-5, 502-yard 10th is one of Hawaii's best driving holes. With tight fairways and narrow doglegs, the par-72, 6,914-yard North Course is more difficult and more spectacular because it sits higher up the slope of Haleakala. Facilities include a clubhouse, driving range, two putting greens, a pro shop, lockers, and lessons. Additional bonuses include a gorgeous rural setting and spectacular views.

5415 Makena Alanui Dr., Makena (south of Wailea). ☎ *808-879-3344.* www.makena golf.com. *Greens fees: $110–$175, $85–$105 after 2 p.m.*

Pukalani Country Club

This par-72, 6,962-yard course (at a cool elevation of 1,100 feet) offers a break from the resorts' sky-high greens fees, and it's really fun to play. The third hole offers golfers two different options: a tough iron shot from the tee (especially into the wind), across a gully to the green; or a shot down the side of the gully across a second green into sand traps below. (Most people choose to shoot down the side of the gully; it's actually easier than shooting across a ravine.) High handicappers love this course, and more experienced players can make it more challenging by playing from the back tees. Facilities include club and shoe rentals, practice areas, lockers, a pro shop, and a restaurant.

360 Pukalani St., Pukalani (south of Haliimaile on Highway 37, Upcountry). ☎ *808-572-1314.* www.pukalanigolf.com. *Greens fees, including cart: $60 for 18 holes before 11 a.m.; $55 11 a.m.–2 p.m.; $45 after 2 p.m. Take the Hana Highway (Highway 36) to Haleakala Highway (Highway 37) to the Pukalani exit; turn right onto Pukalani Street and go 2 blocks.*

Wailea Golf Club

Most difficult among Wailea's courses is the par-72, 7,070-yard Gold Course, the new home of the Champions Skins Game. This classic Robert Trent Jones, Jr., design boasts a rugged layout, narrow fairways, several tricky dogleg holes, daunting natural hazards, and only-in-Hawaii features like lava outcroppings and native grasses. Both the Blue and the Emerald are easy for most golfers to enjoy, but the par-72, 6,407-yard Emerald Course — another Trent Jones, Jr., design — is both the prettiest and easiest for high handicappers to enjoy. The par-72, 6,700-yard Blue Course, an open course designed by Arthur Jack Snyder, has wide fairways that also appeal to beginners, but bunkers, water hazards, and undulating terrain make it a course that all can enjoy. Facilities include two clubhouses, two pro shops, restaurants, lockers, club rentals, and a complete training facility.

Call to inquire about discounted afternoon rates, money-saving triple- and unlimited-play passes, and other specials, including junior golf rates.

Off Wailea Alanui Drive, Wailea. ☎ *888-328-MAUI, 800-322-1614, or 808-875-7450. www.waileagolf.com. Greens fees: $175–$185 ($135–$145 for Wailea Resort guests); twilight rates $90–$100.*

Enjoying Guided Nature Hikes

Maui's oldest and best-guided hiking company is Ken Schmitt's **Hike Maui** (☎ **808-879-5270;** www.hikemaui.com). Hike Maui has been universally lauded for the quality of its hikes; you can't go wrong with it. The expert guides are all trained naturalists who really know their stuff. Hiking is a fabulous way to see beautiful Maui at its natural best. Hike Maui offers nine hikes ranging from 1½ to 8 miles and from easy to strenuous, but most fall in the moderate category:

✔ **Rainforest and waterfall hikes:** A 1½-mile, easy-to-moderate, half-day option and a 4½-mile, full-day, moderate option are avaliable. Both hikes take you through lush rainforests to gorgeous waterfalls; the full-day trip visits dramatic Kipahulu and includes time for swimming in the waterfall pools.

✔ **Haleakala Volcano hikes:** A moderate 4-mile walk and a strenuous 8-mile walk are available. Both offer an excellent way to see this splendid national park, which can be difficult to appreciate if you don't know what you're seeing. If you're an accomplished hiker and fit for it, don't miss the longer hike. It takes you all the way to the crater floor — which looks so much like the moon that the lunar astronauts trained there — for a truly otherworldly experience.

✔ **Additional hikes:** Hike Maui also offers these outings:

  • A moderate 4½-mile West Maui Mountain Ridge Trail hike that offers a good workout and fabulous views

  • A 3-mile, marine-biologist-led Coastline Hike that combines a moderate hike with an archaeological tour of ancient Hawaiian villages and some terrific snorkeling

  • A 5-mile, full-day, moderate Cloud Forest Hike to Polipoli State Park, where you spot rare birds and wildflowers

  • A moderate 4-mile sea cliff hike

  • A "Do It All in a Day" hike that includes 2½ miles of hiking plus kayaking and snorkeling

---

Maui pineapples: *No ka oi!* (The best!)

Everybody thinks of the pineapple as a genuine Hawaiian treat, but the sad fact is that not many pineapples are grown in Hawaii these days. However, the Maui Pineapple Company — one of the last relevant vestiges of Hawaii's plantation era — still harvests some of the world's sweetest, most succulent pineapples in the rich uplands of Kapalua. You can tour this 23,000-acre working plantation in the company of the company's own field workers, learning about the history of the pineapple in Hawaii and the unique cultivation of these sun-sweet fruits. You even have an opportunity to pick your own luscious fruit to take home. This tour isn't a touristy, faux plantation experience — it's the real deal for folks who are genuinely interested in Hawaii's pineapple history. The two and a half hour tour is offered weekdays at 9:30 a.m.; tickets are $29, and you must be at least 10 years old to attend. Call ☎ 808-669-8088 for reservations or go to www.maui pineapple.com/contact and click on "Tours."

Trips range from $94 to $155 per person. Prices include equipment and transportation from Central Maui (one of the company's air-conditioned vans takes you from the office to the trailhead), and a simple, healthy lunch of sandwiches and fruit. You can book as late as a couple of days in advance, but your best bet is to call before you arrive on the island for the greatest flexibility and to avoid disappointment.

If Hike Maui's schedules don't suit your needs, call **Maui Eco-Adventures** (☎ 877-661-7720 or 808-661-7720; www.ecomaui.com), which specializes in guided cultural and hiking adventures that explore untrammeled areas of the island, including the little-known Maunalei Arboretum; Nakele Point, the northernmost point on Maui; and more, including waterfall hikes and hike/kayak combos. Prices run $75 to $160 per person, including continental breakfast, lunch, a day's supply of water, and pickup from West Maui hotels.

Maui Hiking Safaris (☎ 888-445-3963 or 808-573-0168; www.maui.net/~mhs), another reputable company, offers guided hikes for all levels, including waterfall hikes and guided hikes of Haleakala. Prices run from $59 to $109 per person (10-percent discount for kids 13 and under).

Maui Hiking Safaris extends 10-percent discounts to hikers who book more than two weeks in advance, as well as for groups of six or more.

Getting a Bird's-Eye View: Helicopter Tours

Flightseeing is an excellent way to explore Maui's stunning, untouched natural areas that simply aren't viewable by any other means. Maui-based helicopter tours also offer you the opportunity to see a neighbor island — Molokai, Lanai, or even the Big Island — from the air in addition to the Valley Isle.

You need to take into account some considerations. Although the company I recommend in this section features skilled pilots and helicopters with excellent safety records, the truth is that flightseeing can be a risky business. Twenty-eight people have died in commercial helicopter crashes in Hawaii over the last decade, seven in a Maui crash in July 2000. Of course, just getting into your rental car and driving to dinner — or even getting into the shower in your condo with a renegade bar of soap — is far more dangerous than catching a copter ride. Still, you should make informed decisions.

When reserving a helicopter tour with any company, check to make sure that safety is its first concern. The company should be an FAA-certified Part 135 operator, and the pilot should be Part 135 certified as well. The 135 license guarantees more stringent maintenance requirements and pilot-training programs than those programs that are only Part 91 certified. And any time weather conditions look iffy, reschedule. You can certainly make arrangements before your vacation begins, but it isn't necessary. The concierge at your hotel can help you make an appointment.

Blue Hawaiian Helicopters

This top-notch flightseeing company is my Hawaii favorite. Family run by David and Patti Chevalier and a loyal, long-employed staff, Blue Hawaiian flies a fleet of superb American Eurocopter AStar 350 helicopters that carry six passengers, providing each with a 180° view and a Bose noise-cancelling headset that lets you enjoy a surprisingly quiet ride. A world leader in the flightseeing industry, Blue Hawaiian also flies Hawaii's only EC-130B4 Eco-Stars. These shiny, new cutting-edge copters lower noise pollution with a super-quiet design and maximize comfort and views with state-of-the-art design, technology, and materials. These copters offer one phenomenal ride.

A range of available flight options include some or all of the following spectacular sights: the misty, green West Maui Mountains; otherworldly Haleakala Volcano; luxuriant, unspoiled East Maui and Hana; and Molokai, where you fly by the highest seacliffs in the world. I say go for the whole shebang and book the fantastic 80-minute Maui Spectacular, which includes a complete island tour as well as a midflight landing at an exclusive perch at the Ulupalakua Ranch, on the grassy slopes of Haleakala. The view is simply stunning, as is the landing and takeoff from this remote spot. This trip is one of my best hours spent in Hawaii *ever* — and I've spent plenty of hours in Hawaii. But don't miss out if you can't afford the grand tour; opt for a West Maui/Molokai combo, or a Hana/Haleakala tour (especially if you're not going to have time to hit the road to Hana).

Honored annually by the FAA with its Certificate of Excellence, Blue Hawaiian boasts an excellent safety record, as well as a fleet of other top safety and customer-satisfaction certifications and awards. The pilots (mostly decorated veterans) boast thousands upon thousands of flight hours. The pilots are also well-trained and certified tour guides who are extremely knowledgeable narrators. A state-of-the-art in-flight video is on board in case you want to preserve the sights and sounds of your thrill-a-minute flight for posterity. An expensive adventure, sure — but money well spent.

If you book seven days or more in advance via e-mail, or call and mention that you visited its Web site, Blue Hawaiian will award you a 15-percent price break.

Blue Hawaiian tours depart from Kahului Airport. ☎ *800-745-BLUE or 808-871-8844.* www.bluehawaiian.com. *30- to 100-minute tours: $125–$280 per person.*

If Blue Hawaiian is booked, try **Sunshine Helicopters** (☎ 800-469-3000 or 808-871-5600; www.sunshinehelicopters.com), which offers a variety of flights, from short hops around the West Maui Mountains to island tours. Prices range from $125 to $290 per person.

Saddling Up

Maybe you have a tropical fantasy of riding horseback through rugged ranchlands, into tropical forests, and to remote swimming holes. Maui is the place to make it come true.

Call ahead to reserve a spot on the trail rides that I mention in this section because group size is limited. Also confirm times, prices, and routes, which are subject to change.

If you want to ride down into Haleakala's crater, contact **Pony Express Tours** (☎ 808-667-2200; www.ponyexpresstours.com), which offers a variety of rides down to the crater floor and back up, from $155 to $190 per person. Shorter one- and two-hour rides are also offered at Haleakala Ranch, located on the volcano's beautiful lower slopes, for $60 and $105. Internet discounts of 10 percent are available if you book online. Pony Express provides well-trained horses and experienced guides and accommodates all riding levels. You must be at least 10 years old, weigh no more than 230 pounds, and wear long pants and closed-toe shoes.

Mendes Ranch & Trail Rides, 3530 Kahekili Hwy., 4 miles past Wailuku (☎ 808-244-7320; www.mendesranch.com), is based on the 300-acre Mendes Ranch, a real working ranch complete with waterfalls, palm trees, coral-sand beaches, lagoons, tide pools, a rainforest, and its own volcanic peak. Allan Mendes, a third-generation wrangler, takes you from the rainforest's edge out to the sea. On the way, you cross tree-studded meadows where Texas longhorns sit in the shade and pass a dusty corral where Allan's father, Ernest, a champion roper, may be breaking a wild horse. The Paniolo Adventure morning ride, which lasts three hours and ends with a barbecue back at the corral, is $130; the two and a half hour Aloha ride, which leaves at 8:15 a.m. or 12:15 p.m., costs $89, and includes snacks but not the barbecue.

If you're out in Hana, call **Maui Stables** (☎ 808-248-7799; www.maui stables.com), which will take you out to explore the lush scenery of the Kipahulu district. Half-day tours are $150 per person, including a deli lunch. Reservations are a must.

If you enjoy your ride, remember to kiss your horse and tip your guide.

Serving Up Some Tennis

Most resorts and nicer condo complexes in Maui offer private tennis courts.

If you need a court in West Maui, contact the **Kapalua Tennis Garden,** Kapalua Resort (☎ 808-669-5677; www.kapaluamaui.com), which features ten Plexipave courts for both day and night play ($12 for nonresort guests), plus group and private instruction.

In South Maui, book a court at the **Wailea Tennis Club** (☎ 808-879-1958; www.waileatennis.com). Consistently chosen as one of the finest tennis facilities in the country, Wailea has 11 hard courts available for $12 per person, or a maximum of $48 per court for nonresort guests, plus a full calendar of lessons, clinics, round robins, and the like. The club also rents racquets, shoes, and hall machines.

Relaxing at a Spa

What's the icing on the cake of any vacation? A good, long, pampering spa day, of course. Hawaii's spas have raised the art of relaxation and healing to a new level, showcasing Hawaiian products and traditional treatments available only in the islands.

Spas simply don't come any finer than the luxurious **Spa Grande** at the Grand Wailea Resort (☎ 800-888-6100 or 808-875-1234; www.grand wailea.com), regularly recognized as one of the top ten spas in the United States. This 50,000-square-foot temple to the good life boasts a massive East-meets-West spa menu, a first-rate army of therapists, 40 individual treatment rooms (many with ocean views), and a full Terme hydrotherapy circuit consisting of a variety of healthful baths (including mud, seaweed, aromatherapy, tropical enzyme, and mineral salt, each with their own rejuvenating powers), Roman pools, and Swiss-jet showers that are worth the treatment price of admission alone. (They're included with every treatment, so I recommend coming a full hour or more before your appointment). For a one-of-a-kind experience, don't miss the celestial Coconut Euphoria bath, a multistep moisturizing treatment that makes you feel like a piña-colada-scented queen for a day. Honestly, you can't go wrong anywhere on this menu. Book a full day's package for the ultimate indulgence — you deserve it. Reserve well ahead.

The Spa at the **Four Seasons Resort Maui** (☎ 808-874-8000; www.four seasons.com/maui/index.html) is another good place to spoil yourself with pure pampering. The intimate and sophisticated facility features 13 indoor treatment rooms, a state-of-the-art gym, a healing garden, and three outdoor *hale* with idyllic ocean views. Imagine the sounds of the waves rolling on Wailea Beach as you're soothingly massaged in the privacy of your own thatch-roofed hut, tucked into the beachside foliage.

For an intimate, personalized experience in South Maui, book treatments at **Spa Kea Lani,** at the Fairmont Kea Lani Maui (☎ 800-257-7544 or 808-875-4100; www.kealani.com). A terrific signature experience infused with local character is the Awapuhi Ginger Treatment, which includes full body exfoliation, a body masque applied using Hawaiian *lomi lomi* massage, and a foot, scalp, and face massage.

In West Maui, your top choice is **Spa Moana** at the Hyatt Regency Maui (☎ 800-233-1234 or 808-661-1234; www.maui.hyatt.com), a newly expanded 15,000-square-foot oceanview spa with 15 treatment rooms, a full-service salon with prime views, an open-air relaxation lounge, and an extensive treatment menu that includes some dynamite facials, as well as soothing body work. Two couples suites allow for romantically infused relaxation. The adjacent Moana Athletic Club has the finest views of any fitness center on the island.

In April 2004, Kaanapali's Westin Maui unveiled **The Spa at Westin Maui** (☎ 808-667-2525; www.westinmaui.com), the first Westin Heavenly Spa, with 13,000 square feet of celestial pampering and relaxation. Many treatments are infused with island scents, including Maui-grown lavender. If you're in Lahaina and in the mood for some storefront pampering, visit **Lei Spa Maui,** 505 Front St. complex (☎ 808-661-1178; www.leispa.com).

In Paia, if you're looking for an excellent, low-key, and affordable massage, visit **Northshore Chiropractic,** 16 Baldwin Ave. (☎ 808-579-9134), on the west side of the main street, a few doors from the highway. They charge a mere $40 an hour and have fabulous therapists.

Chapter 14

Shopping the Local Stores

In This Chapter

▶ Finding the best places to buy fabulous, colorful aloha wear
▶ Introducing Maui's art galleries
▶ Discovering unique island gifts for the folks back home

*I*n terms of shopping opportunities, the Valley Isle is the reigning king among the neighbor islands. Shoppers may really find themselves in paradise.

Central Maui: Wailuku

Although Kahului is the island's hub and the place to go for practical items, the historic town of Wailuku immediately to its west offers reasonably good hunting grounds for antique hounds. Like most Maui shopping destinations, Wailuku is a mixed bag — it has never really taken off like some had hoped — but you can find a few quality shops featuring both new and used treasures on North Market Street; to get there, simply go west from Kahului on Kaahumanu Avenue and turn right when you reach Market, in the heart of Wailuku.

Highlights include **Brown-Kobayashi,** 38 N. Market St. (☎ **808-242-0804** or 808-242-0805), a treasure trove of graceful Asian antiques (mostly large pieces, but affordable prices make the shipping worth it for committed collectors); **Bird of Paradise Unique Antiques,** 54 N. Market St. (☎ **808-242-7699**), for a jumble of collectible glassware, pottery, and Hawaiiana; and **If the Shoe Fits,** 12 N. Market St. (☎ **808-249-9710**), for unique footwear.

Wailuku's top stop is **Sig Zane**, 53 N. Market St. (☎ **808-249-8997;** www.sigzane.com). Mauians cheered when this Big Island designer set up a Valley Isle outpost. Sig's distinctive, two-color, all-cotton aloha wear is the height of simple style and good taste. The stunningly beautiful fabrics are sold in a variety of clean-lined, easy-to-wear styles as well as off the bolt if you want to take some home. If you buy one article of aloha wear to bring home, buy it at Sig Zane's. And if you've already visited the Big Island boutique, stop in anyway, because you can find unique patterns and colors here.

West Maui: Lahaina, Kaanapali, and Kapalua

Shopping in West Maui consists of three main parts: Lahaina, Kaanapali, and Kapalua. The following sections give you the lowdown on these areas.

Lahaina

Lahaina's main drag, Front Street, overflows with surf-wear shops, contemporary art galleries, trendy boutiques, cheesy T-shirt shops, and much more — you'll tire of browsing well before you run out of places to flex your credit card.

Your best bet is to just start at one end of Front Street and browse. Highlights include **Serendipity**, 752 Front St. (☎ **808-667-7070**), for casual women's wear in comfortable, loose-fitting island styles. Next door is **Tropical Blues**, 754 Front St. (☎ **808-667-4008**), specializing in high-quality tropical wear for women, plus a small men's collection; you also find fun tropical-themed accessories, bags, and sandals. **Honolua Surf Co.**, 845 Front St. (☎ **808-661-8848;** www.honoluasurf.com), carries its own fabulous line of surf wear and gear. **Kamehameha Garment Company**, in the Pioneer Inn, 109 Hotel St. (just off Front Street; ☎ **808-667-2269**), sells the company's own line of gorgeous new aloha wear in vintage patterns; all the telltale signs of quality aloha wear are there, including patterns that match on the seams and coconut-shell buttons.

Célébrités, 764 Front St. (☎ **800-428-3338** or 808-667-0727; www.celebrityfineart.com), features art by and about celebrities. It's the height of over-the-top conspicuous consumption, but it's a compelling browse nonetheless. **Vintage European Posters**, 744 Front St. (☎ **808-662-8688**), boasts a fantastic array of original poster art from

1890 to 1950, mostly European and all in mint condition; prices are excellent considering the stock's quality. For a hand-painted original, visit the **Curtis Wilson Cost Gallery,** 710 Front St. (☎ 808-661-4140; www.costgallery.com). The Maui-based painter is a landscape traditionalist; his islandscapes are luminescent and alive with detail.

If you want to stock up on contemporary island tunes, stop by the **Hawaiian Music Store,** in an open-air kiosk at the north end of Front Street next to Longhi's, across from the Bubba Gump Shrimp Co. (☎ 808-661-9225; www.hawaiianmusicstore.com).

An island of artistic integrity in the sea of Lahaina kitsch is **Na Mea Hawaii Store,** in the Baldwin House, 120 Dickenson St., at Front Street (☎ 808-661-5707), which sells only fine-quality island-made crafts and gifts. That doesn't mean expensive, though; you can find a surprising number of affordable prizes among the bounty.

For marine-themed goods and educational gifts for kids, you can't do better than the nonprofit **Pacific Whale Foundation** store, 143 Dickenson St., a block up from Front Street (☎ 808-667-7447; www.pacificwhale.org). Members save 15 percent off all whale- and ecothemed goodies as well as whale-watch cruises and snorkel tours that you can book right at the shop (see Chapter 12), so consider joining up for a good cause. You can find a second Pacific Whale Foundation shop in South Maui at Maalaea Harbor Village, 300 Maalaea Rd. (in the same complex as the Maui Ocean Center), at the north end of Kihei (☎ 808-249-8977).

At the far-south end of Front Street, in the 505 Front St. complex, is **Lei Spa Maui** (☎ 808-661-1178; www.leispa.com), which carries a wonderful line of fragrant and rejuvenating Hawaii-made bath and body products, while therapists offer massages, body wraps, and facials. Tucked away in the mall's south end is **Old Lahaina Book Emporium** (☎ 808-661-1399), for used and new fiction, nonfiction, music, and videos.

At the opposite, north end of Front Street are a couple of shopping centers, including **Lahaina Cannery Mall,** 1221 Honoapiilani Hwy. (☎ 808-667-0592; www.lahainacannerymall.com), for practical items and a few special names like **Lahaina Printsellers** and the **Totally Hawaiian Gift Gallery.** The **Lahaina Center,** 900 Front St. (☎ 808-667-9216; www.lahainacenter.com), is a pleasant open-air mall that boasts **Local Motion** for surf wear and gear; **Hilo Hattie,** Hawaii's biggest name in affordable aloha wear; and mall standards like **Banana Republic.**

Kaanapali

On the beach, in Kaanapali, **Whaler's Village,** 2435 Kaanapali Pkwy.
(☎ **808-661-4567;** www.whalersvillage.com), has blossomed into
quite an upscale shopping and dining complex, offering an appealing
open-air shopping experience (once you get past the ordeal of parking).
Although it has become the Rodeo Drive of Maui in recent years — with
Gucci, Dior, Chanel, Prada, Louis Vuitton, Tiffany & Co., and **Versace**
all represented — it also has some surprisingly excellent midrange boutiques, including two branches of **Honolua Surf Co.,** whose stylish surf
gear and wear I just love; **Sandal Tree,** for an excellent collection of
women's footwear, sunhats, and handbags; **Clio Blue** for whimsically
elegant silver jewelry, much of it shaped like fish (despite the fish theme,
it's a Parisian import); **Vintage European Posters,** for artful browsing;
Dolphin Galleries, for high-quality island-themed and locally designed
jewelry, including a 14-carat collection designed in a clever petroglyph
style; **Noa Noa,** for attractive batik clothing and Indonesian-style home-
wares; a branch of **Reyn's,** the Hawaii-based company that makes my
second-favorite contemporary aloha wear (after Sig Zane; see Wailuku,
earlier in this section); and **Martin & MacArthur** for island crafts. Meeting
your practical needs are such stops as **The Body Shop** and **Waikiki Aloe,**
in case you need to stock up on ecofriendly sunscreen or nature's best
sunburn antidote; **Ritz Camera; Maui Dive Shop;** and **Waldenbooks,** in
case you need a fresh beach read.

Kapalua

The quiet, upscale **Kapalua Shops,** adjacent to the Kapalua Bay Hotel
on Bay Drive, don't pack the same punch as Whaler's Village, but a few
unique highlights are worth seeking out. For fine jewelry designs in gold,
most done by local artisans, visit **Haimoff and Haimoff** (☎ **808-669-5213;**
www.haimoffandhaimoff.com). **Bella Vitri Gallery** (☎ **808-665-0916**)
showcases fine studio-quality art glass. **Hawaiian Quilt Collection**
(☎ **808-665-1111**) offers fine handmade quilts in the boldly artistic
Hawaiian style, while **Trouvaville** (☎ **808-669-8508**) focuses on primitive art and textiles.

South Maui: Wailea

The lovely open-air **Shops at Wailea,** 3750 Wailea Alanui Dr. (☎ **808-**
891-6770; www.shopsatwailea.com), has been an excellent addition
to the Wailea resort, bringing in both much-needed practical retailers
and elegant gift outlets. Stores run the gamut from familiar names ranging from **Tiffany & Co.** to **The Gap.** Specialty stores worth seeking out
include **Footprints** for an excellent selection of sandals for men, women,
and children; **Tori Richard** and **Reyn's** for high-quality aloha wear in fun

and funky prints; **Martin & MacArthur** for hand-crafted koa and other Hawaii crafts; **Na Hoku** for fine jewelry done in the Hawaiian heritage style, plus beautiful Tahitian pearls; **Blue Ginger,** which has brought batik into the 21st century with its bold prints and flowing modern cuts; the new **Wailea Body & Bath;** and **Tommy Bahama's,** whose tropically sophisticated clothing emporium also boasts a winning oceanview cafe and bar (see Chapter 11), and much more. Art lovers can find a wealth of upscale art galleries, including outlets of such Lahaina favorites as **Célébrités,** showcasing art by and about, yes, celebrities; and **Elizabeth Doyle Gallery,** whose large-scale treasures include the monumental art glass of Dale Chihuly; plus **Eclectic Image Gallery** for high-quality photographic art. You find all this and much, much more in a pleasant oceanview setting.

Off the Beaten Path: Paia, Makawao, and Kula

Just because you're off the beaten path, doesn't mean you won't find great shopping. Shopping fanatics can have a ball in Paia, Makawao, and Kula.

Shopping Paia

 The hip little surf town of **Paia** (pa-*ee*-ah), just 15 minutes east of Kahului on the Hana Highway (Highway 36), has evolved into my favorite Maui shopping stop of late. It makes an eclectic but appealing stop for shoppers looking for funky, fun, and fashion-forward goods. The boutiques sprawl in a T-shape from the intersection of the Hana Highway and Baldwin Avenue, and the choices range from the sublime to the ridiculous.

On the sublime end is **Maui Crafts Guild,** on the ocean side of Hana Highway at No. 43 (☎ **808-579-9697;** www.mauicraftsguild.com), an artist-owned cooperative that represents some of the finest artists and craftspeople on Maui; you find artworks and gifts in all price ranges there.

At the opposite end of the spectrum is **Big Bugga Sportswear,** 18 Baldwin Ave. (☎ **808-579-6216;** www.bigbugga.com), which carries the largest men's casual wear you've ever seen in your life — from XL to a sumo-sized 10XL. In between, you can find **Moonbow Tropics** at 20 and 36 Baldwin Ave. (☎ **808-579-8775** or 808-579-8592; www.moonbow tropicsmaui.com), which offers the finest contemporary aloha-wear lines available, and more good stuff.

Necessories Boutique, 21 Baldwin Ave. (☎ 808-579-9805), bills itself as "Hawaiian Bohemian funk," but the collection of home décor and wearables is surprisingly well chosen and creatively displayed, making this one of my favorite stops in a shopping-rich town.

You also can choose from the **Paia Trading Co.,** 106 Hana Hwy. (☎ 877-218-8763 or 808-579-9472), for good, old-fashioned vintage collectibles. **Nuage Bleu,** 76 Hana Hwy. (☎ 808-579-9792), specializes in cutting-edge clothing and accessories for women and children, carrying such brands as Juicy Couture, Miss Sixty, Diane Von Furstenberg, and others. You also find chic island-style fashions from names like Sanctuary and Jil Stuart at **Bahama Mamma,** 62 Baldwin Ave. (☎ 808-579-8188), while the island's hottest bikinis are at **Maui Girl Beachwear,** 12 Baldwin Ave. (☎ 808-579-9266). Moonbow Tropics, 20 and 36 Baldwin Ave. (☎ 808-579-8592), carries an excellent collection — possibly the island's best — of high-end tropical clothing for men and women. There's plenty more good stuff; just park and browse.

Shopping Makawao

From Paia, drive on Baldwin Avenue (Highway 390), toward the mountain, and in 7 miles, you reach **Makawao** (ma-*ka*-wow), a cowboy-town-turned-New-Age-village that's another petite shopper's paradise.

The shopping is so good in Makawao that the whole *town* is a highlight. Serious shoppers should definitely save an afternoon to explore. Seek out **Hurricane,** 3639 Baldwin Ave. (☎ 808-572-5076), a wonderful split-level boutique that carries a well-displayed selection of fine casuals for women, including such fine labels as Sigrid Olsen; and **Tropo,** next door (☎ 808-573-0356), Hurricane's boutique for men. **The Courtyard,** at 3620 Baldwin Ave., houses a number of interesting craft shops of varying quality, including **Maui Hands** (☎ 808-352-4278; www.mauihands.com) and **Hot Island Glass Studio & Gallery** (☎ 808-572-4527; www.hot islandglass.com), a fascinating glassblower's studio that's worth a peek; the **Master Touch Gallery,** 3655 Baldwin Ave. (☎ 808-572-6000; www.saccojewelry.com), carrying the extraordinary one-of-a-kind jewelry of designer David Sacco; and much, much more. Highlights of the numerous visual arts galleries include **R. Groden Gallery,** 1152 Makawao Ave. (☎ 808-573-5311; www.rgroden.com), which showcases the beautiful, intricate, female-focused visual art of local artist Randy Groden.

The highlight of Makawao is the **Hui Noeau Visual Arts Center,** a mile outside of town at 2841 Baldwin Ave. (☎ 808-572-6560; www.hui noeau.com). A tree-lined driveway leads to the 1917 estate (designed by noted Hawaii architect C.W. Dickey) that houses the island's most renowned artists' collection and features rotating exhibits by both established and up-and-coming island artists, plus an excellent shop featuring original works. The center has a $2 suggested donation for the exhibit gallery. The artistically active among you may also want to inquire about workshops, demonstrations, visiting-artist events, and other short-term opportunities for study.

Kula

Want to send some of those gorgeous Maui flowers back home to someone special — maybe yourself? Head Upcountry to the slopes of Haleakala, to the **Upcountry Harvest Gift Shop,** on Haleakala Highway (Highway 377; ☎ **800-575-6470;** www.upcountryharvest.com), adjacent to the Kula Lodge & Restaurant (see Chapter 11). The stunning protea — those oversized flowers that look like they came to Maui from another planet — are grown on the owners' own Sunrise Protea Farm. The shop also features a nice collection of island-style gifts and local crafts.

Chapter 15

Living It Up After the Sun Goes Down

In This Chapter
▶ Indulging in sunset cocktails
▶ Catching a spectacular show
▶ Going Upcountry

*M*aui's nightlife certainly doesn't rival the after-dark scene on the island of Oahu. Many of Maui's restaurants — particularly the oceanfront ones — do double duty as post-dinner hot spots, often hosting lively bar scenes, live music, and dancing. The epicenter of island nightlife is lively Lahaina.

Finding Your Way Out of the Dark

For the most complete calendar of what's happening while you're on Maui, pick up a copy of the weekly *MauiTime Weekly* newspaper, available for free at kiosks all over the island.

If you're interested in the more refined performing arts, look for a copy of *Centerpiece,* the free bimonthly magazine published by the **Maui Arts and Cultural Center,** the finest cultural venue in the islands; hotel concierges usually have copies. You can also call the center, which is located in Kahului, at ☎ 808-242-7469 or visit the Web site at www.mauiarts.org for a current schedule. The Maui Arts and Cultural Center dominates the performing-arts scene on the island, featuring a visual-arts gallery, an outdoor amphitheater, a 300-seat theater for experimental performances, and a 1,200-seat main theater. The diverse calendar sometimes features big names like Melissa Etheridge, Natalie Cole, or George Winston; Maui Film Festival screenings; or performances by Hawaii's most renowned musicians. (Don't miss Amy Hanaialii Gilliom if she's on the calendar.)

The island's best sunset cruises are offered by **Paragon Sailing Charters** (☎ **800-441-2087** or 808-441-2087; www.sailmaui.com). From Lahaina Harbor (on Front Street), you'll sail into the sunset on a state-of-the-art, high-performance catamaran. These two-hour sails are intimate affairs (only 24 passengers). Prices are $51 for adults, $34 for kids ages 4–12, with hors d'oeuvres and beverages (including champagne, wine, and beer). A 15-percent online advance-booking discount was available at press time. Departure times vary seasonally, and cruises aren't offered every day, so call ahead.

And, of course, don't forget that Maui is home to the finest examples of the ultimate island form of after-dark entertainment: the **luau!** I highly recommend planning to participate in one while you're on the Valley Isle, because it's home to the best commercial luaus in all of Hawaii. For details, see Chapter 11.

Partying in West Maui

West Maui is the Valley Isle's party central. Lahaina, in particular, takes on a festive atmosphere as sunset nears. The restaurants along ocean-front Front Street boast stellar views and energetic bar scenes, some with live music; just stroll the street and join whatever party suits your fancy.

Among the best spots to join the party are **Cheeseburger in Paradise,** 811 Front St. (☎ **808-661-4855**), a regular forum for live-and-lively music; the **Hard Rock Cafe,** 900 Front St. (☎ **808-667-7400**); and **Kimo's,** 845 Front St. (☎ **808-661-4811**). Lahaina's hottest new club is **The Breakwater,** in Lahaina Center at 900 Front St., next to the Front Street Theaters (☎ **808-667-7794**), which offers Lahaina's largest on-tap selection, sexy low lighting, comfy couches, a sushi bar, and an eclectic calendar of DJ dance parties and live music that makes this one of the most thrilling clubs in town. Call to see what's on. Every Friday from 7 to 10 p.m., as part of **Friday Night Is Art Night** in Lahaina, the town's galleries open their doors for special shows, demonstrations, and refreshments; you can even enjoy strolling musicians wandering the streets.

Lahaina is also home to two nightly shows that are well worth seeking out. If you love the performing arts — and even if you don't think you do — don't pass up an opportunity to see '*Ulalena* at the Maui Myth & Magic Theatre, in Old Lahaina Center, 878 Front St. (☎ **877-688-4800** or 808-661-9913; www.ulalena.com or www.mauitheatre.com). This incredible, Broadway-quality, 75-minute live show interweaves the natural, historical, and mythological tales of the birth of Hawaii using a near-perfect mix of original contemporary music and dance, ancient chant and hula, and creative lighting, gorgeous costumes, visual artistry (including some mind-blowing puppets), and live musicianship. This universally lauded production is bold, mesmerizing, and like nothing Hawaii has ever seen before — sort of like Laurie Anderson hooks up with Cirque du Soleil in Hawaii. Lest you think it all sounds too artsy for you, *'Ulalena* has been so popular among tourists and visitors alike that two shows are performed nightly (except on Tuesdays) at 6 p.m. Tickets are $48 to $75 for adults, $28 to $45 for kids ages 3 to 10 — yes, they'll love *'Ulalena,* too. Don't miss it! Packages that include dinner and/or VIP access to go backstage and meet the performers are now also available.

On my last visit to *'Ulalena,* I saved about 10 percent on my tickets by purchasing them at the **Hawaiian Music Store,** which also serves as an official ticket outlet for the show. You can find it just around the corner from Old Lahaina Center on Front Street (next to Longhi's, across from the Bubba Gump Shrimp Co.; ☎ **808-661-9225;** www.hawaiianmusic store.com).

For something completely different, spend an evening at **Warren & Annabelle's,** 900 Front St., in Lahaina (☎ **808-667-6244;** www.hawaii magic.com). This genuinely fun and surprisingly not cheesy mystery-and-magic cocktail show stars illusionist Warren Gibson and "Annabelle," a ghost from the *previous* turn of the century who plays a grand piano — and even takes your requests. Expect the requisite audience participation, of course. Tickets are $45 per person, with dinner packages ranging from $73 to $80 per person; you must be 21 or older to enter. Food and drinks are available for an additional charge. The show is very popular, so book at least a few days in advance to avoid disappointment; no shows are scheduled on Sundays.

An early-evening family-friendly show is sometimes added to the Warren & Annabelle's schedule; call for details.

Kaanapali has its own family-friendly entertainment as well. **Kupanaha** is the terrific magic show at the Kaanapali Beach Hotel (☎ **808-667-0128;** www.kbhmaui.com), starring husband-and-wife illusionists Jody and Kathleen Baran and their daughters, child prodigy magicians Katrina and Crystal. The dazzling show interweaves illusions, Hawaiian hula and chant, and the stories and myths of ancient Hawaii into a show that the whole family will love. No kidding — the show has been a huge hit. Shows are offered Tuesday through Saturday at the family-friendly hour of 5 p.m.; dinner is included, and you'll be out by 8 p.m. Tickets are $69 to $79 for adults, $49 for teens, $29 for kids 6 to 12, including the three-course dinner; a kids' menu is available.

For live music in Kaanapali, head to **Whaler's Village,** on Kaanapali Beach at 2435 Kaanapali Pkwy., where you can take an open-air seat facing the ocean at the bar at **Hula Grill** (☎ 808-667-6636), which features Hawaiian music and hula. Or head next door to **Leilani's on the Beach** (☎ 808-661-4495), where the party starts every afternoon with live music at 2:30 p.m. or so. With tiki torches flickering and the waves rolling in, you can't go wrong at either spot.

Also in Kaanapali, on the *mauka* (mountain) side of Highway 30, you'll find the **Sugar Cane Train** (☎ 808-667-6851; www.sugarcanetrain.com), a vintage, open-air steam train — a vestige of Maui's old plantation days — that offers a dinner ride for the entire family Tuesday and Thursday evenings at 5 p.m. You'll enjoy a sunset train ride complete with singing conductor aboard the historic steam engine and then disembark for a Hawaiian-style *paniolo* (cowboy) barbecue and hoe down complete with live music. Think of it as a luau, upcountry cowboy style; sure, it's cheesy, but the kids will love it. Tickets are $69 for adults and $39 for kids 3 to 12, including an all-you-can-eat buffet.

Up in Kapalua, every Tuesday evening comes alive with traditional and contemporary Hawaiian music thanks to the **Masters of Hawaiian Slack Key Guitar Concert Series.** Hosted by George Kahumoku, Jr., the weekly event hosts the islands' finest musicians, including such local luminaries as Ledward Kaapana, Cyril Pahinui, Dennis Kamakahi, and others, who come to play music and talk story in genuine local style. It's an event not to be missed, especially if you're a live music fan. Shows take place at the amphitheater at the Ritz-Carlton, Kapalua, every Tuesday at 6 and 8:30 p.m. Check www.slackkey.com for the current performance calendar; call ☎ 888-669-3858 or 808-669-3858 for reservations.

Sipping a Beverage in South Maui

South Maui is a tad quieter overall, but boasts a couple of hopping joints.

Hapa's Nightclub, in the Lipoa Shopping Center, 41 E. Lipoa St. (between South Kihei Road and Piilani Highway), Kihei (☎ 808-879-9001; www.hapasmaui.com), serves up live music and microbrews nightly from 9 p.m. to 1:30 a.m. This large, popular place is simple and lively, boasting good sound and a big dance floor. Call to see what's on: It may be jazz, blues, rock, reggae, funk, or Hawaiian.

A DJ spins Top-40 hits at chic **Tsunami,** one of Hawaii's biggest and best dance clubs, at the Grand Wailea Resort, 3850 Wailea Alanui Dr., Wailea (☎ 808-875-1234), where a well-heeled crowd shakes its collective booty Friday and Saturday nights from 9:30 p.m. to 2 a.m.

Bocalino Bistro & Bar, at 1279 S. Kihei Rd. (☎ **808-874-9299**), is a great place to boogie down to live music from 10 p.m. to 1 a.m. nightly except Thursday; the tempo varies from Hawaiian contemporary to Latin to rock, depending on the night, so call for the schedule.

In the mood for a taste o' the Emerald Isle while you're on the Valley Isle? Head on over to **Mulligan's on the Blue,** located on the Wailea Blue Golf Course on Wailea Alanui Drive, across from the Fairmont Kea Lani (☎ **808-874-1131;** www.mulligansontheblue.com). Mulligan's is an authentic Irish pub, complete with Guinness on tap, traditional pub fare (in case you're in the mood for bangers and mash or a potato boxty while you're in the islands) and seven TVs complete with satellite sports channels, plus the kind of panoramic ocean view that only Maui can offer. Pubgoers enjoy high-quality live music nightly, with a Celtic spin on Sundays. It's an all-around excellent place to hang out!

Hitting the Dance Floor Upcountry

Somewhat unexpectedly, one of the hottest party spots on the island is Upcountry, in the cowboy town of Makawao. The party never ends at **Casanova,** 1188 Makawao Ave. (☎ **808-572-0220;** www.casanovamaui. com), a popular Italian restaurant (see Chapter 11). The bar area has large booths, all the better for socializing around the stage and dance floor. Wednesday nights usually feature the venue's famous ladies' night disco, while Friday and Saturday nights boast the top names in local and visiting entertainment, which generally starts at 9:45 p.m. and continues to 1:30 a.m. Out in quiet Hana, your best place for entertainment is the Hotel Hana-Maui, where the **Paniolo Lounge (☎ 808-248-8211)** hosts live Hawaiian music Thursday through Sunday from 6:30 to 9:30 p.m. Live hula also occurs in the hotel's main dining room every Thursday and Sunday from 7:30 to 8:15 p.m. (Call to confirm the current schedule.)

Chapter 16

Taking a Side Trip to Molokai

By Jeanette Foster

In This Chapter

▶ Introducing Molokai
▶ Deciding where to stay and dine
▶ Knowing what to see and do

*B*orn of volcanic eruptions 1.5 million years ago, Molokai remains a time capsule at the dawn of the 21st century. It has no deluxe resorts, no stoplights, and no buildings taller than a coconut tree. Molokai is the least developed, most "Hawaiian" of all the islands, making it especially attractive to adventure travelers and peace seekers.

Molokai lives up to its reputation as the most Hawaiian place chiefly through its lineage; more people of Hawaiian blood live there than anywhere else. This slipper-shaped island was the cradle of Hawaiian dance (the hula was born there) and the ancient science of aquaculture. An aura of ancient mysticism clings to the land, and the old ways still govern life. The residents survive by taking fish from the sea and hunting wild pigs and axis deer on the range. Some folks still catch fish in throw nets and troll the reef for squid.

Not everyone loves Molokai. It's a rustic, rural place — don't expect sophisticated resorts and restaurants, or much in the way of shopping and diversions. It's about communing with nature and standing in awe of Hawaii's highest waterfall and greatest collection of fishponds, the world's tallest sea cliffs, sand dunes, coral reefs, rainforests, hidden coves, and gloriously empty beaches. The slow-paced, simple life and the absence of modern development attract people in search of the "real" Hawaii. If you want a bustling nightlife, you're in the wrong place; Molokai shuts down after sunset. The only public diversions are softball games under the lights of Mitchell Pauole Field, movies at Maunaloa, and the few restaurants that stay open after dark, often serving local brew and pizza.

Rugged, red-dirt Molokai isn't for everyone, but anyone who likes to explore remote places and seek their own adventures should love it. The "friendly island" is a funky place that may enchant you as the real Hawaii of your dreams. On the other hand, you may leave shaking your head, never to return. Regardless of how you approach Molokai, remember our advice: Take it slow.

Getting to Know Molokai

Kaunakakai (Ka-oo-na-ka-keye) could be any small town, but it's the closest thing Molokai has to a business district. Friendly Isle Realty and Friendly Isle Travel offer islanders dream homes and vacations; Rabang's Filipino Food posts bad checks in the window; antlered deer-head trophies guard the grocery aisles at Misaki's Market; and Kanemitsu's, the town's legendary bakery, churns out fresh loaves of onion-cheese bread daily. With its Old West–style storefronts laid out in a three-block grid on a flat, dusty plain, Kaunakakai is a town from the past. At the end of Wharf Road is Molokai Wharf, a picturesque place to fish, photograph, and just hang out. Kaunakakai is the dividing point between the lush, green East End and the dry, arid West End. On the west side of town stands a cactus, and on the east side of town you find thick, green vegetation.

On the **North Coast,** upland from Kaunakakai, the land tilts skyward and turns green, with scented plumeria in yards and glossy coffee trees all in a row, until it blooms into a true forest — and then abruptly ends at a great precipice, falling 3,250 feet to the sea. The green sea cliffs are creased with five V-shaped crevices so deep that light is seldom seen (to paraphrase a Hawaii poet). The North Coast is a remote, forbidding place, with a solitary peninsula — **Kalaupapa** — which was once the home for exiled lepers (it's now a national historical park). This region is easy on the eyes but difficult to visit. It lies at a cool elevation, and frequent rainsqualls blow in from the ocean. In summer, the ocean is calm, providing great opportunities for kayaking, fishing, and swimming, but during the rest of the year, giant waves come rolling onto the shores.

Molokai

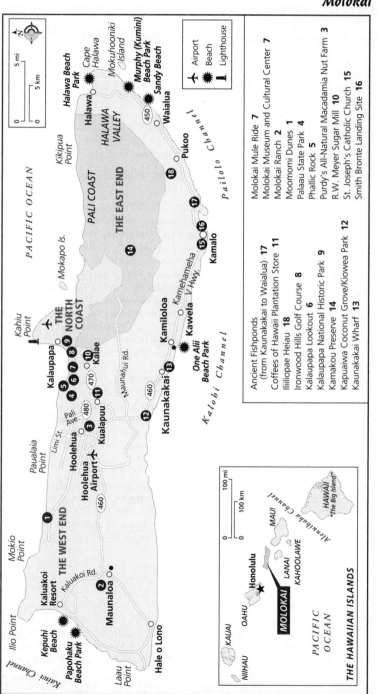

Molokai Mule Ride **7**
Molokai Museum and Cultural Center **7**
Molokai Ranch **2**
Moomomi Dunes **1**
Palaau State Park **4**
Phallic Rock **5**
Purdy's All-Natural Macadamia Nut Farm **3**
R.W. Meyer Sugar Mill **10**
St. Joseph's Catholic Church **15**
Smith Bronte Landing Site **16**

Ancient Fishponds
(from Kaunakakai to Waialua) **17**
Coffees of Hawaii Plantation Store **11**
Iliiliopae Heiau **18**
Ironwood Hills Golf Course **8**
Kalaupapa Lookout **6**
Kalaupapa National Historic Park **9**
Kamakou Preserve **14**
Kapuaiwa Coconut Grove/Kiowea Park **12**
Kaunakakai Wharf **13**

Kalaupapa National Historic Park

Molokai's top attraction is Kalaupapa National Historic Park, where Father Damien established his famous leper colony. Touring this remote, poignant site is a memorable journey best made on the back of a trusty mule, who will safely carry you down a spectacular, steep trail. It's an all-day adventure, and the trip of a lifetime. The mule ride can be done as a daytrip from Maui. If you're only visiting Molokai briefly, don't miss it. See "The legacy of Father Damien: Kalaupapa National Historic Park" near the end of this chapter for complete details. Read about it and decide if you'd like to sign up before you arrive — it's important to make reservations *well* in advance of your visit.

The **West End** of the island, home to **Molokai Ranch,** is miles of stark desert terrain, bordered by the most beautiful white-sand beaches in Hawaii. The rugged rolling land slopes down to Molokai's only destination resort, **Kaluakoi,** a cul-de-sac of condos clustered around a nearly three-decades-old seafront hotel (which closed in 2001 and was still closed when we went to press) near 3-mile-long **Papohaku,** the island's biggest beach. On the way to Kaluakoi, you find **Maunaloa,** a 1920s-era pineapple-plantation town that's in the midst of being transformed into a master-planned community, Maunaloa Village, with an upscale lodge, triplex theater, restaurants, and shops. The West End is dry. The area hardly ever receives rain, but when it does (usually in the winter), expect a downpour and plenty of red mud.

The area **east** of Kaunakakai becomes lush, green, and tropical, with golden pocket beaches and a handful of cottages and condos that are popular with thrifty travelers. With this voluptuous landscape comes rain. However, most storms are brief (15-minute) affairs that blow in, dry up, and disappear. Winter is Hawaii's rainy season, so expect more rain during January to March, but even then, the storms usually are brief and the sun comes back out.

Beyond Kaunakakai, the two-lane road curves along the coast past pig farms, palm groves, and a 20-mile string of fishponds as well as an ancient *heiau* (sacred Hawaiian religious site), Damien-built churches, and a few contemporary condos by the sea. The road ends in the glorious **Halawa Valley,** one of Hawaii's most beautiful valleys.

Settling into Molokai

When you arrive on Molokai and are searching for visitor information, look for a sun-faded, yellow building on the main drag, Kamehameha V Highway (Highway 460), on the right just past the town's first stop sign, at mile marker 0. It houses the **Molokai Visitors Association,** P.O. Box 960, Kaunakakai, HI 96748 (☎ **800-800-6367** from the mainland and

Canada, 800-553-0404 interisland, or 808-553-3876; www.molokai-hawaii.com). The staff can give you all the information you need on what to see and do while you're on Molokai.

Arriving on Molokai

Molokai has two airports, but you'll most likely fly into **Hoolehua Airport,** which everyone calls "the Molokai Airport." It's on a dusty plain about 6 miles from Kaunakakai town. If you're going to Lanai (see Chapter 17) from Molokai, jet service is now available, but only on **Hawaiian Airlines** (☎ **800-367-5320** or 808-565-6977; www.hawaiianair.com), which offers one flight a day. Twin-engine planes take longer and are sometimes bumpier, but they offer great views because they fly lower. **Island Air** (☎ **800-323-3345** from the mainland, or 800-652-6541 interisland; www.islandair.com) has eight direct flights a day from Honolulu and two direct flights from Maui. **Molokai Air Shuttle** (☎ **808-545-4988**) and **Pacific Wings** (☎ **888-575-4546** from the mainland, or 808-873-0877 from Maui; www.pacificwings.com) have one daily flight from Honolulu to Hoolehua and one flight a day from Maui to Molokai.

You can also get to Molokai by taking a ferry from Maui. Island Marine's *Molokai Princess* ferry (☎ **800-275-6969** or 808-667-6165; www.mauiprincess.com) runs from Maui's Lahaina Harbor to Molokai's Kaunakakai Wharf. It makes the 90-minute journey from Lahaina to Kaunakakai daily; the cost is $40 per adult one-way and $20 per child one-way. Or you can choose to tour the island from two different package options: Cruise-Drive, which includes round-trip passage and a rental car for $149 for the driver, $80 per additional adult passenger and $40 for children; or the Alii Tour, which is a guided tour in an air-conditioned van plus lunch for $149 for adults and $89 for children.

Getting around

Getting around Molokai isn't easy if you don't have a rental car, and rental cars are often hard to find. On holiday weekends — and remember, Hawaii celebrates some additional holidays not observed in the rest of the United States (see Chapter 3) — car-rental agencies simply run out of cars. Book before you go.

Molokai doesn't have any municipal transit or shuttle service, but a 24-hour taxi service is available (see the section "Taking a taxi or tour").

Renting a car

Rental cars are available from **Budget** (☎ **808-567-6877**) and **Dollar** (☎ **808-567-6156**); both agencies are located at the Molokai Airport. Nonchain operators include **Molokai Rentals and Tours,** Kaunakakai (☎ **800-553-9071** or 808-553-5663; www.molokai-rentals.com), which has compacts for $34 a day ($224 a week) and four-wheel-drive Jeeps for $70 a day ($455 a week).

We also recommend **Island Kine** (☎ 808-553-5242; www.molokai-car-rental.com) — not only are the cars cheaper, but Barbara Shonely and her son, Steve, also give personalized service. They meet you at the Molokai Airport, take you to their office in Kaunakakai, and recommend specific outfitters for your activities. Their used cars are in perfect condition and are air-conditioned. Vans and pick-up trucks are also available. You don't need a four-wheel-drive vehicle unless you're planning some specialized hiking, but if that's the case, Island Kine has what you're looking for.

Taking a taxi or tour

Molokai Off-Road Tours & Taxi (☎ 808-553-3369; www.molokai.com/offroad) offers regular taxi service, an airport shuttle ($7 per person, one way, to the Lodge at Molokai Ranch, based on four people; otherwise, the shuttle is $28 for two, one way; and $7.50 per person to Kaunakakai, based on three people), and a variety of island tours.

Finding a Place to Stay

Molokai doesn't offer many places to stay — mostly B&Bs, condos, a few quaint oceanfront vacation rentals, an aging resort, and a very expensive lodge.

Molokai is Hawaii's most affordable island, especially for hotels. And because few restaurants are on the island, most hotel rooms and condo units come with kitchens, which can save you a bundle on dining costs.

In the following listings, each accommodation's name is followed by a number of dollar signs, ranging from one ($) to five ($$$$$). Each represents the median rack-rate price range for a double room per night, as follows:

Symbol	Meaning
$	Super cheap — less than $100 per night
$$	Still affordable — $100 to $175
$$$	Moderate — $175 to $250
$$$$	Expensive but not ridiculous — $250 to $375
$$$$$	Ultraluxurious — more than $375 per night

Don't forget that the state adds 11.42 percent in taxes to your hotel bill.

Molokai Accommodations and Dining

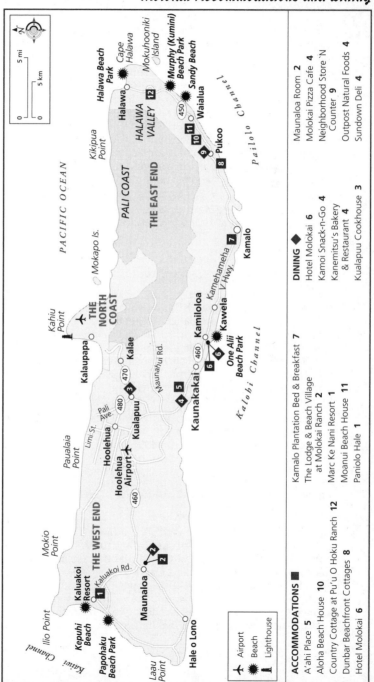

ACCOMMODATIONS ■
A'ahi Place **5**
Aloha Beach House **10**
Country Cottage at Pu'u O Hoku Ranch **12**
Dunbar Beachfront Cottages **8**
Hotel Molokai **6**
Kamalo Plantation Bed & Breakfast **7**
The Lodge & Beach Village at Molokai Ranch **2**
Marc Ke Nani Resort **1**
Moanui Beach House **11**
Paniolo Hale **1**

DINING ◆
Hotel Molokai **6**
Kamoi Snack-n-Go **4**
Kanemitsu's Bakery & Restaurant **4**
Kualapuu Cookhouse **3**
Maunaloa Room **2**
Molokai Pizza Cafe **4**
Neighborhood Store 'N Counter **9**
Outpost Natural Foods **4**
Sundown Deli **4**

✈ Airport
✹ Beach
🗼 Lighthouse

A'ahi Place
$ Kaunakakai

Just outside the main town of Kaunakakai and up a small hill lies this nice but simple vacation cottage, complete with a wicker-filled sitting area, a kitchen, and two full-size beds . Two lanais make great places to just sit and enjoy the stars at night. Tropical plants, flowers, and fruit trees surround the entire property. You can choose to forgo breakfast or, for $10 more per night (for two), get all the fixings for a continental breakfast (home-grown Molokai coffee, fresh-baked goods, and fruit from the property) placed in the kitchen so that you can enjoy it at your leisure. It's not fancy by any means, but for people who seek a quiet vacation with no phone or TV to distract you, this place is for you. And for people who want to explore Molokai, the central location is perfect.

See map p. 265. P.O. Box 528, Kaunakakai, HI 96748. ☎ *808-553-8033.* www.molokai. com/aahi. *Rack rates: $75 double without continental breakfast, $85 double with breakfast. Extra person $20. Three-night minimum stay. Seventh night free. No credit cards.*

Aloha Beach House
$ The East End

Nestled on the lush East End, this Hawaiian-style beach house sits right on the white-sand beach of Waialua. Perfect for families, this impeccably decorated two-bedroom, 1,600-square-foot beach house can sleep up to five people. The huge living/dining/kitchen area opens out to an old-fashioned porch for meals or just sitting in the comfy chairs and watching the clouds roll by. It's fully equipped, from the complete kitchen (including a dishwasher) to a VCR (plus a library of videos) to all the beach toys you can think of. It's located close to the Neighborhood Store.

See map p. 265. Located just after mile marker 19. Reservations c/o The Rietows, P.O. Box 79, Kilauea. ☎ *888-828-1008 or 808-828-1100. Fax: 808-828-2199.* www.molokai vacation.com. *$220 per night plus $95 cleaning fee. Three-night minimum. No credit cards.*

Country Cottage at Pu'u O Hoku Ranch
$$ The East End

Escape to a working cattle ranch! *Pu'u o Hoku* ("Star Hill") Ranch, which spreads across 14,000 acres of pasture and forests, is the last place to stay before Halawa Valley — the cottage is at least an hour's drive from Kaunakakai along the shoreline. Two acres of tropically landscaped property circle the ranch's rustic cottage, which boasts breathtaking views of rolling hills and the Pacific Ocean. The wooden cottage features comfortable country furniture, a full kitchen, two bedrooms (one with a double bed, one with two twin beds), two bathrooms, and a separate dining room on the enclosed lanai. TVs and VCRs are available on request. You can stargaze at night, watch the sunrise in the morning, and hike, swim, or play a game of croquet in the afternoon. (And, of course, horseback riding is available at the ranch.) Larger groups can choose a four-bedroom, three-bathroom house that sleeps up to eight.

See map p. 265. Kamehameha V Highway, at mile marker 25. Reservations: P.O. Box 1889, Kaunakakai. ☎ ***808-558-8109.*** *Fax: 808-558-8100.* www.puuohoku.com/ cottage *or* www.puuohoku.com/grove. *$125 double for 2-bedroom cottage or for 4-bedroom cottage. Weekly rate $750. Extra person $10. Two-night minimum stay. No credit cards.*

Dunbar Beachfront Cottages
$$ The East End

This property is one of the most peaceful, comfortable, and elegant on Molokai's East End, and the setting is simply stunning. Each of these two green-and-white plantation-style cottages sits on its own secluded beach (good for swimming) — you feel like you're on your own private island. The Puunana Cottage has a king bed and two twin beds, while the Pauwalu has a queen bed and two twin beds. Each has a full kitchen, VCR, ceiling fans, comfortable tropical furniture, large furnished deck (perfect for whale-watching in winter), and views of Maui, Lanai, and Kahoolawe across the channel.

See map p. 265. Kamehameha V Highway, past mile marker 18. Reservations c/o Kip and Leslie Dunbar, HC01 Box 901, Kaunakakai, HI 96748. ☎ ***800-673-0520*** *or 808-558-8153. Fax: 808-558-8153.* www.molokai-beachfront-cottages.com. *Parking: Free. Rack rates: $140 cottage, plus 1-time $75 cleaning charge. Three-night minimum. No credit cards.*

Hotel Molokai
$–$$ Kaunakakai

This nostalgic Hawaiian motel complex is composed of a series of modified A-frame units, nestled under coco palms along a gray-sand beach with a great view of Lanai. The rooms are basic (ask for one with a ceiling fan), with a lanai. The mattresses are on the soft side, the sheets thin, and the bath towels rough, but you're on Molokai — and this hotel is the only one in Kaunakakai. The kitchenettes, with a coffeemaker, a toaster, pots, and a two-burner stove, can save you money on eating out. The front desk is open only from 7 a.m. to 8 p.m; late check-ins or visitors with problems have to go to security.

See map p. 265. Kamehameha V Highway (P.O. Box 1020), Kaunakakai, HI 96748. ☎ ***800-535-0085*** *or 808-553-5347. Fax: 800-477-2329.* www.hotelmolokai.com. *Parking: Free. Rack rates: $90–$140 double; $150 suite with kitchenette (sleeps 4). Extra bed/crib $17. AE, DC, DISC, MC, V.*

Kamalo Plantation Bed & Breakfast
$ The East End

Glenn and Akiko Foster's (no relation to the author) 5-acre spread includes an ancient heiau ruin in the front yard, plus leafy tropical gardens and a working fruit orchard. Their Eden-like property is easy to find: The B&B is right across the East End Road from Father Damien's historic St. Joseph church. There are two rentals here: a cottage and the Moanui Beach House. The plantation-style cottage is tucked under flowering trees and surrounded by swaying palms and tropical foliage. It has its own lanai, a big living room with a queen sofa bed, and a separate bedroom with a king bed, so it can sleep four comfortably. The kitchen is fully equipped (it even has spices), and you can use a barbecue outside. A breakfast of fruit and freshly baked bread is served every morning. You can't get TV reception, but the cottage does have a VCR, radio, and a CD and cassette player. The secluded Moanui Beach House offers incredible ocean views, open and screened lanais, vaulted ceilings, two bedrooms with king-size beds, one and a half baths, a fully equipped kitchen, a barbecue grill, and a TV/VCR.

See map p. 265. Kamehameha V Highway, just past mile marker 10 (HC01, Box 300), Kaunakakai, HI 96748. ☎ *and fax **808-558-8236.*** www.molokai.com/kamalo. *Parking: Free. Rack rates: $85 cottage for 2, $140 beach house for 2. Rates include continental breakfast fixings. Extra person $20. Two-night minimum stay for cottage, 3-night minimum for beach house. No credit cards.*

The Lodge & Beach Village at Molokai Ranch
$$$$$ The West End

Designed to resemble a 1930s-style Hawaii ranch owner's private home, the Lodge features a giant fireplace, huge wooden-beam construction, panoramic views, and plenty of details — cuffed cowboy boots beside the door, old books lining the shelves — to make it look and feel like a real ranch. Guests step back in time to a Hawaii of yesteryear. The 22 guest rooms, each with individual country décor, are of two types: deluxe and luxury. The lovely luxury rooms are spacious corner units that feature either greenhouse-type skylights or a cozy king daybed nestled in a comfy alcove. There's an upscale dining room, a small but practical spa (with massage treatments, men's and women's sauna, and locker facilities), a gorgeous infinity swimming pool, a fabulous network of mountain biking trails, and access to a host of activities (which require an extra fee; there's ocean kayaking, guided hikes, horseback riding, beach activities, and more, ranging in price from $30–$125). You can also enjoy wonderful local entertainment in the Great Room; even if you don't stay here, come for the live music on Friday and Saturday nights. There's a complimentary shuttle to the beach (a 20- to 25-minute ride away); ten minutes away is the newly renovated Kaluakoi Golf Course, where greens fees are $70.

The other half of this operation is the Beach Village, which is a sort of luxury eco-camping setup on the beach. You stay in comfortable safari-type tents mounted on wooden platforms, with ceiling fans, private bathrooms, solar-powered lights, hammocks, and daily maid service. Guests dine on three buffet-style meals each day at the beach pavilion (meal prices are $12 for breakfast, $15 for lunch, and $29 for dinner) and gather for nightly entertainment. It's a nice idea, but the prices seem awfully high (adding on activities makes the tab start to soar) for what is essentially a fancy camping experience.

The Lodge is the most expensive place to stay on Molokai and is priced as high as oceanfront resorts on Maui. Despite some nice features, it can't compete with the amenities (not to mention the beachfront location) offered by other similarly priced Hawaii resorts. After changing hands a couple of times in recent years, the Lodge was taken over by new management as we went to press. It's now a member of Small Luxury Hotels of the World. Call ahead and ask questions before booking here; the new management may very well implement changes in prices, amenities, and policies in the coming months. Hopefully, they'll introduce some new money-saving packages.

See map p. 265. P.O. Box 259, Maunaloa, HI 96770. ☎ *888-627-8082 or 808-552-2741. Fax: 808-552-2773.* www.molokairanch.com. *Parking: Free. Rack rates: $360–$425 double for Lodge rooms; $275–$299 Beach Village tent lodgings. Mandatory $10 per day "resort fee" for transportation to beach, use of facilities at Lodge, and use of beach equipment at the beach camp. Activities cost extra. AE, DISC, DC, MC, V.*

Nani Kai Resort
$$–$$$ The West End

This place is great for families, who appreciate the space. The large apartments are set up for full-time living with real kitchens, washer/dryers, VCRs, attractive furnishings, and breezy lanais. You also have access to a huge pool, a hot tub, a volleyball court, tennis courts, and golf on the neighboring Kaluakoi course. These condos are farther from the sea than other local accommodations, but still just a brief walk from the beach. Parking and garden areas surround the two-story buildings. The only downside: Maid service is only every third day.

See map p. 265. In the Kaluakoi Resort development, Kaluakoi Road, off Highway 460 (P.O. Box 289), Maunaloa, HI 96770. ☎ *800-535-0085 or 808-552-2761. Fax: 808-552-0045.* www.marcresorts.com. *Parking: Free. Rack rates: $179–$189 1-bedroom apartment (sleeps up to 4); $199–$219 2-bedroom apartment (sleeps up to 6). Deals: Check for Internet specials (as low as $134 at press time) and discounts on Dollar rental cars. AE, DC, DISC, MC, V.*

Paniolo Hale
$$–$$$ The West End

The Paniolo Hale is far and away Molokai's most charming lodging, and probably its best value — be sure to ask about discounted weekly rates and special condo/car packages when making your reservations. The two-story, old Hawaiian ranch-house design is airy and homey, with oak floors and walls of folding-glass doors that open to huge screened verandas, doubling your living space. The one- and two-bedroom units come with two bathrooms and accommodate three or four people easily. Some units have hot tubs on the lanai. All are spacious, comfortably furnished, and well equipped, with full kitchens and washer/dryers. The whole place overlooks the Kaluakoi Golf Course, a green barrier that separates these condos from the rest of Kaluakoi Resort. Out front, Kepuhi Beach is a scenic place for walkers and beachcombers, but the seas are too hazardous for most swimmers. A pool, paddle tennis, and barbecue facilities are on the property, which adjoins open grassland. As with most condominiums in a rental pool, the quality and upkeep of the individually owned units can vary widely. When booking, spend some time talking with the friendly people at Molokai Vacation Rentals so that you can get a top-quality condo that has been renovated recently.

See map p. 265. Next door to Kaluakoi Resort, Lio Place (P.O. Box 190), Maunaloa. ☎ *800-367-2984 or 808-552-2731. Fax: 808-552-2288.* www.molokai-vacation-rental.com. *Parking: Free. Rack rates: $95–$155 studio; $125–$175 1-bedroom apartment; $150–$225 2-bedroom apartment. Extra person $10. Three-night minimum stay; 1-week minimum Dec 20–Jan 5. AE, MC, V.*

Dining

Molokai is strong on adventure, the outdoors, and the get-away-from-it-all feeling. But when it comes to dining, the offerings are sparse. That's just par for the course on a rugged and undeveloped island.

Mom-and-Pop eateries dominate the scene. They're nothing fancy — most of them are fast-food or take-out places and many of them come with a home-cooked touch. Food and wine connoisseurs had best lower their expectations upon arrival.

Molokai's restaurants are inexpensive or moderately priced, and several of them don't accept credit cards. Regardless of where you eat, you certainly don't have to dress up. In most cases, I list just the town rather than the street address — street addresses are as meaningless on this island as fancy cars and sequins. Reservations aren't accepted unless otherwise noted.

In the restaurant listings that follow, each restaurant name is followed by a number of dollar signs, ranging from one ($) to five ($$$$$). The dollar signs are meant to give you an idea of what a complete dinner for one person — with appetizer, main course, a drink, tax, and tip — is likely to cost. The price categories go like this:

Symbol	Meaning
$	Cheap eats — less than $15 per person
$$	Still inexpensive — $15 to $25
$$$	Moderate — $25 to $40
$$$$	Pricey — $40 to $70
$$$$$	Ultraexpensive — more than $70 per person

To give you a further idea of how much you can expect to spend, I also include the price range of main courses or items in the listings. (Prices can change at any time, of course, but restaurants usually don't raise their prices by more than a dollar or two at any given time.)

Note: The restaurants that I review in this chapter are plotted on the "Molokai Accommodations and Dining" map in this chapter.

Hotel Molokai
$$$ Kaunakakai   American/Island

On the ocean, with a view of Lanai, torches flickering under palm trees, and tiny fairy lights lining the room and the neighboring pool area, the Hotel Molokai's dining room has a nice tropical vibe. It's a casual room for dinner or cocktails, with the most pleasing ambience on the island. Lunch choices stick to the basics; most promising are salads (Big Island organic greens) and sandwiches, from roast beef to grilled mahimahi. As the sun sets and the torches are lit for dinner, the menu turns to heavier meats, ribs, fish, and pasta. Try the fresh catch, Korean kalbi ribs, barbecued pork ribs, New York steak, coconut shrimp, or garlic chicken. It's simple hearty fare — a solid, satisfying meal in a lovely setting.

See map p. 265. On Kamehameha V Highway. ☎ _808-553-5347. Reservations recommended for dinner. Main items: $7–$8 lunch, $12–$19 dinner. AE, DC, MC, V. Open: Breakfast, lunch, and dinner daily; bar until 10:30 p.m._

Kamoi Snack-N-Go
$ Kaunakakai   Ice Cream/Snacks

The Kamoi specialty: sweets and icy treats. Ice cream made by Dave's on Oahu comes in flavors like green tea, lychee sherbet, *ube* (a brilliant purple color, made from Okinawan sweet potato), haupia, mango, and many other tropical — and traditional — flavors. Schoolchildren and their parents line up for the cones, shakes, sundaes, and popular Icee floats, and to peruse the aisles of candy at this tiny snack shop.

See map p. 265. In Kamoi Professional Center. ☎ *808-553-3742. Ice cream $1.65–$3.40. MC, V. Open: Mon–Sat 9 a.m.–9 p.m.; Sun noon to 9 p.m.*

Kanemitsu's Bakery & Restaurant
$ Kaunakakai   Bakery/Deli

Morning, noon, and night, this local legend fills the Kaunakakai air with the sweet smells of baking. Taro lavosh and Molokai bread (developed in 1935 in a cast-iron, kiawe-fired oven) are the hot sellers. Flavors range from apricot-pineapple to mango (in season), but the classics remain the regular white, wheat, cheese, sweet, and onion-cheese breads. For people who like their bread warm, the bread mixes offer a way to take Molokai home with you. In the adjoining coffee shop/deli, all sandwiches come with their own freshly baked buns and breads. The hamburgers, egg-salad sandwiches, mahi burgers, and honey-dipped fried chicken are popular and cheap.

See map p. 265. 79 Ala Malama St. ☎ *808-553-5855. Most items under $6. No credit cards. Restaurant open for breakfast and early lunch Wed–Mon, bakery Wed–Mon 5:30 a.m.–6:30 p.m.*

Kualapuu Cook House
$$ En route to north coast   American

An old wagon in front of a former plantation house marks this down-home eatery, now take-out only. Local residents flock there, not only for the family atmosphere but also for the oversized servings. Breakfasts feature giant omelets, homemade corned beef hash, and, for diners who dare, The Works — buttermilk pancakes, eggs, and home fries (you'll either be fueled for the day or ready to take a nap). Lunch can either be a burger or sandwich or one of their humongous plate lunches of pork katsu or chicken, served up with rice, of course.

See map p. 265. Farrington Highway, 1 block west of Highway 470, Kalapuu. ☎ *808-567-9655. Main items: Mostly under $15. No credit cards. Open: Breakfast and lunch Mon–Sat.*

Maunaloa Room
$$$ The West End   Molokai Regional

Molokai has never had anything resembling fine dining, but this restaurant changes the picture. It's in the island's first upscale hotel, a 22-room lodge fashioned after a ranch owner's private home in the cool hills of Maunaloa, where you can see Oahu (Diamond Head under the best of conditions) past the rolling ranch lands and the ocean. Because the hotel is under new management, the menu is likely to change in the coming months, but you can bet that it will remain the most upscale and sophisticated dining option on Molokai.

See map p. 265. In the Lodge at Molokai Ranch, Maunaloa. ☎ *808/660-2824. Reservations recommended for dinner. Main courses: $20–$28. AE, DC, DISC, MC, V. Open: daily 7–10 a.m. and 6–9 p.m. (Sunday brunch, 11 a.m.–1:30 p.m., $23), lunch served 10 a.m.–4 p.m. in the bar (most sandwiches under $10).*

Molokai Pizza Cafe
$$ Kaunakakai   Pizza

The excellent pizzas and sandwiches make this a major gathering place for locals. The best-selling pies are the Molokai (pepperoni and cheese), the Big Island (pepperoni, ham, mushroom, Italian sausage, bacon, and vegetables), and the Molokini (plain cheese slices). Pasta, sandwiches, and specials round out the menu; the fresh-baked submarine and pocket sandwiches and the gyro pocket with spinach pie are hits. Sunday is prime-rib day, Wednesday is Mexican, and Hawaiian plates are sold on Thursdays. Coin-operated cars and a toy airplane follow the children's theme, but adults feel equally at home with the very popular barbecued baby-back-rib plate and the fresh fish dinners. Children's art and letters in the tiled dining room add an entertaining and charming touch.

See map p. 265. In Kahua Center, on the old Wharf Road. ☎ *808-553-3288. Main items: Large pizzas $13–$23. No credit cards. Open: Lunch and dinner daily.*

Neighborhood Store 'N Counter
$ The East End   American

The Neighborhood Store is nothing fancy, and that's what folks love about it. This store/lunch counter appears like a mirage near mile marker 16 in the Pukoo area en route to the East End. Picnic tables under a royal poinciana tree are a wonderful sight, and the food doesn't disappoint. The place serves omelets, Portuguese sausage, and other breakfast specials (brunch is very popular) and then segues into sandwiches, salads, mahimahi plates, and varied over-the-counter lunch offerings. Favorites include the mahimahi plate lunch, the chicken katsu, and the Mexican plate, each one with a tried-and-true home-cooked flavor. The Neighborhood Store offers daily specials, ethnic dishes, and some vegetarian options, as well as burgers (including a killer veggie burger), saimin, and legendary desserts. Made-on-Maui Roselani ice cream is a featured attraction, and customers rave over the Portuguese doughnut dessert, a deep-fried doughnut filled with ice cream. A Molokai treasure, the Neighborhood Store is also the only grocery store on the East End.

See map p. 265. Pukoo. ☎ *808-558-8498. Main items: Less than $6.95; bento box $7.30. No credit cards. Open: Breakfast, lunch, and all afternoon daily.*

Outpost Natural Foods
$ **Kaunakakai   Vegetarian**

The healthiest and freshest food on the island is served at this health store's lunch counter, around the corner from the main drag on the ocean side of Kaunakakai town. The tiny store abounds in Molokai papayas, bananas, herbs, potatoes, watermelon, and other local produce, complementing its selection of vitamins, cosmetics, and health aids, as well as bulk and shelf items. But the real star is the closet-size lunch counter. The salads, burritos, tempeh sandwiches, vegetarian potpie, tofu-spinach lasagna, and mock chicken, turkey, and meatloaf (made from oats, sprouts, seeds, and seasonings) are testament to the fact that vegetarian food need not be boring. It's a must for health-conscious diners and shoppers.

See map p. 265. 70 Makaena Place. ☎ *808-553-3377. Main courses: Most items less than $5. AE, DISC, MC, V. Open: Breakfast and lunch Sun–Fri.*

Sundown Deli
$ **Kaunakakai   Deli**

From "gourmet saimin" to spinach pie, Sundown's offerings are home-cooked and healthful, with daily specials that include vegetarian quiche, vegetarian lasagna, and club sandwiches. The sandwiches (like smoked turkey and chicken salad) and several salads (Caesar, oriental, and stuffed tomato) are served daily, with the soup of the day. Vitamins, T-shirts, and snacks are sold in this tiny cafe, but most of the business is take-out.

See map p. 265. 145 Puali St. (across the street from Veteran's Memorial Park). ☎ *808-553-3713. Main items: Sandwiches, soups, and salads $4–$9. AE, MC, V. Open: Breakfast and lunch Mon–Sat.*

Having Fun On and Off the Beach

With imposing sea cliffs on one side and lazy fishponds on the other, Molokai has little room for beaches along its 106-mile coast — but the beaches that are accessible certainly provide an array of watersports. If land sports are more your speed, all the usual suspects are present for your enjoyment, including golf and biking.

Discovering Molokai's beaches

A big gold-sand beach awaits on the West End, in addition to tiny pocket beaches on the East End. The emptiness of Molokai's beaches is both a blessing and a curse: The seclusion means no lifeguards on any of the beaches.

At the foot of scenic Halawa Valley is **Halawa Beach Park,** a beautiful black-sand beach with a palm-fringed lagoon, a wave-lashed island offshore, and a distant view of the West Maui Mountains across the Pailolo Channel. The swimming is safe in the shallows close to shore, but where the waterfall stream meets the sea, the ocean is often murky and unnerving. A winter swell creases the mouth of Halawa Valley on the north side of the bay and attracts a crowd of local surfers. Facilities are minimal; bring your own water. To get there, take King Kamehameha V Highway (Highway 450) east to the end.

Golfers see **Kepuhi Beach,** a picturesque golden strand in front of the Kaluakoi Resort and Golf Course, as just another sand trap, but sunbathers like the semiprivate grassy dunes; they're seldom, if ever, crowded. Beachcombers often find what they're looking for there, but swimmers have to dodge lava rocks and risk rip tides. Oh, yes — look out for errant golf balls. The beach doesn't have any facilities or lifeguards, but cold drinks and restrooms are handy at the resort.

Murphy Beach Park was formerly Kumimi Beach Park, but some old-timers still call it Kumimi Beach, and, just to make everything confusing, some people call it Jaycees Park. No matter what you call it, ironwood trees line this white-sand beach and shade the small, quaint park. Swimming is generally safe. On calm days, snorkeling and diving are great outside the reef. You may spot some fishermen there, looking for papio and other island fish.

One Alii Beach Park, a thin strip of sand, once reserved for the *alii* (chiefs), is the oldest public beach park on Molokai. You find One Alii Beach Park (*One* is pronounced *o-nay,* not *won*) by a coconut grove on the outskirts of Kaunakakai. Safe for swimmers of all ages and abilities, families often crowd the beach on weekends, but it can be all yours on weekdays. Facilities include outdoor showers, restrooms, and free parking.

Nearly 3 miles long and 100 yards wide, gold-sand **Papohaku Beach** is one of the biggest in Hawaii. It's great for walking, beachcombing, picnics, and sunset-watching year-round. The big surf and rip tides make swimming risky except in summer, when the waters are calmer. Go early in the day when the tropical sun is less fierce and the winds are calm. The beach is so big that you may never see another soul except at sunset, when a few people gather on the shore in hopes of spotting the elusive green flash, a natural wonder that takes place when the horizon is cloud free. Facilities include outdoor showers, restrooms, picnic grounds, and free parking.

Sandy Beach is Molokai's most popular swimming beach — ideal for families with small kids. The beach is a roadside pocket of gold sand protected by a reef, with a great view of Maui and Lanai. You find it off the King Kamehameha V Highway (Highway 450) at mile marker 20. The beach doesn't have any facilities — just you, the sun, the sand, and the surf.

Enjoying the water

The best places to rent beach toys (snorkels, boogie boards, beach chairs, fishing poles, kayaks, and more) are **Molokai Rentals and Tours,** Kaunakakai (☎ 800-553-9071 or 808-658-1717; www.molokai-rentals.com), and **Molokai Outdoors,** in the lobby of Hotel Molokai, just outside Kaunakakai (☎ 877-553-4477 or 808-553-4477; www.molokai-outdoors.com). Both operators have everything you need for a day at the beach and can also can give you advice on where to find a great swimming beach or where the waves are breaking. Another good place to check out is **Molokai Fish & Dive,** Kaunakakai (☎ 808-553-5926; www.molokaifishanddive.com), a mind-boggling store filled with outdoor gear. You can rent snorkels, fishing gear, and even ice chests. This place is also a hot spot for fishing news and tips on what's running where.

Body boarding and bodysurfing

Molokai has only three beaches that offer rideable waves for body boarding (also know as boogie boarding) and bodysurfing: Papohaku, Kepuhi, and Halawa. Even these beaches are only for experienced bodysurfers due to the strength of the rip currents and undertows. You can rent boogie boards with fins for $7 a day or $21 a week from **Molokai Rentals and Tours,** Kaunakakai (☎ 808-658-1717; www.molokai-rentals.com). Boards go for $5 a day or $20 a week at **Molokai Outdoors,** in the lobby of Hotel Molokai, just outside Kaunakakai (☎ 877-553-4477 or 808-553-4477; www.molokai-outdoors.com).

Ocean kayaking

During the summer months, when the waters on the North Shore are calm, Molokai offers some of the most spectacular kayaking in Hawaii. However, most of Molokai is for the experienced kayaker. You must be adept in paddling through open ocean swells and rough waves.

  ✔ **Molokai Rentals and Tours,** Kaunakakai (☎ 808-658-1717; www.molokai-rentals.com), has a kayak tour of the south side of Molokai for $45 for adults and $25 for children under 16, which includes snorkeling. They also offer kayak rentals, singles $25 a day ($100 a week) and doubles $35 a day ($150 a week), which include life jackets, roof rack, paddles, and leashes.

✔ **Molokai Outdoors,** in the lobby of Hotel Molokai, just outside Kaunakakai (☎ 877-553-4477 or 808-553-4477; www.molokai-outdoors.com), has several different kayak tours, including routes that explore the ancient Hawaii fishponds and the inshore reefs. It offers outings suitable for beginners and others that challenge more experienced kayakers; some include stops for snorkeling. Call or check the Web site for the latest offerings; prices range from $47 for a sunset tour to $141 for a bike-and-kayak combo. The company also rents kayaks from $10 a day.

Scuba diving

Want to see turtles or manta rays up close? How about sharks? Molokai resident Bill Kapuni has been diving the waters around the island his entire life; he'll be happy to show you whatever you're brave enough to encounter. **Bill Kapuni's Snorkel & Dive,** Kaunakakai (☎ 808-553-9867), can provide gear, a boat, and even instruction. Two-tank dives in his 22-foot Boston whaler cost $125 and include Bill's voluminous knowledge of the legends and lore of Hawaii.

Snorkeling

Molokai offers excellent snorkeling. You see a wide range of butterfly fish, tangs, and angelfish. Most of the island's beaches are too dangerous for snorkeling in winter, when big waves and strong currents are generated by storms that sweep down from Alaska. From mid-September to April, stick to Murphy Beach Park (also known as Kumimi Beach Park) on the East End. In summer, roughly May to mid-September, when the Pacific Ocean takes a holiday and turns into a flat lake, the whole west coast of Molokai opens up for snorkeling.

Molokai Rentals and Tours (☎ 808-658-1717; www.molokai-rentals.com) and **Molokai Outdoors** (☎ 877-553-4477 or 808-553-4477; www.molokai-outdoors.com) offer the least-expensive snorkel gear for rent ($6 a day or $24 a week). Molokai Outdoors also offers prescription masks in case you have less than 20-20 vision.

For snorkeling tours, contact **Bill Kapuni's Snorkel & Dive,** Kaunakakai (☎ 808-553-9867), which charges $65 for a two and a half hour trip. Bill also rents snorkeling gear for $10 a day (see "Scuba diving," earlier in this chapter). Walter Naki of **Molokai Action Adventures** (☎ 808-558-8184) offers leisurely snorkeling, diving, and swimming trips in his 21-foot Boston whaler for $100 per person for a four- to six-hour custom tour.

Sportfishing

Molokai's waters can provide prime sporting opportunities, whether you're looking for big-game sportfishing or bottom fishing. When customers are scarce, Captain Joe Reich, who has been fishing the waters around Molokai for decades, goes commercial fishing, so he always knows where the fish are biting. He runs **Alyce C Sportfishing** out of Kaunakakai Harbor (☎ **808-558-8377;** www.alycecsportfishing.com). A full day of fishing for up to six people is $400, three-quarters of a day is $350, and a half day is $300. You can usually persuade him to do a whale-watching cruise during the winter months.

For fly-fishing or light-tackle reef-fish trolling, contact Walter Naki at **Molokai Action Adventures** (☎ **808-558-8184**). Walter has been fishing his entire life and loves to share his secret spots with visiting fishermen — he knows *the* place for bonefishing on the flats. A full-day trip in his 21-foot Boston whaler is $300 for up to four people.

For deep-sea fishing, **Fun Hogs Hawaii** (☎ **808-567-6789;** www.molokai-rentals.com/funhogs.html) has fishing excursions on a 27-foot, fully equipped sportfishing vessel. For six passengers, prices are $350 for four hours, $400 for six hours, and $450 for eight hours.

If you just want to try your luck casting along the shoreline, **Molokai Outdoors,** in the lobby of Hotel Molokai, just outside Kaunakakai (☎ **877-553-4477** or 808-553-4477; www.molokai-outdoors.com), rents fishing poles for $5 a day and can tell you where the fish are biting.

Hitting the links

Golf is one of Molokai's best-kept secrets; it's challenging and fun, tee times are open, and the rates are lower than your score will be. After being closed for a number of years, the **Kaluakoi Golf Course** (☎ **808-552-0255**) is open again. After extensive renovation, the 18-hole course has just reopened (the back nine was just completed in May 2004). Most of the work was cosmetic, and the Ted Robinson–designed course is still as challenging as ever, especially the par-3 16th hole, where you tee off over a gulch. The distraction of the incredible Papohaku Beach from the 3rd tee is a particularly delightful challenge. Greens fees are $70, including cart.

The real find is the **Ironwood Hills Golf Course,** off Kalae Highway (☎ **808-567-6000**). You can locate it just before the Molokai Mule Ride Mule Barn, on the road to the Lookout. Del Monte Plantation built Ironwood Hills (named after the two predominant features of the course, ironwood trees and hills) in 1929 for its executives. This unusual course, which sits in the cool air at 1,200 feet, delights with its rich foliage, open fairways, and spectacular views of the island. If you play there, use a trick developed by the local residents: After teeing off on the sixth hole, just take whatever clubs you need to finish playing the hole and a driver for the seventh hole and park your bag under a tree. The climb to the seventh hole is steep — you'll be glad that you're only carrying a few clubs. Greens fees are only $15 for nine holes and $20 for 18 holes. Cart fees are $7 for nine holes and $14 for 18. You can also rent a handcart for just $2.50. Club rentals are $7 for nine holes and $12 for 18.

If you didn't bring your clubs, you can also rent them from **Molokai Rentals and Tours,** Kaunakakai (☎ **808-658-1717;** www.molokai-rentals.com). Prices start at $6 a day ($24 for the week).

Exploring the island on two wheels

Molokai is a great place to tour by bicycle. The roads aren't very busy, and you can choose to pull off the road and take a quick dip at several great places. **Molokai Rentals and Tours,** Kaunakakai (☎ **808-658-1717;** www.molokai-rentals.com), offers a great tour of the 500 cultivated acres of Coffees of Hawaii fields. With numerous ups and downs, the tour rounds the coffee fields' perimeter and ventures up to an overlook and back to the plant where you get a walking tour of the process. The tour includes taste testing different varieties, a delicious Mocha Mama or Smoothie, and a 2-ounce bag of coffee. The Two and a half hour tours are Monday through Friday starting at 8:30 a.m., $45 for adults and $25 for children under 16. The more adventurous may want to try the All Day Bike Tours — either up to the Forest Reserve or off the beaten paths. Both tours start at 8 a.m. and go until the tour has seen everything (usually around 3 p.m.); lunch is also provided. Cost is $80 and includes bikes, helmets, and water bottles. Or if you want to explore the island on your own, you can rent bikes for $20 a day or $80 a week.

Molokai Outdoors, in the lobby of Hotel Molokai, just outside Kaunakakai (☎ **877-553-4477** or 808-553-4477; www.molokai-outdoors.com), offers a bike-kayak tour of the East End. It can take you into the rainforest in a four-wheel-drive vehicle and then set you up on a mountain bike so that you can ride to the ocean for kayaking on a secluded beach. Your gear, lunch, guide, and transportation cost $157. If you prefer to bike on your own, you can rent good-quality road and mountain bikes for $13 an hour, $26 a day, or $113 a week, including helmet.

The best mountain biking in the state is on the extensive network of trails at the **Lodge and Beach Village at Molokai Ranch** (☎ **888-627-8082** or 808-552-2741; www.molokairanch.com). Imagine 53,000 acres with intercrossing trails that weave up and down the West End to the beach. They're simply spectacular, and you don't have to be a guest of the hotel to enjoy them. The equipment is good, and the guides are excellent. Sheraton also offers courses on how to mountain bike, conducted on specially constructed wooden trails for teaching ($45). Guided tours range from $45 for two to three hours, to full-day rides with a guide and lunch for $85. Bike rentals are $35 a day.

Seeing the Sights

Molokai has plenty of history and beauty that you don't want to miss. I list some of my favorites in the following section. I divide the section into the different areas of Molokai. *Note:* The following attractions are plotted on the "Molokai" map in this chapter.

In and around Kaunakakai

Kapuaiwa Coconut Grove/Kiowea Park

This royal grove — 1,000 coconut trees on 10 acres planted in 1863 by the island's high chief Kapua'iwa (later, King Kamehameha V) — is a major roadside attraction. The shoreline park is a favorite subject of sunset photographers and visitors who delight in a hand-lettered sign that warns: "DANGER: FALLING COCONUTS." In its backyard, across the highway, stands Church Row: seven churches, each a different denomination — clear evidence of the missionary impact on Hawaii.

See map p. 261. Along Maunaloa Highway (Highway 460), 2 miles west of Kaunakakai.

Post-A-Nut

Postmaster Margaret Keahi-Leary can help you say "Aloha" with a dried Molokai coconut. Just write a message on the coconut with a felt-tip pen, and she'll send it via U.S. mail over the sea. Coconuts are free, but postage is $3.95 (and up) for a mainland-bound 2-pound coconut.

See map p. 261. Hoolehua Post Office, Puu Peelua Avenue (Highway 480), near Maunaloa Highway (Highway 460). ☎ *808-567-6144. Mon–Fri 7:30–11:30 a.m. and 12:30–4:30 p.m.*

Purdy's All-Natural Macadamia Nut Farm (Na Hua O'Ka Aina)

The Purdys have made macadamia-nut buying an entertainment event, offering tours of the homestead and giving lively demonstrations of nut-shell cracking in the shade of their towering trees. The tour of the 70-year-old nut farm explains the growing, bearing, harvesting, and shelling processes, so that by the time you bite into the luxurious macadamia nut, you'll have more than a passing knowledge of its entire life cycle.

See map p. 261. Lihi Pali Avenue (behind Molokai High School), Hoolehua. ☎ *808-567-6601.* www.molokai-aloha.com/macnuts. *Free admission. Mon–Fri 9:30 a.m.–3:30 p.m.; Sat 10 a.m.–2 p.m.; closed on holidays.*

The North Coast

Even if you don't get a chance to see Hawaii's most dramatic coast in its entirety — not many people do — don't miss the opportunity to glimpse it from the **Kalaupapa Lookout** at Palauu State Park. On the way, I list the few diversions, arranged in geographical order en route to the North Coast.

Coffees of Hawaii Plantation Store

The defunct Del Monte pineapple town of Kualapuu is rising again — only this time, coffee is the catch, not pineapple. Located in the cool foothills, Coffees of Hawaii has planted coffee beans on 600 acres of former pineapple land. The company is irrigating the plants with a high-tech, continuous water and fertilizer drip system. You can see it all on the walking tour; call 24 hours in advance to set up a tour. The Plantation Store sells arts and crafts from Molokai. Stop by the Espresso Bar for a Mocha Mama (Molokai coffee, ice, chocolate ice cream, chocolate syrup, whipped cream, and chocolate shavings on top). The Mocha Mama will keep you going all day — maybe even all night.

See map p. 261. Highway 480 (near the junction of Highway 470). ☎ *800-709-BEAN or 808-567-9241.* www.molokaicoffee.com. *Walking tour $7 adults, $3.50 children 5–12. Tours Mon–Sat 9:30 a.m. and 11:30 a.m.; Sun 11:30 a.m. only. Store open Mon–Fri 7 a.m.–4 p.m.; Sat 8 a.m.–4 p.m.; Sun 10 a.m.–4 p.m.*

Molokai Museum and Cultural Center

En route to the California Gold Rush in 1849, Rudolph W. Meyer, a German professor, came to Molokai, married the high chieftess Kalama, and began to operate a small sugar plantation near his home. Now on the National Register of Historic Places, this restored 1878 sugar mill, with its century-old steam engine, mule-driven cane crusher, copper clarifiers, and redwood evaporating pan (all in working order), is the last of its kind in Hawaii. The mill also houses a museum that traces the history of sugar growing on Molokai and features special events, such as wine tastings every two months, taro festivals, an annual music festival, and occasional classes in ukulele making, loom weaving, and sewing. Call for a schedule.

See map p. 261. Meyer Sugar Mill, Highway 470 (just after the turnoff for the Ironwood Hills Golf Course, and 2 miles below Kalaupapa Overlook), Kalae. ☎ *808-567-6436. Admission $2.50 adults, $1 students. Mon–Sat 10 a.m.–2 p.m.*

Palaau State Park

This 234-acre piney-woods park, 8 miles out of Kaunakakai, doesn't look like much until you get out of the car and take a hike, which literally puts you between a rock and a hard place. Go right, and you end up on the edge of Molokai's magnificent sea cliffs, with its panoramic view of the well-known Kalaupapa leper colony; go left, and you come face to face with a stone phallus.

If you have no plans to scale the cliffs by mule or on foot, the **Kalaupapa Lookout** is the only place from which to see the former place of exile. The trail is marked, and historic photos and interpretive signs explain what you're seeing.

The ironwood forest is airy and cool. Camping is free at the designated state campground. You need a permit from the **State Division of Parks** (☎ **808-567-6618**). Not many people seem to camp there, probably because of the legend associated with the **Phallic Rock.** Six feet high, pointed at an angle that means business, Molokai's famous Phallic Rock is a legendary fertility tool that appears to be working today. According to Hawaiian legend, a woman who wants to become pregnant need only spend the night near the rock and, *voilà!* It's probably just a coincidence, of course, but Molokai does have a growing number of young, pregnant women.

Phallic Rock is at the end of a well-worn uphill path that passes an iron-wood grove and several other rocks that vaguely resemble sexual body parts. No mistaking the big guy, though. Supposedly, it belonged to Nanahoa, a demigod who quarreled with his wife, Kawahuna, over a pretty girl. In the tussle, Kawahuna was thrown over the cliff, and both husband and wife were turned to stone. Of all the phallic rocks in Hawaii and the Pacific, this rock is the one to see. The rock is also featured on a postcard with a tiny, awestruck Japanese woman standing next to it.

See map p. 261. At the end of Highway 470.

The legacy of Father Damien: Kalaupapa National Historic Park

An old tongue of lava that sticks out to form a peninsula, Kalaupapa became infamous because of man's inhumanity to victims of a once-incurable contagious disease.

King Kamehameha V sent the first lepers — nine men and three women — into exile on this lonely shore, at the base of ramparts that rise like temples against the Pacific, on January 6, 1866. By 1874, more than 11,000 lepers had been dispatched to die in one of the world's most beautiful — and lonely — places. They called Kalaupapa "The Place of the Living Dead."

Leprosy is actually one of the world's least contagious diseases, trans-mitted only by direct, repetitive contact over a long period of time. A germ, *Mycobacterium leprae,* that attacks the nerves, skin, and eyes, causes leprosy. The germ is found mainly, but not exclusively, in tropical regions. American scientists found a cure for the disease in the 1940s.

Before science found a cure, Father Damien intervened. Born to wealth in Belgium, Father Damien (born Joseph de Veuster) traded a life of excess for exile among lepers; he devoted himself to caring for the afflicted at Kalaupapa. Father Damien volunteered to go out to the Pacific in place of his ailing brother. Horrified by the conditions in the leper colony, Father Damien worked at Kalaupapa for 11 years, building houses, schools, and churches, and giving hope to his patients. He died on April 15, 1889, in Kalaupapa, of leprosy. He was 49.

A hero nominated for Catholic sainthood, Father Damien is buried not in his tomb next to Molokai's St. Philomena Church but in his native Belgium. (Well, most of him anyway. His hand was recently returned to Molokai and was buried at Kalaupapa as a relic of his martyrdom.)

This small peninsula is probably the final resting place of more than 11,000 souls. The sand dunes are littered with grave markers, sorted by the religious affiliation — Catholic, Protestant, Buddhist — of those people who died there. But because so many are buried in unmarked graves, no accurate census of the dead exists.

Kalaupapa is now a National Historic Park (☎ **808-567-6802;** www.nps. gov/kala) and one of Hawaii's richest archaeological preserves, with sites that date from A.D. 1000. About 60 former patients chose to remain in the tidy village of whitewashed houses with statues of angels in their yards. The original name for their former affliction, leprosy, was officially banned in Hawaii by the state legislature in 1981. The name used now is "Hansen's Disease," for Dr. Gerhard Hansen of Norway, who discovered the germ in 1873. The few remaining residents of Kalaupapa still call the disease leprosy, although none are too keen on being called lepers.

Kalaupapa welcomes visitors who arrive on foot, by mule, or by small plane. Father Damien's St. Philomena church, built in 1872, is open to visitors, who can see it from a yellow school bus driven by resident tour guide Richard Marks, an ex-seaman and sheriff who survived the disease. You can't roam freely, and you can only enter the museum, the craft shop, and the church.

Visitors must be 16 years of age or older; you can't bring the kids along for this adventure.

Taking a mule ride to Kalaupapa

Riding a mule to Kalaupapa is quite memorable. The first turn is a gasp, and it's downhill from there. You can close your eyes and hold on for dear life, or slip the reins over the pommel and sit back, letting the mule do the walking down the precipitous path to Kalaupapa National Historic Park.

Even if you have only one day on Molokai, spend it on a mule. This ride is a once-in-a-lifetime adventure. The cliffs are taller than a 300-story skyscraper, but Buzzy Sproat's mules go safely up and down the narrow 3-mile trail daily, rain or shine. Starting at the top of the nearly perpendicular ridge (1,600 feet high), the surefooted mules step down the muddy trail, pausing often on the 26 switchbacks to calculate their next move — and always, it seems, veering close to the edge. Each switchback is numbered; by the time you get to number four, you'll catch your breath, put the mule on cruise control, and begin to enjoy Hawaii's most awesome trail ride.

The mule tour starts daily at 7:50 a.m. and lasts until about 3:15 p.m. The tour costs $150 per person for the all-day adventure, which includes the round-trip mule ride, a guided tour of the settlement, a visit to Father Damien's church and grave, lunch at Kalawao, and souvenirs. To go, you must be at least 16 years old and physically fit. Contact **Molokai Mule Ride,** 100 Kalae Highway, Suite 104, on Highway 470, 5 miles north of Highway 460 (☎ **800-567-7550** or 808-567-6088 between 8 and 10 p.m.; www.muleride.com). *Note: Advance reservations (at least two weeks ahead) are required,* as space is limited to 18 visitors. The friendly folks at Molokai Mule Ride can also provide airport transfers for $9 per person. They also offer packages from Maui that include round-trip airfare, airport transfers, lunch, and the mule tour, for $289.

Seeing Kalaupapa by plane

The fastest and easiest way to get to Kalaupapa is by hopping on a plane (from Honolulu or Maui) and zipping to Kalaupapa airport. From there, you can pick up the same Kalaupapa tour that the mule riders and hikers take. **Father Damien Tours** (☎ and fax **808-567-6171**) picks you up at Kalaupapa airport and takes you to some of the area's most scenic spots, including Kalawao, where Father Damien's church still stands, and the town of Kalaupapa. A round-trip flight from the Molokai Airport to Kalaupapa, entry permits, a historical park tour with Damien Tours, and a light picnic lunch costs $119. Contact **Molokai Mule Ride** (see earlier in this chapter) for details.

Molokai Mule Ride can also arrange fly-in tours (without the mule ride) that include airfare from Maui or Honolulu. Round-trip airfare, entry permits, Historical Park tour, and a light picnic lunch are $234 from Maui and $225 from Honolulu.

Seeing Kalaupapa by ferry/hiking

From Maui, you can take the *Molokai Princess* ferry to Molokai (☎ **866-307-6524** or 808-662-3355 on Maui; www.mauiprincess.com), where a van meets you and transports you to the top of the 1,700-foot sea cliffs. You then hike down the 3-mile trail to the Kalaupapa National Historic Park. At the park, Father Damien Tours meets you and gives you a van tour of the peninsula, during which you visit Father Damien's St. Philomena Church and hear the stories of struggle and courage of Kalaupapa's residents. Then you have the option of taking an air shuttle back to the top, or physically fit participants can hike back up the 1,700-foot cliffs, where the van picks you up and returns you to the ferry dock for the trip back to Maui. It takes about an hour hiking down and another one and a half hours to hike back up. Cost for ferry, transportation, tour, and lunch is $215. (As with all the other tours, participants must be 16 years and older.)

The West End

In the first and only urban renewal on Molokai, the 1920s-era pineapple-plantation town of **Maunaloa** is being reinvented. Streets are getting widened and paved, and curbs and sidewalks are being added to serve a new tract of houses. Historic Maunaloa is becoming Maunaloa Village — the area already has a town center with a park, a restaurant, a triplex movie theater, a gas station, a KFC, and an upscale lodge. This master-planned village will also have a museum and artisans' studios — uptown stuff for Molokai.

On the northwest shore

Undisturbed for centuries, the **Moomomi Dunes,** on Molokai's northwest shore, are a unique treasure chest of great scientific value. The area may look like just a pile of sand as you fly over on the final approach to Hoolehua Airport, but Moomomi Dunes are much more. Archaeologists have found quarries, ancient Hawaiian burial sites, and shelter caves; botanists have identified five endangered plant species; and marine biologists are finding evidence that endangered green sea turtles are coming out from the waters once again to lay eggs there. The greatest discovery, however, belongs to Smithsonian Institute ornithologists, who have found bones of prehistoric birds — some of them flightless — that existed nowhere else on earth.

Accessible by Jeep trails that thread downhill to the shore, this wild coast is buffeted by strong afternoon breezes. It's hot, dry, and windy, so take water, sunscreen, and a windbreaker.

At Kawaaloa Bay, a 20-minute walk to the west, you find a broad golden beach that you can have all to yourself. ***Warning: Due to the rough seas, stay out of the water.*** Within the dunes, you find a 920-acre preserve accessible via monthly guided nature tours led by the **Nature Conservancy of Hawaii;** call ☎ **808-553-5236** or 808-524-0779 for an exact schedule and details.

To get there, take Highway 460 (Maunaloa Highway) from Kaunakakai, turn right onto Highway 470, and follow it to Kualapuu. At Kualapuu, turn left on Highway 480 and go through Hoolehua Village; it's 3 miles to the bay.

The East End

The East End is a cool and inviting green place that's worth a drive to the end of King Kamehameha V Highway (Highway 450). Unfortunately, the trail that leads into the area's greatest natural attraction in Halawa Valley, the Hipuapua Falls, is off-limits because it's located on private property.

Riding horseback to Iliiliopae Heiau

On horseback (where the elevated view is magnificent), you bump along a dirt trail through an incredible mango grove, bound for an ancient temple of human sacrifice. This temple of doom — right out of *Indiana Jones* — is Iliiliopae, a huge rectangle of stone made of 90 million rocks, overlooking the once-important village of Mapulehu and four ancient fishponds. The horses trek under the perfumed mangoes, and then head uphill through a kiawe forest filled with Java plums to the *heiau* (temple), which stands across a dry streambed under cloud-spiked Kaunolu, the 4,970-foot island summit.

Hawaii's most powerful heiau attracted *kahuna* (priests) from all over the islands. They came to find out the rules of human sacrifice at this university of sacred rites. Contrary to Hollywood's version, historians say that the chosen victims were always men, not young virgins, and that they were strangled, not thrown into a volcano, while priests sat on *Lauhala* mats watching silently. Spooky, eh?

After the visit to the temple, your horse takes you back to the mango grove. Contact **Molokai Wagon Rides,** King Kamehameha V Highway (Highway 450), at mile marker 15, Kaunakakai, HI 96748 (☎ **808-558-8380**). The tour and horseback ride are $50 per person. The hour-long ride goes up to the heiau, then beyond it to the mountaintop for those breathtaking views, and finally back down to the beach.

Kamakou Preserve

The nearly mile-high summit receives more than 80 inches of rain a year — enough to qualify as a rainforest. The Molokai Forest, as it was historically known, is the source of 60 percent of Molokai's water. The Nature Conservancy, which has identified 219 Hawaiian plants that grow there exclusively, owns nearly 3,000 acres, from the summit to the lowland forests of eucalyptus and pine. The preserve is also the last stand of the endangered Molokai thrush *(olomao)* and Molokai creeper *(kawawahie).*

To get to the preserve, take the Forest Reserve Road from Kaunakakai. The road is a 45-minute, four-wheel-drive trip on a dirt trail to Waikolu Lookout Campground. From there, you can venture into the wilderness preserve on foot across a boardwalk on a one and a half hour hike. For more information, contact the **Nature Conservancy** (☎ **808-553-5236**).

En route to Halawa Valley

No visit to Molokai is complete without at least a passing glance at the island's **ancient fishponds,** a singular achievement in Pacific aquaculture. With their hunger for fresh fish and lack of ice or refrigeration, Hawaiians perfected aquaculture in 1400, before Christopher Columbus "discovered"

America. They built gated, U-shaped stone and coral walls on the shore to catch fish on the incoming tide; they then raised them in captivity. The result: a constant, ready supply of fresh fish.

The ponds, which stretch for 20 miles along Molokai's south shore and are visible from Kamehameha V Highway (Highway 450), offer insight into the island's ancient population. Approximately a thousand people tended a single fishpond, and more than 60 ponds once existed on this coast. All the fishponds are named; a few are privately owned. Some are silted in by red-dirt runoff from south coast gulches, while some folks, who raise fish and seaweed, have revived some.

A 3-foot-high, 2,000-foot-long stone wall surrounds the largest, 54-acre Keawa Nui Pond. You can spot **Alii Fish Pond,** reserved for kings, through the coconut groves at One Alii Beach Park. From the road, you can see **Kalokoeli Pond,** 6 miles east of Kaunakakai on the highway.

Smith Bronte Landing Site

In 1927, Charles Lindbergh soloed the Atlantic Ocean in a plane called *The Spirit of St. Louis* and became an American hero. That same year, Ernie Smith and Emory B. Bronte took off from Oakland, California, on July 14, in a single-engine Travelair aircraft named *The City of Oakland,* and headed across the Pacific Ocean for Honolulu, 2,397 miles away. The next day, after running out of fuel, they crash-landed upside down in a kiawe thicket on Molokai, but emerged unhurt to become the first civilians to fly to Hawaii from the U.S. mainland. The 25-hour, 2-minute flight landed Smith and Bronte a place in aviation history — and on a roadside marker on Molokai.

See map p. 261. King Kamehameha V Highway (Highway 450), at mile marker 11, on the makai (ocean) side.

Halawa Valley

Of the five great valleys of Molokai, only Halawa, with its two waterfalls, golden beach, sleepy lagoon, great surf, and offshore island, is easily accessible. Unfortunately, the trail through fertile Halawa Valley, which was inhabited for centuries, and on to the 250-foot Moaula Falls has been closed for some time. One operator conducts very expensive tours, but I have received so many letters of complaint (and have been personally stood up by him after a confirmed reservation) that I no longer recommend you use him.

You can spend a day at the county beach park (see earlier in this chapter), but don't venture into the valley on your own. The valley's private landowners, worried about slip-and-fall lawsuits, have posted "No Trespassing" signs on their property.

To get to Halawa Valley, drive north from Kaunakakai on Highway 450 for 30 miles along the coast to the end of the road, which descends into the valley past Jersalema Hou Church. If you want to catch a glimpse of the valley on your way to the beach, take a moment at the scenic overlook along the road: After Puuo Hoku Ranch at mile marker 25, the narrow two-lane road widens at a hairpin curve, and you find the overlook on your right; the drive is 2 miles more to the valley floor.

Shopping the Local Stores

Because many visitors stay in condos or vacation rentals, it's especially important to find the local grocery stores, so I include them in this section. But serious shoppers won't find much to do on Molokai.

In downtown Kaunakakai, most of the retail shops sell T-shirts, muumuus, surf wear, and informal apparel. The **Imamura Store** (☎ 808-553-5615) is a jumble of Hawaiian-print tablecloths, Japanese tea plates, ukulele cases, and even coconut bikini tops. **Molokai Surf,** 130 Kamehameha V Highway (☎ 808-553-5093), offers a broad range of clothing, gear, and accessories for life in the surf and sun.

You can't miss the salmon-colored wooden storefront of the **Friendly Market Center** (☎ 808-553-5595), on the main drag of Kaunakakai, which has an especially good range of produce and healthy foods — better than standard grocery-store fare. You can also stock up your kitchen at **Misaki's Grocery and Dry Goods** (☎ 808-553-5505), established in 1922. You'll find fresh produce, Boca Burgers, a good fish counter, and more. **Molokai Wines & Spirits** (☎ 808-553-5009) is your best bet on the island for a decent bottle of wine.

And don't forget to treat yourself to a loaf of hot bread from **Kanemitsu Bakery's,** 79 Ala Malama St. in Kaunakakai (☎ 808-553-5855). It's a late-night ritual for local residents, who line up at the bakery's back door beginning at 10:30 p.m. You can order your fresh bread with butter, jelly, cinnamon, or cream cheese, and the bakers will cut the hot loaves down the middle and slather on the works so that it melts in the bread.

En route to the North Coast, the **Coffees of Hawaii Plantation Store and Espresso Bar,** Highway 480 (near the junction of Highway 470), Kualapuu (☎ 800-709-BEAN or 808-567-9023), is a combination coffee bar, store, and gallery for more than 30 artists and craftspeople from Molokai, Maui, and the Big Island. A stone's throw away is the **Kualapuu Market** (☎ 808-567-6243), where you can pick up wine, food, and necessities.

On the West End, the stand-out store is the **Big Wind Kite Factory & the Plantation Gallery** in Maunaloa (☎ 808-552-2364). Not only can you purchase beautifully designed kites (and take free kite-flying classes when conditions are right), but the adjoining gallery features local and Balinese handicrafts and Hawaiian-music CDs. The **Maunaloa General Store** (☎ 808-552-2346) is the place to stock up on food and basics.

On the East End, the only place for groceries is **The Neighborhood Store 'N Counter,** in Pukoo (☎ 808-558-8498), where you can enjoy a solid breakfast or lunch at the counter, too.

Enjoying Molokai After Dark

The **Hotel Molokai,** in Kaunakakai (☎ 800-367-5004 or 808-553-5347), offers live entertainment from local musicians, poolside and in the dining room. With its South Seas ambience and poolside setting, the hotel has become the island's premier venue for local and visiting entertainers.

Movie buffs can catch a flick at **Maunaloa Cinemas** (☎ 808-552-2707), a triplex theater that shows first-run movies in the middle of Maunaloa town.

Also in Maunaloa, the lounge at the **Lodge and Beach Village at Molokai Ranch** (☎ 808-552-2741; www.molokairanch.com) is a nice setting for cocktails and occasional live Hawaiian music.

Fast Facts: Molokai

Banks

Molokai has several banks, including the Bank of Hawaii (☎ 808-553-3273), which has a 24-hour ATM.

Emergencies/Hospitals

Molokai and Lanai are both part of Maui County. For **local emergencies,** call ☎ **911.** For nonemergencies, call the **police** at ☎ 808-553-5355, the **fire department** at ☎ 808-553-5601, or **Molokai General Hospital,** in Kaunakakai, at ☎ 808-553-5331.

Mail

Downtown Kaunakakai has a **post office** (☎ 808-553-5845).

Pharmacies

Head to **Molokai Drugs** in the Kamoi Professional Center, downtown Kaunakakai (☎ **808-553-5790**). Not only can you stock up on essentials, but this drugstore, which has been family-run since 1935, is a friendly stop for guidebooks, books about Molokai, maps, paperbacks, flip-flops, and other handy items.

Chapter 17

Taking a Side Trip to the Island of Lanai

By Jeanette Foster

. . . .

In This Chapter

▶ Introducing Lanai
▶ Deciding where to stay and dine
▶ Knowing what to see and do

. . . .

*L*anai (lah-*nigh*-ee), the nation's biggest defunct pineapple patch, now claims to be one of the world's top tropical destinations. The claim is bold because so little is there. Don't expect lots of dining or accommodations choices — Lanai has even fewer than Molokai. Lanai doesn't have any stoplights and has barely 30 miles of paved road. This almost-virgin island is unspoiled by modern intrusions, except for a tiny 1920s-era plantation village — and, of course, the village's fancy new arrivals: two first-class luxury hotels where room rates hover around $400 a night.

As soon as you arrive on Lanai, you feel the small-town coziness. Residents stop to talk to friends and wave to every passing car. Fishing and working in the garden are considered priorities in life, and leaving the car keys in the ignition is standard practice. But this island is also a place where people come looking for dramatic beauty, quiet, solitude, and an experience with nature. It's a far cry from the action and development found on Maui. Come to Lanai if you crave the chance to be away from it all in a peaceful tropical setting.

Getting to Know Lanai

Inhabited Lanai is divided into three parts: Lanai City, Koele, and Manele. One climate zone is hot and dry, while the other region is cool and misty. **Lanai City** (population 2,800) sits at the heart of the island at 1,645 feet above sea level. It's the only place on the island with any services. Built in 1924, this plantation village is a tidy grid of quaint tin-roofed cottages in bright pastels, with roosters penned in tropical gardens of banana, lilikoi, and papaya. Many of the residents are Filipino immigrants who worked the pineapple fields and imported the art, culture, language, food, and lifestyle of the Philippines. Their clapboard homes, now worth $200,000 or more, are excellent examples of historic preservation; the whole town looks like it's been kept under a bell jar.

Norfolk and Cook Island pines line the charming Dole Park Square, with towering, plantation buildings that house general stores with basic necessities as well as a U.S. Post Office, two banks, and a police station with a jail that consists of three outhouse-sized cells with padlocks.

In the nearby, cool, upland district of **Koele** is The Lodge at Koele, standing alone on a knoll overlooking pastures and the sea at the edge of a pine forest, like a grand European manor. The other bastion of luxury, the Manele Bay Hotel, is on the sunny southwestern tip of the island at **Manele.** You get more of what you expect from Hawaii there — beaches, swaying palms, mai tais, and the like.

If you're not planning to stay on Lanai, you can visit the island on a daytrip from Maui. See Chapter 12 for complete details on the highly recommended snorkel cruises to Lanai offered by **Trilogy Excursions.** It's a great way to go, with a stop at Lanai's Hulopoe Beach; for an extra fee, you can add on guided tours of the island as well. Note that these trips are very popular, so you'll need to book your spot well in advance.

Settling into Lanai

Destination Lanai (☎ 800-947-4774 or 808-565-7600; www.visitlanai. net) and the **Hawaii Visitors and Convention Bureau** (☎ 800-GO-HAWAII or 808-923-1811; www.gohawaii.com) provide brochures, maps, and island guides. For a free *Road and Site Map* of hikes, archaeological sites, and other places to visit, contact **Castle and Cooke Resorts** (which manages the Manele Bay and the Koele Lodge), P.O. Box 310, Lanai, HI 96763 (☎ **808-565-3000;** www.lanai-resorts.com).

Arriving on Lanai

There are no flights to Lanai from the mainland — only from Honolulu or Kahului, Maui. From either of these airports, it's a 25-minute trip to Lanai. Jet service is now available, but only on **Hawaiian Airlines** (☎ **800-367-5320** or 808-565-6977; www.hawaiianair.com), which offers one flight a day. Twin-engine planes take longer and are sometimes bumpier, but they offer great views because they fly lower. **Island Air** (☎ **800-652-6541** or 808-565-6744; www.islandair.com) offers seven flights a day. Prop or jet, you touch down in Puuwai Basin, once the world's largest pineapple plantation. From the airport, it's about 10 minutes by car to Lanai City and 25 minutes to Manele Bay.

If you prefer traveling by boat, round-trip excursions on **Expeditions Lahaina/Lanai Passenger Ferry** (☎ **808-661-3756**) take you between Maui and Lanai for $52. The ferry service runs five times a day, 365 days a year, between Lahaina and Lanai's Manele Bay harbor. The ferry leaves Lahaina at 6:45 a.m., 9:15 a.m., 12:45 p.m., 3:15 p.m., and 5:45 p.m.; the return ferry from Lanai's Manele Bay Harbor leaves at 8 a.m., 10:30 a.m., 2 p.m., 4:30 p.m., and 6:45 p.m. The 9-mile channel crossing takes 45 minutes to an hour, depending on sea conditions. Reservations are strongly recommended. Baggage is limited to two checked bags and one carryon.

See Chapter 12 for details on visiting Lanai on a daytrip outing from Maui with **Trilogy Excursions.**

Getting around

With so few paved roads on Lanai, you need a four-wheel-drive vehicle if you plan on exploring the island's remote shores, its interior, or the summit of Mount Lanaihale. Even if you have only one day on Lanai, rent a four-wheel-drive and see the island. You can also arrange a four-wheel-drive adventure tour from **Adventure Lanai Ecocentre** (☎ **808-565-7373;** www.adventurelanai.com), which offers three- to four-hour off-road tours for $99.

Both cars and four-wheel-drive vehicles are available at the **Dollar Rent-A-Car** desk at **Lanai City Service/Lanai Plantation Store,** 1036 Lanai Ave. (☎ **800-588-7808** for Dollar reservations, or **808-565-7227** for Lanai City Service). Expect to pay about $60 a day for the least expensive car available, a Nissan Sentra, and up to $129 a day for a four-wheel-drive Jeep. **Adventure Lanai Ecocentre** (☎ **808-565-7373;** www.adventurelanai.com) has four-wheel-drive Jeeps for rent (complete with towels, masks, fins, snorkel, ice chest, and an island map) for $124.

 Gas is expensive on Lanai, and those four-wheel-drive vehicles get terrible mileage. Because everything in Lanai City is within walking distance, rent a Jeep only for the days you want to explore the island.

Although renting a car and exploring the island is fun, you can stay on Lanai and get to the beach without one. The two big resort hotels run shuttle vans around the island, but only for their guests. The shuttles between The Lodge at Koeleand Manele Bay Hotel run every hour (sometimes on the half hour if it's busy). The pick-up spot is at Hulopoe Beach.

If you're staying elsewhere, you can walk to everything in Lanai City and take a taxi to the beach. **Lanai Plantation Store** (☎ **808-565-7227**) provides transportation from Lanai City to Hulopoe Beach for $10 per person one-way. (You can arrange with them when you want to be picked up, or you can walk over to the Manele Bay Hotel and phone them to come and get you — or you can most likely get a ride back up to Lanai City with a local.) Whether or not you rent a car, sooner or later you'll find yourself at Lanai City Service/Lanai Plantation Store. This all-in-one grocery store, gas station, rental-car agency, and souvenir shop serves as the island's Grand Central Station. Here's where you can pick up information, directions, maps, and all the local gossip.

Finding a Place to Stay

Most accommodations are located "in the village," as residents call Lanai City. Above the village is the luxurious Lodge at Koele, while down the hill at Hulopoe Bay are two options: the equally luxurious Manele Bay Hotel, or tent camping under the stars at the park.

In the following listings, each accommodation's name is followed by a number of dollar signs, ranging from one ($) to five ($$$$$). Each represents the median rack-rate price range for a double room per night, as follows:

Symbol	Meaning
$	Super cheap — less than $100 per night
$$	Still affordable — $100 to $175
$$$	Moderate — $175 to $250
$$$$	Expensive but not ridiculous — $250 to $375
$$$$$	Ultraluxurious — more than $375 per night

Don't forget that the state adds 11.42 percent in taxes to your hotel bill.

Dreams Come True
$ **Lanai City**

This quaint plantation house is tucked away among papaya, banana, lemon, and avocado trees in the heart of Lanai City, at 1,620 feet. Hosts Susan and Michael Hunter have filled their house with Southeast Asian antiques collected on their travels. Both are jewelers; they operate a working studio on the premises. Two of the four bedrooms feature a four-poster canopied bed and an additional single bed (perfect for a small family). The other rooms have just one queen bed. The common area looks out on the garden and is equipped with both a TV and VCR. Breakfast usually consists of freshly baked bread with homemade jellies and jams, tropical fruit, juice, and coffee. The Hunters also rent nearby two-, three-, and four-bedroom homes for $250 to $350 a night.

See map p. 295. 1168 Lanai Ave., Lanai City. ☎ *800-566-6961 or 808-565-6961. Fax: 808-565-7056.* http://circumvista.com/dreamscometrue.html. *Rack rates: $99 double. Rates include continental breakfast. Extra person $25. AE, DISC, MC, V.*

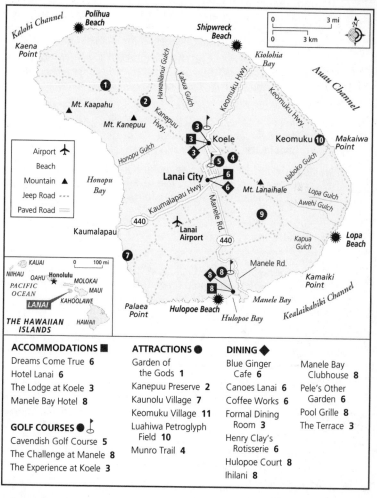

Lanai

ACCOMMODATIONS ■
Dreams Come True **6**
Hotel Lanai **6**
The Lodge at Koele **3**
Manele Bay Hotel **8**

GOLF COURSES ● ⛳
Cavendish Golf Course **5**
The Challenge at Manele **8**
The Experience at Koele **3**

ATTRACTIONS ●
Garden of
  the Gods **1**
Kanepuu Preserve **2**
Kaunolu Village **7**
Keomuku Village **11**
Luahiwa Petroglyph
  Field **10**
Munro Trail **4**

DINING ◆
Blue Ginger
  Cafe **6**
Canoes Lanai **6**
Coffee Works **6**
Formal Dining
  Room **3**
Henry Clay's
  Rotisserie **6**
Hulopoe Court **8**
Ihilani **8**

Manele Bay
  Clubhouse **8**
Pele's Other
  Garden **6**
Pool Grille **8**
The Terrace **3**

Hotel Lanai
$$–$$$ Lanai City

If you're looking for the old-fashioned aloha that Lanai City is famous for, this moderately priced hotel is great. Built in the 1920s for VIPs, this clapboard plantation-era relic has retained its quaint character and lives on as a country inn. A well-known chef from Maui, Henry Clay Richardson, is the inn's owner and the dining room's executive chef (see review later in this chapter). The ten guest rooms are extremely small, but clean and newly decorated, with Hawaiian quilts, wood furniture, and ceiling fans (but no air-conditioning or televisions). The most popular are the lanai units, which feature a lanai shared with the room next door. All rooms have ceiling fans and private, shower-only bathrooms. The small, one-bedroom cottage, with a TV and bathtub, is perfect for a small family.

See map p. 295. 828 Lanai Ave. (P.O. Box 630520), Lanai City. ☎ 800-665-2724 or 808-565-7211. Fax: 808-565-6450. www.hotellanai.com. Rack rates: $105–$135 double; $175 cottage double. Rates include continental breakfast. Extra person $10. AE, MC, V. Airport shuttle $25 round-trip.

The Lodge at Koele
$$$$$ Lanai City

Guests come here looking for relaxation in the cool mist of the mountains. Relax on the porch and watch the turkeys mosey across the manicured lawns; stroll through the Japanese hillside garden; or watch the sun sink into the Pacific and the stars light up at night. The Lodge, as folks here call it, stands in a 21-acre grove of Norfolk Island pines at 1,700 feet above sea level, 8 miles from any beach.

The 102-room resort resembles a grand English country estate. Inside, heavy timbers, beamed ceilings, and the two huge stone fireplaces of the Great Hall complete the look. Overstuffed furniture sits invitingly around the fireplaces, richly patterned rugs adorn the floor, and museum-quality art hangs on the walls. The guest rooms continue the English theme with four-poster beds, flowery wallpaper, formal writing desks, and luxury bathrooms with oversize tubs. The atmosphere is informal during the day, more formal after sunset. (Jackets are required in the main dining room; see review later in this chapter.)

You have plenty of activities to choose from at the Lodge and at the sister resort down the hill, Manele Bay, so that you get the best of both hotels. Other pluses: complimentary shuttle to the acclaimed golf courses, beach, and Manele Bay Hotel; complimentary coffee and tea in the lobby; formal tea every afternoon; twice-daily maid service; turndowns; and some rooms with butler service. Additional activities include croquet lawns, horseback riding, Upcountry hiking trails, and garden walks.

 Both the Lodge at Koele (see earlier listing) and the Manele Bay Hotel (see upcoming listing) are slated to become members of the ultraposh **Four Seasons** chain — arguably the finest hotel and resort brand in the world — sometime in 2005. This luxury takeover will certainly enhance the Lanai experience for those looking for a leave-it-all-behind luxury escape. For the latest details, call Four Seasons at ☎ **800-819-5053**, visit www.fourseasons.com, or call the hotels directly and ask for an update.

See map p. 295. P.O. Box 630310, Lanai City. ☎ 800-321-4666 or 808-565-7300. Fax: 808-565-4561. www.lodgeatkoele.com. Rack rates: $400–$575 double; from $725 suites. Extra person $75. Children under 18 stay free in parent's room. Numerous packages (such as fifth night free, adventure, golf, and wedding) available. AE, DC, MC, V. Airport shuttle $25 round-trip.

Manele Bay Hotel
$$$$$ Lanai City

Located on a sun-washed southern bluff overlooking Hulopoe Beach, one of Hawaii's best stretches of golden sand, this U-shaped hotel steps down the hillside to the pool and that great beach and then fans out in ocean-front wings separated by gardens with lush flora, manmade waterfalls, lotus ponds, and streams. On the other side, golf greens on a hillside of dry scrub border the hotel. The place is a real oasis against the dry Arizona-like heat of Lanai's arid South Coast. The oversized guest rooms are done in the style of an English country house on the beach: sunny chintz fabrics, mahogany furniture, Audubon prints, huge marble bath-rooms, and semiprivate lanais. This resort is much less formal than the Lodge up the hill. Its attracts more families, and because it's warmer here, people wander through the lobby in shorts and T-shirts. The small spa offers a variety of massages, facials, and wraps. There's also a fitness center with cardiovascular equipment, free weights, a multistation gym, and yoga classes.

See map p. 295. P.O. Box 630310, Lanai City. ☎ *800-321-4666 or 808-565-7700. Fax: 808-565-2483.* www.manelebayhotel.com. *Rack rates: $400–$800 double; $795–$3,500 suite. Additional person $75. Numerous packages (such as fifth night free, adventure, golf, and wedding) available. AE, DC, MC, V. Airport shuttle $25 round-trip.*

Dining on Lanai

Lanai is a curious mix of innocence and sophistication, with strong cross-cultural elements that liven up its culinary offerings. You can dine like a sultan on this island, but be prepared for high prices. The tony hotel restaurants require deep pockets (or bottomless expense accounts), and you have only a handful of other options.

In the restaurant listings that follow, each restaurant name is followed by a number of dollar signs, ranging from one ($) to five ($$$$$). The dollar signs give you an idea of what a complete dinner for one person — with appetizer, main course, a drink, tax, and tip — is likely to cost. The price categories go like this:

Symbol	Meaning
$	Cheap eats — less than $15 per person
$$	Still inexpensive — $15 to $25
$$$	Moderate — $25 to $40
$$$$	Pricey — $40 to $70
$$$$$	Ultraexpensive — more than $70 per person

To give you a further idea of how much you can expect to spend, I also include the price range of main courses or items in the listings. (Prices can change at any time, of course, but restaurants usually don't raise their prices by more than a dollar or two at any given time.)

Blue Ginger Cafe
$ Lanai City   Coffeeshop

Famous for its mahimahi sandwiches and inexpensive omelets, Blue Ginger is a local, casual, and inexpensive alternative to Lanai's fancy hotel restaurants. The four tables on the front porch face the cool Norfolk pines of Dole Park and are always filled with locals who "talk story" from morning to night. The tiny cafe is often jammed from 6 to 7 a.m. with construction workers on their way to work. The offerings are solid, no-nonsense, every-day fare: fried saimin (no MSG, a plus), very popular hamburgers on home-made buns, and mahimahi with capers in a white-wine sauce. Blue Ginger also serves a tasty French toast made with homemade bread, vegetable lumpia (the Filipino version of a spring roll), and Mexican specials. The stir-fried vegetables — a heaping platter of fresh, perfectly cooked veg-gies, including summer squash and fresh mushrooms — are a hit.

See map p. 295. 409 Seventh St. (at Lilima Street), Lanai City. ☎ *808-565-6363. Main courses: Breakfast items under $6.50; lunch under $10; dinner under $12. No credit cards. Open: Daily 6 a.m.–8 p.m.*

Canoes Lanai
$ Lanai City   Local

This mom-and-pop joint may have recently changed its name, but it's been a landmark since the 1920s. In those days, the tiny storefront sold canned goods and cigarettes; the ten tables, hamburgers, and Filipino food came later. This hole-in-the-wall is a local institution, with a reputation for serving local-style breakfasts. The fare — fried rice, omelets, short stacks, burgers, and simple ham and eggs — is more greasy spoon than gourmet, but it's friendly to the pocketbook.

See map p. 295. 419 Seventh St., Lanai City. ☎ *808-565-6537. Reservations not accepted. Main courses: Breakfast less than $8.50; lunch items $2.50–$8.50. No credit cards. Open: 6:30 a.m.–1 p.m. Thurs–Tues.*

Coffee Works
$ Lanai City   Coffeehouse

Oahu's popular Ward Warehouse coffeehouse has opened a new branch in Lanai City with a menu of espresso coffees and drinks, ice cream (from gelatos to local brands like Lapperts and Roselani), and a small selection of pastries. It's Lanai City's gathering place, a tiny cafe with tables and benches on a pleasing wooden deck surrounded by tall pines, and a stone's throw from Dole Park. Formerly a plantation house, the structure fits in with the surrounding plantation homes in the heart of Lanai City. Coffee Works also has some nice gift items available, including T-shirts, tea infusers, Chai, teapots, cookies, and gourmet coffees.

See map p.295. 604 Ilima, Lanai City (across from Post Office). ☎ *808-565-6962. Most items: under $5. MC, V. Open: Mon–Fri 7 a.m.–6 p.m.; Sat 7 a.m.–2 p.m.*

Formal Dining Room
$$$$ Lanai City Rustic American/Upcountry Hawaiian

The setting: a roaring fire, bountiful sprays of orchids, sienna-colored walls, and well-dressed women in pearls sitting across from men in jackets, with wine buckets tableside. The menu highlights American favorites with intense flavors. Foie gras has a strong presence on the seasonally changing menu, as do venison, local seafood, wild mushrooms, rack of lamb, and the vaunted threadfish. During fall and winter months, expect to see pumpkins, beans, ragouts, and braised items offered in creative seasonal preparations. The Dining Room is known for its use of fresh herbs, vegetables, and fruit grown on the island, harvested just minutes away.

See map p. 295. In the Lodge at Koele. ☎ *808-565-4580. Reservations required. Jackets requested for men. Main courses: $44–$45. AE, DC, MC, V. Open: daily 6–9:30 p.m.*

Henry Clay's Rotisserie
$$$ Lanai City Country Cuisine

Henry Clay Richardson, a New Orleans native, operates this rustic inn in the middle of Lanai City. It's very popular and always full. Maybe that's because the restaurant is the only option on Lanai that occupies the vast gap between deli-diner and upscale-deluxe. The menu focuses on French country fare: fresh meats, seafood, and local produce in assertive preparations. Appetizers and entrees reflect Cajun, regional, and international influences, particularly the Rajun Cajun Clay's shrimp, a fiery concoction of hefty shrimp in a spiced tomato broth, or the "Almost Grandma's Gumbo," straight from his New Orleans roots. The meats, which could be rabbit, duck, quail, venison, osso bucco, beef, or chicken, are spit-roasted on the rotisserie. Gourmet pizzas and salads occupy the lighter end of the spectrum. Diners rave about the fresh catch in lemon-butter caper sauce. I love the eggplant Creole, presented with perfect sugar snap peas on a bed of herbed angel-hair pasta. Don't leave without a piece of the New Orleans–style pecan pie. The décor consists of plates on the pine-paneled walls, chintz curtains, peach tablecloths and hunter-green napkins, and fireplaces in both rooms.

See map p. 295. In the Hotel Lanai. 828 Lanai Ave., Lanai City. ☎ *808-565-7211. Main courses: $14–$38. MC, V. Open: Daily 5:30–9 p.m.*

Hulopoe Court
$$$–$$$$ Lanai City Hawaii Regional

Hulopoe is casual compared to the Manele Bay Hotel's fine dining room, Ihilani, but more formal than the Pool Grille, the hotel's lunchtime spot. The 17th-century palanquin in the adjoining lower lobby, the Asian accents, the tropical murals by gifted Lanai artists, and the vaulted ceilings add up to an eclectic ambience. The new menu showcases local ingredients, such as Maui asparagus, hearts of palm, locally caught fresh fish, and gourmet breakfasts, including an impressive buffet. Crab-coconut soup or mahimahi with poblano mashed potatoes are excellent choices.

See map p. 295. In the Manele Bay Hotel. ☎ *808-565-2290. Reservations recommended. Collared shirt required for men. Main courses: $28–$35. AE, DC, MC, V. Open: daily 7–11 a.m. and 6–9:30 p.m.*

Ihilani
$$$–$$$$$ Lanai City Mediterranean

Chef Mark Tsuchiyama melds together Mediterranean and island styles. Standouts include appetizers like homemade goat cheese and spinach ravioli with roasted eggplant and asparagus salad, in a sun-dried-tomato-cilantro sauce, or terrine of foie gras with pear d'anjou, Madeira wine gele, and warm, toasted black truffle brioche. Entrees include baked onaga and citrus in a seasalt crust and lavender-honey-glazed duck breast. The prix-fixe menu is very complete and comes with selected wines.

See map p. 295. In the Manele Bay Hotel. ☎ *808-565-2296. Reservations strongly recommended. Jackets requested for men. Main courses: $23–$40; set menu $100 without wine, $150 with wine. AE, DC, MC, V. Open: dining Tues–Sat 6–9:30 p.m.*

Manele Bay Clubhouse
$$ Lanai City Pacific Rim

The view from the alfresco tables may be the best on the island, encompassing Kahoolawe, Haleakala on Maui, and, on an especially clear day, the peaks of Mauna Kea and Mauna Loa on the Big Island. Lighter fare prevails at lunch: salads and sandwiches, burgers, Caesar salad with chicken, herbed chicken sandwich on sourdough, fish and chips, and excellent dim sum and calamari salad. The clubhouse is casual, specializing in cold and warm pupu (appetizers), which you can enjoy as a light meal or combine to create a large feast, such as soft-shell-crab sushi rolls, crispy calamari with fried seagreens, Chinese barbecue chicken salad, and pan-seared foie gras with sushi rice.

See map p. 295. In the Challenge at Manele Clubhouse. ☎ *808-565-2230. Reservations recommended. Main courses: $10–$16. AE, DC, MC, V. Open: Lunch 11 a.m.–5 p.m.; dinner 5–9 p.m.*

Pele's Other Garden
$ Lanai City   Deli/Pizzeria/Juice Bar

This popular Lanai City eatery, featuring a patio with umbrella tables outside, is a full-scale New York–style deli that also offers box lunches and picnic baskets to go. At lunch, the first-rate pizzas and sandwiches are popular; in the evening, the place becomes a full-fledged dining room where you can also order pastas (butterfly pasta with garlic shrimp, fettuccine with smoked salmon) and salads. Daily soup and menu specials, excellent pizza, fresh organic produce, fresh juices, and special touches, such as top-quality black-bean burritos, roasted red peppers, and stuffed grape leaves, are some of the features that make Pele's Other Garden a must. Sandwiches are made with whole-wheat, rye, sourdough, or French bread, baked on the island and delivered fresh daily; the turkey is free-range. The bright yellow building is easy to spot along tree-shaded Dole Park.

See map p. 295. Dole Park, 811 Houston St., Lanai City. ☎ **808-565-9628.** *Most items: less than $7. AE, DISC, MC, V. Open: Mon–Sat 9:30 a.m.–3 p.m. and 5–9 p.m.*

Pool Grille
$$ Lanai City   Eclectic

At the most casual of Manele Bay Hotel's restaurants, you dine poolside under beach umbrellas, feasting on huge hamburgers (homemade buns, of course) and gourmet salads. Salad choices include spicy chicken, grilled tiger prawns, and cobb. The Lanai venison pastrami sandwich and grilled Hawaiian taro burger are popular options. Even nonguests drop by — this joint is one of only two restaurants on the beach open for lunch.

See map p. 295. In the Manele Bay Hotel. ☎ **808-565-7700.** *Main courses: $11–$16. AE, DC, MC, V. Open: Daily 11 a.m.–5 p.m.*

The Terrace
$$$–$$$$ Lanai City   American

Located next to the Formal Dining Room in the Lodge at Koele, between the 35-foot-high Great Hall and a wall of glass looking out over prim English gardens, the Terrace is far from your typical hotel dining room. The menu may be fancy for comfort food, but it does, indeed, comfort. Hearty breakfasts of waffles and cereals, fresh pineapple from the nearby Palawai Basin, frittata, and Kauai Shrimp Benedict (sautéed Kauai shrimp, grilled taro bread, and wilted spinach with poached eggs and blue crab hollandaise) are a grand start to the day. Dinner choices are the American classics, created by Executive Chef Andrew Manion-Copley, such as roasted veal chop on herb mashed potatoes with fava beans and carrots, pepper roasted rib-eye steak with blue cheese mashed potatoes, and garlic-herb roasted chicken with potato onion cake.

See map p. 295. In the Lodge at Koele. ☎ **808-565-4580.** *Reservations recommended. Main courses: $12–$16 at breakfast, $28–$35 at dinner. AE, DC, MC, V. Open: Daily 6 a.m.–9:30 p.m.*

Having Fun on and off the Beach

If you like big, wide, empty gold-sand beaches and crystal-clear, cobalt-blue water full of bright tropical fish — and who doesn't? — then go to Lanai. There is something for just anyone and plenty to see and experience.

Relaxing on Lanai's best beaches

With 18 miles of sandy shoreline, Lanai has some of Hawaii's least crowded and most interesting beaches. One spot in particular is perfect for swimming, snorkeling, and watching spinner dolphins play: **Hulopoe Beach,** Lanai's best. Black-lava fingers, protecting swimmers from the serious ocean currents that sweep around Lanai, border this palm-fringed, gold-sand beach. In summer, Hulopoe is perfect for swimming, snorkeling, or just lolling about; the water temperature is usually in the mid-70s. Swimming is usually safe, except when swells kick up in winter. The bay at the foot of the Manele Bay Hotel is a protected marine preserve, and the schools of colorful fish know it. So do the spinner dolphins that go there to play, as well as the humpback whales that cruise by in winter. Hulopoe is also Lanai's premier beach park, with a grassy lawn, picnic tables, barbecue grills, restrooms, showers, and ample parking. You can camp there, too.

You can find some of the best **lava-rock tide pools** in Hawaii along Hulopoe Bay's south shore. These miniature underwater worlds are full of strange creatures: *asteroids* (sea stars) and *holothurians* (sea cucumbers), not to forget spaghetti worms, Barber Pole shrimp, and Hawaii's favorite local delicacy, the opihi, a tasty morsel also known as the limpet. Youngsters enjoy swimming in the enlarged tide pool at the bay's eastern edge.

When you explore tide pools, do so at low tide. Never turn your back on the waves. Wear tennis shoes or reef walkers because wet rocks are slippery. Collecting specimens in this marine preserve is forbidden, so don't take any souvenirs home.

The 8-mile-long, windswept **Shipwreck Beach** on Lanai's northeastern shore — named for the rusty ship *Liberty* stuck on the coral reef — is a sailor's nightmare and a beachcomber's dream. The strong currents yield all sorts of flotsam, from Japanese handblown-glass fish floats and rare pelagic paper nautilus shells to plenty of junk. This place is also great for spotting whales from December to April, when the Pacific humpbacks cruise in from Alaska to winter in the calm offshore waters. The road to the beach is paved most of the way, but you really need a four-wheel-drive to get to this deserted beach at the end of Polihua Road, a 4-mile off-road trail.

The area doesn't have facilities except fishermen's huts and driftwood shelters. Bring water and sunscreen. Beware the strong currents, which make the water unsafe for swimming.

Enjoying the water

Lanai has Hawaii's best water clarity because it lacks major development, and has low rainfall and runoff, and because its coast is washed clean daily by the sea current known as "The Way to Tahiti." But the strong sea currents pose a threat to swimmers, and the waters have few good surf breaks. Most of the aquatic adventures — swimming, snorkeling, and scuba diving — are centered on the somewhat-protected south shore, around Hulopoe Bay.

The two main outfitters for watersports are **Trilogy Lanai Ocean Sports** (☎ **888-MAUI-800** or 808-565-9303; www.visitlanai.com) and **Adventure Lanai Ecocentre** (☎ **808-565-7373;** www.adventurelanai.com).

Body boarding, bodysurfing, and board surfing

When the surf's up on Lanai, catching the waves is a real treat. Under the right conditions, Hulopoe and Polihua are both great for catching waves. Boogie boards ($10 a day) are available through **Adventure Lanai Ecocentre** (☎ **808-565-7373;** www.adventurelanai.com). The beach shack at Hulopoe Beach has complimentary boogie boards for guests of the Manele Bay Hotel and the Lodge at Koele.

Ocean kayaking

Discover the thrill of kayaking with **Trilogy's** guided trips into Lanai's complex ecosystems and unique flora and fauna (☎ **888-MAUI-800** or 808-565-9303; www.visitlanai.com), Monday through Saturday, from 7:30 a.m. to 2 p.m. The trips paddle along Lanai's magnificent south shore, exploring the water and sea caves at Kahekili Ho'e, where thousand-foot sea cliffs still hide the bones of ancient Hawaiians, or along the north shore at Shipwreck Beach, one of the longest barrier reefs in Hawaii, where you can explore the shipwreck and paddle your kayak among the numerous turtles who frequent it. Both trips offer lunch, sodas, and snacks, as well as single and double kayaks and snorkeling gear. Cost is $125 (half price for children ages 3 to 15).

Trilogy offers 10 percent off excursions and activities booked online.

The **Adventure Lanai Ecocentre** (☎ **808-565-7373;** www.adventure lanai.com) offers half-day sea kayak/snorkel adventures (as well as kayak/scuba trips) aimed at introducing beginners to the world of ocean kayaking. The center provides state-of-the-art kayaks (with lightweight graphite paddles and full back-support seats), life vests, the latest in snorkel equipment, dry bags, towels, water, and snacks. After receiving instruction on how to kayak, your group will set off to explore the waters around Lanai, with stops for snorkeling, snacks, and beachcombing. The four-hour trip costs $99. Rental kayaks are also available, starting at $30 a day for a single kayak or $50 a day for a double kayak.

Catchin' a wave

Everyone, from small kids to grandparents, can learn to surf with **Adventure Lanai Ecocentre** (☎ 808-565-7373; www.adventure lanai.com). The four-hour "Surf Safari" is $99, and surfboard rental is $45 a day.

Sailing

Trilogy Lanai Ocean Sports (☎ 888-MAUI-800 or 808-565-9303; www.visitlanai.com) offers a two-hour sunset sail three times a week (Tuesday, Thursday, and Saturday). Appetizers and beverages are included, and views of spinner dolphins are likely. The trips leave at 4 p.m. from October to April; 5 p.m. the rest of the year. Price is $59 for adults, or $30 for children ages 3 to 15. See also the upcoming section on snorkeling for Trilogy's morning sail and snorkel trip.

Scuba diving

You can find two of Hawaii's best-known dive spots in Lanai's clear waters, just off the south shore: **Cathedrals I** and **II,** so named because the sun lights up an underwater grotto like a magnificent church. **Trilogy Lanai Ocean Sports** (☎ 888-MAUI-800 or 808-565-9303; www.visitlanai.com) offers several different kinds of sailing, diving, and snorkeling trips on catamarans and from their 32-foot, high-tech jet-drive ocean raft. At 6:30 a.m. on Tuesday and Thursday, or 7:30 a.m. on Saturday, Trilogy has its own version of "sunrise services" at the Cathedrals. Not only is the morning the best time of day to dive this incredible area, but virtually no other dive boats are available in the water at this time. The 90-minute dives costs $95.

For those wanting to sleep in, **Trilogy** offers a couple of other dive experiences: an afternoon dive (3 to 6 p.m.) on Monday, Wednesday, and Friday for the serious diver looking for a two-tank dive in the areas that have made Lanai famous. Cost is $130 and includes sodas, snacks, scuba gear, and a dive master. Noncertified divers can check out Trilogy's Daily Beach Dives (Monday through Friday, 10 a.m.) from the beach at Hulopoe Bay for $75; certified divers can join in for $65.

The **Adventure Lanai Ecocentre** (☎ 808-565-7373; www.adventure lanai.com) has a four-hour diving tour, with instructor, to the top dive spots on Lanai for $99; scuba gear rental a la carte or package deals are also at their store, 338 Eighth St. in Lanai City.

Snorkeling

Hulopoe is Lanai's best snorkeling spot. Fish are abundant and friendly in the marine-life conservation area. Try the lava-rock points at either end of the beach and around the lava pools. Snorkel gear is free to guests of the two resorts. You can also rent for $10 a day from the **Adventure Lanai Ecocentre**(☎ 808-565-7373; www.adventurelanai.com), which also offers ocean kayaking/snorkeling trips.

Trilogy Lanai Ocean Sports (☎ **888-MAUI-800** or 808-565-9303; www. visitlanai.com), which has built a well-deserved reputation as the leader in sailing/snorkeling cruises in Hawaii, has a snorkel sailing trip from 8:45 a.m. to 1 p.m. on Monday, Wednesday, and Friday, and 10 a.m. to 2:30 p.m. on Saturday, on board luxury custom sailing catamarans. The trips along Lanai's protected coastline include sailing past hundreds of spinner dolphins and into some of the best snorkeling sites in the world. The $110 price (half price for children ages 3 to 15) includes breakfast, lunch, sodas, snacks, snorkel gear, and instruction.

Sportfishing

Jeff Menze takes you out on the 28-foot Omega boat *Spinning Dolphin* (☎ **808-565-6613**). His fishing charters cost $400 for six people for four hours, or $600 for six people for eight hours. He also offers exclusive three-hour whale-watching tours in season, which cost $300 for six passengers.

Whale-watching

Year round, **Trilogy** (☎ **888-MAUI-800** or 808-565-9303; www.visitlanai. com) offers one and a half hour adventures on a 32-foot, 26-passenger rigid-hulled inflatable boat. From late December through April, Trilogy is on the lookout for whales, but during the remainder of the year, the Blue Water Marine Mammal Watch goes in search of schools of spinner dolphins. The cost is $75 (half price for children ages 3 to 15).

Hitting the links

The **Challenge at Manele,** next to the Manele Bay Hotel in Hulopoe Bay (☎ **800-321-4666** or 808-565-2222; greens fees: $225, $185 for guests), is a target-style, desert-links course, designed by Jack Nicklaus, and one of the most challenging courses in the state. Check out the local rules: "No retrieving golf balls from the 150-foot cliffs on the ocean holes 12, 13, or 17," and "All whales, axis deer, and other wild animals are considered immovable obstructions." If that doesn't give you a hint of the unique-ness of this course, maybe the fact that you must reserve tee times 90 days in advance will confirm it. Facilities include a clubhouse, a pro shop, rentals, a practice area, lockers, and showers.

The **Experience at Koele,** next to the Lodge at Koele in Lanai City (☎ **800-321-4666** or 808-565-4653; greens fees: $225, $185 for guests) is a traditional par-72 course designed by Greg Norman with fairway archi-tecture by Ted Robinson. The course has very different front and back nine holes. All goes well until you hit the signature hole, No. 8, where you tee off from a 250-foot elevated tee to a fairway bordered by a lake on the right and trees and dense shrubs on the left. To level the playing field, you can choose from four different sets of tees. Facilities include a clubhouse, a pro shop, rentals, a practice area, lockers, and showers. Book tee times a minimum of 90 days in advance.

Cavendish Golf Course (next to the Lodge at Koele in Lanai City; no phone) is a quirky par-36, nine-hole public course that not only *doesn't* have a clubhouse or club pros, but also no tee times, scorecards, or club rentals. To play, just show up, put a donation into the little wooden box next to the first tee ($5–$10 is appropriate), and hit away.

Bicycling around Lanai

Road-bike treks are available through the **Adventure Lanai Ecocentre** (☎ 808-565-7373; www.adventurelanai.com) for $99 per person for four hours and are perfect for beginners — they're all downhill. A four-wheel-drive van meets you at the bottom with snacks, takes you on a tour of the petroglyphs, and then gives you a ride back up to the top. Trips for more advanced riders are also available. The center rents 21-speed front-suspension mountain bikes starting at $25 a day.

The **Lodge at Koele** (☎ 808-565-7300) also has mountain bikes to rent for $8 an hour, $35 for four hours, and $40 to $55 for eight hours.

For general information about bike trails, check out www.bikehawaii.com.

Seeing the sights

You need a four-wheel-drive to reach all the sights that I list in this section. Renting one is an expensive proposition on Lanai — from $129 to $179 a day — so I suggest that you rent one just for the day (or days) you plan on sightseeing; otherwise, you can easily get to the beach and around Lanai City without your own wheels. For details on vehicle rentals, see the section "Getting around," earlier in this chapter.

For a guided four-wheel-drive tour, contact **Adventure Lanai Ecocentre** (☎ 808-565-7373; www.adventurelanai.com), which offers four-hour off-road tours for $99 per person.

If you decide to rent a four-wheel-drive, take some of these suggested tours:

✔ **Garden of the Gods:** A dirt four-wheel-drive road leads out of Lanai City, through the now uncultivated pineapple fields, past the Kanepuu Preserve (a dry-land forest preserve teeming with rare plant and animal life), to the so-called Garden of the Gods, out on Lanai's north shore. This place has little to do with gods, Hawaiian or otherwise. It is, however, the ultimate rock garden: a rugged, barren, beautiful place full of rocks strewn by volcanic forces and shaped by the elements into a variety of shapes and colors — brilliant reds, oranges, ochers, and yellows. Go early in the morning or just before sunset, when the light casts eerie shadows on the mysterious lava formations. Drive west from the Lodge on Polihua Road; in about 2 miles, you see a hand-painted sign that points you in the right direction, left down a one-lane, red-dirt road through a kiawe forest and past sisal and scrub to the site.

✔ **Kanepuu Preserve:** Don't expect giant sequoias big enough to drive a car through; this ancient forest on the island's western plateau is so fragile, you can visit only once a month. Kanepuu, which has 49 species of plants unique to Hawaii, survives under the Nature Conservancy's protective wing. Botanists say the 590-acre forest is the last dry lowland forest in Hawaii; the others have all vanished, trashed by axis deer, agriculture, or "progress." Among the botanical marvels of this dry forest are the remains of *olopua* (native olive), *lama* (native ebony), *mau hau hele* (a native hibiscus), and the rare aiea trees, which were used for canoe parts. The self-guided tour takes about 10 to 15 minutes to walk. Guided hikes must be arranged in advance. Contact the **Nature Conservancy Oahu Land Preserve** manager at 923 Nuuatel (☎ **808-565-7430** http://nature.org/wherewework/northamerica/states/hawaii) to reserve.

✔ **Kaunolu Village:** Out on Lanai's nearly vertical, Gibraltar-like sea cliffs is an old royal compound and fishing village. Now a national historic landmark and one of Hawaii's most treasured ruins, historians believe that King Kamehameha the Great and hundreds of his closest followers inhabited the area about 200 years ago. The drive is a hot, dry, dusty, slow-going 3 miles in a four-wheel-drive from Lanai City to Kaunolu, but the mini-expedition is worth it. Take plenty of water, don a hat for protection against the sun, and wear sturdy shoes.

✔ **Off the tourist trail in Keomoku Village:** Visiting Keomoku Village, on Lanai's east coast, is really getting away from it all. All that's in Keomoku, a ghost town since the mid-1950s, is a 1903 clapboard church in disrepair, an overgrown graveyard, an excellent view across the 9-mile Auau Channel to Maui's crowded Kaanapali Beach, and some very empty beaches that are perfect for a picnic or a snorkel. This former ranching and fishing village of 2,000 was the first non-Hawaiian settlement on Lanai, but it dried up after droughts killed off the Maunalei Sugar Company. The village is a great little escape from Lanai City. Follow Keomoku Road for 8 miles to the coast, turn right on the sandy road, and keep going for 5¾ miles.

✔ **Luahiwa Petroglyph Field:** With more than 450 known petroglyphs in Hawaii at 23 sites, Lanai is second only to the Big Island in its wealth of prehistoric rock art, but you have to search a little to find it. Some of the best examples are on the outskirts of Lanai City, on a hillside site known as Luahiwa Petroglyph Field. The characters you see incised on 13 boulders in this grassy 3-acre knoll include a running man, a deer, a turtle, a bird, a goat, and even a rare, curly-tailed Polynesian dog. (A latter-day wag has put a leash on him — some joke.) To get there, take the road to Hulopoe Beach. About 2 miles out of Lanai City, look to the left, up on the slopes of the crater, for a cluster of reddish-tan boulders (believed to form a rain *heiau*, or shrine, where people called up the gods Ku and Hina to nourish their crops). A cluster of spiky century plants marks the spot. Look for the Norfolk pines on the left side of the highway, turn

left on the dirt road that veers across the abandoned pineapple
fields, and after about a mile, take a sharp left by the water tanks.
Drive for another half mile and then veer to the right at the V in the
road. Stay on this upper road for about a third of a mile until you
come to a large cluster of boulders on the right side. Take a short
walk up the cliffs (wear walking or hiking shoes) to the petroglyphs.
Exit the same way you came. Go between 3 p.m. and sunset for
ideal viewing and photo ops.

✔ **Five islands at a single glance on the Munro Trail:** In the first
golden rays of dawn, when lone owls swoop over abandoned
pineapple fields, hop into a four-wheel-drive and head out on the
two-lane blacktop toward Mount Lanaihale, the 3,370-foot summit
of Lanai. Your destination is the Munro Trail, the narrow, winding
ridge trail that runs across Lanai's razorback spine to the summit.
From there, you may get a rare Hawaii treat: On a clear day, you can
see all the main islands in the Hawaiian chain except Kauai.

Shopping on Lanai

Lanai is small, so you can imagine that visitors don't go there to shop.
However, the island does have some treasures you don't want to miss.

Central Bakery, 1311 Fraser Ave., Lanai City (☎ 808-565-3920), is the
mother lode of the island's baked delights. Although Central Bakery isn't
your standard retail outlet, you can call in advance, place your order,
and pick it up. The staff prefers as much notice as possible, and it's
worth it. The guava chiffon and chocolate chantilly cakes are in great
demand, and the breads are legendary.

Gifts with Aloha, Dole Park, 363 Seventh St. at Ilima Street (☎ 808-565-
6589), ships minigardens, fountains, and lamps to the mainland and sells
fabulously stylish hats and hatbands, T-shirts, swimwear, quilts, dresses,
children's books and toys, Hawaii-themed books, *pareus* (long, wrap-
around skirts usually made from a colorful or decorative fabric), candles,
aloha shirts, and much more.

Stop by **International Food & Clothing,** 833 Ilima Ave. (☎ 808-565-6433),
for groceries, housewares, T-shirts, fishing supplies, over-the-counter
drugs, wine and liquor, paper goods, and hardware. There's even a take-
out lunch counter.

A local landmark for two generations, **Pine Isle Market,** 356 Eighth St.
(☎ 808-565-6488), specializes in locally caught fresh fish, but you can
also find fresh herbs and spices, canned goods, ice cream, toys, zoris,
and other basic essentials of work and play. The fishing section is out-
standing, with every lure imaginable.

Richard's Shopping Center, 434 Eighth St. (☎ **808-565-6047**), is, in fact, a general store with a grocery section, liquor, film, cosmetics, sunscreens, clothing, and other miscellaneous items. Half a wall is lined with an extraordinary selection of fishhooks and anglers' needs.

At the **Lanai Marketplace** on Dole Square, farmers sell their dewy-fresh produce, home-baked breads, plate lunches, and handicrafts from 7 to 11 a.m. or noon on Saturday.

The Local Gentry, 363 Seventh St., behind Gifts with Aloha, facing Ilima Street (☎ **808-565-9130**), is a wonderful boutique and first of its kind on the island, featuring clothing and accessories that aren't the standard resort-shop fare.

Enjoying Lanai After Dark

Except for special programs, such as the annual **Pineapple Festival** in May, when some of Hawaii's best musicians arrive to show their support for Lanai, the only regular nightlife venues are the **Lanai Playhouse** (☎ **808-565-7500**), at the corner of Seventh and Lanai avenues in Lanai City, and the two resorts, the Lodge at Koele and Manele Bay Hotel.

Fast Facts

Dentists

For emergency dental care, call **Dr. Nick's Family Dentistry** (☎ 808-565-7801).

Doctors/Hospitals

If you need a doctor, contact the **Lanai Family Health Center** (☎ 808-565-6423) or the **Lanai Community Hospital** (☎ 808-565-6411).

Emergencies

Call the police, fire department, or ambulance services at ☎ **911,** or the **Poison Control Center** at ☎ 800-362-3585. For nonemergencies, call the **police** (☎ 808-565-6428).

Weather

For a weather report, call the **National Weather Service** at ☎ 808-565-6033.

Part V
The Part of Tens

The 5th Wave   By Rich Tennant

In this part . . .

*I*t wouldn't be a *For Dummies* book without a couple of these lists of ten! In the first of the three chapters, I introduce you to the wonderful world of dining, Maui style. Next, you find insider tips on how to ditch the tourist trappings and fit in like a local. In the final chapter, I share the secrets of creating romance on Maui.

Chapter 18

Ten Steps to Incredible Island Dining

. . . .

In This Chapter

▶ Knowing what you're eating
▶ Maximizing your dining experiences

. . . .

*B*elieve me, eating well on Maui isn't a problem. Hawaii has lured some of the world's finest chefs to its kitchens and managed to cultivate some stars of its own in the process — and the largest and finest bunch of them has chosen the Valley Isle as muse. Anyone who loves quality seafood, fresh-grown veggies, sweet tropical fruits, and even artisan-crafted cheeses will think they've died and gone to heaven, because Maui is the bounteous breadbasket of the Hawaiian Islands.

However, you may want to know a few facts about island dining before you sit down to a meal — the first being that Hawaii has two brands of homegrown cuisine. Local food is the traditional everyday eats of the locals, while Hawaii Regional (or Hawaii Island) Cuisine is the gourmet version. But both are hybrid cuisines, informed by both European and Asian influences. This chapter tells you more about island cuisine — and what else to expect on the culinary front.

Savoring Hawaii's Freshest Foods

If you love seafood, you've come to the right place. In fact, Hawaii's **seafood** may be the best in the world — some of the world's finest chefs think so — and the selection is generally much more diverse than what you find in your average mainland supermarket. And Maui's chefs definitely know how to select, prepare, and serve the fruits of the sea. (For details on the variations you may find on island menus, see the section "Working Your Way around the Menu: A Translation List for Seafood Lovers," later in this chapter.)

But Maui's bounty isn't limited to the sea. A wealth of **fresh-grown vegetables** — including leafy lettuces, vine-ripened tomatoes, and sweet Maui onions — thrives in the lava-rich soil.

Maui's verdant Upcountry plays host to Surfing Goat Dairy, which crafts some of the finest **goat cheeses** in all the land. The hard and soft chèvres come in a range of creatively ripened and herbed varieties. If you spot one of these extraordinary chèvres on a local menu, don't pass it up. The charming goat farm has even developed into a tourist attraction in its own right, so you can also go right to the source (see Chapter 13).

And **fruits** are Maui's real forte. All you need to do is head to the local supermarket to discover a whole new world of citrus, more varieties of banana than you ever knew existed, and other colorful tropical treats. (See the section "Shopping at a Maui Supermarket," later in this chapter, for more details.)

Tropical fruit comes as no surprise, of course — but who knew that Hawaii offered so much island-raised meat? The Big Island is home to the largest privately owned cattle ranch in the United States: Parker Ranch, covering 225,000 acres, including more than 50,000 cattle, and serving as the heart of Hawaii's *paniolo* (cowboy) country. Ranch-raised beef and lamb appear on fine-dining menus all over the state.

Tasting Traditional Island Eats

Local food is a casual, catch-all affair. As evidenced by the list of food terms that appears later in this chapter (see the section "Mastering More Everyday Hawaiian Food Terms," later in this chapter), outsider influences on the local cuisine arrived in Hawaii from all over the map, from Portugal to Japan and just about everywhere in between.

Lomilomi salmon is the perfect example of local food as a hybrid cuisine. Islanders didn't have natural access to the cold-water fish, but they accepted it in trade from globetrotting explorers and traders. Discovering how to prepare it ceviche-style for short-term preservation, they quickly became accustomed to accepting it in trade and incorporated it into their diet as a staple.

Local food is generally starch heavy and high in calories, so don't expect it to have a positive impact on your waistline. Local food is most commonly served as a **plate lunch,** which usually consists of a main dish (anything from fried fish to teriyaki beef), "two scoops rice," an ice-cream-scoop serving of macaroni salad, and brown gravy, all served on a paper plate. Plate lunches are cheap and available at casual restaurants and beachside stands. An excellent place to indulge in this local tradition is Maui's **Aloha Mixed Plate** (see Chapter 11).

Another great place to try local food is at a *luau,* a traditional feast that's not a tourist trap but a genuine part of island culture, thrown to celebrate everything from a baby's birth to a college graduation. For more on luaus, see "Knowing What to Expect at a Luau," later in this chapter.

Finding Maui's Gourmet Side

About a dozen or so years ago, Hawaii's kitchens underwent a culinary revolution: the birth of Hawaii Regional Cuisine. Island chefs were tired of preparing stodgy continental fare that was unsuited to Hawaii living, so they created a new standard of gourmet cuisine using fresh local ingredients in creative combinations and preparations.

Hawaii Regional Cuisine is often disguised under other names — Euro-Asian, Pacific Rim, Indo-Pacific, Pacific Edge, Euro-Pacific, Island Fusion, and so on — but it all falls under the jurisdiction of Hawaii Regional Cuisine. Although it has variations, you can expect the following keynotes: plenty of fresh island fish, Asian flavorings (ginger, soy, wasabi, seaweed, and so on) and cooking styles galore (searing, grilling, panko crust, and wok preparations), and fresh tropical fruit sauces (mango, papaya, and the like).

Hawaii Regional Cuisine has really matured in recent years, with the finest HRC chefs putting clever multicultural spins on the established canon, based on their training and heritage. You may already know of Roy Yamaguchi, who has installed outposts of his **Roy's Restaurant** chain not only on each island but also around the world, from New York to Guam. Maui stars include Beverly Gannon (of **Haliimaile General Store** and **Joe's Bar & Grill**), Peter Merriman (of **Hula Grill**), and David Paul (of **David Paul's Lahaina Grill**).

In 1999, the next generation of island chefs banded together under the label Hawaiian Island Chefs, taking their craft to the next level — and they've succeeded in spades. Instead of emphasizing broad-based fusion in island cuisine, these upstarts generally start from an ethnic or thematic base, incorporating Hawaii ingredients and adding their own individual stamp. The stellar James MacDonald works his magic at chic sister seafood restaurants **I'o** and **Pacific'o**. D.K. Kodama, who reinvented sushi for adoring gourmands at Maui's **Sansei Seafood Restaurant and Sushi Bar,** has not taken on the Tuscan tradition at his warm and wonderful trattoria **Vino.** Although eating at some of these restaurants may be a splurge, I encourage you to treat yourself to a gourmet island meal at least once during your trip. See Chapter 11 for reviews of these establishments and more of Maui's top choices.

Working Your Way around the Menu: A Translation List for Seafood Lovers

Even savvy seafood eaters can become confused when confronted with a Hawaiian menu. Although the mainland terms are sometimes included, many menus only use the Hawaiian names to tout their daily catches. Furthermore, some types of seafood that make regular appearances in Hawaii's kitchens simply don't show up on mainland menus.

You're likely to encounter many of the following types of seafood while you're in Maui:

- **ahi:** This dense, ruby-red bigeye or yellowfin tuna is a Hawaiian favorite — and it may be one of yours too, as popular as it has become on the mainland. Ahi is regularly served raw, as sushi and sashimi, or panko-crusted and seared in Hawaii Regional Cuisine. Yellowfin is the beefier of the two.

- **aku:** This meaty, robust skipjack tuna is also known as bonito (which may be familiar to sushi fans). Aku is best as raw sushi, because it can get too dry if not expertly cooked.

- **au** (ow): This firm-fleshed marlin or broadbill swordfish sometimes stands in for ahi in local dishes. Pacific blue marlin is sometimes called kajiki, while striped marlin often shows up as nairagi.

- **hebi** (*heh*-bee): This mildly flavored, almost lemony, spearfish is sometimes the day's catch in upscale restaurants.

- **mahimahi:** Like ahi, this white, sweet, moderately dense fish is likely to also be familiar to you; it's Hawaii's most popular fish and shows up regularly on mainland menus.

- **monchong** (*mon*-chong): This exotic fish boasts a flaky, tender texture and a simple flavor. It's best served broiled, sautéed, or steamed.

- **onaga** (o-*na*-ga): This mild, moist, and tender ruby-red snapper is served in many fine restaurants; sample it if it's available.

- **ono** (*oh*-no): "Ono" means "good to eat" in Hawaiian, and this mackerel-like fish sure is. Also called wahoo, it's similar to snapper, but firmer and drier. You should have multiple opportunities to try this popular, distinctly flavored fish; it's often served grilled and in sandwiches.

- **opah** (*oh*-pa): This rich, almost creamy moonfish is good served just about any way, from sashimi to baked.

- **opakapaka** (oh-pa-ka-*pa*-ka): Either pink or crimson snapper, this light, flaky, elegant fish is very popular on fine-dining menus.

- **shutome** (shuh-*toe*-me): This fish is what mainlanders call swordfish. It's a sweet and tender steaklike fish that is great grilled or broiled.

- **tombo:** Tombo is albacore tuna — but this firm, flavorful whitefish surpasses the canned stuff by miles when prepared appropriately.

- **uku** (*oo*-koo): This gray — pale pink, really — snapper is flaky, moist, and delicate.

- **ulua** (oo-*loo*-ah): Ulua is large jack trevally, a firm-fleshed, flavorful fish also known as pompano.

Demand for fish has driven down the populations of certain fish species, such as Chilean seabass and Hawaiian grouper (hapuupuu), to dangerously low levels. If you'd like to know which fish are relatively abundant and which ones are overfished before you make your menu choices, you may want to pack a copy of the **Audobon/Pacific Whale Foundation Seafood Wallet Card.** The printable card — available at www.pacific whale.org/printouts/fish_card.pdf — makes it easy to make the environmentally correct choice at a glance. The color-coded card indicates which menu-common species are abundant and relatively well managed, which are not currently in danger but are under watch, and which are in danger of severe depletion.

Mastering More Everyday Hawaiian Food Terms

All the following foods are common in plate lunches and at luaus. A number of them also pop up on gourmet menus — usually with expensive ingredients and prepared with a twist, of course:

- ✔ **bento:** A Japanese box lunch.

- ✔ **haupia** (how-*pee*-ah): Creamy coconut pudding, usually served in squares.

- ✔ **kalua pork:** Pork slow-cooked in an *imu,* or underground oven; listed on menus as "luau pig" on occasion. Sometimes it's served in a pulled kalua pork sandwich, much like barbecue pork in the Southeast or Texas.

- ✔ **kiawe** (kee-*ah*-vay): An aromatic mesquite wood often used to fire the wood-burning ovens.

- ✔ **laulau:** Pork, chicken, or fish wrapped in ti leaves and steamed.

- ✔ **lilikoi** (lil-*ee*-koy): Passion fruit.

- ✔ **lomilomi** (low-mee-*low*-mee) **salmon:** Salted salmon marinated, sevichelike, with tomatoes and green onions.

- ✔ **lumpia** (lum-*pee*-ah): The Portuguese version of a spring roll, but spicier, doughier, and deep-fried (and usually stuffed with pork and veggies).

- ✔ **malassada** (mah-lah-*sah*-da): The Portuguese version of a donut, usually round, deep-fried, and generously sprinkled with powdered sugar.

- ✔ **manapua** (man-ah-*poo*-ah): A bready, doughy bun with sweetened pork or sweet beans inside, like Chinese bao.

- ✔ **ohelo** (oh-*hay*-low): A berry very similar to a cranberry that commonly appears in Hawaii Regional Cuisine sauces.

- ✔ **panko:** Japanese bread crumbs, most commonly used to prepare *katsu* (deep-fried pork or chicken cutlet). Creative chefs often use it for other purposes, most commonly as a tempura-like crust on sushi-grade ahi rolls.

- ✔ **poi:** The root of the taro pounded into a purple, starchy paste; a staple of the island diet, but generally tasteless to most outsiders.

- ✔ **poke** (*po*-kay): Cubed raw fish — usually ahi or marlin — seasoned with onions, soy, and seaweed.

- ✔ **ponzu:** A soy-and-citrus dipping sauce popular with Hawaii Regional Cuisine chefs.

- ✔ **pupus:** Appetizers or hors d'oeuvres.

- ✔ **saimin** (*sai*-min): A brothy soup with ramenlike noodles, topped with bits of fish, chicken, pork, and/or vegetables. Saimin is served almost everywhere in Hawaii, from plate-lunch stands to museum cafes to McDonald's.

- ✔ **shave ice:** The island version of a snow cone, best enjoyed with ice cream and sweet *azuki* (red) beans at the bottom.

- ✔ **taro:** A green leafy vegetable grown in Hawaii; the root is used to make poi (see earlier in this list), while the leafy part of the vegetable is often steamed like spinach.

Enjoying Other Local Favorites

Lest all this unfamiliar food talk makes you think otherwise, remember that the majority of Hawaii islanders are red-blooded, flag-waving Americans — and they love a good burger just as much as your average mainlander.

My favorite burgers on Maui are served at **Cheeseburger in Paradise.** See Chapter 11 for all the juicy details.

Hawaii has also co-opted Mexican cuisine and made the burrito its own, most successfully at **Maui Tacos,** where island-grown ingredients and fresh-caught fish provide top-quality surf-style filling. Again, see Chapter 11 for details.

Discovering Maui's Ethnic Eats

Thanks to its proximity to the Eastern Hemisphere and its large, multifaceted Asian population, the Hawaiian Islands boast a wealth of fabulous Asian restaurants — Chinese, Thai, Vietnamese, Japanese, and so on. With the exception of Japanese (of course), most Asian restaurants tend to be very affordable. Furthermore, because island palates are more accustomed to dining Asian style, you find that dishes aren't Americanized for a mainland population; flavors are bold and strong, ingredients fresh and crisp. While dining out on Maui, you may just find yourself enjoying the finest ethnic food you've ever eaten.

Maui's ethnic standout is **A Saigon Cafe,** whose piquant flavors and friendly service make it well worth seeking out in off-the-tourist-track Wailuku. I never miss it when I'm on the island. See Chapter 11.

Shopping at a Maui Supermarket

Whenever I'm in a foreign country, I always take the time to visit the local supermarket. And even though Hawaii is part of the United States, its grocery stores are a world apart — a trip to the market is an entertaining culinary adventure. If you're staying in a condo or a vacation rental, you'll want to stock the pantry, but even if you're not, I highly recommend an excursion to your local Safeway, KTA, Star Market, or Foodland.

Hawaii supermarkets offer a number of treats that you don't find at your average mainland supermarket. **Poi** (taro root mixed with water and pounded into a paste — similar to polenta in consistency), for example, comes in instant, premade, and make-your-own forms; I defy you to find poi in *any* form in your hometown supermarket.

The bounty in the seafood case is amazing. Hawaii refrigerator cases regularly contain such taste treats as sushi-grade tuna, fresh Pacific octopus, and whole squid (insert "yum!" or "yuck!" here, depending on your taste buds). If you have access to a barbecue at your hotel or condo complex, grilling up a fresh fish filet is a simple but magnificent dinner.

Just about any Hawaii supermarket has multiple aisles devoted to Asian foods, from noodles to bizarre candies. The juice refrigerator case is also a treat, so don't be afraid to try something new. My husband never misses an opportunity to chug **POG** (passion fruit-orange-guava juice) when he's in the islands.

Java lovers, rejoice. Maui's local brew is available in just about any average market. All Hawaii-grown coffees are delicious, but the world-famous **Kona coffee,** grown on the Big Island, is the top of the heap (and it makes a great, affordable gift to bring home to your favorite caffeine addict).

You can find the greatest bounty among the fresh fruits, where you uncover such tropical treats as mangoes, guava, star fruit, lychee, lilikoi (passion fruit), and much more. Whenever I go to Hawaii, I eat as much papaya as I can. (Mainland imports just don't equal the island-grown fruits.) Cut your papaya in half, dig out the seeds, and serve with a squirt of lime — island breakfast doesn't get any better than this. Pineapples are another Hawaii taste treat; the small white pineapples are sweetest, and you usually find them clearly labeled at the market. The Big Island's lava-rich soil produces extra-flavorful citrus fruits; Kau oranges, for example, are legendary for their sweetness. Even watermelon is an extra-special treat; Molokai-grown watermelons are the best in the world — full of seeds, but fabulous.

Among Hawaii-grown vegetables, Maui onions are the ultimate treat. They're very sweet, like Vidalias, but with a distinctive flavor all their own. Slice 'em thick and throw 'em right on the barbecue. Dense, purple, Molokai-grown sweet potatoes are another of my favorites.

Don't shy away from tropical fruits or other foods just because you're unfamiliar with them. Islanders are friendly and talkative folks. Supermarket attendants — or even your fellow shoppers — can advise you on how to cut or clean island fruits. Just ask, and you're likely to find yourself on the receiving end of some friendly conversation.

Hawaii shopping does have a downside — namely, high prices. Although you can save quite a few bucks by stocking up and cooking for yourself back at the condo instead of eating in restaurants for three meals a day, you still have to be prepared to pay more for staples than you would back home. The general rule is: Expect anything that has to wing its way across the Pacific to be more than you usually pay.

Unfortunately, Maui's supermarket prices are high all across the board. Fish is about the same price as on the mainland, and the quality is generally better — but pick up some ground beef for burgers, and expect to pay $2.50 a pound. Your average breakfast cereal goes for $5 or $6 a box. At first glance, you may think the prices of milk and bread are a joke: Expect to pay about $6 a gallon for milk, and around $4.50 for a loaf of bread.

Sipping a Tropical Cocktail

California entrepreneur Vic Bergeron — more popularly known as Trader Vic — may have been responsible for the birth of the mai tai, but it's practically the official state cocktail in Hawaii. The classic mai tai is a magical sweet-tart concoction of Jamaican rum, fresh limejuice, and chunky ice, generally served in a tumbler and topped with a fresh sprig of mint.

A mai tai is a simple blend, and any bar worth its salt in Hawaii can mix you a well-balanced drink. But score an out-of-sorts bartender on the wrong night, however, and you end up with either a sickly sweet syrup that couldn't do justice to a stack of flapjacks, or a thick, face-distorting blend strong enough to power up a sports utility vehicle.

For the perfect blend of ideal mai tai–making and only-in-Maui ambience, the bar at any of the big resorts can satisfy your sunset cravings. In Lahaina, **Cheeseburger in Paradise** is the place to go for the top concoction. See Chapter 11.

Of course, mai tais may not be your drink of choice. If that's the case, don't worry — you can find plenty of other ways to toast your time in paradise. Personally, I'm a big fan of the piña colada — not a Hawaii cocktail, sure, but it never fails to put me in the tropical mood, especially when a colorful paper umbrella and a generous slice of pineapple are included in the picture. Again, **Cheeseburger in Paradise** makes the island's best.

Hawaii is no Portland, Oregon, but microbrews are serious business on the islands. The finest wear the **Kona Brewing Company** label.

Knowing What to Expect at a Luau

A luau is the ideal place to experience island traditions — but only to a degree, of course. Any commercial luau (read: any luau you're likely to attend) will be tainted by its commercialism. But a few luaus do a great job of bringing genuine island culture into the mix.

You're in luck! The best luaus — offering the best mix of good food, amenities, setting, and authentic culture — are on Maui. The **Old Lahaina Luau** and the **Feast at Lele** are the best luaus Hawaii has to offer, hands down. Be sure to reserve right away; see Chapter 11.

What should you plan for when attending a luau? Luckily, most luau feasts are self-sufficient, idiot-proof ventures, so after you make your reservations, all you need to bring is your appetite and aloha spirit. Dress for the festivities in bright, bold colors, even if you don't own any aloha wear because bright colors really suit the mood. Other than that, just wear what's comfortable for you, and bring a sweater if the weather is expected to cool down after dark. (All luaus take place outdoors, and most in breezy oceanfront settings.)

When you make your reservations, you're usually told when the gates open and when you should plan to arrive. Come in plenty of time to wander the grounds because the best luaus feature authentic craft making, games, and the like in the hour before the festivities formally begin. The luau pig, which has been baking all day in its *imu,* or underground oven, is also unearthed early in the program, and unless you're squeamish, you don't want to miss it.

Upon arrival, the Hawaiians typically greet you with a lei, made of either fresh flowers or shells, and a cocktail, often a **mai tai** (or fruit juice, if you're too young or a teetotaler). They lead you to your assigned seat, usually at a communal table with chairs (although the Old Lahaina Luau now features some traditional seating, on cushions facing low-slung tables).

Cocktails are usually included in the pay-one-price admission fee to a luau. Open bars are common, but some luaus limit you to a certain number or kind of drink. If it matters to you, be sure to ask when booking.

After your hosts unearth the luau pig from the imu, they will ask everyone to take a seat and then invite you to fill your plate from the buffet luau spread; the best luaus clearly mark the dishes so that you know what you're sampling. In addition to the kalua pork (shredded from the bone after the luau pig is unearthed), you can expect traditional dishes, such as poi, the tasteless purple paste that's the staple starch of Hawaii. Poi is worth trying for its iconic status, but you're unlikely to become a fan. People usually don't eat poi alone, but with other starches; ask an attendant what's best in the night's feast for poi dipping. You're likely to prefer such dishes as lomilomi salmon, poke, and haupia (see "Mastering More Everyday Hawaiian Food Terms," earlier in this chapter). If you're a less-than-adventurous diner, don't worry — you can find plenty of familiar dishes on hand, including chicken teriyaki, long rice, and salad. You can refill your plate as often as you like. After dinner, the evening's entertainment begins, usually a hula show that lasts an hour or so before the evening winds down.

Most luau food is satisfactory at best, so don't expect a gourmet feast (the exception being the Feast at Lele, which eschews the standard setting for intimate seating, food prepared by one of Hawaii's best chefs, and full table service). Top-notch luaus like the Old Lahaina Luau serve well-prepared fare, but remember that they're still cooking in bulk for hundreds. Come for the party and plan to have a first-rate dinner at a standard restaurant on another night.

What kind of luau is right for you is entirely up to you; some luaus are more suited to couples, for example, while others are great for families with kids. Some luaus feature wholly authentic Hawaiian entertainment (primarily chanting and dancing), while others blow the wad on glitzy Vegas-style extravaganzas with glittering costumes. (***Note:*** Any luau that calls itself authentically Hawaiian shouldn't have fire-knife dancers, which is a Samoan tradition.)

Luaus are pricey — usually $50 to $100 a head, depending on the fête — so choose carefully. Before you commit, see Chapter 11 and ask your reservations agent to make sure that you end up at the party that's right for you.

Chapter 19

Ten Ways to Lose the Tourist Trappings and Look Like a Local

. . . .

In This Chapter

▶ Fitting in on Maui
▶ Making yourself at home in paradise

. . . .

*H*awaii may be the 50th state, but it's an ocean — and a world — apart from its 49 mainland brethren. In fact, because it didn't join the star-spangled party until 1959, Hawaii came into the Union as an adopted adult, complete with its own unique personality, fully formed (indeed, ancient) culture, and distinct world view.

Maui sits closer to Tokyo than it does to Washington, D.C. — or even Chicago. The islands don't always share the Eurocentric perspective that many Americans have of the world.

Even the population is dramatically different. Unlike the rest of the United States, no one ethnic group forms a majority in Hawaii. Although Caucasian and Japanese are the two largest ethnic groups (each accounts for roughly 22% of the population), nearly 35% of islanders consider themselves of mixed ethnicity. Hawaii's residents, as a group, don't consider race a factor in marriage; they're just as likely to marry someone from a different race as not.

The fact that Maui is both exotic and familiar is one of its greatest appeals; however, it's also one of the biggest pitfalls for visitors. Because Hawaii is part of the good ol' U.S. of A., many first-time visitors think they have it all figured out. What else do they need to know?

A few things, it turns out. If you want to come across as an *akamai* (a-*kay*-my; smart) traveler instead of advertising your status as a *malihini* (ma-li-*hee*-nee; newcomer), read on.

Mastering the Two Most Important Words

Everyone in Hawaii speaks English, of course. But a few Hawaiian words and phrases have made their way into the common vernacular, and regularly pop up in everyday conversation.

You probably already know the Hawaiian word *aloha* (a-*lo*-ha), which serves as an all-purpose greeting — hello, welcome, or goodbye. Aloha is a warm and wonderful word full of grace and compassion and good feeling, so use it liberally. I can't think of a better way to get caught up in Hawaii's true spirit.

A second word that every visitor needs to know is *mahalo* (ma-*ha*-low), which means "thank you" and is used extensively throughout Hawaii. If you want to say "Thanks very much!" or "Thank you *so* much," say *mahalo nui loa* (ma-*ha*-low *noo*-ee *low*-ah). You'll impress the locals with your efforts, and you'll flatter them with your graciousness, too.

Learning More Hawaiian Words

If you only know *aloha* and *mahalo,* you'll do just fine. But if you consider yourself ahead of the curve and want to know a few more useful words, take a few minutes to study the following list. That way, when you're in a restaurant and the waiter offers your little ones a *keiki* menu, describes today's lunch special as particularly *ono,* or asks you if you're *pau* when he comes to clear your plate, you'll feel like a regular *kamaaina:*

- ✔ **alii** (ah-*lee*-ee): Hawaiian royalty

- ✔ **halau** (ha-*lau*): School

- ✔ **hale** (*ha*-lay): House

- ✔ **haole** (*how*-lee): Foreigner or Caucasian (literally "out of breath" — pale, or paleface); a common reference, not an insult (usually)

- ✔ **heiau** (heh-*ee*-ow): Hawaiian temple

- ✔ **hui** (*hoo*-ee): A club, collective, or assembly (for example, an artists' collective is an artists' hui)

- ✔ **hula** (*hoo*-lah): Native dance

- ✔ **imu** (*ee*-moo): Underground oven lined with hot rocks that's used for cooking the luau pig

- ✔ **kahuna** (ka-*hoo*-nah): Priest or expert

- ✔ **kamaaina** (ka-ma-*eye*-nah): Local person

- ✔ **kane** (*ka*-nay): Man (you may see this word on a restroom door)

- ✔ **kapu** (*ka*-poo): Anything that's taboo, forbidden

- ✔ **keiki** (*keh*-kee): Child

- ✔ **kupuna** (koo-*poo*-nah): An elder, leader, grandparent, or anyone who commands great respect

- ✔ **lanai** (*lah*-nigh): Porch or veranda

- ✔ **lei** (lay): Garland (usually of flowers, leaves, or shells)

- ✔ **luau** (*loo*-ow): A celebratory feast

- ✔ **malihini** (ma-li-*hee*-nee): Stranger or newcomer

- ✔ **mana** (*ma*-na): Spirit, divine power

- ✔ **muumuu** (moo-oo-*moo*-oo): A loose-fitting dress, usually in a tropical print

- ✔ **ono** (*oh*-no): Delicious

- ✔ **pau** (pow): Finished or done

- ✔ **pali** (*pah*-lee): Cliff

- ✔ **pupu** (*poo*-poo): Starter dish, appetizer

- ✔ **wahine** (wa-*wee*-nay): Woman (again, you may see this word on a restroom door)

Pronouncing Those Pesky Hawaiian Words and Place Names

Because the Hawaiian language has only 12 characters to work with — the five vowels (*a, e, i, o,* and *u*), plus seven consonants (*h, k, l, m, n, p,* and *w*) — Hawaiian words and names tend to be long and difficult, with plenty of repetitive syllables that can really twist your tongue. Master just a few basic rules, however, and "Honoapiilani Highway" and "Haliimaile" will be rolling out of your mouth like "Main Street" and "Anytown, USA" in no time.

Half of the letters in the Hawaiian language — *h, k, l, m, n,* and *p* — sound just like they do in English. The one consonant that sounds different in Hawaiian is *w. W* usually carries the "v" sound when it follows *i* or *e*; for example, the Oahu town of Haleiwa is "Ha-lay-*ee*-vah." At the beginning of words and after *a, u,* and *o,* though, it's usually your standard "w" sound — hence Wailea (why-*lay*-ah) and Makawao (mah-*kah*-wow), two Maui destinations.

The vowels are pronounced like this:

a	*ah* (as in father) or *uh* (as in above)
e	*eh* (as in bed) or *ay* (as in they)
i	*ee* (as in police)
o	*oh* (as in vote)
u	*oo* (as in too)

You sound almost all vowels separately, although you do pronounce some together, as in the name of Waikiki's main thoroughfare, Kalakaua Avenue, which is pronounced, "Kah-lah-*cow*-ah."

Remember this tip when trying to pronounce a Hawaiian word or name: Get into the habit of seeing long words or names as a collection of short syllables, and you can find them much easier to say. (Accents almost always fall on the second-to-last syllable.)

The trick is knowing where to put on the "breaks." That leads me to important tip No. 2: All syllables end with vowels, so a consonant always indicates the start of a new syllable. An example: The tongue-twisting Kealakekua Bay (the famous marine preserve off the Big Island's Kona coast), which throws nearly everyone for a loop. Break the syllables down by reading the consonants as red flags, though, and see how easy it becomes: "Kay-ah-lah-keh-*koo*-ah."

Discovering more about the Hawaiian language

If the vocabulary list and pronunciation key in this chapter whet your appetite for the Hawaiian language, a few Web sites can help you discover more. Probably most comprehensive — and the best place to start — is the **Hawaiian Language** Web site (www.hawaiianlanguage.com).

If you want to translate specific words or terms, use the searchable online dictionaries at the **Coconut Boyz' Hawaiian Dictionary** (www.hisurf.com/hawaiian/dictionary.html) or the Hawaiian Language Center's **Mamaka Kaiao** dictionary (www.olelo.hawaii.edu/eng/dictionary).

If you prefer a hard-copy Hawaiian-language reference or dictionary, you can find several at online bookstores, including Arthur Schultz's pocket-size *All About Hawaiian,* and the comprehensive *New Pocket Hawaiian Dictionary,* published by the University of Hawaii and generally considered the standard; you can order it online at www.uhpress.hawaii.edu.

The Hawaiian language actually has a 13th character: the glottal stop, which looks exactly like a single opening quotation mark (') and is meant to indicate a pause. I've chosen not to use the glottal stop throughout this book; it's often left out in printed Hawaiian and on store and street signs. Although serious Hawaiian-language students study volumes about the glottal stop and its equal importance to its fellow consonants and vowels, you don't need to worry about it for your purposes; you can basically ignore it when you see it.

I lay out these basics so that you can understand how the language works, but don't expect to become an expert at pronouncing Hawaiian words anytime soon. Whenever I return to Hawaii, I always feel that it takes me a day or two to get my tongue back in working order — and I *know* this stuff. Still, I have fun practicing — and with these basic tools under your belt, you'll quickly get the hang of it. Practice with *aloha* and *mahalo* and you'll really impress the locals when you get to Maui.

Knowing How to Give and Take Directions

Leave your compass at home, because islanders have a different sense of direction than mainlanders do. Even though locals think of the islands as having north shores and south shores, west coasts and east coasts, seldom does anybody direct you using the most common directional terms.

Instead, they send you either **makai** (ma-*kai*), a directional meaning toward the sea, or **mauka** (*mow*-kah), meaning toward the mountains. Because each island is basically a volcano with a single coastal road circling it, those two terms are often enough to do the trick.

When they don't, locals are likely to invoke relative terms rather than "north," "south," "east," or "west."

Remembering That You're in the United States

Don't say "back home in the U.S." when you're talking to folks in Maui. This tip seems like a real no-brainer, but that long flight across the Pacific and the one-of-a-kind Hawaii ambience and culture can really play tricks with your mind. Islanders are, by and large, a patriotic bunch, so they don't take kindly to being left off the national map. Refer to the continental United States as the mainland, which is what they do.

Another very important point in the same vein: Locals are always called "islanders," never Hawaiians, unless they have native blood, which not that many islanders do. (Hawaiian is an ethnic label.)

Wearing Sunscreen

You don't need a trained eye to spot the newest arrivals — they're lobster-red from their excruciating sunburns. Way too many newcomers fry themselves on day one of their vacations in an overzealous quest to tan, putting a major damper on their trip — and, sometimes, their long-term health — in the process.

Hawaii's sun-loving population has achieved the dubious distinction of having the highest incidence of skin cancer in the United States, and as a result, has developed quite an attachment to sunscreen. Deep-tanning Coppertone days are a thing of the past — so islanders will merely look on in horror rather than admiration if you whip out a bottle of SPF 8 to spread on your just-flown-in virgin skin.

Most locals I know use SPF 25 or 30 sunscreen on a daily basis; you should, too. Never go out in the sun, not even for ten minutes, wearing anything less than SPF 15. Stick with an SPF 30 or 45 if you have a light complexion.

You don't need a high-ticket brand. In fact, I've had some of the best luck with garden-variety drugstore brands (although I do love the California Tan Heliotherapy line). Just find something that works for you and stick with it. Conversely, if you find that a certain sunscreen doesn't jive with your skin's chemistry, don't lament the 8 bucks you spent; simply toss the bottle and switch to something else before you find yourself with a burn.

Your best bet is to apply sunscreen — liberally — first thing in the morning, before you get dressed (to avoid missing those inch-below-the-cuff spots, which can result in nasty burns). Apply more sunscreen before you head to the beach, and do regular reapplications (every hour or two) as you sit on the sand, no matter how high the SPF. Don't throw on a T-shirt and consider yourself covered; the average white T-shirt only offers coverage equal to SPF 6 sunscreen. And ignore all claims of "waterproof" — always give yourself a fresh coat immediately after swimming.

Always make sure you apply sunscreen under bathing-suit straps, on the tops of your feet, on the back of your neck, and on your ears and lips — all spots that are the easiest to forget but the most sensitive to painful burns. To prevent sunscreen from dripping into your eyes, use a waxy sunscreen stick around your eyes and a high-SPF lip balm; both are available at just about any Hawaii convenience store.

Additionally, always wear sunglasses and a hat while you're in the sun. Throw away those $5 shades and splurge on a decent pair with UV filters to protect your corneas from sunburn and to prevent cataracts. Wear a hat with a wide brim that goes all the way around because baseball caps leave some of your most vulnerable areas — your ears and neck — exposed to the sun's harsh rays.

Dressing the Part

You probably can't think of anything more tacky-touristy than a bold tropical-patterned aloha shirt, right? Wrong!

Invented by an enterprising Honolulu tailor looking for a new way to drum up business in 1936, the aloha shirt has spawned a whole wardrobe of bright, tropical-print clothing for men, women, and children, collectively known as aloha wear. In the process, aloha wear has developed into a way of life in the Hawaiian Islands. Spirited, beautiful, easy to wear, and comfortable, aloha wear is the embodiment of the Hawaii lifestyle.

Aloha wear is acceptable just about anywhere in Hawaii, from the beach to the boardroom to the best table at a four-star restaurant. Of course, the key to wearing aloha wear well is understanding the line that separates sublime from goofy — or, in plainer terms, how to tell good aloha wear from bad aloha wear.

You can find aloha wear in any shape, from traditional aloha shirts (wearable by men and women alike) to generous women's muumuus or sexy minidresses. Basically, the key is quality. Silk is top of the line, and great for evening, but skip it for daywear on warm days (when you may perspire). Quality rayon and cotton are terrific alternatives for day and evening.

Look for beautiful, well-designed prints with strong colors and no bleeding. Look for quality buttons (coconut or wood are best, but not a must) and pattern matching at the seams and pockets. Excellent brands that offer consistently top-quality aloha wear include **Kahala Sportswear, Kamehameha Garment Co.,** and the **Paradise Found** and **Diamond Head** labels, all which have revived vintage designs; **Reyn's,** which boasts beautiful patterns in a range of flattering styles, especially for women; **Tommy Bahama's,** whose top-quality clothing lines are generically tropical but suit the Hawaii mood perfectly; and, one of my all-time favorites, **Tori Richard,** which employs some of Hawaii's finest artists to design their patterns. **Sig Zane's** all-cotton aloha wear is the height of subdued sophistication and nature-inspired beauty. **Hilo Hattie** is the largest manufacturer and distributor of aloha wear (producing more than 300,000 shirts annually); while Hilo Hattie's stuff isn't the height of aloha fashion, its quality has increased substantially in recent years while remaining very affordable.

What's the cardinal rule of wearing aloha wear like a local rather than a tourist? No matching. No themed husband-and-wife shirts, no mom-and-daughter muumuus, no two garments on one person in the same pattern. Period.

At some of the high-end resorts or fancier restaurants — the big-money places, the kind that would require a jacket and tie if you were on the mainland — they request that you wear "resort attire." For women, resort attire generally means a long or short dress or coordinating pants and top — more dressy-casual than full dressy, if you know what I mean. For men, it generally translates to pants (not shorts) and a collared shirt. Neatly presented aloha wear always does the trick, of course.

(A tiny handful of Maui's most expensive resort restaurants do require men to wear a jacket, but I don't recommend them. Go to Europe if you want to pack a blazer.)

 Don't let a flower lei outstay its welcome. Fresh-flower leis are a short-term treat, enjoyed at the height of their fragrance and beauty and disposed of after the moment has passed. So don't wear old, dying leis; nothing will peg you as a tourist with a capital T quite so blatantly. Most leis only last a day — which provides you with the perfect excuse to find a fresh one tomorrow!

Remembering Your Island-Style Manners

In many Eastern cultures, the common practice is to remove your shoes when you enter a private home. Hawaii homeowners follow the same practice — which is one reason why flip-flops and other slip-on-style shoes are so common in the islands. You find that this practice is almost always upheld in bed-and-breakfasts, and even condos may request that you leave your shoes at the door. No one is policing you, of course, but be sure to honor the request.

Islanders pride themselves on their laidback manner and friendliness, and they really show it in their driving habits — so leave your need for speed at home. Take it easy. Don't be in a hurry. And don't honk your horn to chastise other drivers, which islanders consider the height of rudeness. If the car in front of you isn't moving quickly enough, or someone cuts you off, just let it slide. Use your car horns to greet friends in Hawaii.

Leaving Your Laptop at Home and Turning Your Phone Off

Even the newly minted mainland millionaires who are buying up Maui real estate left and right understand the meaning of Hawaii. Don't cart your business worries halfway around the world; an island vacation is far too precious for that. Conveniently forget to give your boss your itinerary. Leave your work behind and relax.

And don't just leave the work behind — dump the rat-race attitude, too. The quickest way to label yourself a "tourist" in Maui is to be pushy, aggressive, or demanding.

Islanders tend to take life nice and easy. The clock doesn't rule them, and they don't like to rush. They call it "island time." Buy into it — lock, stock, and barrel — while you're there. Do as the locals do: Take life as it comes, don't stress if things don't happen with the utmost timeliness, and leave plenty of space in your day to do nothing but appreciate the beauty that surrounds you.

Smiling a Lot and Saying "Aloha" to Strangers

Who knows? You may even get yourself mistaken for a local.

Chapter 20

Ten Ways to Enjoy Maui's Romance

Don't cart your worries and everyday stresses halfway around the world; an island getaway with your partner is far too precious for that. Maui is the place to leave it all behind. Relax and bask in the romance. In this chapter, I give you the ten best ways to forget it all and find Hawaiian happiness no matter how you define romance.

Luxuriating in the Lap of Luxury

Sometimes you just gotta suck it up and spend the big bucks — especially if this trip is your honeymoon. Theoretically, you only do this once, so you may as well do it right. If staying in an oceanfront room that lets the sound of the waves lull you to sleep and the caress of the ocean breeze kiss you awake is important to you, or if you've found the luxury B&B of your dreams tucked away in a rainforest hideaway, don't visit Maui on the cheap. Spend the extra money and make memories.

If you really want to splurge on that ultradeluxe beach resort or a zippy convertible sports car but you're worried about the cost, consider splurging for just *part* of your trip. Book the oceanfront suite or red convertible Mustang for a few days (cruising the road to Hana with the top down is the ultimate Hawaii vacation dream), and make more budget-friendly choices during the rest of your stay (perhaps by moving to a still-romantic but more affordable B&B in Upcountry Maui). You won't regret it — and you won't feel quite so guilty about it after you add up your total costs.

Discovering That You Don't Need Tons of Luxury for Maui to Feel Like Paradise

But maybe your budget just doesn't allow for a big splurge. Don't despair — despite all those luxury resorts, Maui doesn't have to be a superexpensive destination.

To find true Hawaii happiness, follow this rule: The simpler, the better. You don't need flat-screen TVs, 24-hour butler service, or a telephone in the bathroom to be content. Some of my happiest times on Maui have been spent sitting on the lanai of a budget condo, watching the sunrise as I sipped home-brewed Kona coffee and nibbled on fresh papaya bought from a farm stand. Room service and Frette bed linens wouldn't have improved the moment one iota. So you don't have to overdo it — save the extra dough for having fun!

Booking the Hot Spots Before You Leave Home

After you've booked your airfare, accommodations, and rental car, you're set until you get to Maui — unless you're dying to partake in some specific activity after you arrive.

If you have your heart set on dining at a particular special-occasion restaurant, catching a highly recommended snorkel cruise, or attending a certain live performance, special event, or luau, make your reservations from home; otherwise, you may miss out, which would be a crying shame.

Certain popular activities — such as the terrific Old Lahaina Luau or Trilogy snorkel cruises — book up weeks in advance, as do tee times at the top golf courses and tables at in-demand restaurants. Make any can't-miss plans before you leave home. See Chapter 8 for more details.

Setting Aside Time for Relaxation

Work plenty of do-nothing time into your plans. Keep your time loose and go with the flow; don't plan your days in the same detailed way you'd map out your itinerary on a grand tour of Europe, with its myriad museums and historical sites.

A romantic getaway to Maui is less about seeing everything and more about leaving the conventions of regular life — including a hardcore commitment to time management — behind. Don't feel guilty that you're not doing or seeing enough. You do enough the other 50 weeks out of the year, don't you?

Enjoying a Heavenly Drive

No Hawaii road is more celebrated than the "heavenly" **Hana Highway** (Highway 36), the supercurvaceous road that winds along Maui's northeastern shore, offering some of the most stunning natural sightseeing in the entire state.

The Hana Highway winds for some 52 miles east from Kahului, crossing more than 50 one-lane bridges, passing greener-than-green taro patches, magnificent seascapes, waterfalls, botanical gardens, and rainforests before passing through the little town of Hana and ultimately ending up in one of Hawaii's most beautiful tropical places: the Kipahulu section of Haleakala National Park. Kipahulu is home to Oheo (oh-*hay*-oh) Gulch, a series of waterfall pools that tumble down to the ocean. Just past the town of Hana is romantic Hamoa Beach. (See more about Hamoa Beach in the section "Spending a Day at Maui's Most Romantic Beach.")

 Despite the draws at the end of the road, remember that this drive isn't so much about the destination as it is about the journey. The drive takes at least three hours — but allow all day to do it. If you race to arrive in Hana as quickly as you can, you'll be as perplexed as so many others who just don't understand the drive. Start out early, take it slow and easy, stop at scenic points along the way, and let the Hana Road work its magic on you. It will — I promise. In fact, for the ultimate romantic getaway, I suggest staying overnight in Hana (see Chapter 10 for recommendations).

See Chapter 13 for full coverage of the drive, including great stops along the way.

Making Mornings Your Ocean Time

Maui's beaches tend to be less crowded, and the surf and winds tend to be calmer, in the morning hours — particularly in winter. Always take the day's first snorkel and dive cruise, when conditions are calmest and clearest — outfitters don't offer discounts on their afternoon sails either.

Spending a Day at Maui's Most Romantic Beach

Off the Hana Highway (see earlier in this chapter), about 2½ miles past the town of Hana, Hamoa Beach is a remote, romantic spot. This half-moon-shaped beach at Maui's easternmost point is breathtakingly lovely, with surf the color of turquoise, golden-gray sand, and verdant hills providing a postcard-perfect backdrop. The Hotel Hana-Maui likes to maintain the beach as its own, but it has to share, so march down the steps from the lava-rock lookout point and stake out your spot. The beach is generally good for swimming and waveriding in the gentle seasons, but stick close to the shore because the ocean is open and unprotected. Stay out of the water entirely in winter. The hotel maintains minimal facilities for nonguests, including a restroom.

Toasting the Sunset Every Evening

You can't get closer to the ocean than the alfresco tables at **I'o,** 505 Front St., Lahaina (☎ **808-661-8422;** www.iomaui.com; $$$$). Overseen by the award-winning chef James McDonald, I'o is a multifaceted joy, with a winningly innovative, mostly seafood menu, first-rate service, and a top-notch wine list.

My favorite Kaanapali restaurant, the more casual **Hula Grill,** in Whaler's Village, 2435 Kaanapali Pkwy. (☎ **808-667-6636;** www.hulapie.com; $$$), serves an excellent steak-and-seafood menu and overflows with quintessential Hawaii charm. The indoor/outdoor setting on the sand is ideal for sunset-watchers; tiki torches make the after-dark hours magical as well. Diners on a budget can stick to the bar menu ($) without losing out on ambience.

Despite the high prices, I just love **Mama's Fish House,** just off the Hana Highway at 799 Poho Place, Paia (☎ **808-579-8488;** www.mamasfish house.com; $$$$$). The fresh fish is as fabulous as it can be, and the beachfront tiki-room setting is quintessential romantic Hawaii. The lengthy list of tropical drinks (with umbrellas!) puts you right in the mood.

For romance on a budget, **Cheeseburger in Paradise,** 811 Front St., Lahaina (☎ **808-661-4855;** www.cheeseburgermaui.com; $), offers an idyllic harbor view from every seat, and it comes with a first-class burger. Big, juicy, gooey, and served on fresh-baked buns, the burgers are guaranteed to satisfy even the most committed connoisseur. Two bars boasting a festive tropical-drinks menu and live music nightly round out the appeal.

Dining in Style

Dubbed "Maui's little French jewel" by *Bon Appétit,* **Gerard's,** in the Plantation Inn, 174 Lahainaluna Rd., Lahaina (☎ **877-661-8939** or 808-661-8939; www.gerardsmaui.com; $$$$), is an excellent choice for couples in love. Gerard's may be the perfect special-occasion restaurant; the garden patio tables are the prime place to woo.

David Paul's Lahaina Grill, 127 Lahainaluna Rd., Lahaina (☎ **808-667-5117;** www.lahainagrill.com; $$$$), is consistently voted "Best of Maui." Expect distinctive New American flavors that are bold without being overpowering. The dining room is stylish yet delightfully homey, and the expert service is a nice change of pace from the usual Maui surfer style.

Overlooking luxuriant golf greens and the stunning Kapalua coastline, the **Plantation House,** 2000 Plantation Club Dr., Kapalua (☎ 808-669-6299; www.theplantationhouse.com; $$$$), boasts an utterly glorious setting — and Chef Alex Stanislaw's one-of-a-kind Asian-Mediterranean fusion menu lives up to the setting completely. Book a terrace table and come at sunset to maximize the romance.

Nick's Fishmarket, in the Kea Lani Hotel, 4100 Wailea Alanui Dr., Wailea (☎ 808-879-7224; www.tri-star-restaurants.com; $$$$–$$$$$), is my first choice for romance in South Maui. This top-quality Mediterranean-accented seafooder gets everything right: food, wine list, setting, and service. I prefer the vine-covered, iron-furniture-dressed terrace, but the gorgeous dining room is equally fine.

Joe's Bar & Grill, at the Wailea Tennis Center, 131 Wailea Ike Dr., Wailea (☎ 808-875-7767; $$$$), is another wonderful South Maui choice. Joe's serves a pleasing menu of upscale American home cooking with island twists, and low lighting and well-spaced tables make for a surprisingly romantic ambience after dark.

For a complete listing of all the restaurants I recommend, see Chapter 11.

Mellowing Out Like a Local

Islanders tend to take life nice and easy. A clock doesn't rule them, and they don't like to rush. They call it "island time." While you're in Maui, do as the locals do: Take life as it comes, don't stress if things don't happen with the utmost timeliness, and leave plenty of space in your day for you and your beloved to do nothing but appreciate the beauty that surrounds you.

You probably already know the Hawaiian word aloha, which serves as an all-purpose greeting — hello, welcome, or goodbye. But what it really means is love — and that's the whole purpose of your visit to Hawaii, isn't it? Aloha is a warm and wonderful word full of grace, compassion, and good feeling, so use it liberally; I can't think of a better way to get caught up in Hawaii's true spirit.

Appendix

Quick Concierge

Fast Facts

American Automobile Association (AAA)

Although roadside service is available on Maui, the only AAA office in Hawaii is on Oahu at 1130 Nimitz Hwy., Honolulu (☎ 800-736-2886 from Maui; www. aaa-hawaii.com). The office is open Monday through Friday from 9 a.m. to 5 p.m. and Saturday from 9 a.m. to 2 p.m.

For information on becoming a member before you leave home, call ☎ 800-AAA-HELP or point your Web browser to www. aaa.com, where you'll be linked to your regional club's home page by entering your zip code. See Chapter 4 for details on the many benefits of AAA membership.

American Express

The only American Express office on Maui is located in Kaanapali at the Westin Maui, 2365 Kaanapali Pkwy. (☎ 808-661-7155).

Cardholders and traveler's-check purchasers should call ☎ 800-221-7282 for all money emergencies. To make inquiries with the American Express Travel Agency or to locate other branch offices, call ☎ 800-AXP-TRIP. For more information, visit www.americanexpress.com.

Area Code

All the Hawaiian Islands are in the **808** area code. Note that if you're calling another island from Maui, you must dial 1-808 first, and you'll be billed at long-distance rates (which can be more expensive than calling the mainland — so be sure to use your long-distance calling card). You can leave off the area code when you're on Maui and calling another Maui number.

ATMs

All the major resort areas on Maui have plenty of ATMs. Branches of Hawaii's most popular banks are plentiful, and all are connected to the major global ATM networks. Most supermarkets also have ATMs inside (though these may charge a higher fee). Do yourself a favor and don't set off for a remote area (say, Upcountry or Hana) without stocking up on cash first. These areas do have ATMs, but why waste your precious vacation time tracking them down?

One of Hawaii's most popular banks, with branches throughout the state, is **Bank of Hawaii,** which is linked with all the major worldwide networks. To find the one nearest you, call ☎ 888-643-3888 or point your Web browser to www.boh.com/locations/atmdir.asp. You can also find ATMs on the **Cirrus** network by dialing ☎ 800-424-7787 or going online to www.mastercard.com; to find a **Plus** ATM, call ☎ 800-843-7587 or visit www. visa.com and then click on "ATM locator" at the bottom of the start page.

Baby Sitters and Baby Stuff

Any hotel or condo can refer you to a reliable baby sitter with a proven track record. If yours can't, contact **Happy Kids** (☎ 808-667-5437), **The Nanny Connection** (☎ 808-875-4777 or 808-667-5777;

www.thenannyconnection.com), or **Nana Enterprises** (☎ 888-584-6262). **Baby's Away** (☎ 800-942-9030 or 808-875-9030; www.babysaway.com) rents cribs, strollers, highchairs, playpens, infant seats, and the like; they deliver whatever you need to wherever you're staying, and pick it up when you're done.

Business Hours

Most offices are open from 8 a.m. to 5 p.m. The morning commute usually runs from 6 to 8 a.m., and the evening rush is from 4 to 6 p.m. Bank hours are 8:30 a.m. to 3 p.m., Monday through Thursday, and 8:30 a.m. to 6 p.m. Friday; some banks are open on Saturday. Shopping centers are open 10 a.m. to 9 p.m. Monday through Friday, 10 a.m. to 5:30 p.m. Saturday, and noon to 5 or 6 p.m. Sunday.

Credit Cards

If your Visa card is lost or stolen, call ☎ 800-645-6556. MasterCard holders should call ☎ 800-307-7309. American Express cardholders should call ☎ 800-221-7282 for all money emergencies.

Dentists

Emergency dental care is available at **Maui Dental Center**, 162 Alamaha St., Kahului (☎ 808-871-6283).

Doctors

West Maui Healthcare Center, Whalers Village, 2435 Kaanapali Pkwy., second floor (behind Leilani's, Kaanapali; ☎ 808-667-9721), takes walk-ins 8 a.m. to 9 p.m. daily; note that they charge an additional $30 for visits after 6 p.m. **Doctors on Call** (☎ 808-667-7676) takes appointments at the Hyatt Regency in Lahaina, at the Westin Maui in Kaanapali, and at the Ritz-Carlton in Kapalua.

In Kihei, call **Urgent Care**, 1325 S. Kihei Rd., Suite 103 (at Lipoa Street, across from Star Market), Kihei (☎ 808-879-7781), open daily from 6 a.m. to midnight; doctors are on call 24 hours a day.

If you need medical attention while you're out in Hana, contact the **Hana Community Health Center**, 4590 Hana Hwy. (☎ 808-248-8294).

Your hotel's concierge or front-desk staff can direct you to a reliable doctor in the immediate area, if you need one.

Emergencies

Dial **911** from any phone, just like back home.

Etiquette

Hawaii's customs are much like those on the mainland, but take notice of a few small differences.

In Hawaii, remove your shoes before entering anyone's home. Many bed-and-breakfasts may make the same request of you.

Aloha wear is perfectly acceptable (and wonderfully festive) formal wear in the islands.

When you're driving, don't honk your horn in frustration. Chill out like the locals — honking to hurry someone along or to express anger is considered rude. Islanders only honk to greet friends.

Don't say, "Back home in the U.S. . . . ."

Holidays

In addition to the same national holidays observed in the rest of the United States, Hawaii celebrates a few other special days: Prince Kuhio Day (March 26), King

Kamehameha Day (June 11), and Admission Day (the third Friday in August). All government offices are closed, and some local businesses may close as well, so plan accordingly. See the calendar of events in Chapter 3 for a full rundown of Maui's special celebrations.

Hospitals

Around-the-clock emergency care is available from **Maui Memorial Hospital**, 221 Mahalani St., Wailuku (☎ 808-244-9056), in Central Maui.

Information

The **Maui Visitors Bureau** is located in Central Maui at 1727 Wili Pa Loop, Wailuku, HI 96793 (☎ 800-525-6284 or 808-244-3530; www.visitmaui.com), but it's not really designed as a walk-in office. Call before you leave home to order your free Maui travel planner or check the Web site for a wealth of good information.

Some of Maui's resort areas have dedicated visitor associations that provide information, including the **Kaanapali Beach Resort Association** (☎ 800-245-9229 or 808-661-3271; www.kaanapaliresort.com), the **Kapalua Resort** (☎ 800-527-2482; www.kapaluamaui.com), and the **Wailea Resort** (☎ 800-332-1614).

After you land at Kahului Airport, stop over at the state-operated **Visitor Information Center** while you're waiting for your baggage and pick up a copy of *This Week Maui, 101 Things to Do on Maui,* and other free tourist publications. If you forget, don't worry — you can find them at malls and shopping centers around the island.

In addition, all the big resort hotels are overflowing with printed info. Even if your hotel or condo doesn't have a dedicated concierge, the staff can point you in the

right direction, make recommendations, and give advice.

Internet Access

Many hotels provide access to the Internet. Call your hotel in advance to see whether it has computers available for guests to use for a fee or whether an Internet connection is available in your room.

Liquor Laws

The legal drinking age in Hawaii is 21. Beer, wine, and liquor are sold in grocery and convenience stores at any hour, 7 days a week. It's illegal (though rarely prosecuted) to have an open container on the beach. Bars stay open until 2 a.m.

Maps

AAA supplies excellent free maps of Hawaii to members only. For more information on becoming a member, see Chapter 4.

All rental-car companies hand out good free map booklets of Maui to navigate your way around.

If you want a more complete topographic map, the University of Hawaii Press prints the best. They're available from just about any bookstore on Maui. If you want to order one before you leave home, contact **Basically Books** (☎ 800-903-MAPS; www.basicallybooks.com). Or go straight to the source and order them directly from the UH Press: www.uhpress.hawaii.edu.

Newspapers/Magazines

The *Maui News* (www.mauinews.com) is the island's daily paper; the Web site can provide you with a great source of information before you leave home. Additionally, a number of free newspaper weeklies, such as *Maui Time* and the *Maui Weekly,* are available from racks around town.

If you're interested in the performing arts, look for a copy of *Centerpiece,* the free bimonthly magazine published by the Maui Arts and Cultural Center. Hotel concierges usually have copies.

Hawaii magazine is a glossy monthly that's targeted to visitors; it offers a good introduction to the islands. You can usually find the current issue in the travel magazine section at your local branch of the big chain bookstores, such as Borders and Barnes & Noble.

The *Honolulu Advertiser* (www.honoluluadvertiser.com) and the *Honolulu Star-Bulletin* (www.starbulletin.com) are the two statewide daily newspapers.

Pharmacies

LongsDrugs (www.longs.com), Hawaii's biggest drugstore chain, has a branch in Central Maui at the Maui Mall, 70 Kaahumanu Ave. (between Puunene Avenue and the Hana Highway), Kahului (☎ 808-877-0041). If you're in West Maui, head to the branch at Lahaina Cannery Mall, 1221 Honoapiilani Hwy. (between Kapunkea and Kenui streets), Lahaina (☎ 808-667-4384). In South Maui, head to Long's Kihei Center, 1215 S. Kihei Rd. (just north of Lipoa Street), Kihei (☎ 808-879-2259).

Police

The main headquarters of the **Maui Police Department** is in Wailuku at 55 Mahalani St., near Maui Memorial Hospital (☎ 808-244-6400). District stations are located next to the Lahaina Civic Center, 1760 Honoapiilani Hwy., on the mountain side of the highway, just north of Lahaina (☎ 808-661-4441); and in Hana on the Hana Highway, near Ua Kea Road (☎ 808-248-8311). Of course, if you have an emergency, dial **911** from any phone.

Post Offices

In West Maui, a big branch office is next to the Lahaina Civic Center at 1760 Honoapiilani Hwy. between Kaanapali and Lahaina (on the mountain side of the highway; it's easy to spot), and in downtown Lahaina adjacent to the Lahaina Shopping Center, 132 Papalaua St. (between Front and Wainee streets; ☎ 808-661-0904).

In South Maui, you find a post office at 1254 S. Kihei Rd., across the street from Long's Kihei Center (☎ 808-879-1987).

Satellite post offices are located around the island; to find the one nearest you, call ☎ 800-275-8777 or visit www.usps.com.

Safety

Although Hawaii is generally quite safe, visitors have been crime victims, so stay alert. The most common crime against tourists is rental-car break-ins. Never leave any valuables in your car, not even in your trunk. Thieves can be in and out of your trunk faster than you can open it with your own key.

Be especially careful at high-risk areas, such as beaches and resorts. Never carry large amounts of cash with you. Stay in well-lighted areas after dark. Don't hike on deserted trails alone.

See Chapter 12 for tips on ocean safety and more. Chapter 8 has additional tips on staying healthy when you travel.

Smoking

You can't smoke in public buildings, including airports, grocery stores, retail shops, movie theaters, banks, and all government buildings and facilities. Hotels have non-smoking rooms available, and most B&Bs prohibit smoking altogether. You can't smoke in any part of a restaurant on Maui (even in the bar, although stand-alone bars can allow smoking). Car-rental agencies also have smoke-free cars.

Taxes

Hawaii's sales tax is 4 percent. Expect taxes of about 11.42 percent to be added to your hotel bill.

Taxis

Call **Alii Cab** (☎ 808-661-3688 or 808-667-2605), **Maui Airport Taxi** (☎ 808-877-0907), **Maui Central Cab** (☎ 877-244-7279 or 808-244-7278), **Kihei Taxi** (☎ 808-879-3000), or **Wailea Taxi** (☎ 808-874-5000).

Time

Hawaii standard time is in effect year-round. Hawaii is two hours behind Pacific standard time and five hours behind eastern standard time. In other words, when it's noon in Hawaii, it's 2 p.m. in California and 5 p.m. in New York during standard time on the mainland. Hawaii doesn't use daylight saving time, so when daylight saving time is in effect on the mainland, Hawaii is three hours behind the West Coast and six hours behind the East Coast — so in summer, when it's noon in Hawaii, it's 3 p.m. in California and 6 p.m. in New York.

Hawaii is east of the international date line, putting it on the same day as the U.S. mainland and Canada, and a day behind Australia, New Zealand, and Asia.

Traffic Laws

Hawaii is a no-fault insurance state. If you drive without collision-damage insurance, you're required to pay for all damages before you leave the state, regardless of who is at fault. Your personal auto policy may provide rental-car coverage; read your policy or check with your insurer before you leave home and bring your insurance ID card if you decline the rental-car company's optional insurance. Some credit-card companies also provide collision damage insurance; check with yours.

Seatbelts are mandatory for everyone in the car, all the time, and children under age 4 must be strapped into car seats.

You can turn right on red unless a posted sign specifies otherwise.

Pedestrians always have the right of way, even if they're not on a crosswalk.

Weather and Surf Reports

For Maui's current weather and forecasts, call ☎ 808-877-5111, which also supplies sunrise and sunset times, as well as forecasts for Molokai and Lanai. For marine conditions, dial ☎ 808-877-3477 or 808-877-3949; for wind and surf reports, call ☎ 808-877-3611.

To check the weather forecasts online before you leave home, log on to www.hawaiiweathertoday.com or www.weather.com.

Toll-Free Numbers and Web Sites

Airlines

Air Canada
☎ 888-247-2262
www.aircanada.ca

Air New Zealand
☎ 800-262-1234 in the United States
☎ 800-663-5494 in Canada
☎ 0800-737-000 in New Zealand
www.airnewzealand.com

Alaska Airlines
☎ 800-252-7522
www.alaskaair.com

Aloha Airlines
☎ 800-367-5250
www.alohaair.com

American Airlines
☎ 800-433-7300
www.americanair.com

American Trans Air
☎ 800-435-9282
www.ata.com

Continental Airlines
☎ 800-525-0280
www.continental.com

Delta Air Lines
☎ 800-221-1212
www.delta.com

Hawaiian Airlines
☎ 800-367-5320
www.hawaiianair.com

Island Air
☎ 800-323-3345 from continental
North America
☎ 800-652-6541 from Hawaii
www.islandair.com

Northwest Airlines
☎ 800-225-2525
www.nwa.com

Pacific Wings Airlines
☎ 888-575-4546
www.pacificwings.com

Qantas
☎ 800-227-4500 in the United States
☎ 13-13-13 in Australia
www.qantas.com

United Airlines
☎ 800-864-8331
www.ual.com

Major hotel and motel chains

Aston Hotels and Resorts
☎ 800-997-6667
www.aston-hotels.com

Best Western International
☎ 800-780-7234
www.bestwestern.com

Castle Resorts and Hotels
☎ 800-367-5004
www.castleresorts.com

Four Seasons Hotels and Resorts
☎ 800-819-5053
www.fourseasons.com

Hilton Hotels
☎ 800-HILTONS (445-8667)
www.hilton.com

Hyatt Hotels and Resorts
☎ 800-591-1234
www.hyatt.com

Marc Resorts Hawaii
☎ 800-535-0085
www.marcresorts.com

Marriott Hotels
☎ 888-236-2427
www.marriott.com

Ohana Hotels
☎ 800-462-6262
www.ohanahotels.com

Outrigger Hotels and Resorts
☎ 800-OUTRIGGER (688-7444)
www.outrigger.com

Premier Resorts
☎ 888-774-3533
www.premier-resorts.com

Prince Resorts Hawaii
☎ 800-944-4491
www.princeresortshawaii.com

Renaissance Hotels and Resorts
☎ 800-468-3571
www.renaissancehotels.com

Ritz-Carlton
☎ 800-241-3333
www.ritzcarlton.com

Sheraton Hotels and Resorts
☎ 888-625-5144
www.sheraton-hawaii.com

Starwood's Luxury Collection
☎ 888-625-5144
www.luxurycollection.com

Westin Hotels
☎ 888-625-5144
www.westin.com

Car-rental agencies

Alamo
☎ 800-462-5266
www.alamo.com

Avis
☎ 800-230-4898 in the United States
☎ 800-272-5871 in Canada
www.avis.com

Budget
☎ 800-527-0700
www.budget.com

Dollar
☎ 800-800-4000
www.dollarcar.com

Enterprise
☎ 800-261-7331
www.enterprise.com

Hertz
☎ 800-654-3131
www.hertz.com

National
☎ 800- CAR-RENT (227-7368)
www.nationalcar.com

Thrifty
☎ 800- THRIFTY (847-4389)
www.thrifty.com

Where to Get More Information

Destination Lanai
☎ 800-947-4774
www.visitlanai.net

Haleakala National Park
P.O. Box 369
Makawao, HI 96768
☎ 808-572-4400
www.nps.gov/hale

Hawaii Visitors and Convention Bureau (HVCB)
2270 Kalakaua Ave., 7th Floor
Honolulu, HI 96815
☎ 800-464-2924 or 808-923-1811
www.gohawaii.com

Island of Lanai/Castle & Cooke Resorts
P.O. Box 630310
Lanai City, HI 96763

☎ 800-321-4666
www.lanai-resorts.com

Kaanapali Beach Resort Association
2530 Kekaa Dr., Suite 1-B
Lahaina, HI 96761
☎ 800-245-9229 or 808-661-3271
www.kaanapaliresort.com

Kapalua Resort
800 Kapalua Dr.
Kapalua, HI 96761
☎ 800-527-2582
www.kapaluamaui.com

Maui Visitors Bureau (also issues information on Molokai and Lanai)
1727 Wili Pa Loop
Wailuku, Maui, HI 96793
☎ 800-525-6284 or 808-244-3530
www.visitmaui.com

Maui.net
www.maui.net

Molokai Visitors Association
P.O. Box 960
Kaunakakai, HI 96748
☎ 800-800-6367 or 808-553-3876
www.molokai-hawaii.com

Planet Hawaii
www.planet-hawaii.com

Wailea Resort
161 Wailea Ike Place
Wailea, HI 96753
☎ 800-332-1614
www.kapaluamaui.com

Index

See also separate Accommodations and Restaurant indexes at the end of this index.

General Index

• *L* •

Accommodations Index

Restaurant Index

SINESS, CAREERS & PERSONAL FINANCE

7645-5307-0   0-7645-5331-3 *†

Also available:

✔ Accounting For Dummies †
0-7645-5314-3

✔ Business Plans Kit For Dummies †
0-7645-5365-8

✔ Cover Letters For Dummies
0-7645-5224-4

✔ Frugal Living For Dummies
0-7645-5403-4

✔ Leadership For Dummies
0-7645-5176-0

✔ Managing For Dummies
0-7645-1771-6

✔ Marketing For Dummies
0-7645-5600-2

✔ Personal Finance For Dummies *
0-7645-2590-5

✔ Project Management
For Dummies
0-7645-5283-X

✔ Resumes For Dummies †
0-7645-5471-9

✔ Selling For Dummies
0-7645-5363-1

✔ Small Business Kit For Dummies *†
0-7645-5093-4

ME & BUSINESS COMPUTER BASICS

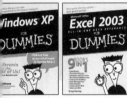

7645-4074-2   0-7645-3758-X

Also available:

✔ ACT! 6 For Dummies
0-7645-2645-6

✔ iLife '04 All-in-One Desk Reference
For Dummies
0-7645-7347-0

✔ iPAQ For Dummies
0-7645-6769-1

✔ Mac OS X Panther Timesaving
Techniques For Dummies
0-7645-5812-9

✔ Macs For Dummies
0-7645-5656-8

✔ Microsoft Money 2004 For Dummies
0-7645-4195-1

✔ Office 2003 All-in-One Desk
Reference For Dummies
0-7645-3883-7

✔ Outlook 2003 For Dummies
0-7645-3759-8

✔ PCs For Dummies
0-7645-4074-2

✔ TiVo For Dummies
0-7645-6923-6

✔ Upgrading and Fixing PCs
For Dummies
0-7645-1665-5

✔ Windows XP Timesaving
Techniques For Dummies
0-7645-3748-2

OD, HOME, GARDEN, HOBBIES, MUSIC & PETS

7645-5295-3   0-7645-5232-5

Also available:

✔ Bass Guitar For Dummies
0-7645-2487-9

✔ Diabetes Cookbook For Dummies
0-7645-5230-9

✔ Gardening For Dummies *
0-7645-5130-2

✔ Guitar For Dummies
0-7645-5106-X

✔ Holiday Decorating For Dummies
0-7645-2570-0

✔ Home Improvement All-in-One
For Dummies
0-7645-5680-0

✔ Knitting For Dummies
0-7645-5395-X

✔ Piano For Dummies
0-7645-5105-1

✔ Puppies For Dummies
0-7645-5255-4

✔ Scrapbooking For Dummies
0-7645-7208-3

✔ Senior Dogs For Dummies
0-7645-5818-8

✔ Singing For Dummies
0-7645-2475-5

✔ 30-Minute Meals For Dummies
0-7645-2589-1

TERNET & DIGITAL MEDIA

7645-1664-7   0-7645-6924-4

Also available:

✔ 2005 Online Shopping Directory
For Dummies
0-7645-7495-7

✔ CD & DVD Recording For Dummies
0-7645-5956-7

✔ eBay For Dummies
0-7645-5654-1

✔ Fighting Spam For Dummies
0-7645-5965-6

✔ Genealogy Online For Dummies
0-7645-5964-8

✔ Google For Dummies
0-7645-4420-9

✔ Home Recording For Musicians
For Dummies
0-7645-1634-5

✔ The Internet For Dummies
0-7645-4173-0

✔ iPod & iTunes For Dummies
0-7645-7772-7

✔ Preventing Identity Theft
For Dummies
0-7645-7336-5

✔ Pro Tools All-in-One Desk
Reference For Dummies
0-7645-5714-9

✔ Roxio Easy Media Creator
For Dummies
0-7645-7131-1

parate Canadian edition also available

parate U.K. edition also available

lable wherever books are sold. For more information or to order direct: U.S. customers
www.dummies.com or call 1-877-762-2974.
customers visit www.wileyeurope.com or call 0800 243407. Canadian customers visit
v.wiley.ca or call 1-800-567-4797.

SPORTS, FITNESS, PARENTING, RELIGION & SPIRITUALITY

0-7645-5146-9   0-7645-5418-2

Also available:
- Adoption For Dummies
  0-7645-5488-3
- Basketball For Dummies
  0-7645-5248-1
- The Bible For Dummies
  0-7645-5296-1
- Buddhism For Dummies
  0-7645-5359-3
- Catholicism For Dummies
  0-7645-5391-7
- Hockey For Dummies
  0-7645-5228-7

- Judaism For Dummies
  0-7645-5299-6
- Martial Arts For Dummies
  0-7645-5358-5
- Pilates For Dummies
  0-7645-5397-6
- Religion For Dummies
  0-7645-5264-3
- Teaching Kids to Read
  For Dummies
  0-7645-4043-2
- Weight Training For Dummies
  0-7645-5168-X
- Yoga For Dummies
  0-7645-5117-5

TRAVEL

0-7645-5438-7   0-7645-5453-0

Also available:
- Alaska For Dummies
  0-7645-1761-9
- Arizona For Dummies
  0-7645-6938-4
- Cancún and the Yucatán
  For Dummies
  0-7645-2437-2
- Cruise Vacations For Dummies
  0-7645-6941-4
- Europe For Dummies
  0-7645-5456-5
- Ireland For Dummies
  0-7645-5455-7

- Las Vegas For Dummies
  0-7645-5448-4
- London For Dummies
  0-7645-4277-X
- New York City For Dummies
  0-7645-6945-7
- Paris For Dummies
  0-7645-5494-8
- RV Vacations For Dummies
  0-7645-5443-3
- Walt Disney World & Orlando
  For Dummies
  0-7645-6943-0

GRAPHICS, DESIGN & WEB DEVELOPMENT

0-7645-4345-8   0-7645-5589-8

Also available:
- Adobe Acrobat 6 PDF
  For Dummies
  0-7645-3760-1
- Building a Web Site For Dummies
  0-7645-7144-3
- Dreamweaver MX 2004
  For Dummies
  0-7645-4342-3
- FrontPage 2003 For Dummies
  0-7645-3882-9
- HTML 4 For Dummies
  0-7645-1995-6
- Illustrator cs For Dummies
  0-7645-4084-X

- Macromedia Flash MX 2004
  For Dummies
  0-7645-4358-X
- Photoshop 7 All-in-One Desk
  Reference For Dummies
  0-7645-1667-1
- Photoshop cs Timesaving
  Techniques For Dummies
  0-7645-6782-9
- PHP 5 For Dummies
  0-7645-4166-8
- PowerPoint 2003 For Dummies
  0-7645-3908-6
- QuarkXPress 6 For Dummies
  0-7645-2593-X

NETWORKING, SECURITY, PROGRAMMING & DATABASES

0-7645-6852-3   0-7645-5784-X

Also available:
- A+ Certification For Dummies
  0-7645-4187-0
- Access 2003 All-in-One Desk
  Reference For Dummies
  0-7645-3988-4
- Beginning Programming
  For Dummies
  0-7645-4997-9
- C For Dummies
  0-7645-7068-4
- Firewalls For Dummies
  0-7645-4048-3
- Home Networking For Dummies
  0-7645-42796

- Network Security For Dummie
  0-7645-1679-5
- Networking For Dummies
  0-7645-1677-9
- TCP/IP For Dummies
  0-7645-1760-0
- VBA For Dummies
  0-7645-3989-2
- Wireless All In-One Desk Refer
  For Dummies
  0-7645-7496-5
- Wireless Home Networking
  For Dummies
  0-7645-3910-8

ALTH & SELF-HELP

645-6820-5 *†   0-7645-2566-2

Also available:
- Alzheimer's For Dummies
  0-7645-3899-3
- Asthma For Dummies
  0-7645-4233-8
- Controlling Cholesterol For Dummies
  0-7645-5440-9
- Depression For Dummies
  0-7645-3900-0
- Dieting For Dummies
  0-7645-4149-8
- Fertility For Dummies
  0-7645-2549-2

- Fibromyalgia For Dummies
  0-7645-5441-7
- Improving Your Memory For Dummies
  0-7645-5435-2
- Pregnancy For Dummies †
  0-7645-4483-7
- Quitting Smoking For Dummies
  0-7645-2629-4
- Relationships For Dummies
  0-7645-5384-4
- Thyroid For Dummies
  0-7645-5385-2

UCATION, HISTORY, REFERENCE & TEST PREPARATION

7645-5194-9   0-7645-4186-2

Also available:
- Algebra For Dummies
  0-7645-5325-9
- British History For Dummies
  0-7645-7021-8
- Calculus For Dummies
  0-7645-2498-4
- English Grammar For Dummies
  0-7645-5322-4
- Forensics For Dummies
  0-7645-5580-4
- The GMAT For Dummies
  0-7645-5251-1
- Inglés Para Dummies
  0-7645-5427-1

- Italian For Dummies
  0-7645-5196-5
- Latin For Dummies
  0-7645-5431-X
- Lewis & Clark For Dummies
  0-7645-2545-X
- Research Papers For Dummies
  0-7645-5426-3
- The SAT I For Dummies
  0-7645-7193-1
- Science Fair Projects For Dummies
  0-7645-5460-3
- U.S. History For Dummies
  0-7645-5249-X

Get smart @ dummies.com®

- Find a full list of Dummies titles
- Look into loads of FREE on-site articles
- Sign up for FREE eTips e-mailed to you weekly
- See what other products carry the Dummies name
- Shop directly from the Dummies bookstore
- Enter to win new prizes every month!